PLANET OF THE Nerds™

PAUL CONSTANT

ALAN ROBINSON

RANDY ELLIOTT

FELIPE SOBREIRO

ROB STEEN

AHOY COMICS

FOR TARA, WHO BUILT THE ROOM
WHERE THIS BOOK WAS WRITTEN.

– PAUL CONSTANT

TO JESSICA, MATILDA AND AGUSTIN.
FOR ALL THEIR SUPPORT AND LOVE.

– ALAN ROBINSON

COMICSAHOY.COM 🐦 @ AHOYCOMICMAGS

HART SEELY - PUBLISHER
TOM PEYER - EDITOR-IN-CHIEF
FRANK CAMMUSO - CHIEF CREATIVE OFFICER
STUART MOORE - OPS
SARAH LITT - EDITOR-AT-LARGE

DAVID HYDE - PUBLICITY
DERON BENNETT - PRODUCTION COORDINATOR
KIT CAOAGAS - MARKETING ASSOCIATE
LILLIAN LASERSON - LEGAL
RUSSELL NATHERSON SR. - BUSINESS

PLANET OF THE NERDS – Published by AHOY Comics LLC, 499 S. Warren St., Suite 612, Syracuse, NY 13202. PLANET OF THE NERDS ©2019 Paul Constant and Alan Robinson. PLANET OF THE NERDS (including all prominent characters herein), its logo and all character licenses, are trademarks of Paul Constant and Alan Robinson. All rights reserved. Ahoy Comics and its logos are trademarks of Ahoy Comics. No part of this publication may be reproduced or transmitted, in any form or by any means (except for short excerpts for review purposes) without the expressed written permission of Ahoy Comics. All names, characters, events and locales in this publication are entirely fictional. Any resemblance to actual persons (living or dead), events or places, without satiric intent, is coincidental.

PRINTED IN THE U.S.A. - FIRST PRINTING - OCTOBER 2019 - ISBN: 978-0-9980442-4-8

TIME, TIME, TIME
SEE WHAT'S BECOME OF ME
WHILE I LOOKED AROUND FOR MY POSSIBILITIES
I WAS SO HARD TO PLEASE
BUT LOOK AROUND
LEAVES ARE BROWN
AND THE SKY IS A HAZY SHADE OF WINTER

– THE BANGLES, "A HAZY SHADE OF WINTER"
(AFTER SIMON & GARFUNKEL)

SAY, YEAH, YEAH, YEAH

– JOHN "COUGAR" MELLENCAMP, "CHERRY BOMB"

PLANET OF THE NERDS

PAUL CONSTANT	WRITER
ALAN ROBINSON	ARTIST
FELIPE SOBREIRO	COLOR
RANDY ELLIOTT	ARTIST (SHORT FEATURES)
LEE LOUGHRIDGE	COLOR ("SUPER MEN")
ROB STEEN	LETTERS
DAVID NAKAYAMA	COVER ARTIST (#1-2)
ALAN ROBINSON	COVER ARTIST (#3-5)
TODD KLEIN	LOGO
JOHN J. HILL	DESIGN
DERON BENNETT	ASSISTANT EDITOR
TOM PEYER	EDITOR
CORY SEDLMEIER	COLLECTION EDITOR

CREATED BY **PAUL CONSTANT** AND **ALAN ROBINSON**

C O N T E N T S

PLANET OF THE NERDS

INTRODUCTION

Speaking of time travel, let me take you back to 2006.

I was on a book tour, and my publisher had booked me to be interviewed on CNN's Headline News channel. This was so long ago that Headline News actually still showed news programming, instead of an endless marathon of true crime reruns. I was going to be interviewed by one of the network's new hires, who was still just a typical cable news blowhard/curmudgeon type, not yet the weepy cult leader and conspiracy theorist he would become a few years later. His real name isn't important. Let's call him Ben Gleck.

So I sit down with Ben Gleck, expecting to talk about my book and the beloved American cultural institution that is *Jeopardy!* To my surprise, Ben's questions go something like this:

"You won seventy-four straight games of *Jeopardy!* Do you consider yourself a nerd?"

"Why are you such a big nerd?"

"What's it like, being a nerd?"

"As a kid, did you get beaten up and bullied a lot? For being a nerd?"

He said "nerd" each time with a tinge of malevolent glee. The whole interview continued in this weird vein.

I gradually realized what was happening: Ben Gleck, born on the cusp of the Baby Boom and Generation X, was a relic of a different time. In his America, there were two main kinds of people, jocks and nerds. For jocks and self-imagined jocks to maintain their status, it was crucial to zing the nerds. Then everyone could be sure which side of the divide you were on. That's how the food chain was maintained.

Ben apparently didn't know that the world had changed since his high school days. The jock/nerd wars had ended with a series of informal treaties in the late '90s—and definitively in favor of the nerds. It was all due to technology, of course. The microcomputer and Internet revolutions meant that nerdy pursuits like video games and "hacker culture" went mainstream. In past centuries, the men who ran the world economy had always been jocks: big, hearty, mutton-chopped tycoons, the kind of figure you'd see in old newspaper engravings standing astride railroads and steel mills like a colossus. Now the richest people in the world were odd, stooped little techies with acne scars and social anxiety. How could any self-respecting jock look at himself in the mirror when these were our new gods?

The Internet also meant that everyone could find their people now. You could form a community, no matter how geeky or obscure your interest. I still remember, as a kid, the distinct shame I would feel about *expertise*. It made you weird to know too much about something: space or Broadway or tropical fish or the X-Men or baseball statistics or The Smiths or *Mystery Science Theater 3000.* In your heart, you knew all that stuff was cool, but it was safer to keep your mouth shut, to pretend to care a lot less than you did. To stay, as it were, in the closet. But no longer! In the new world, expertise was prized. The niches weren't ghettos. They weren't even niches anymore.

That drastic change didn't happen overnight, but it kind of *felt* like it did, which is what makes the hilarious premise of Paul Constant and Alan Robinson's *PLANET OF THE NERDS* resonate. What if three unreconstructed 1980s jocks woke up today, in our weird era when the dusty corners of late-20th-century geek culture (George R. R. Martin fantasy novels, *Pokémon*, the Guardians of the freaking Galaxy) are now mainstream American culture? (That's right: the Planet of the Nerds [SPOILER WARNING]…is actually Earth! *You maniacs! You blew it up! Damn you! God damn you all to hell!!!)* Trust me, a child of the '80s, when I tell you that you're in good hands here. Paul's clever script and Alan's appealing artwork get both eras exactly right.

Make no mistake: the Planet of the Nerds is no utopia. One of the book's funniest conceits is that when the nerds got the keys to our society, many of them turned out to be just as awful as the jocks they displaced. Think about the amoral CEOs and "tech bros," the frightened Gamergaters, the man-child incels. Power corrupts, no matter your somatotype. Meet the new boss, same as the old boss.

Even so, I, for one, welcome our new nerd overlords. A lot of things seem pretty dire right now, but maybe we nerds will learn from the mistakes of the past and begin to turn our planet around.

At least you don't see Ben Gleck around much anymore. That's nice.

Ken Jennings
Seattle, July 2019

Ken Jennings is a computer scientist, author and the second highest-earning contestant in Jeopardy! *history with the series' longest winning streak at 74 wins. He lives in Seattle with his wife Mindy, his son Dylan and daughter Caitlin, and a small, excitable dog named Chance.*

1

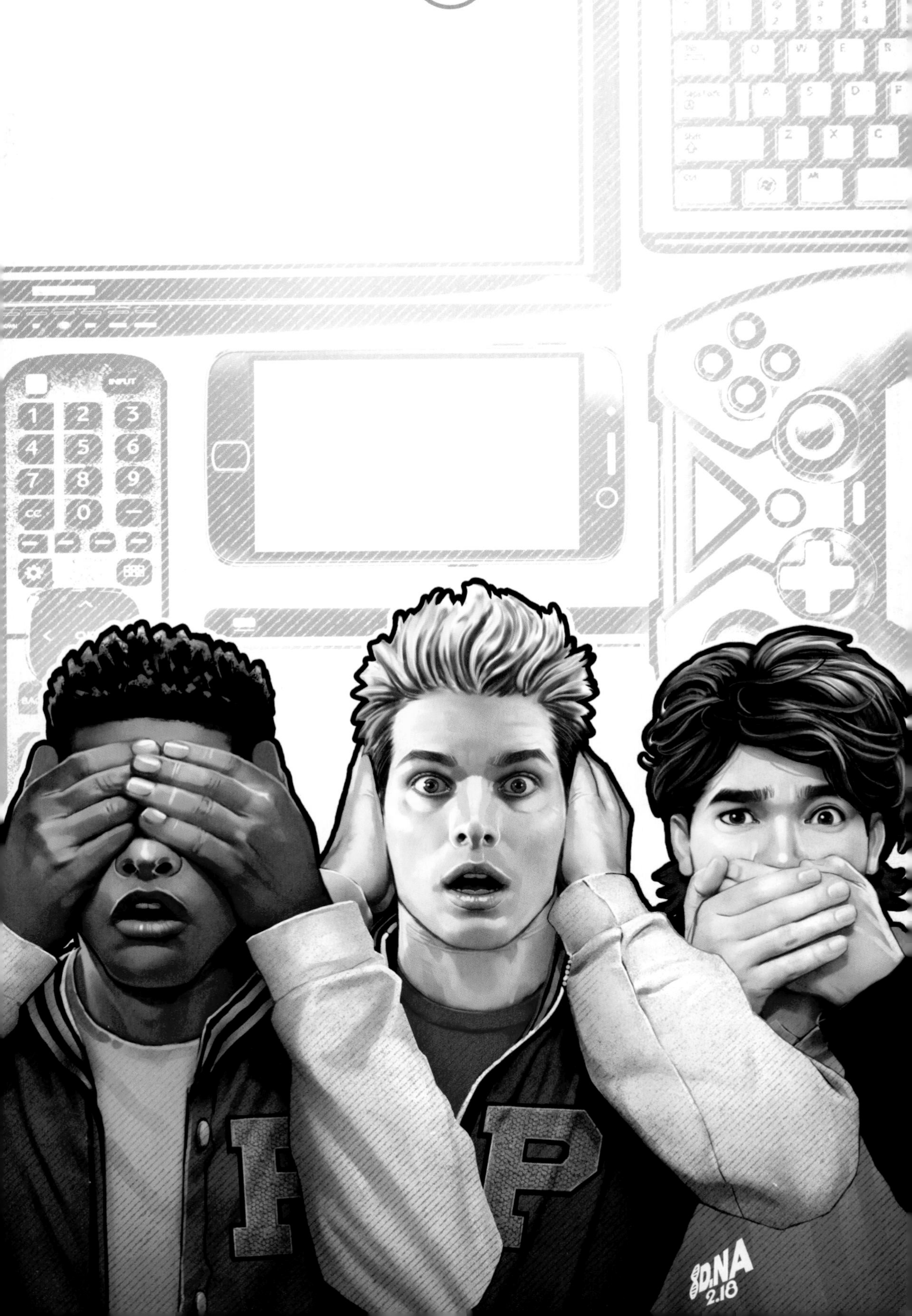
Q W E R
A S D F
Z X C
Shift
INPUT
1 2 3
4 5 6
7 8 9
CC 0
P
D.NA
2.18

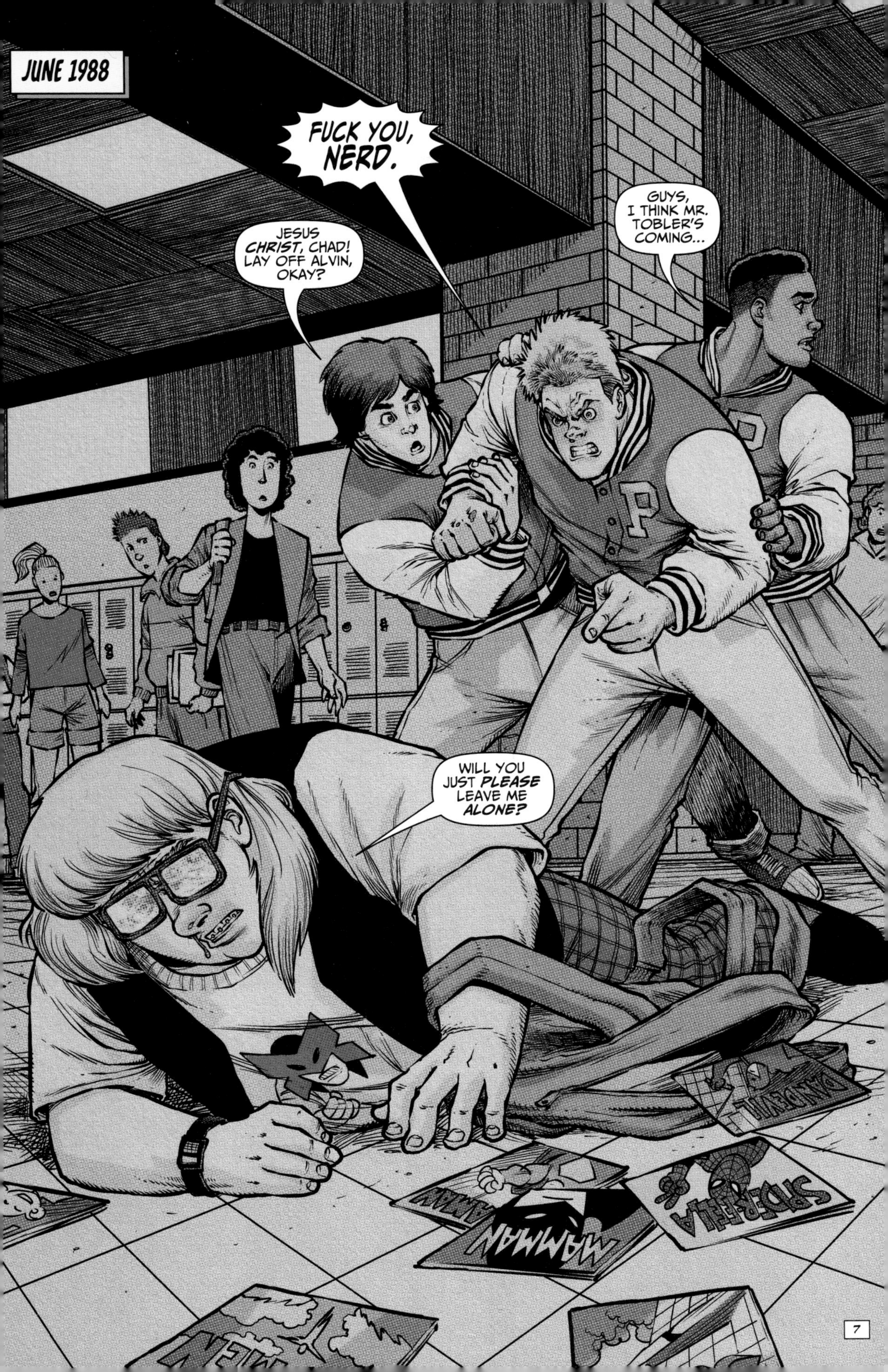
JUNE 1988
FUCK YOU, NERD.
JESUS CHRIST, CHAD! LAY OFF ALVIN, OKAY?
GUYS, I THINK MR. TOBLER'S COMING...
WILL YOU JUST PLEASE LEAVE ME ALONE?

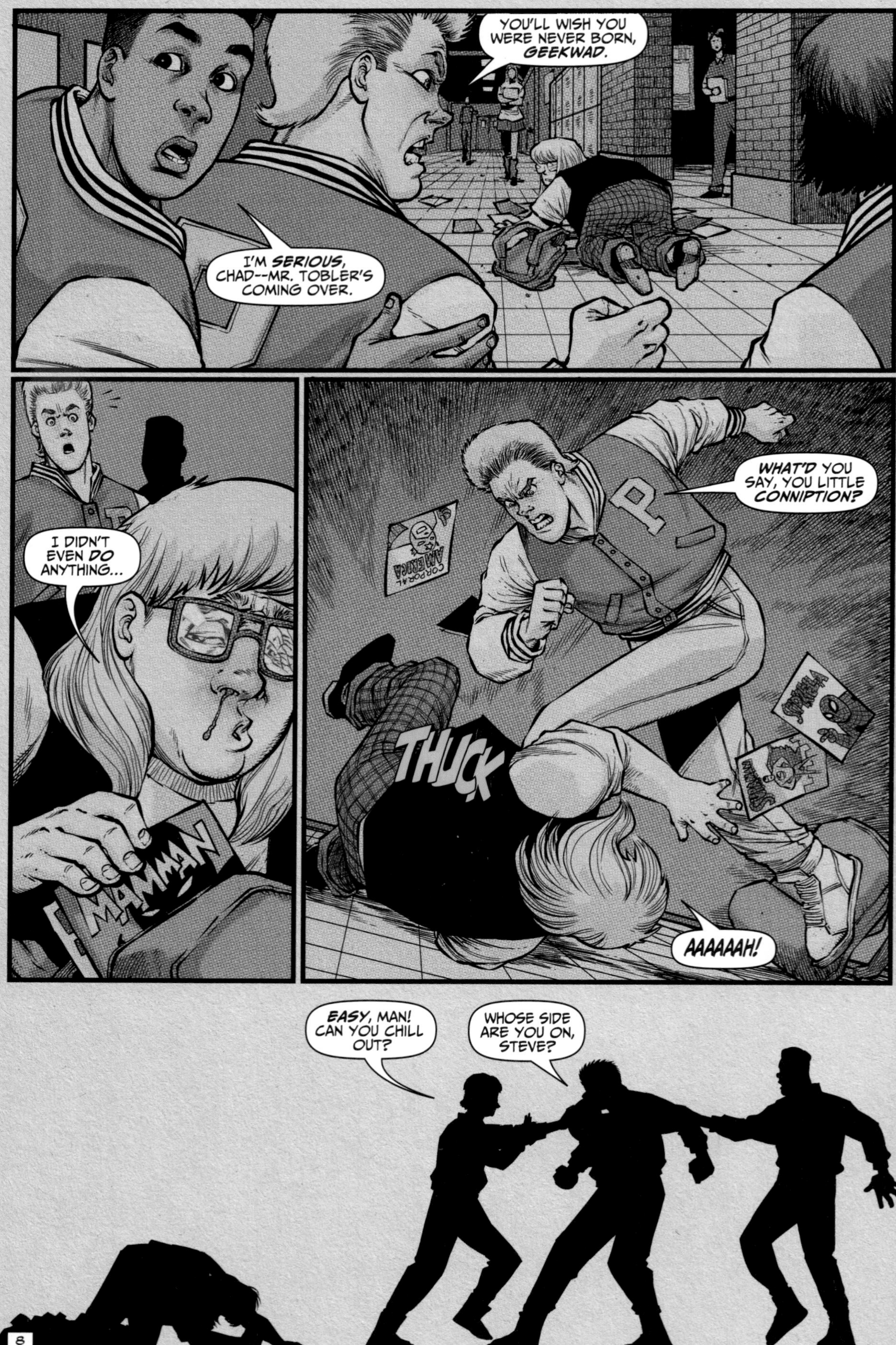
YOU'LL WISH YOU WERE NEVER BORN, GEEKWAD.
I'M SERIOUS, CHAD--MR. TOBLER'S COMING OVER.
I DIDN'T EVEN DO ANYTHING...
WHAT'D YOU SAY, YOU LITTLE CONNIPTION?
CORPORAL AMERICA
THUCK
AAAAAAH!
EASY, MAN! CAN YOU CHILL OUT?
WHOSE SIDE ARE YOU ON, STEVE?

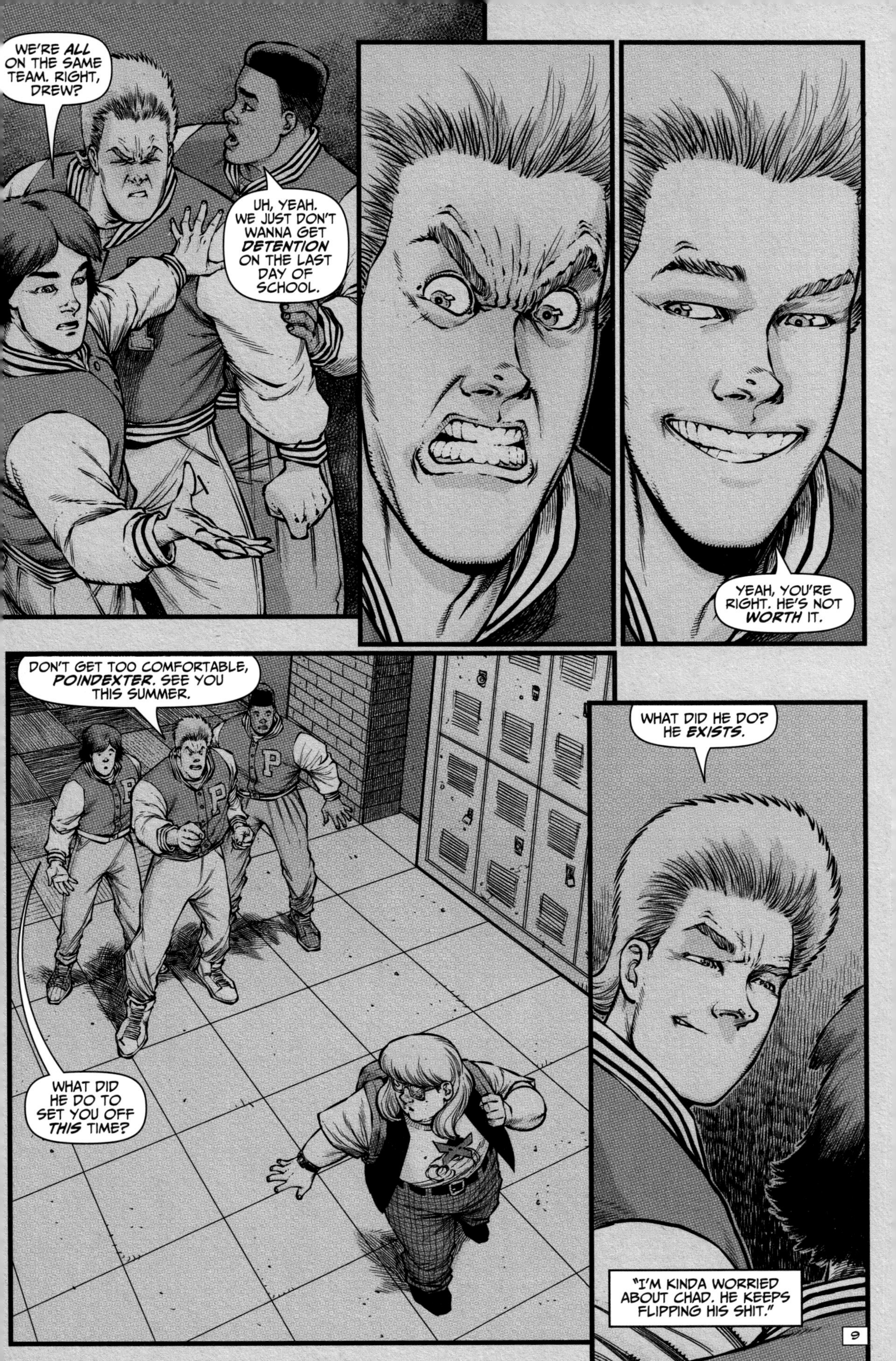
WE'RE *ALL* ON THE SAME TEAM. RIGHT, DREW?
UH, YEAH. WE JUST DON'T WANNA GET *DETENTION* ON THE LAST DAY OF SCHOOL.
YEAH, YOU'RE RIGHT. HE'S NOT *WORTH* IT.
DON'T GET TOO COMFORTABLE, *POINDEXTER*. SEE YOU THIS SUMMER.
WHAT DID HE DO TO SET YOU OFF *THIS* TIME?
WHAT DID HE DO? HE *EXISTS*.
"I'M KINDA WORRIED ABOUT CHAD. HE KEEPS FLIPPING HIS SHIT."

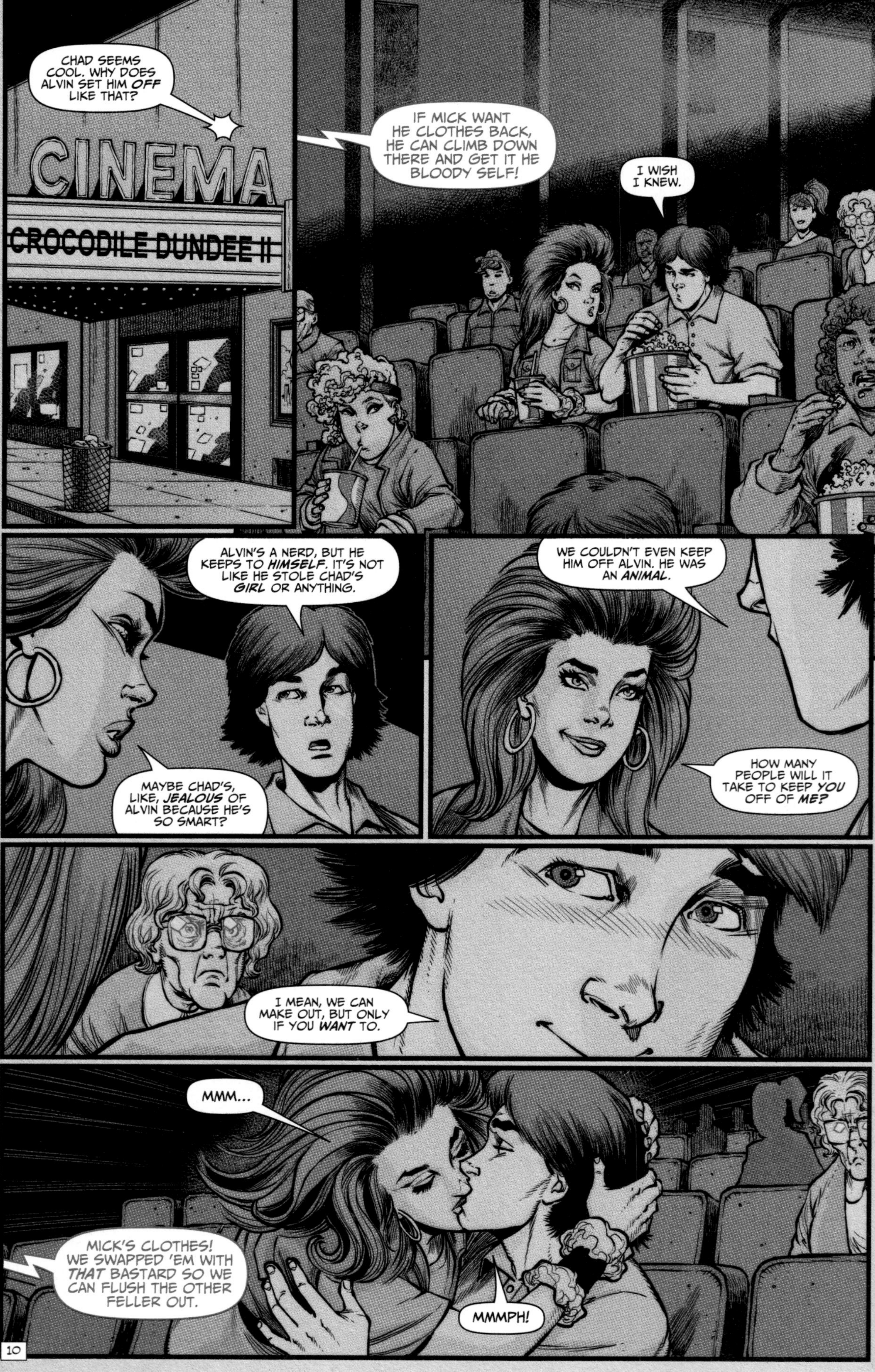
CHAD SEEMS COOL. WHY DOES ALVIN SET HIM OFF LIKE THAT?
CINEMA
CROCODILE DUNDEE II
IF MICK WANT HE CLOTHES BACK, HE CAN CLIMB DOWN THERE AND GET IT HE BLOODY SELF!
I WISH I KNEW.
ALVIN'S A NERD, BUT HE KEEPS TO HIMSELF. IT'S NOT LIKE HE STOLE CHAD'S GIRL OR ANYTHING.
MAYBE CHAD'S, LIKE, JEALOUS OF ALVIN BECAUSE HE'S SO SMART?
WE COULDN'T EVEN KEEP HIM OFF ALVIN. HE WAS AN ANIMAL.
HOW MANY PEOPLE WILL IT TAKE TO KEEP YOU OFF OF ME?
I MEAN, WE CAN MAKE OUT, BUT ONLY IF YOU WANT TO.
MMM...
MICK'S CLOTHES! WE SWAPPED 'EM WITH THAT BASTARD SO WE CAN FLUSH THE OTHER FELLER OUT.
MMMPH!

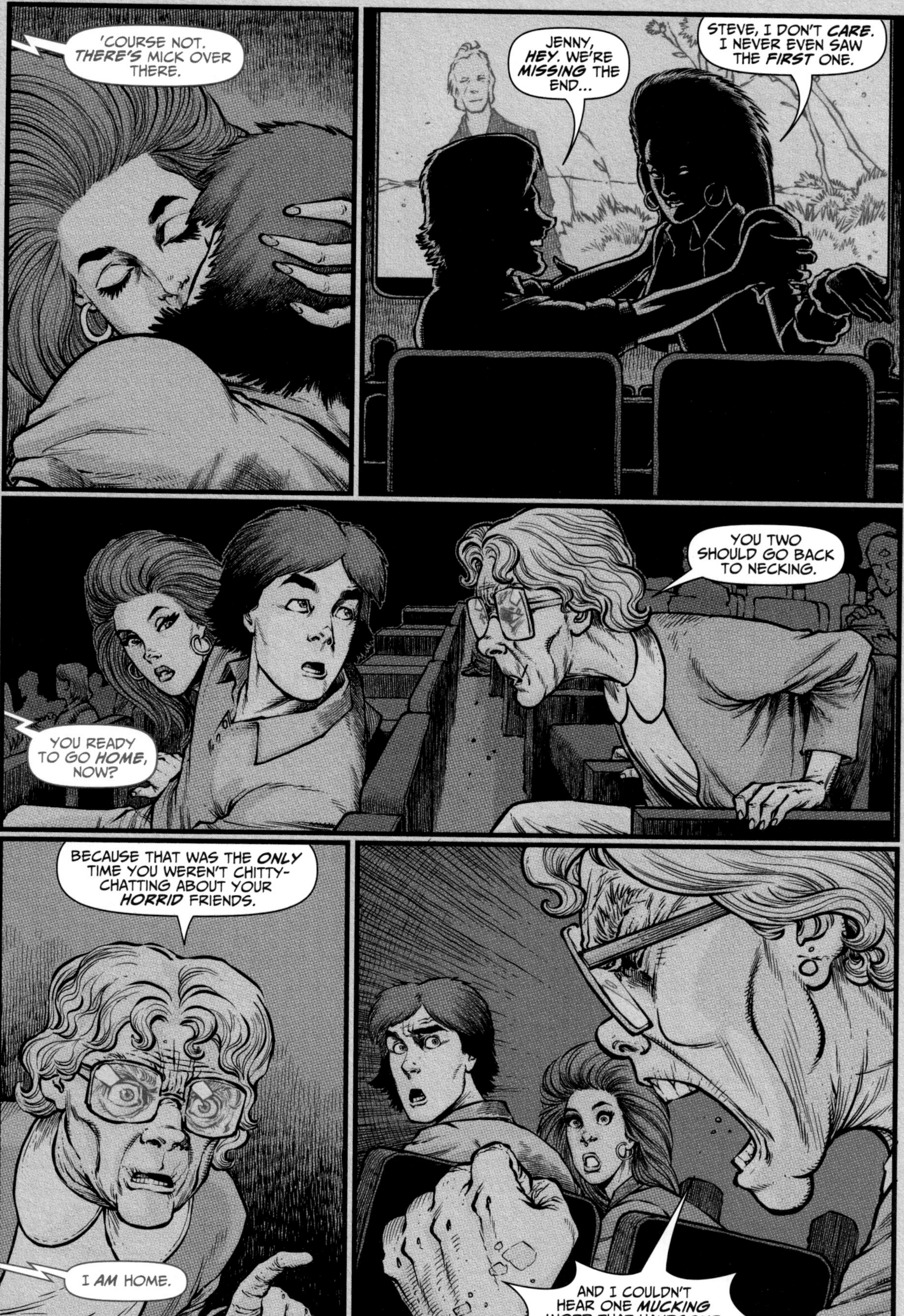
'COURSE NOT. THERE'S MICK OVER THERE.
JENNY, HEY. WE'RE MISSING THE END...
STEVE, I DON'T CARE. I NEVER EVEN SAW THE FIRST ONE.
YOU TWO SHOULD GO BACK TO NECKING.
YOU READY TO GO HOME, NOW?
BECAUSE THAT WAS THE ONLY TIME YOU WEREN'T CHITTY-CHATTING ABOUT YOUR HORRID FRIENDS.
I AM HOME.
AND I COULDN'T HEAR ONE MUCKING WORD THAT HANDSOME PAUL HOGAN SAID BECAUSE OF YOU LITTLE CRASSHOLES!

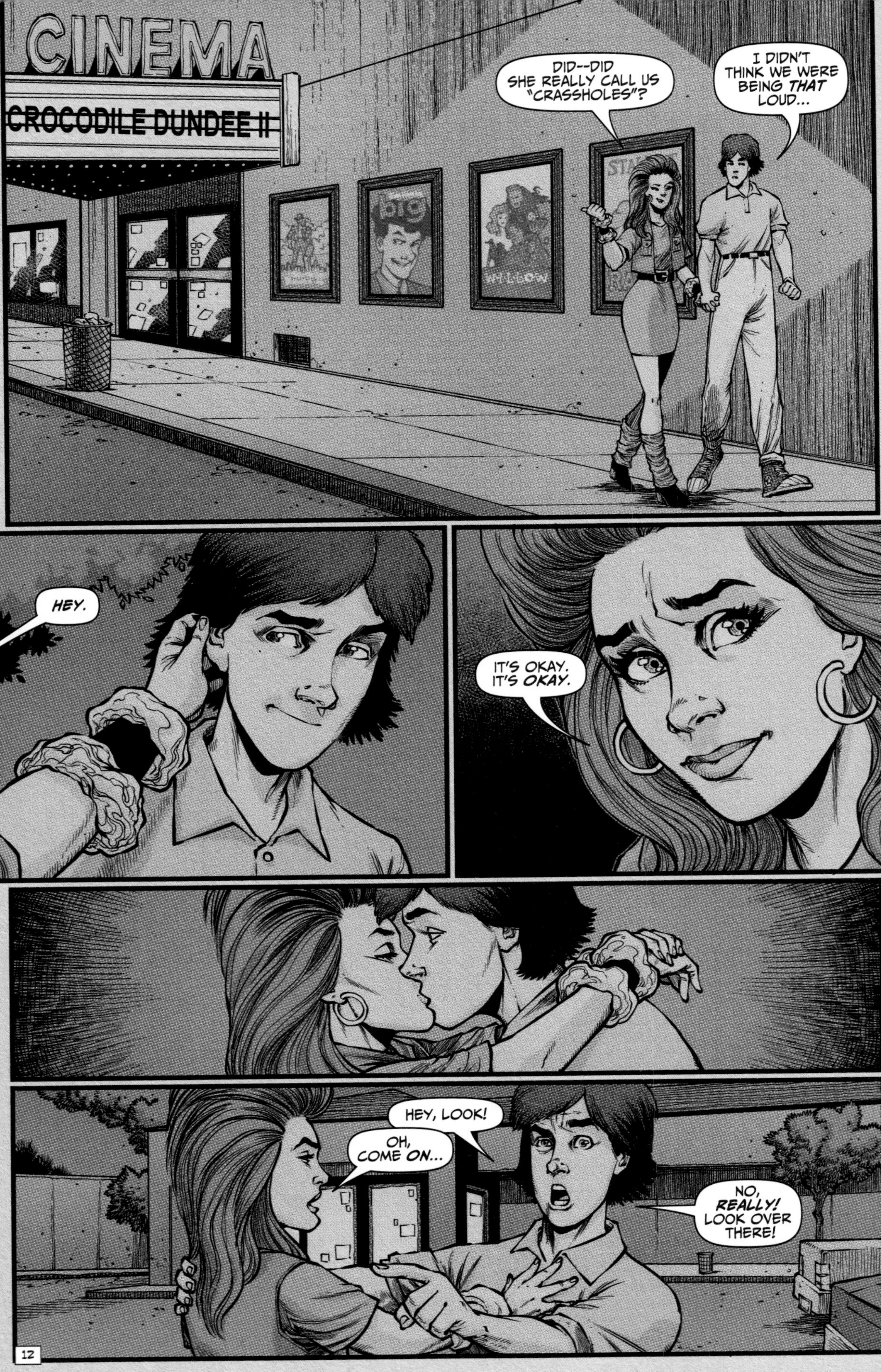
CINEMA
CROCODILE DUNDEE II
DID--DID SHE REALLY CALL US "CRASSHOLES"?
I DIDN'T THINK WE WERE BEING THAT LOUD...
WILLOW
HEY.
IT'S OKAY. IT'S OKAY.
HEY, LOOK!
OH, COME ON...
NO, REALLY! LOOK OVER THERE!

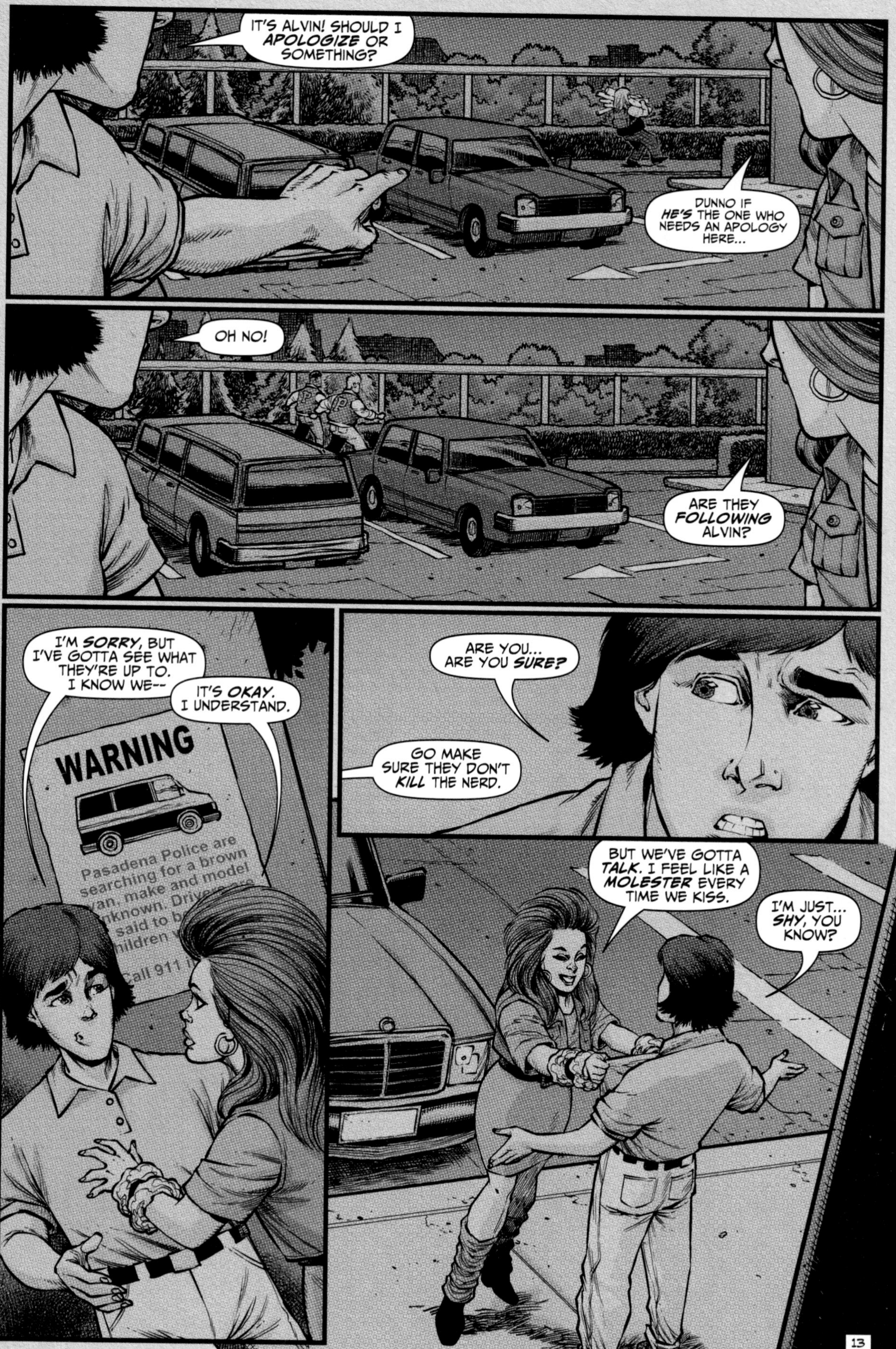
IT'S ALVIN! SHOULD I *APOLOGIZE* OR SOMETHING?
DUNNO IF *HE'S* THE ONE WHO NEEDS AN APOLOGY HERE...
OH NO!
ARE THEY *FOLLOWING* ALVIN?
I'M *SORRY*, BUT I'VE GOTTA SEE WHAT THEY'RE UP TO. I KNOW WE--
IT'S *OKAY*. I UNDERSTAND.
WARNING
Pasadena Police are
searching for a brown
ARE YOU... ARE YOU *SURE?*
GO MAKE SURE THEY DON'T *KILL* THE NERD.
BUT WE'VE GOTTA *TALK*. I FEEL LIKE A *MOLESTER* EVERY TIME WE KISS.
I'M JUST... *SHY*, YOU KNOW?

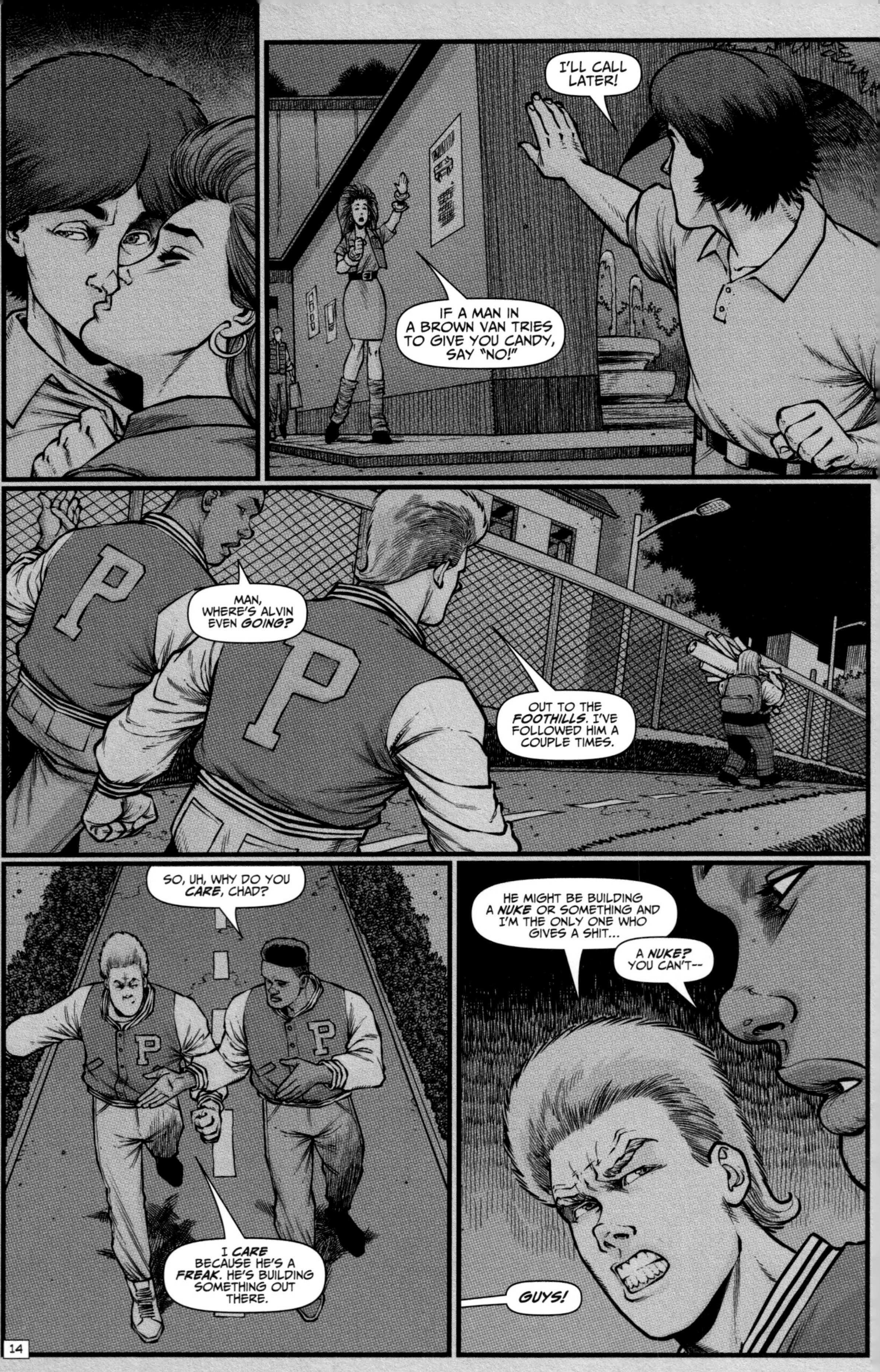
I'LL CALL LATER!
IF A MAN IN A BROWN VAN TRIES TO GIVE YOU CANDY, SAY "NO!"
MAN, WHERE'S ALVIN EVEN GOING?
OUT TO THE FOOTHILLS. I'VE FOLLOWED HIM A COUPLE TIMES.
SO, UH, WHY DO YOU CARE, CHAD?
I CARE BECAUSE HE'S A FREAK. HE'S BUILDING SOMETHING OUT THERE.
HE MIGHT BE BUILDING A NUKE OR SOMETHING AND I'M THE ONLY ONE WHO GIVES A SHIT...
A NUKE? YOU CAN'T--
GUYS!

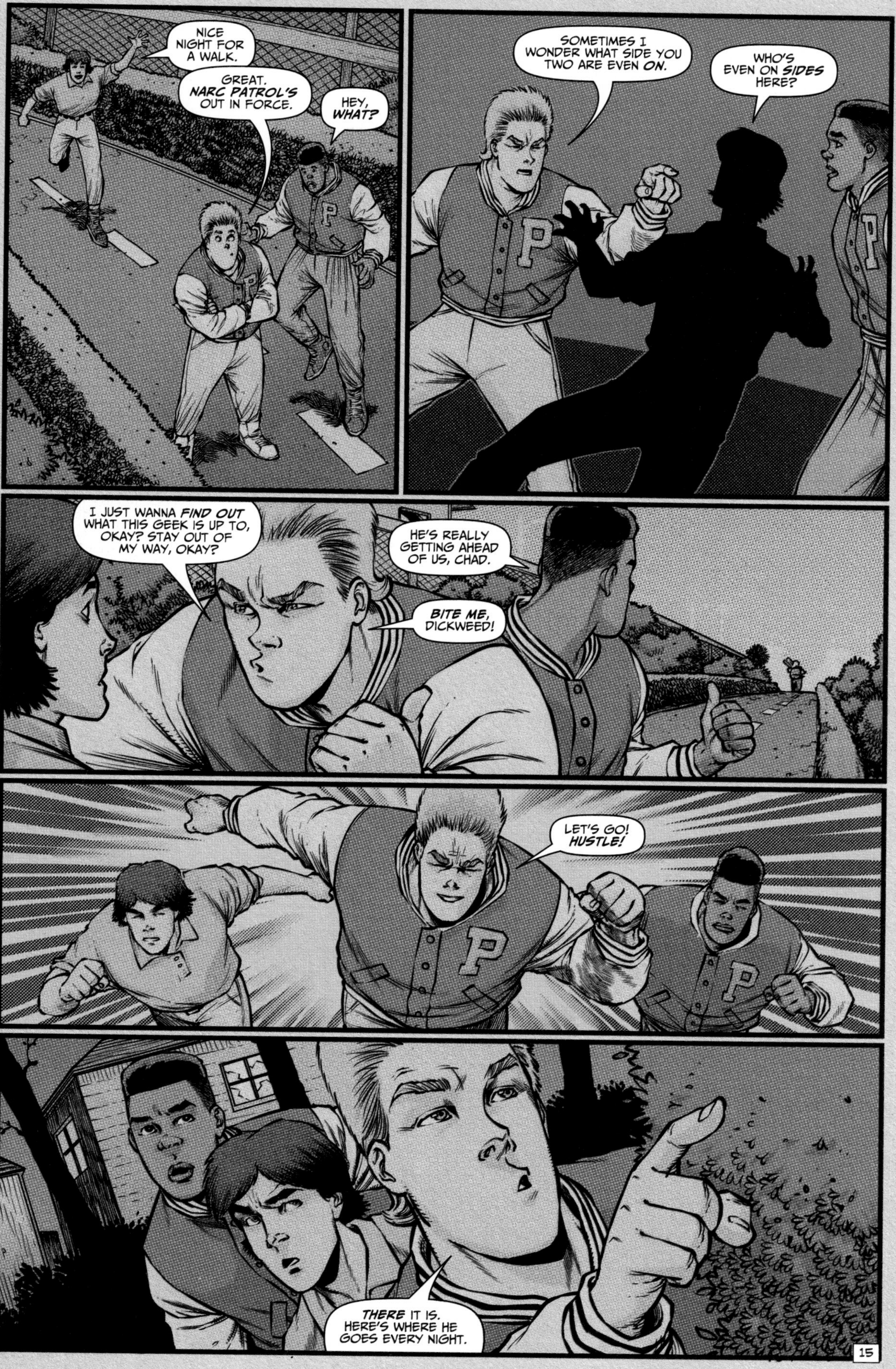

NICE NIGHT FOR A WALK.
GREAT. NARC PATROL'S OUT IN FORCE.
HEY, WHAT?
SOMETIMES I WONDER WHAT SIDE YOU TWO ARE EVEN ON.
WHO'S EVEN ON SIDES HERE?
I JUST WANNA FIND OUT WHAT THIS GEEK IS UP TO, OKAY? STAY OUT OF MY WAY, OKAY?
HE'S REALLY GETTING AHEAD OF US, CHAD.
BITE ME, DICKWEED!
LET'S GO! HUSTLE!
THERE IT IS. HERE'S WHERE HE GOES EVERY NIGHT.

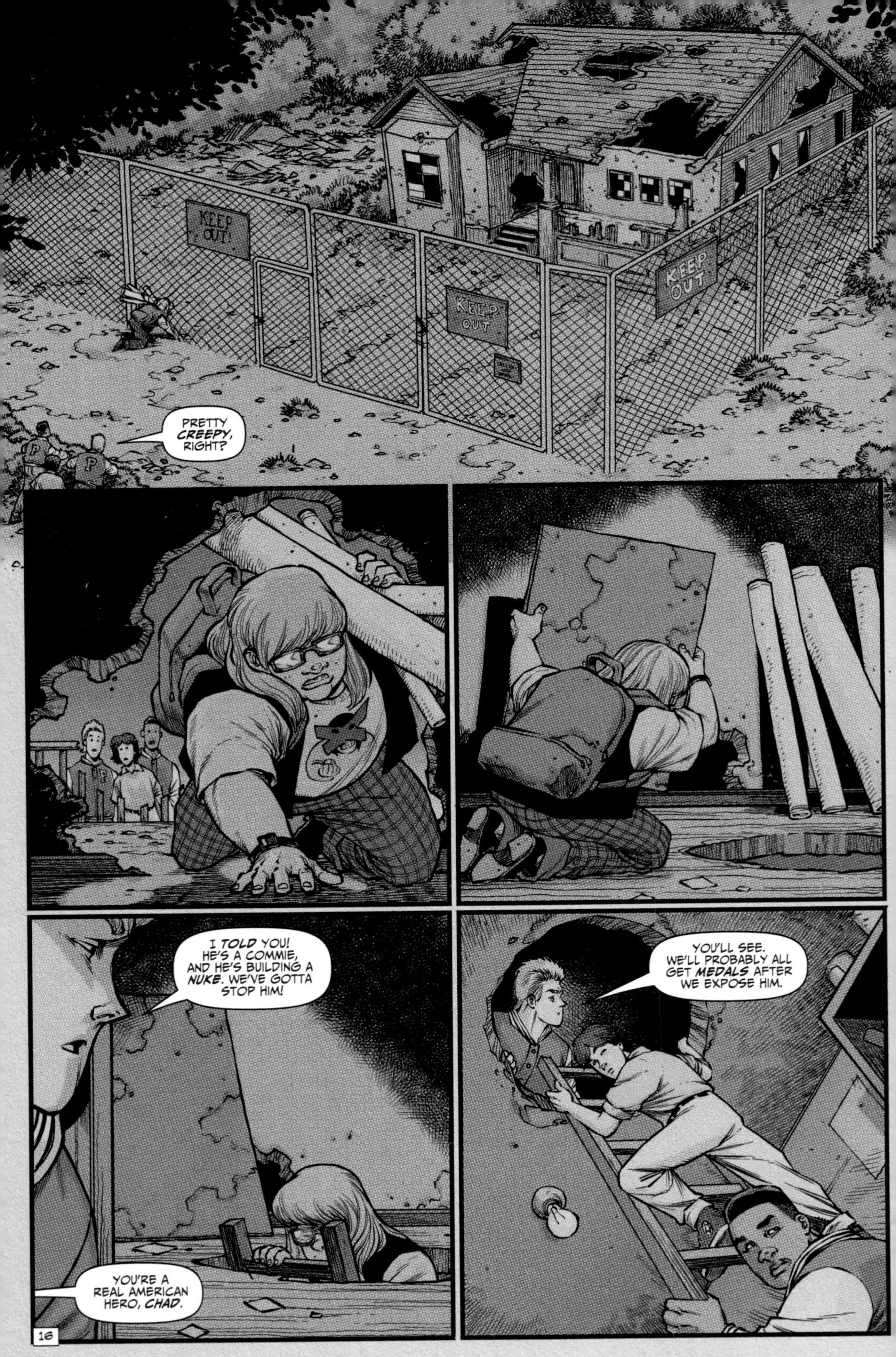
KEEP OUT!
KEEP OUT
KEEP OUT
PRETTY CREEPY, RIGHT?
I TOLD YOU! HE'S A COMMIE, AND HE'S BUILDING A NUKE. WE'VE GOTTA STOP HIM!
YOU'RE A REAL AMERICAN HERO, CHAD.
YOU'LL SEE. WE'LL PROBABLY ALL GET MEDALS AFTER WE EXPOSE HIM.

I'D FEEL BETTER IF I HAD SOMETHING TO *EVEN THE PLAYING FIELD*.

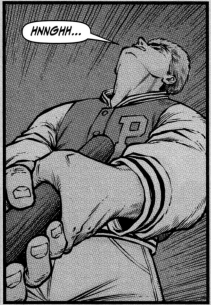

HNNGHH...

GAAAAH!

SPLICHT

HEY, WAIT FOR ME!

WHAT THE HELL IS *THAT?*

17

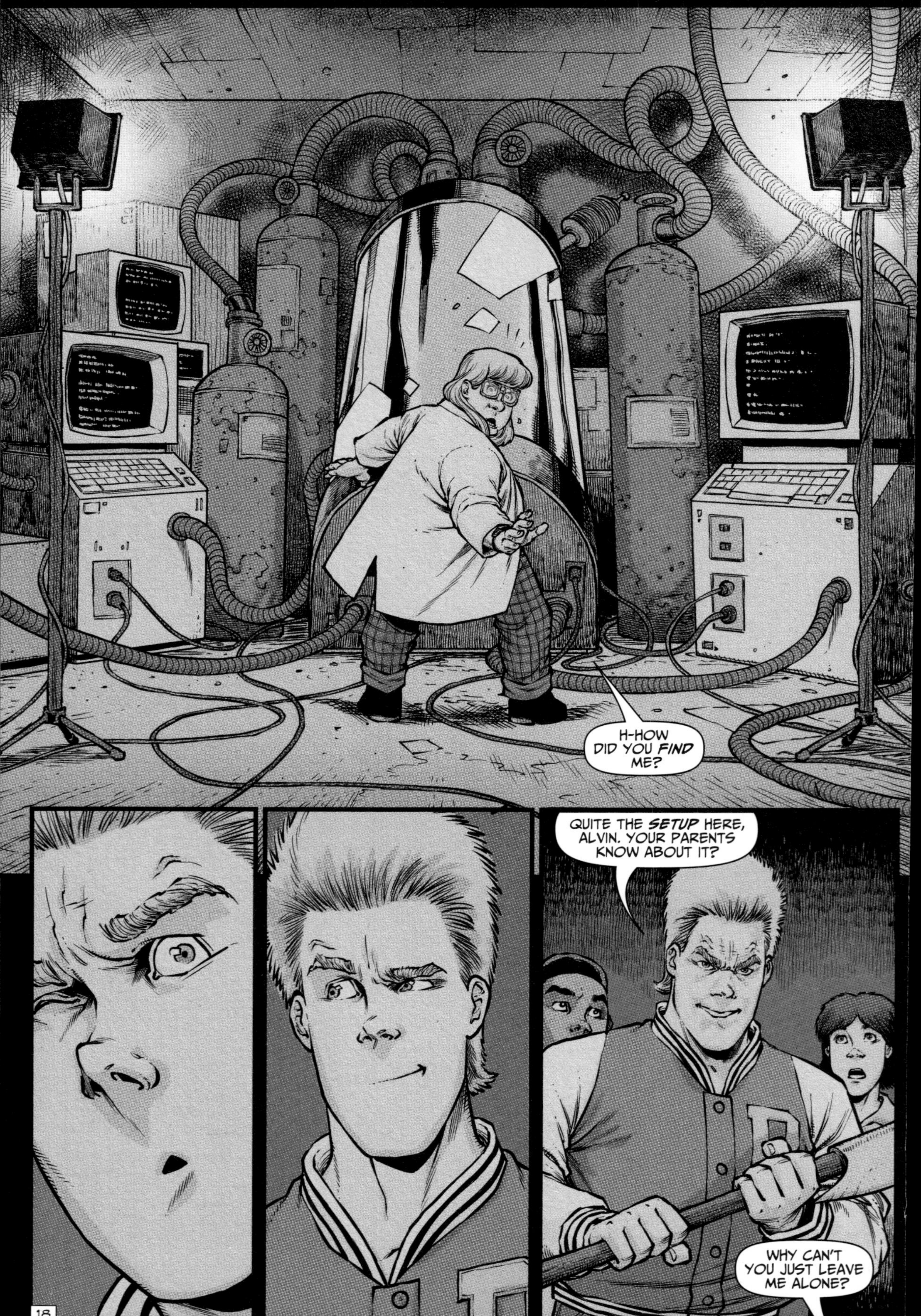
H-HOW DID YOU FIND ME?
QUITE THE SETUP HERE, ALVIN. YOUR PARENTS KNOW ABOUT IT?
WHY CAN'T YOU JUST LEAVE ME ALONE?

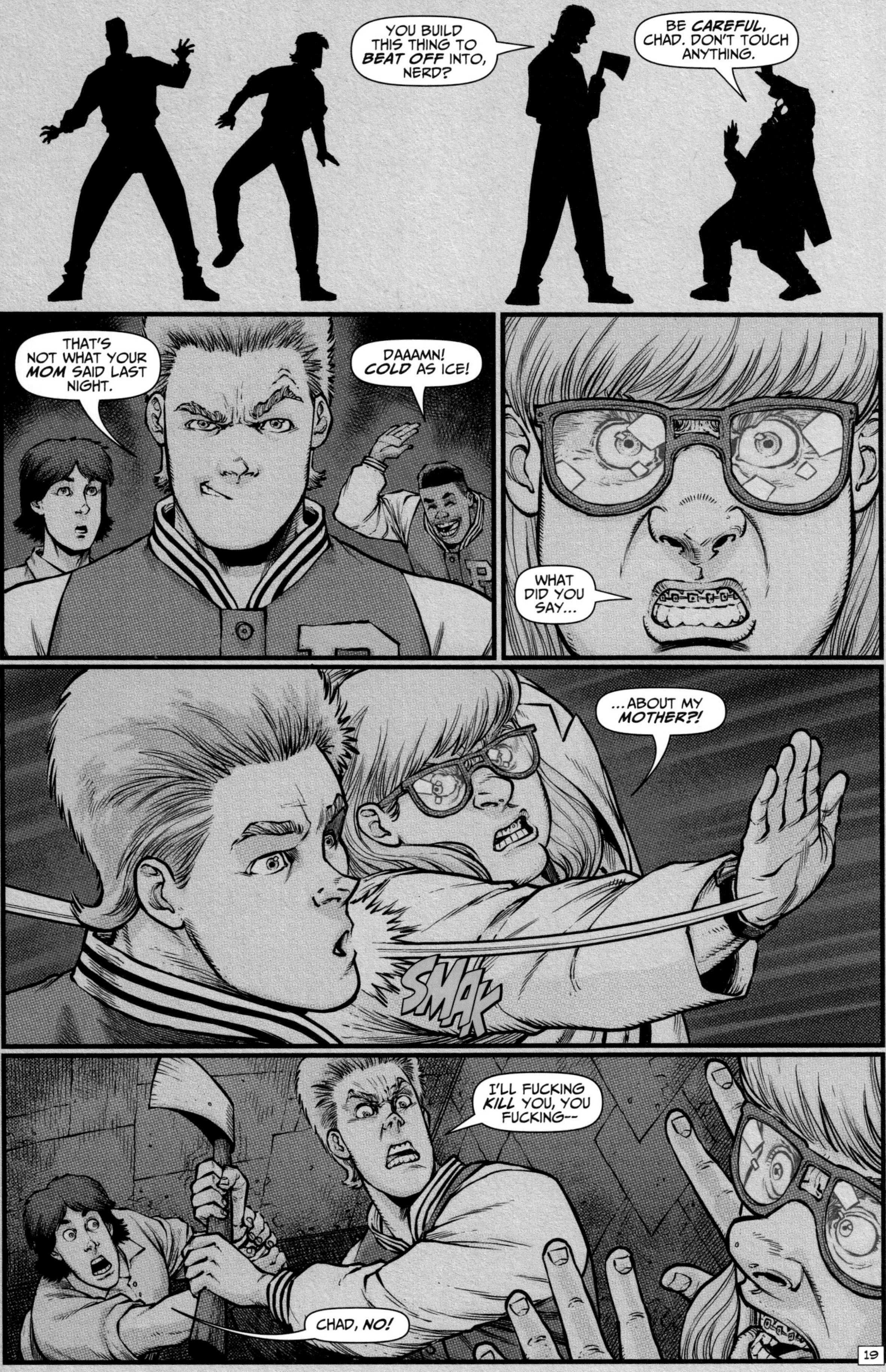
YOU BUILD THIS THING TO BEAT OFF INTO, NERD?
BE CAREFUL, CHAD. DON'T TOUCH ANYTHING.
THAT'S NOT WHAT YOUR MOM SAID LAST NIGHT.
DAAAMN! COLD AS ICE!
WHAT DID YOU SAY...
...ABOUT MY MOTHER?!
SMAK
I'LL FUCKING KILL YOU, YOU FUCKING--
CHAD, NO!

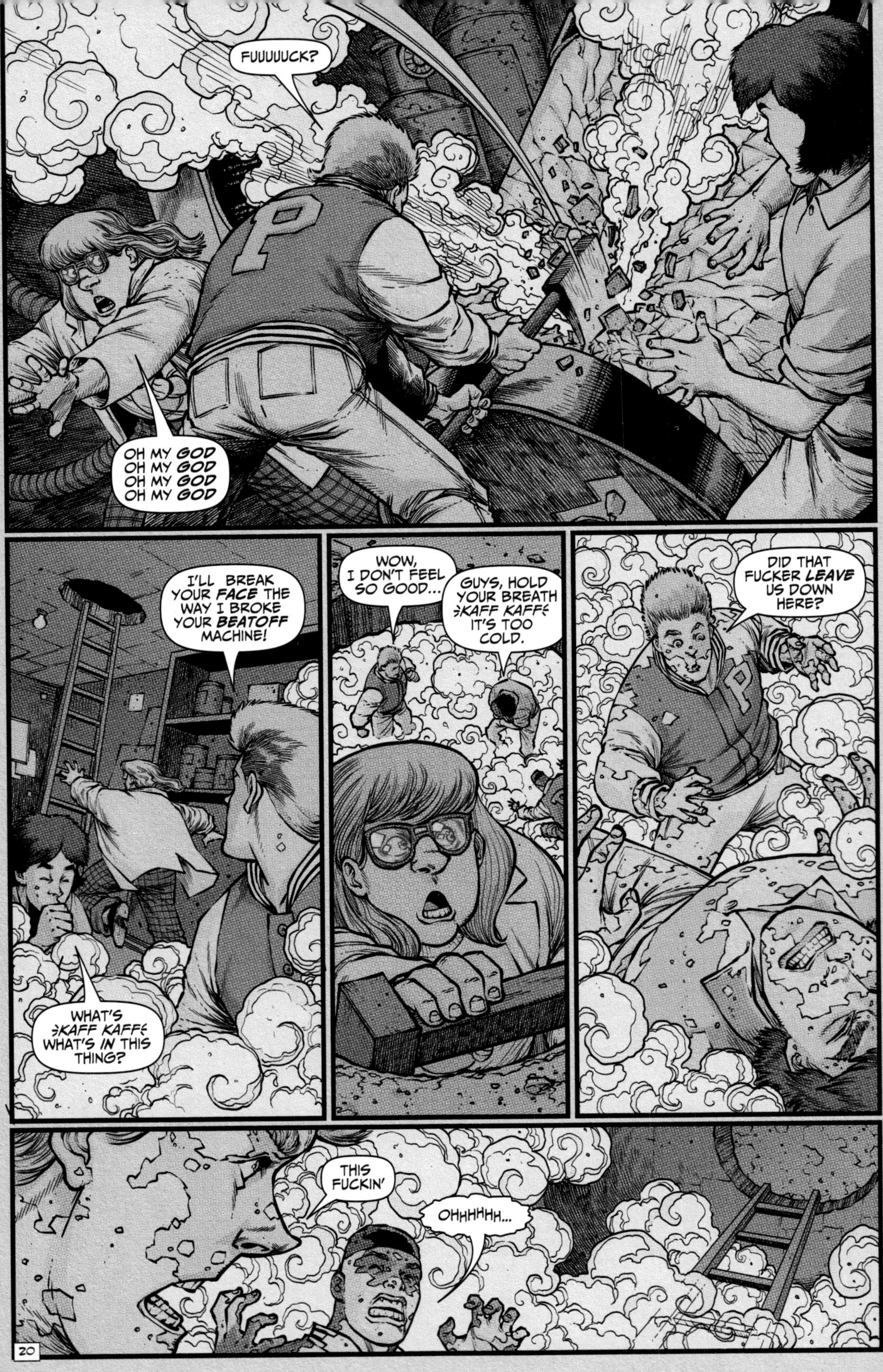
FUUUUUCK?
OH MY GOD OH MY GOD OH MY GOD OH MY GOD
I'LL BREAK YOUR FACE THE WAY I BROKE YOUR BEATOFF MACHINE!
WHAT'S KAFF KAFF WHAT'S IN THIS THING?
WOW, I DON'T FEEL SO GOOD...
GUYS, HOLD YOUR BREATH KAFF KAFF IT'S TOO COLD.
DID THAT FUCKER LEAVE US DOWN HERE?
THIS FUCKIN'
OHHHHHH...

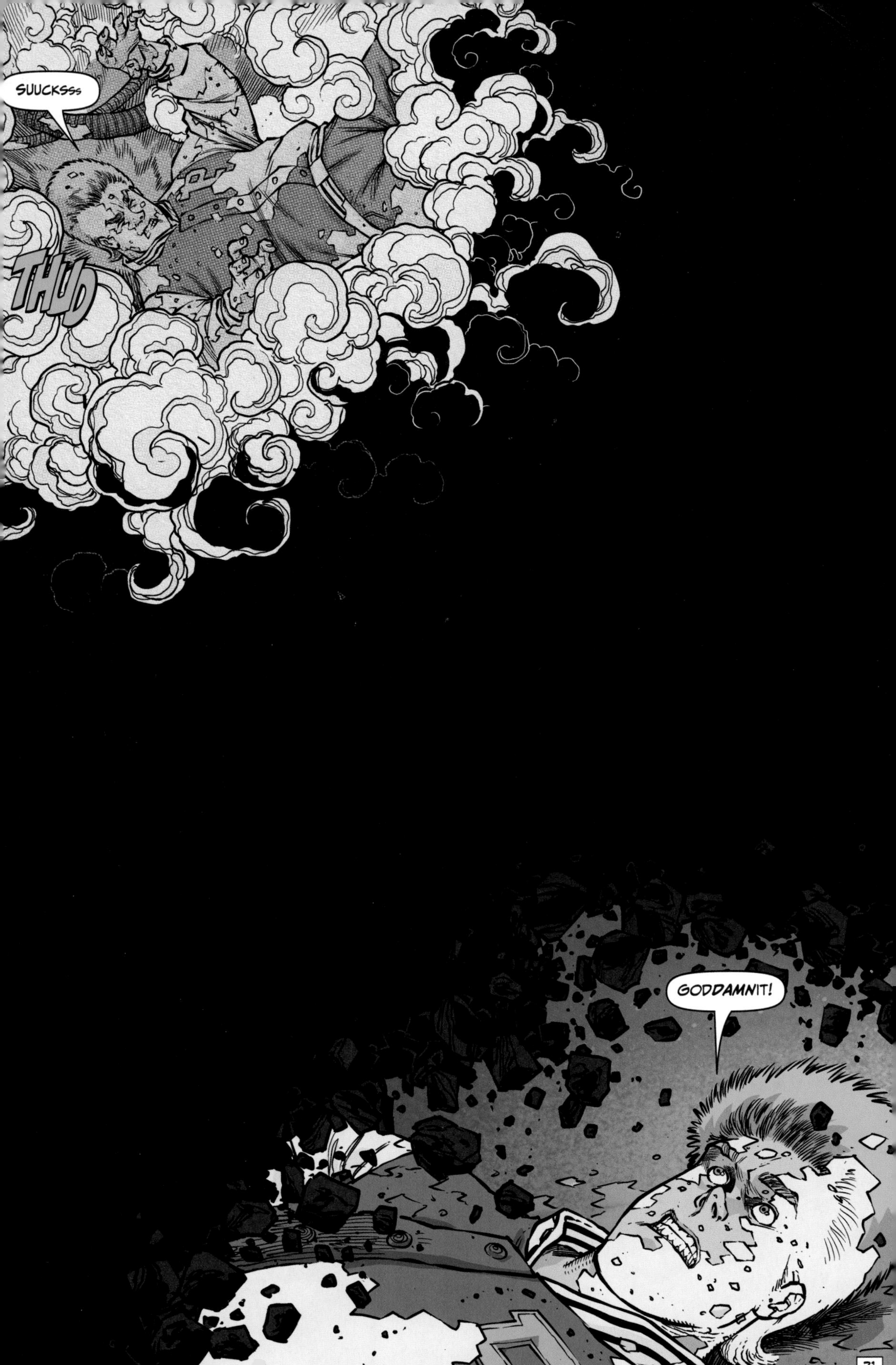
SUUCKSss
THUD
GODDAMNIT!

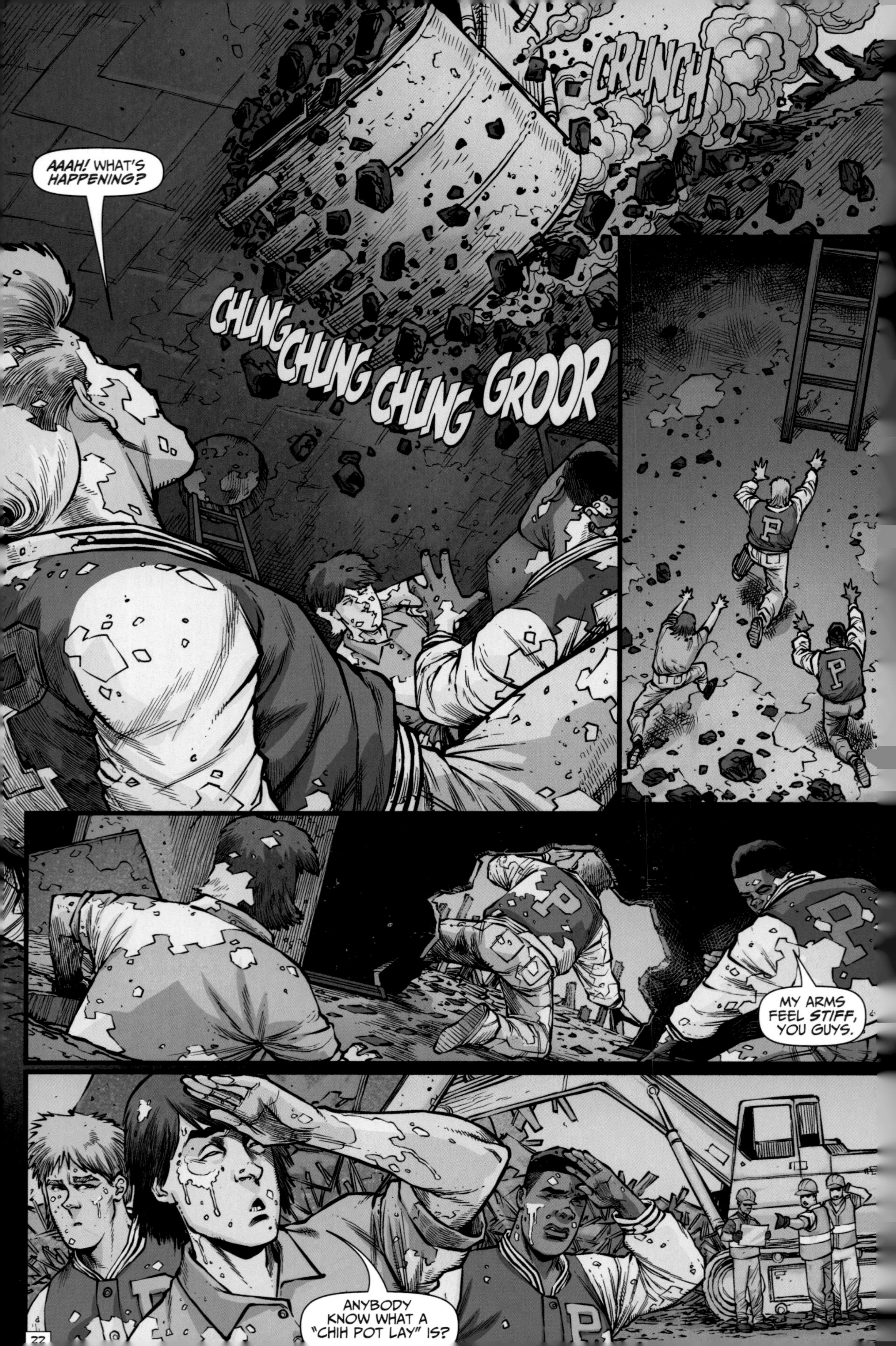
CRUNCH
AAAH! WHAT'S HAPPENING?
CHUNG CHUNG CHUNG GROOR
MY ARMS FEEL STIFF, YOU GUYS.
ANYBODY KNOW WHAT A "CHIH POT LAY" IS?

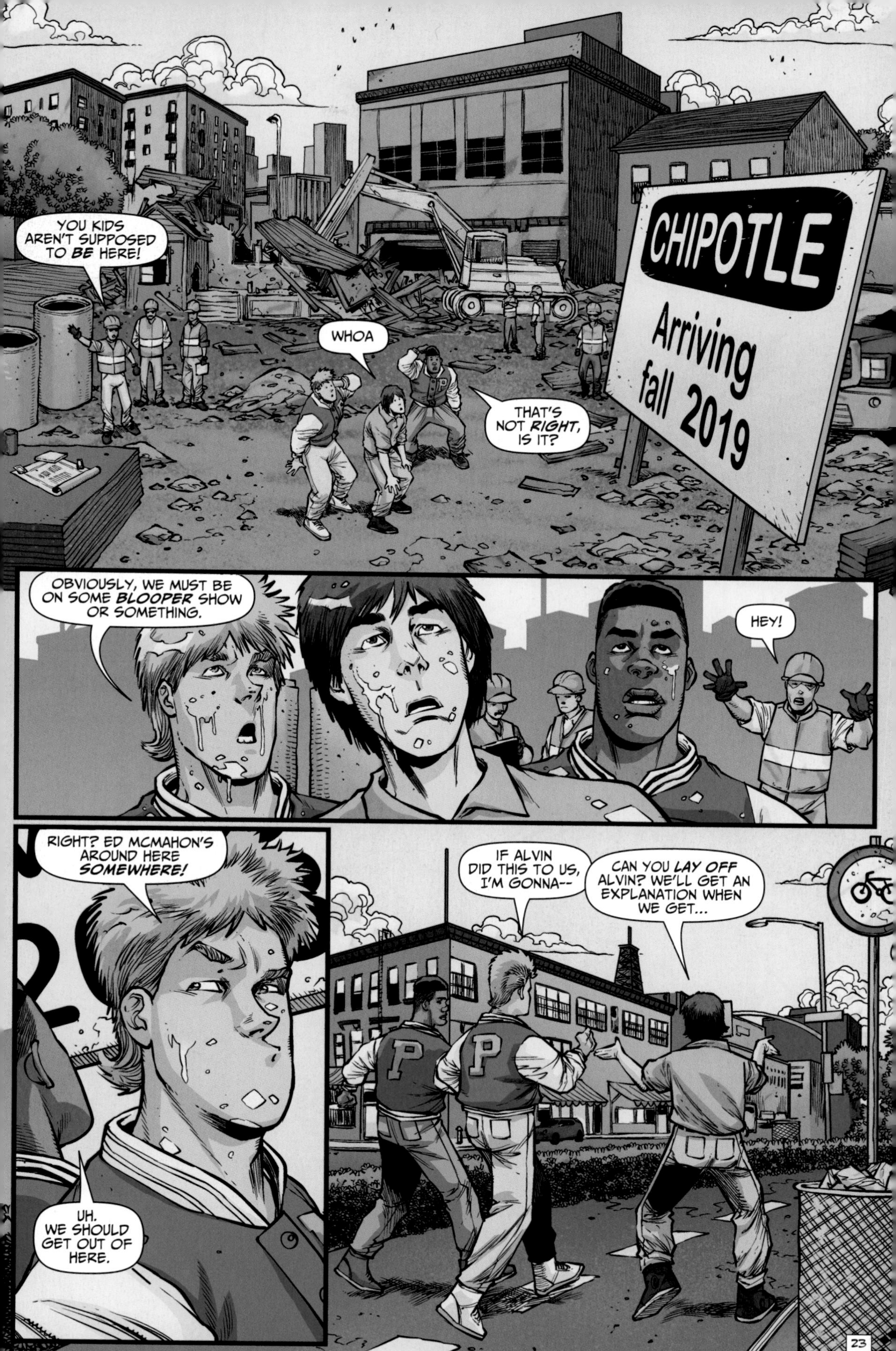

YOU KIDS AREN'T SUPPOSED TO BE HERE!
WHOA
THAT'S NOT RIGHT, IS IT?
CHIPOTLE
Arriving fall 2019
OBVIOUSLY, WE MUST BE ON SOME BLOOPER SHOW OR SOMETHING.
HEY!
RIGHT? ED MCMAHON'S AROUND HERE SOMEWHERE!
UH. WE SHOULD GET OUT OF HERE.
IF ALVIN DID THIS TO US, I'M GONNA--
CAN YOU LAY OFF ALVIN? WE'LL GET AN EXPLANATION WHEN WE GET...

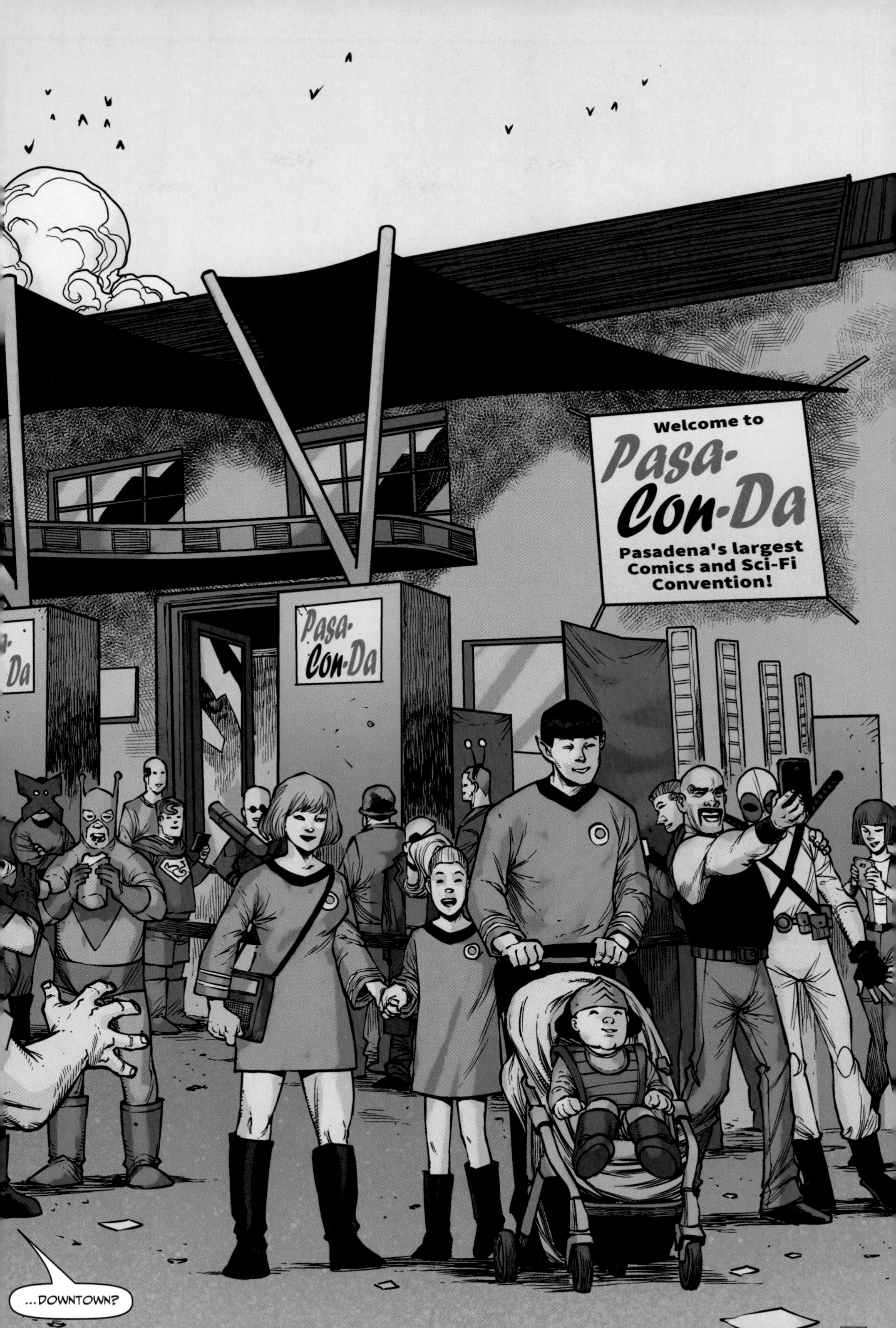

Welcome to
Pasa-Con-Da
Pasadena's largest Comics and Sci-Fi Convention!
Pasa-Con-Da
...DOWNTOWN?

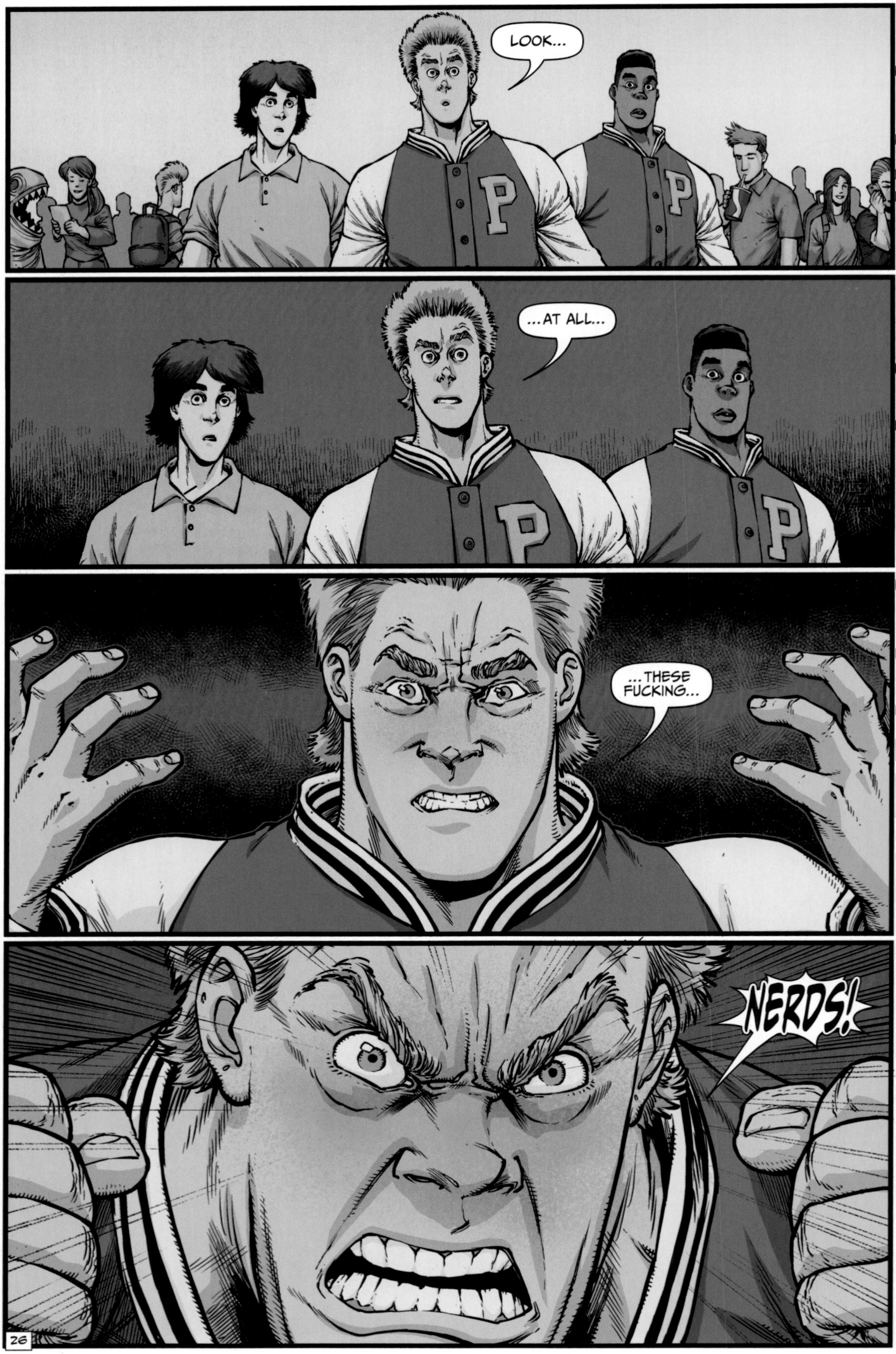
LOOK...
...AT ALL...
...THESE FUCKING...
NERDS!

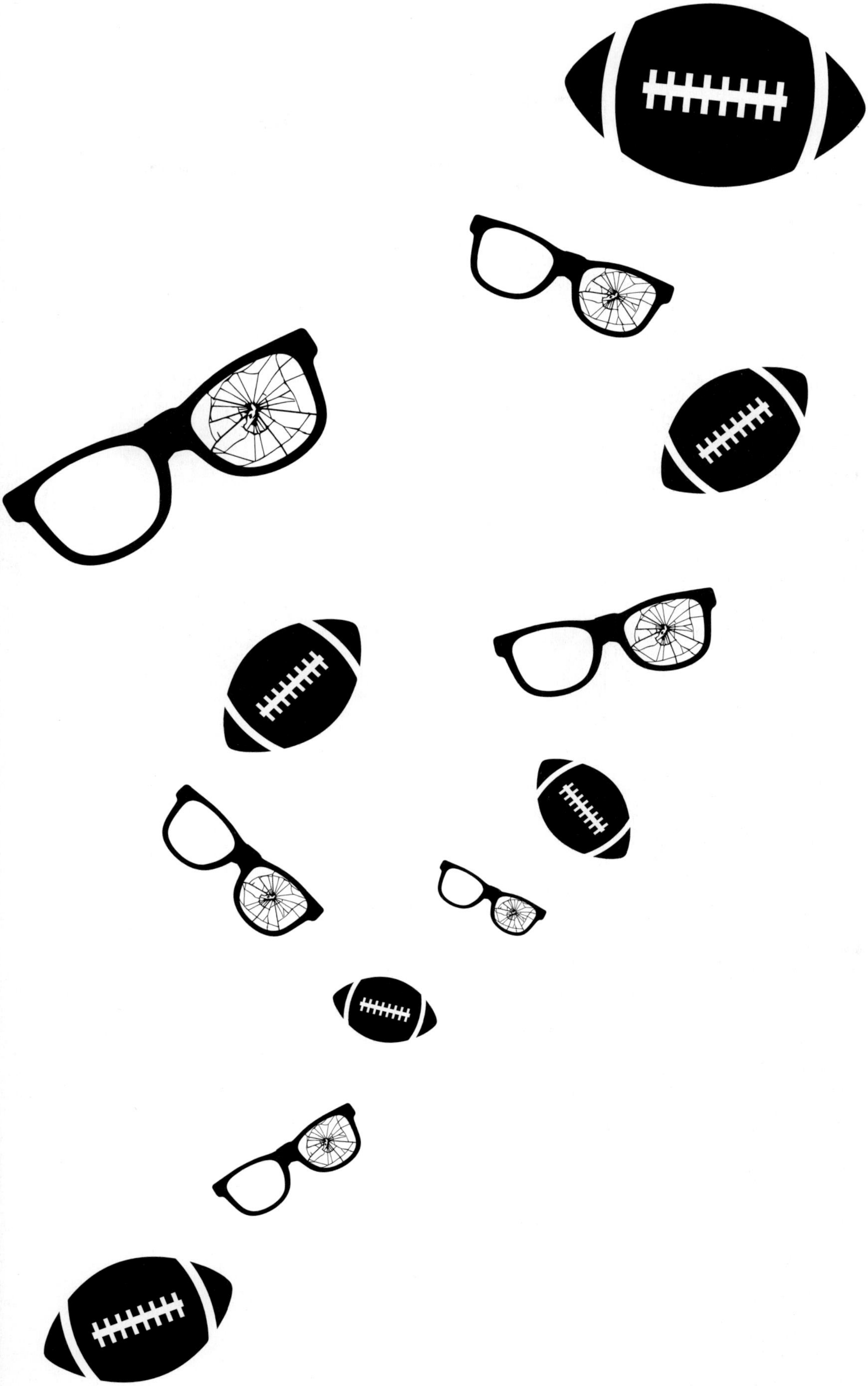

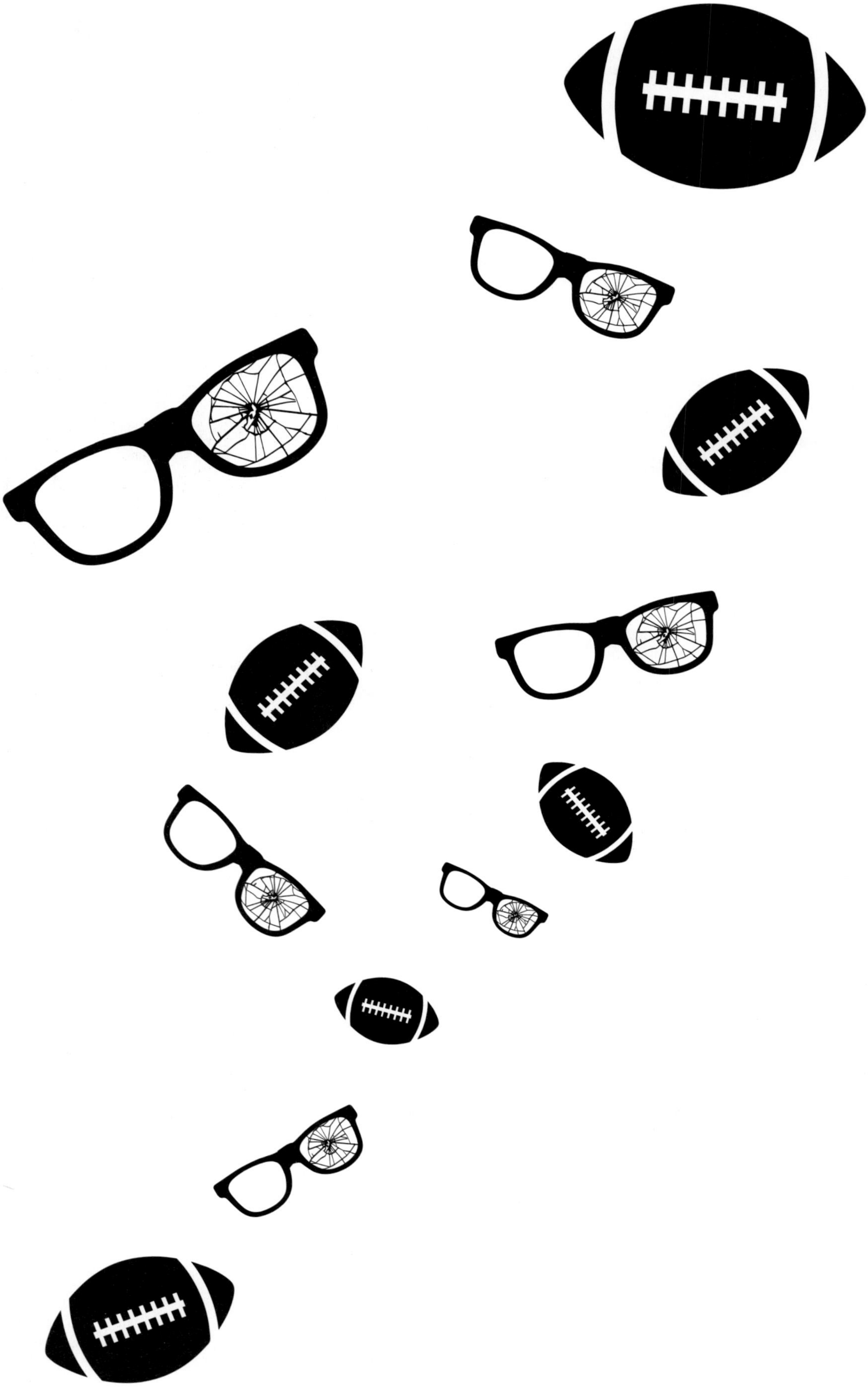

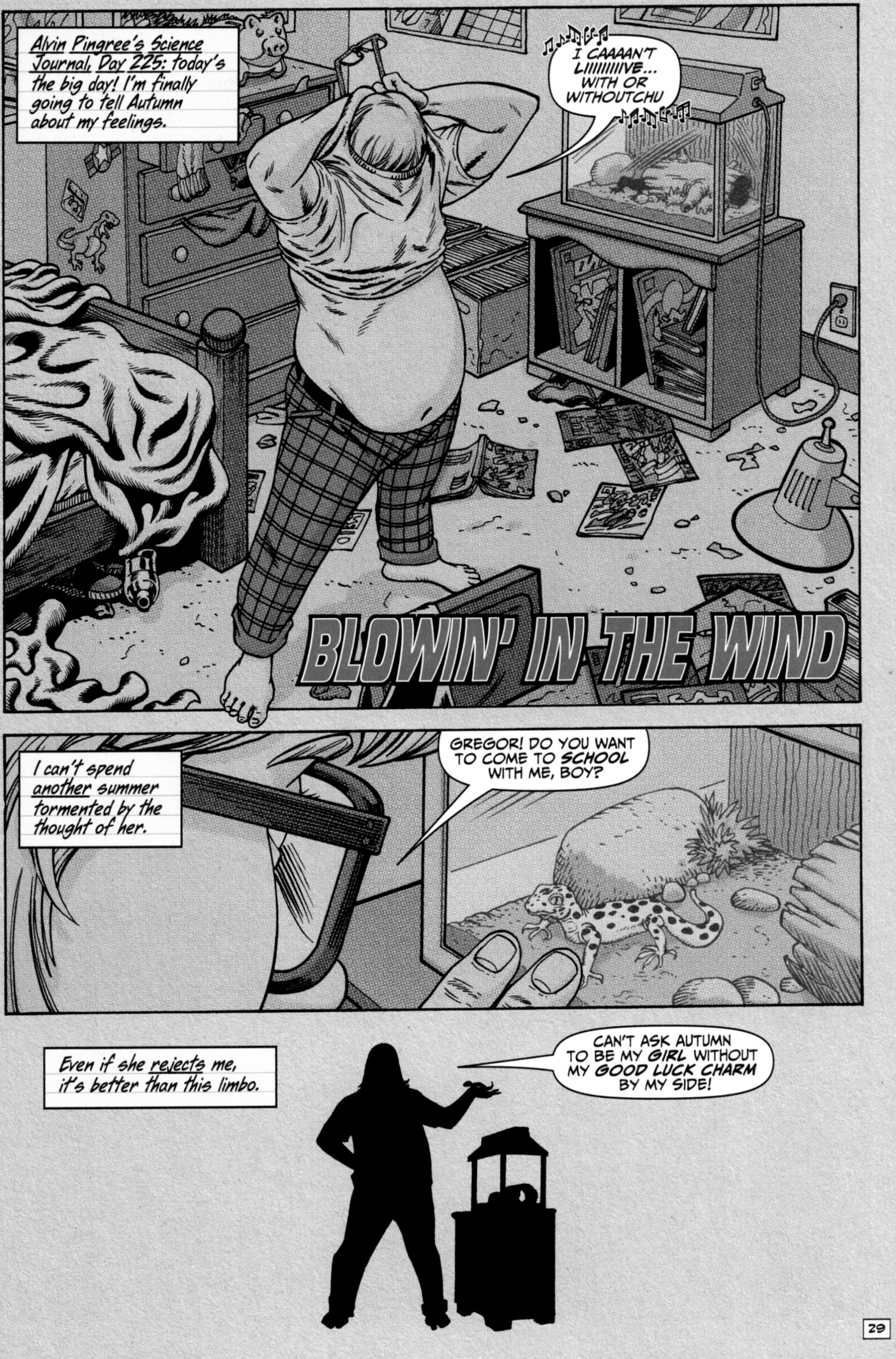

Alvin Pingree's Science Journal, Day 225: today's the big day! I'm finally going to tell Autumn about my feelings.
I CAAAAN'T LIIIIIIIIVE... WITH OR WITHOUTCHU
BLOWIN' IN THE WIND
I can't spend another summer tormented by the thought of her.
GREGOR! DO YOU WANT TO COME TO SCHOOL WITH ME, BOY?
Even if she rejects me, it's better than this limbo.
CAN'T ASK AUTUMN TO BE MY GIRL WITHOUT MY GOOD LUCK CHARM BY MY SIDE!

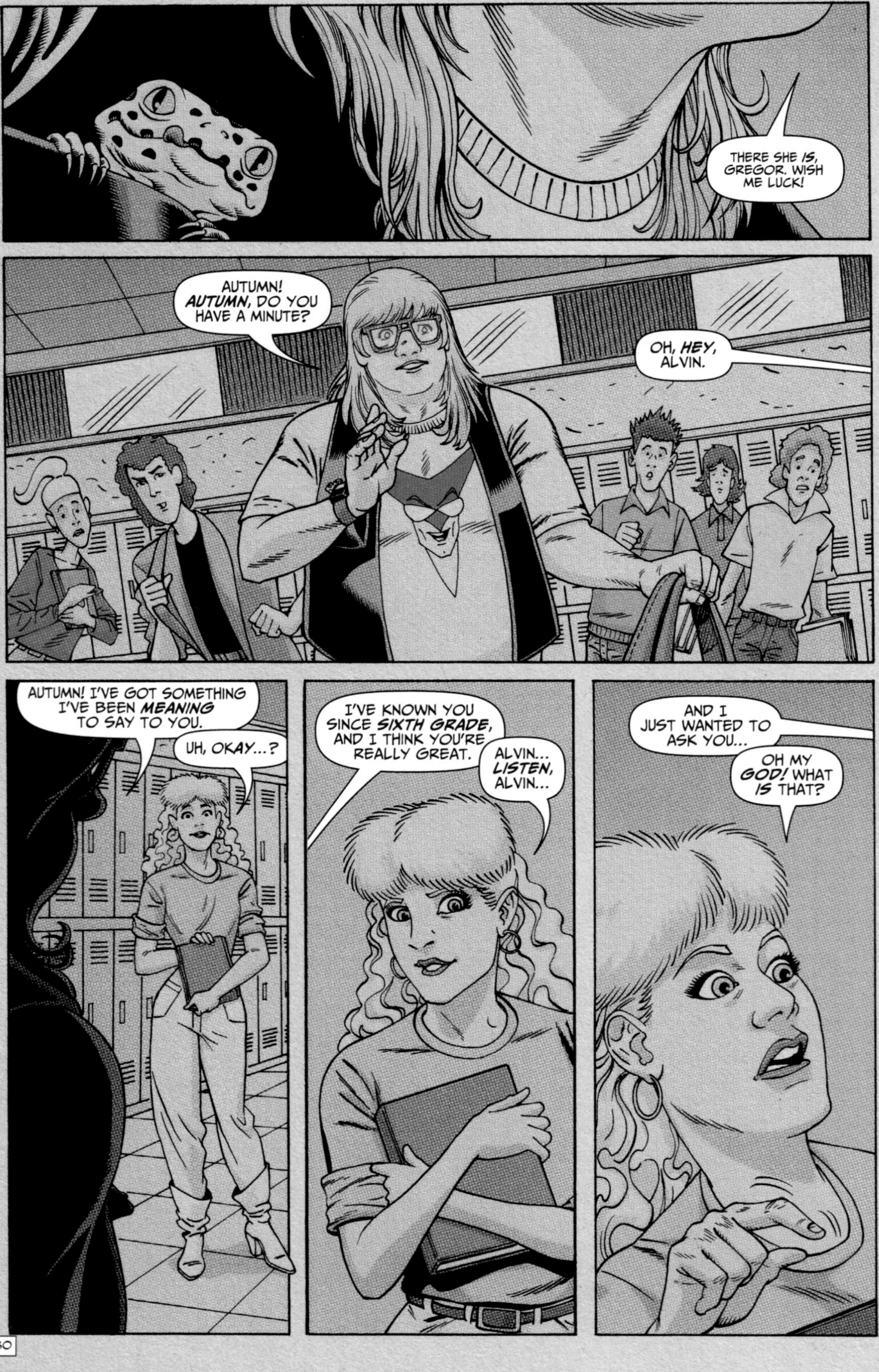
THERE SHE IS, GREGOR. WISH ME LUCK!
AUTUMN! AUTUMN, DO YOU HAVE A MINUTE?
OH, HEY, ALVIN.
AUTUMN! I'VE GOT SOMETHING I'VE BEEN MEANING TO SAY TO YOU.
UH, OKAY...?
I'VE KNOWN YOU SINCE SIXTH GRADE, AND I THINK YOU'RE REALLY GREAT.
ALVIN... LISTEN, ALVIN...
AND I JUST WANTED TO ASK YOU...
OH MY GOD! WHAT IS THAT?

I'M ALLERGIC TO *DOGS*, SO MY PARENTS THOUGHT GREGOR WOULD BE A GOOD COMPROMISE...

GET IT *AWAY!* GET IT AWAY FROM *ME!*

OH, THIS? THIS IS *GREGOR.* HE'S A LEOPARD GECKO.

OH MY *GOD!* OH MY *GOD!*

HEY! LEAVE HER *ALONE!*

SWOCK

FUCK YOU, *NERD.*

JESUS *CHRIST,* CHAD! LAY OFF ALVIN, OKAY?

GUYS, I THINK MR. TOBLER'S COMING...

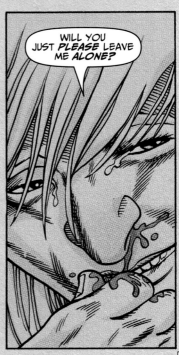

WILL YOU JUST *PLEASE* LEAVE ME *ALONE?*

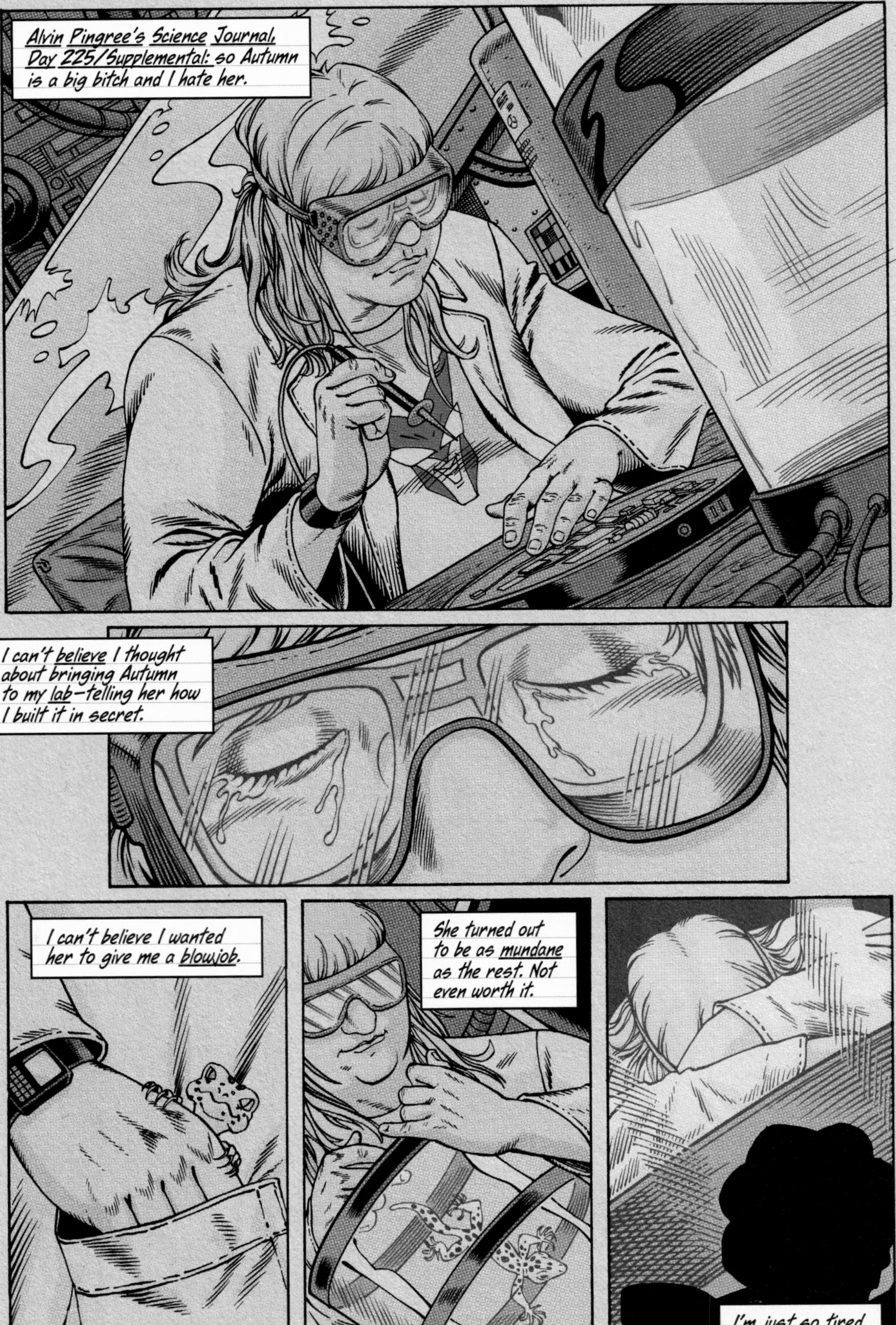
Alvin Pingree's Science Journal, Day 225/Supplemental: so Autumn is a big bitch and I hate her.
I can't believe I thought about bringing Autumn to my lab—telling her how I built it in secret.
I can't believe I wanted her to give me a blowjob.
She turned out to be as mundane as the rest. Not even worth it.
I'm just so tired.

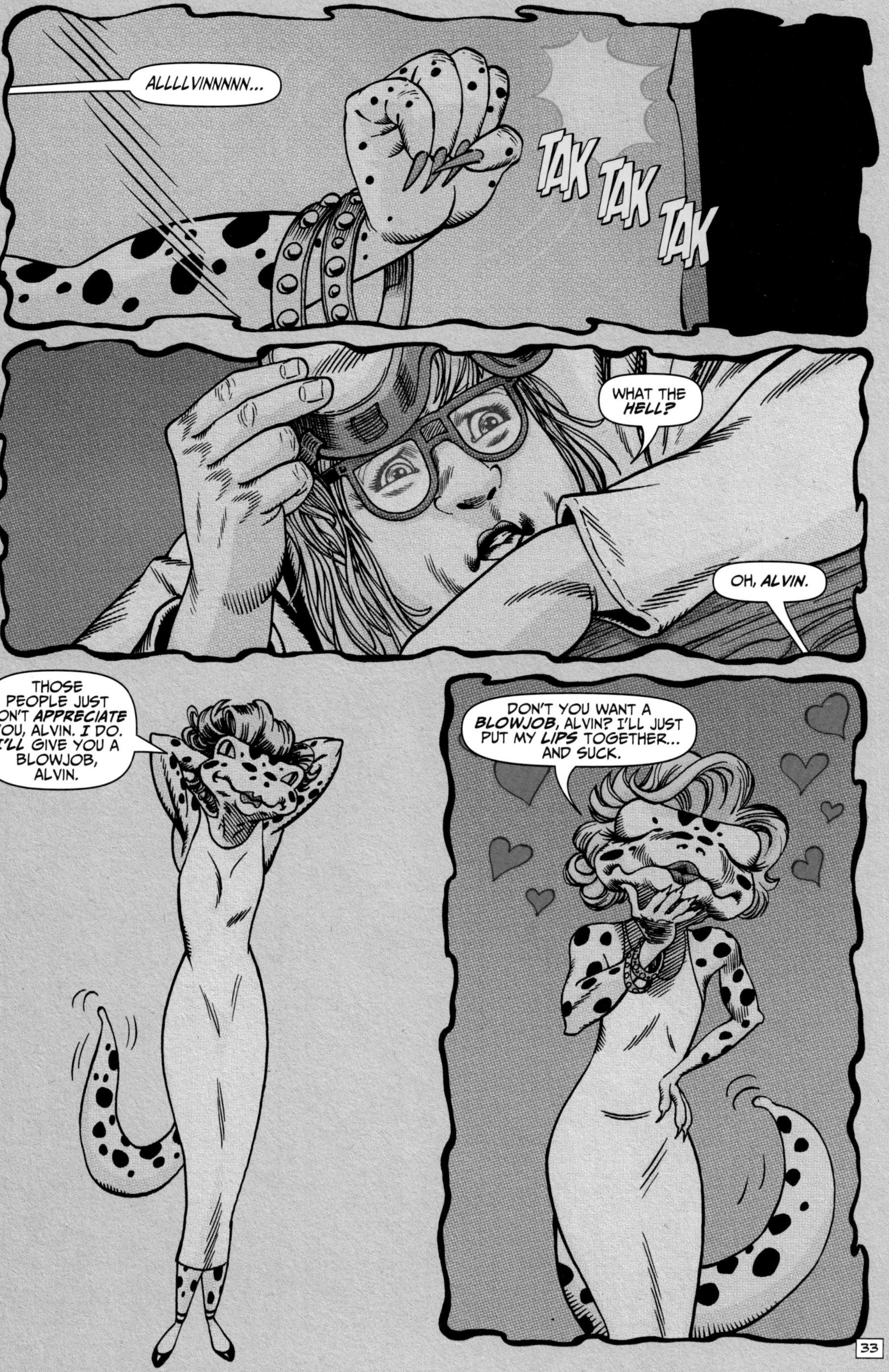
ALLLLVINNNNN...
TAK TAK TAK
WHAT THE HELL?
OH, ALVIN.
THOSE PEOPLE JUST DON'T APPRECIATE YOU, ALVIN. I DO. I'LL GIVE YOU A BLOWJOB, ALVIN.
DON'T YOU WANT A BLOWJOB, ALVIN? I'LL JUST PUT MY LIPS TOGETHER... AND SUCK.

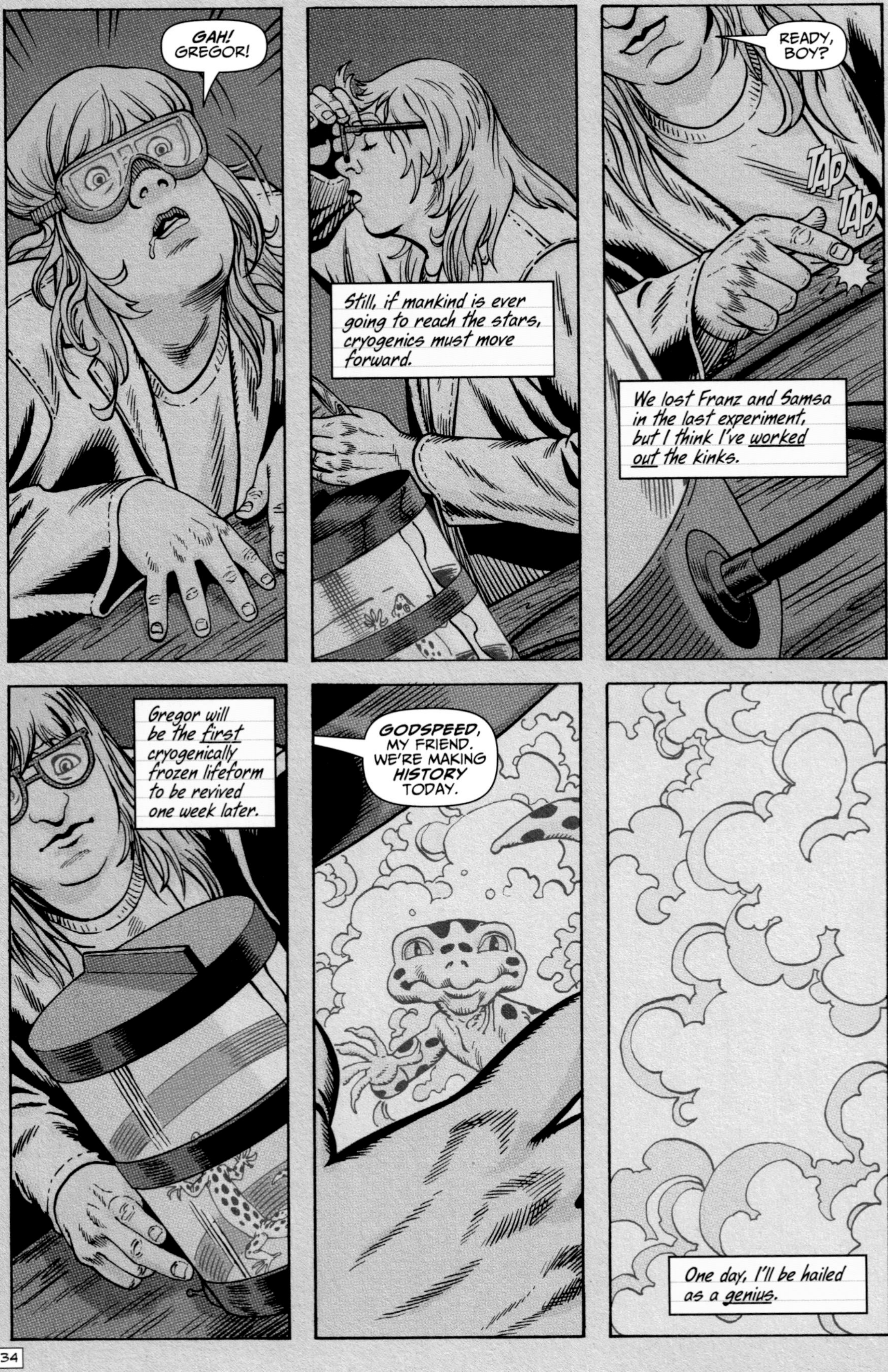
GAH! GREGOR!
Still, if mankind is ever going to reach the stars, cryogenics must move forward.
READY, BOY?
TAP TAP
We lost Franz and Samsa in the last experiment, but I think I've worked out the kinks.
Gregor will be the first cryogenically frozen lifeform to be revived one week later.
GODSPEED, MY FRIEND. WE'RE MAKING HISTORY TODAY.
One day, I'll be hailed as a genius.

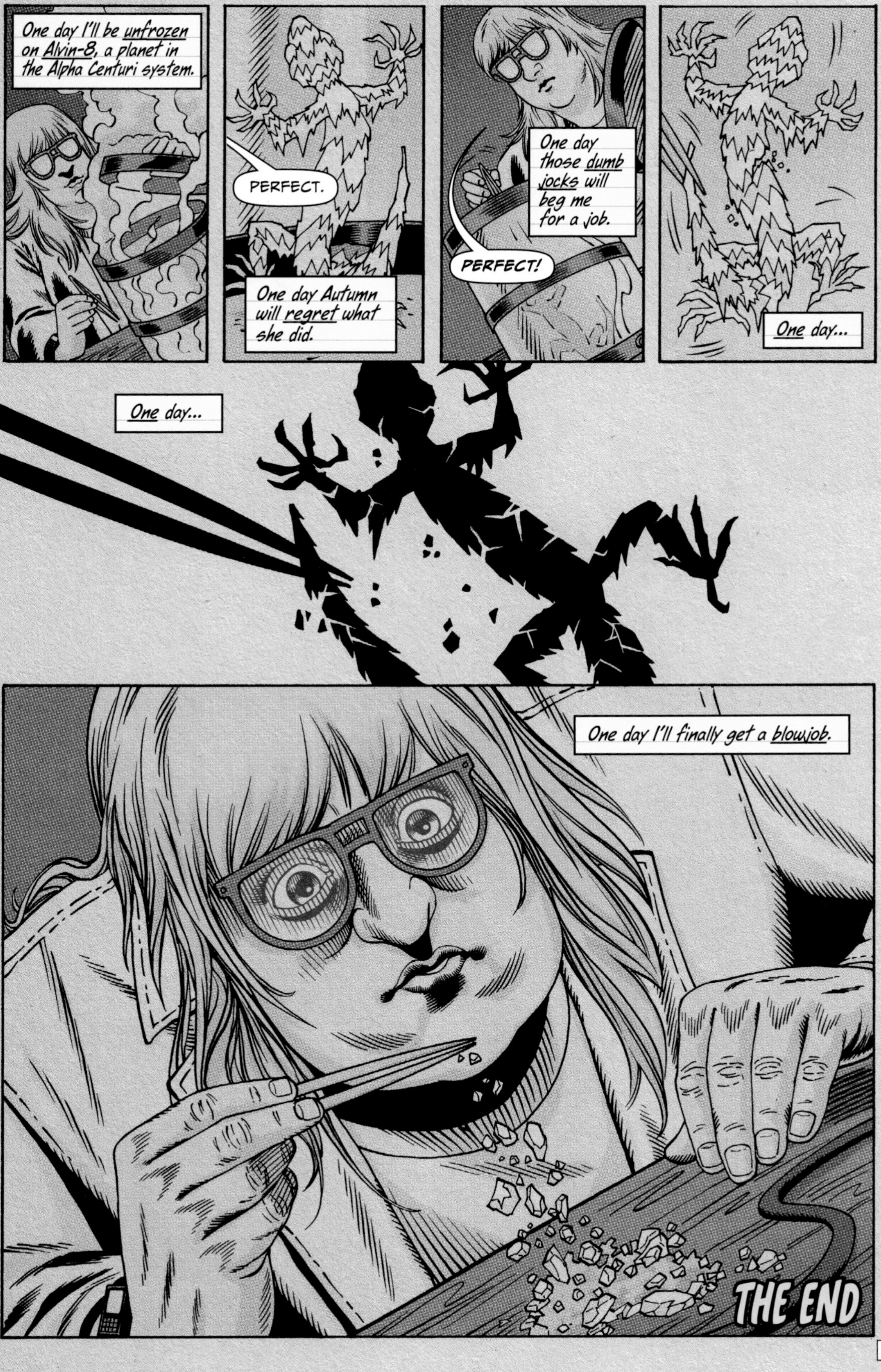
One day I'll be unfrozen on Alvin-8, a planet in the Alpha Centuri system.
PERFECT.
One day Autumn will regret what she did.
One day those dumb jocks will beg me for a job.
PERFECT!
One day...
One day...
One day I'll finally get a blowjob.
THE END

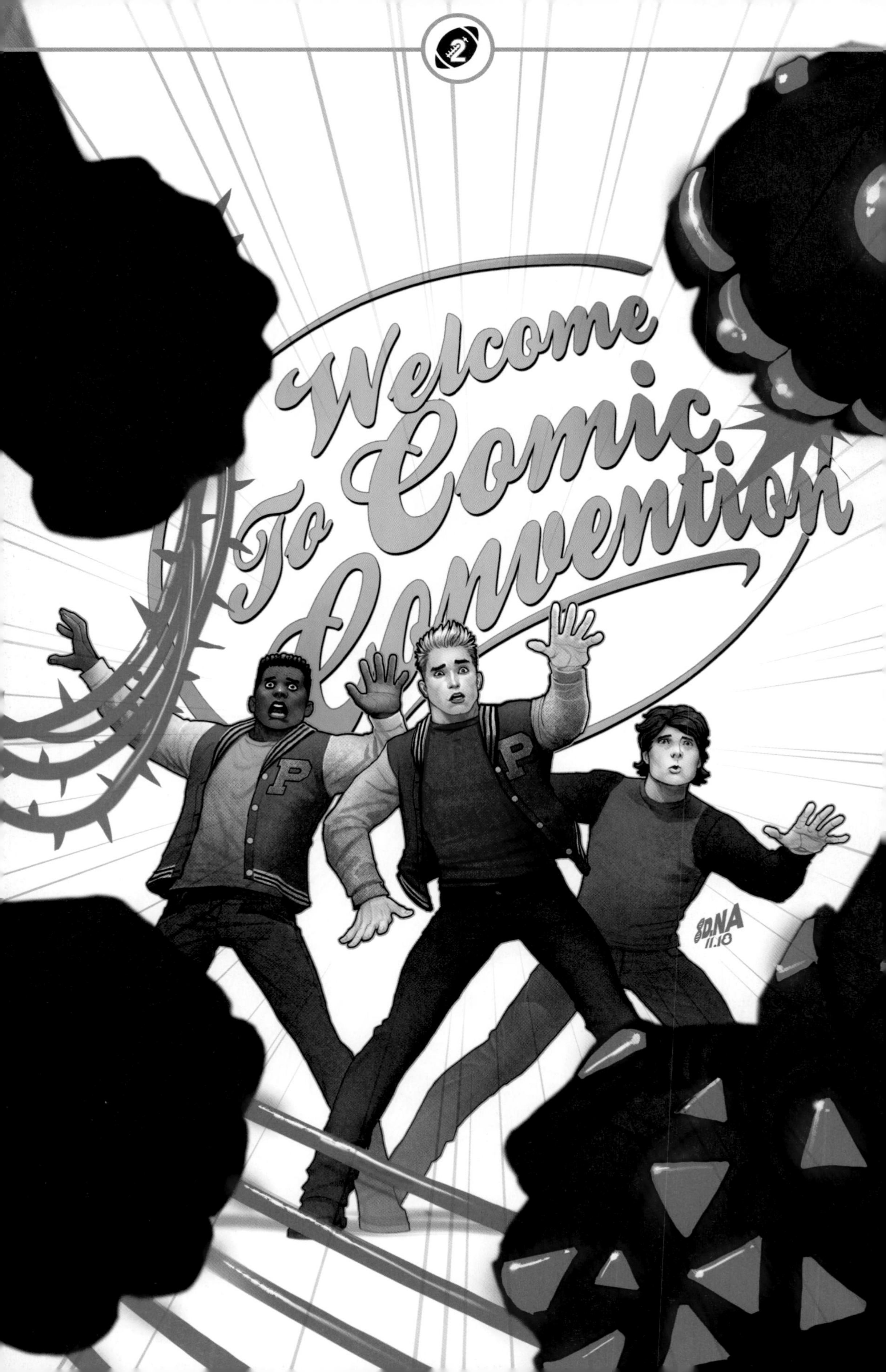
2
Welcome To Comic Convention
DNA 11.18

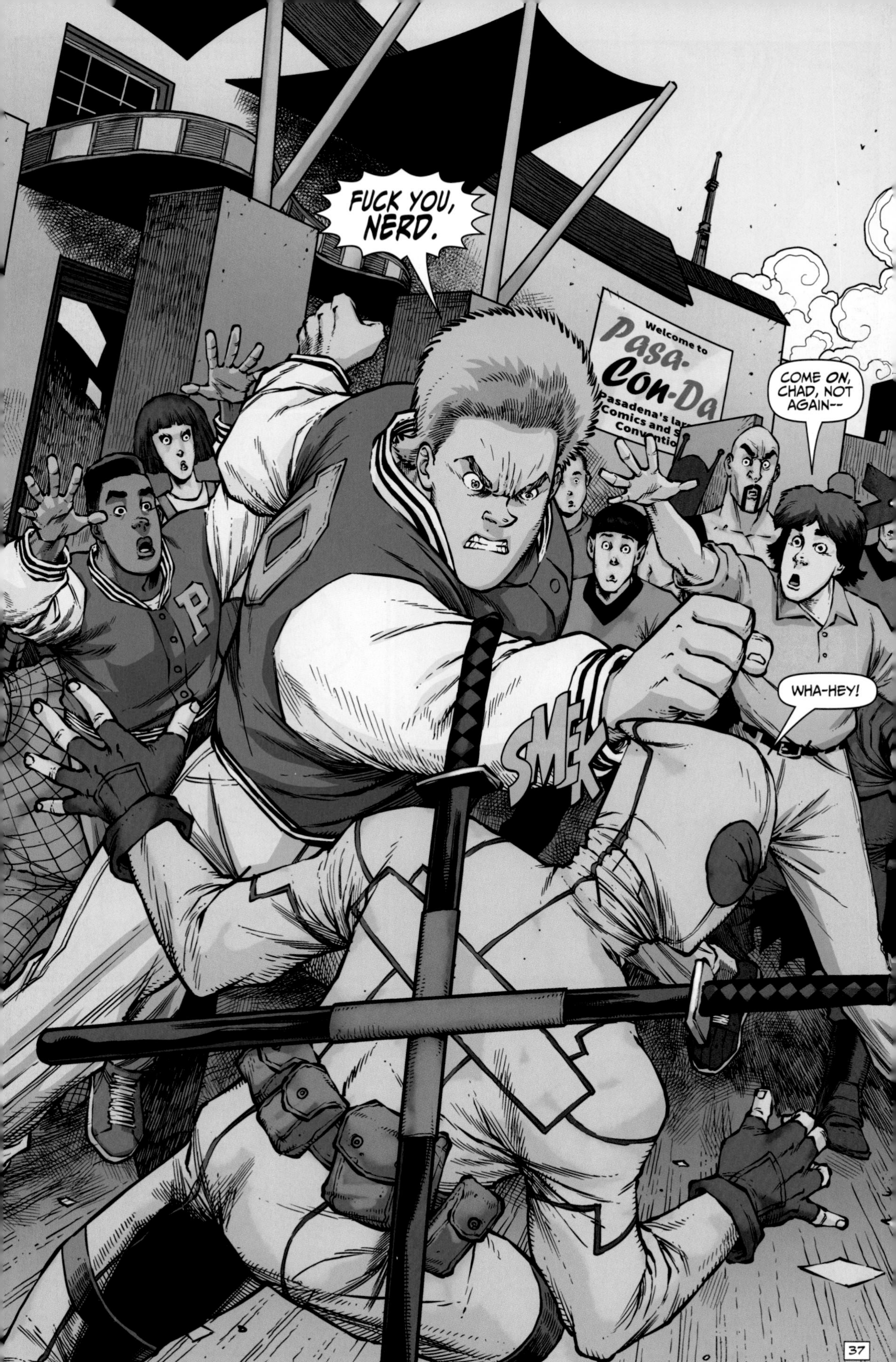
FUCK YOU, NERD.
Welcome to Pasa-Con-Da Pasadena's lar Comics and S Conventio
COME ON, CHAD, NOT AGAIN--
WHA-HEY!
SMEK

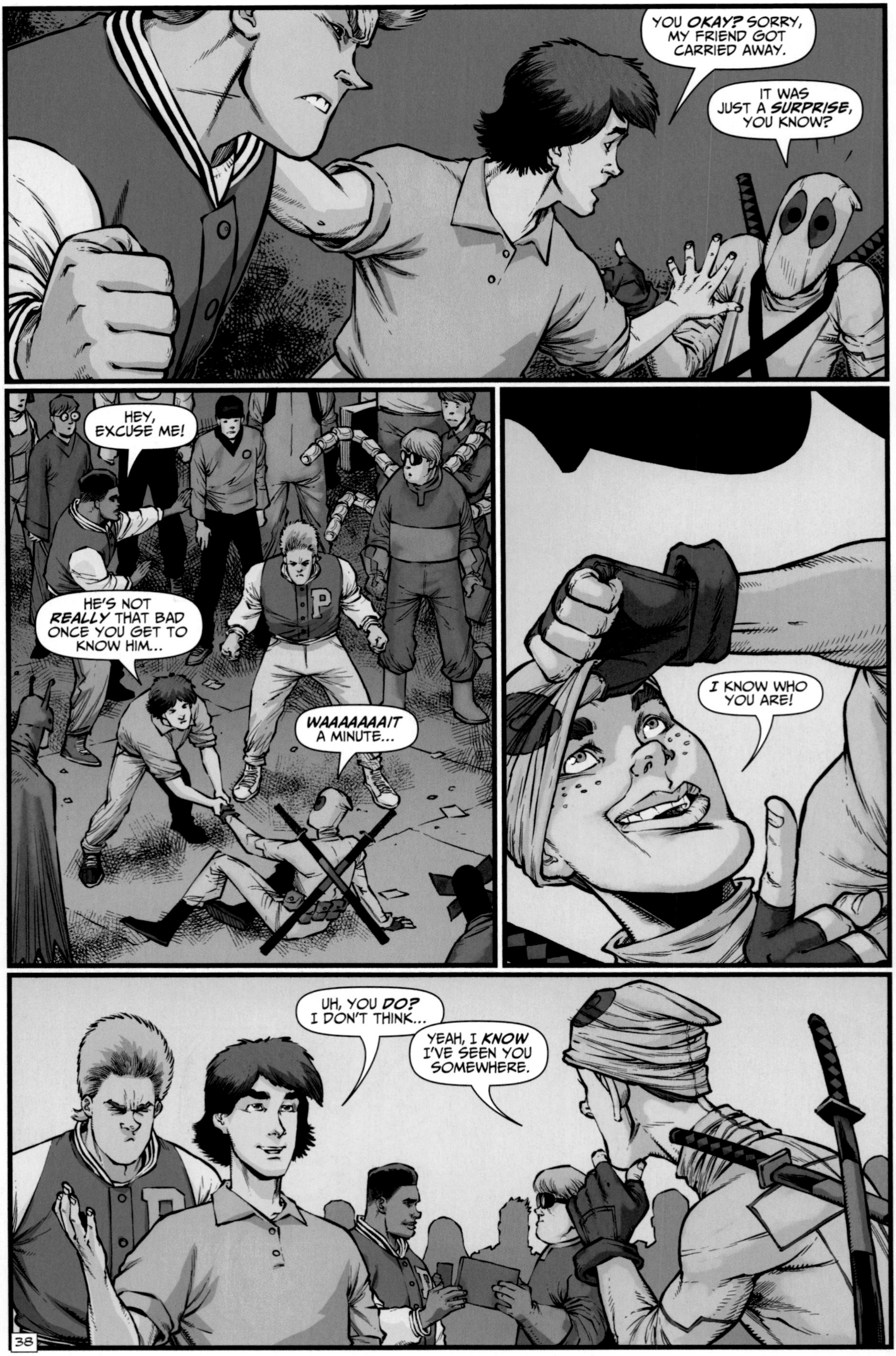
YOU *OKAY?* SORRY, MY FRIEND GOT CARRIED AWAY.
IT WAS JUST A *SURPRISE*, YOU KNOW?
HEY, EXCUSE ME!
HE'S NOT *REALLY* THAT BAD ONCE YOU GET TO KNOW HIM...
WAAAAAAAIT A MINUTE...
I KNOW WHO YOU ARE!
UH, YOU *DO?* I DON'T THINK...
YEAH, I *KNOW* I'VE SEEN YOU SOMEWHERE.

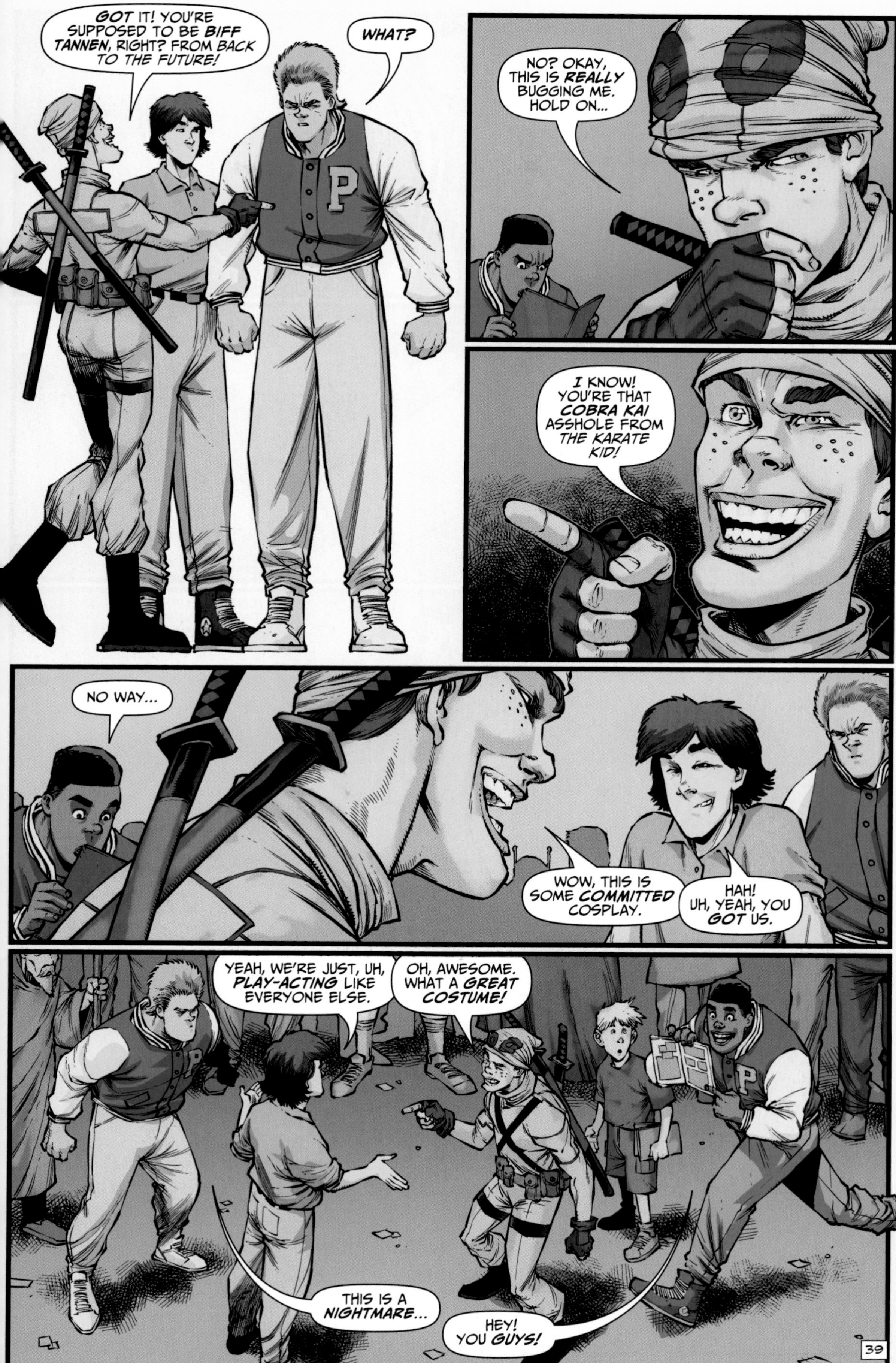
GOT IT! YOU'RE SUPPOSED TO BE BIFF TANNEN, RIGHT? FROM BACK TO THE FUTURE!
WHAT?
NO? OKAY, THIS IS REALLY BUGGING ME. HOLD ON...
I KNOW! YOU'RE THAT COBRA KAI ASSHOLE FROM THE KARATE KID!
NO WAY...
WOW, THIS IS SOME COMMITTED COSPLAY.
HAH! UH, YEAH, YOU GOT US.
YEAH, WE'RE JUST, UH, PLAY-ACTING LIKE EVERYONE ELSE.
OH, AWESOME. WHAT A GREAT COSTUME!
THIS IS A NIGHTMARE...
HEY! YOU GUYS!

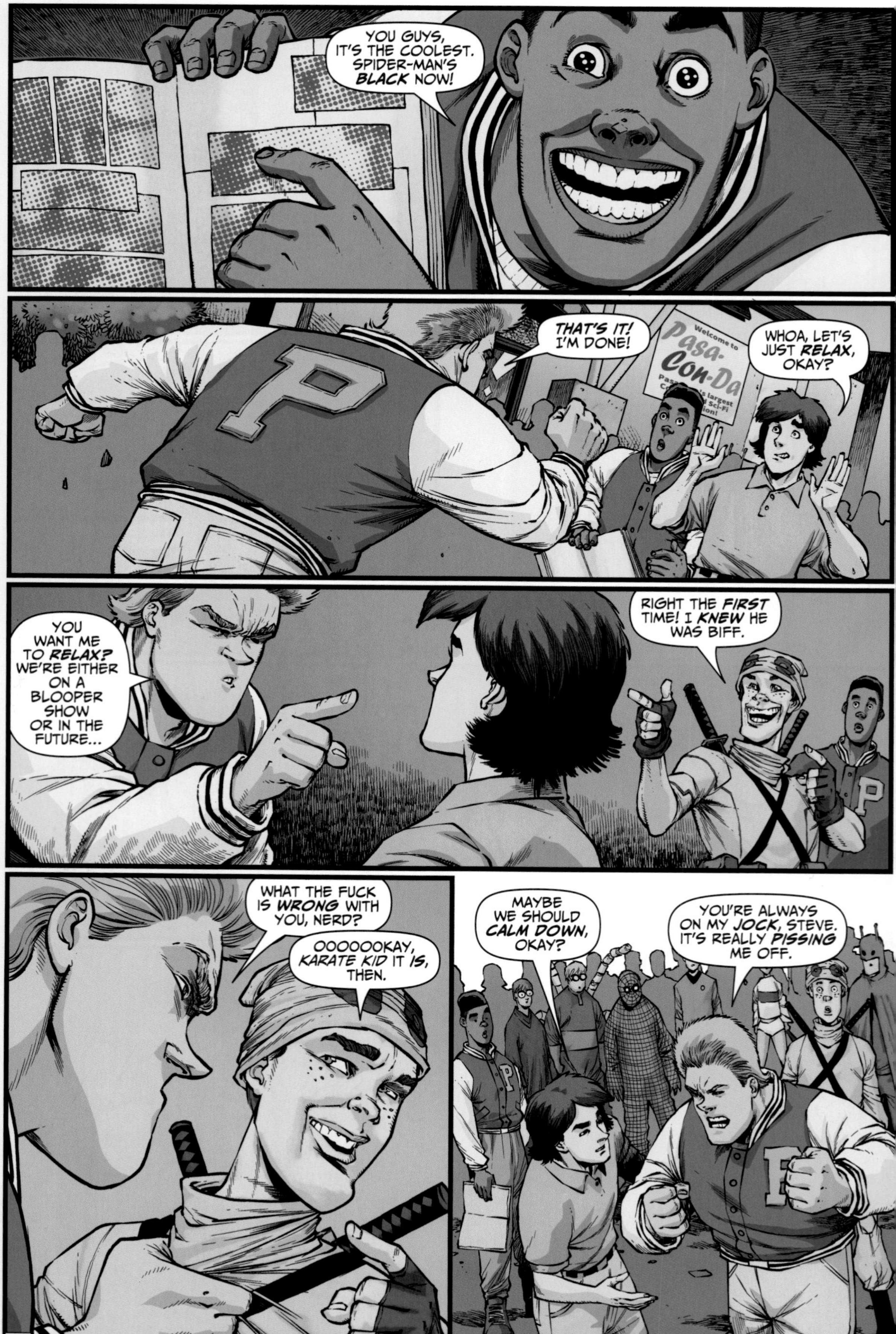

YOU GUYS, IT'S THE COOLEST. SPIDER-MAN'S BLACK NOW!
THAT'S IT! I'M DONE!
Welcome to
Pasa-Con-Da
WHOA, LET'S JUST RELAX, OKAY?
YOU WANT ME TO RELAX? WE'RE EITHER ON A BLOOPER SHOW OR IN THE FUTURE...
RIGHT THE FIRST TIME! I KNEW HE WAS BIFF.
WHAT THE FUCK IS WRONG WITH YOU, NERD?
OOOOOOKAY, KARATE KID IT IS, THEN.
MAYBE WE SHOULD CALM DOWN, OKAY?
YOU'RE ALWAYS ON MY JOCK, STEVE. IT'S REALLY PISSING ME OFF.

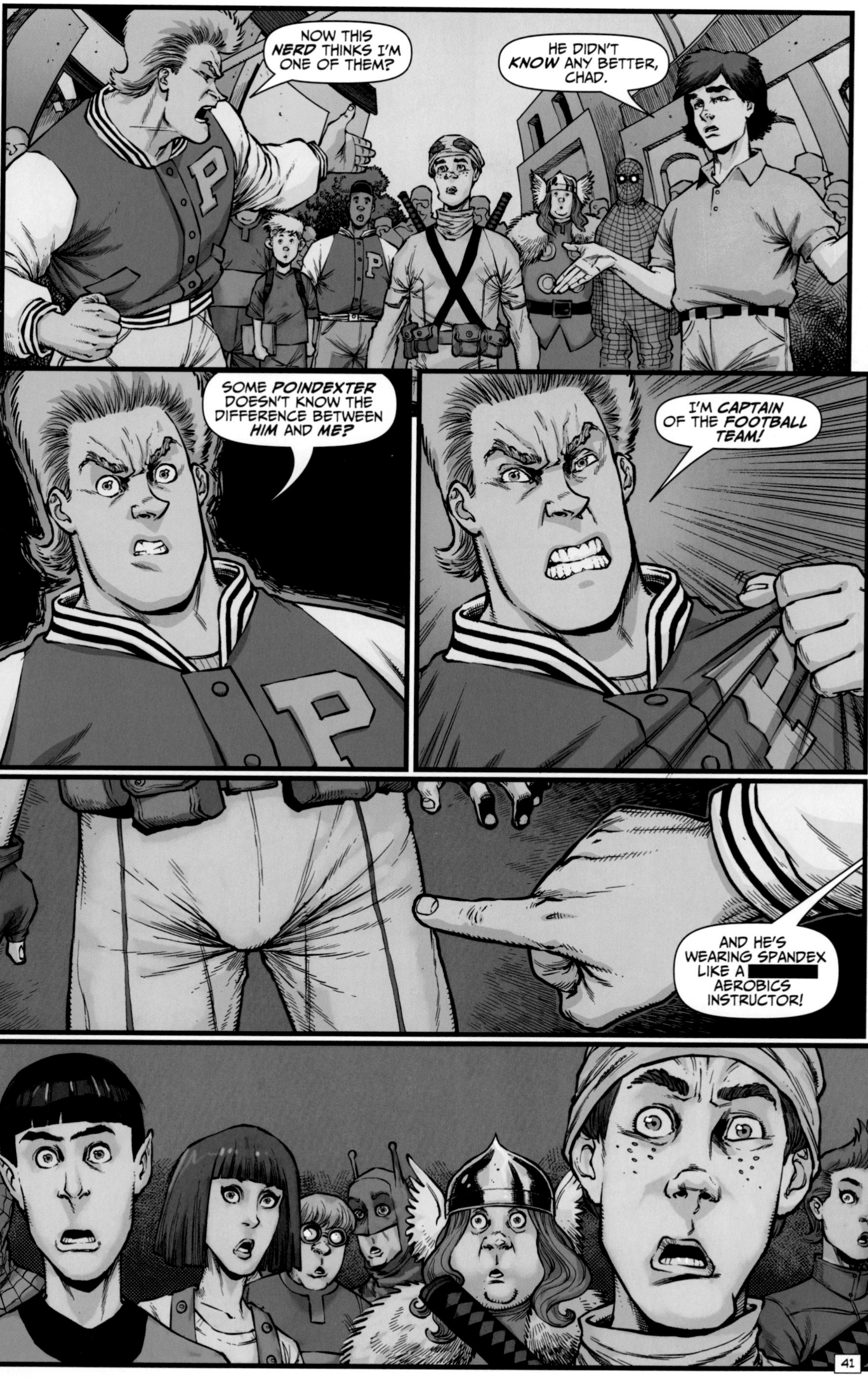
NOW THIS NERD THINKS I'M ONE OF THEM?
HE DIDN'T KNOW ANY BETTER, CHAD.
SOME POINDEXTER DOESN'T KNOW THE DIFFERENCE BETWEEN HIM AND ME?
I'M CAPTAIN OF THE FOOTBALL TEAM!
AND HE'S WEARING SPANDEX LIKE A [redacted] AEROBICS INSTRUCTOR!

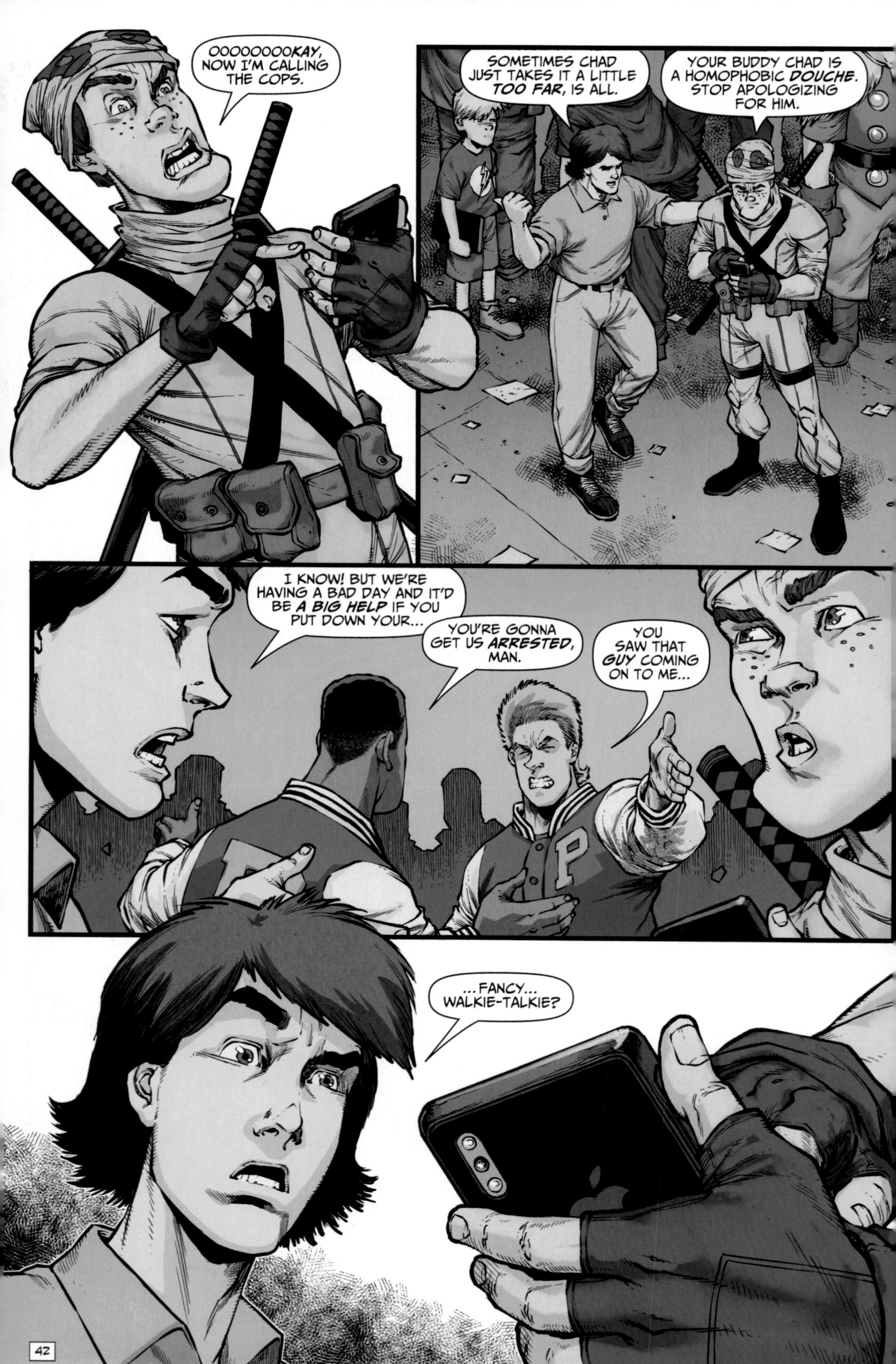
OOOOOOOOKAY, NOW I'M CALLING THE COPS.
SOMETIMES CHAD JUST TAKES IT A LITTLE TOO FAR, IS ALL.
YOUR BUDDY CHAD IS A HOMOPHOBIC DOUCHE. STOP APOLOGIZING FOR HIM.
I KNOW! BUT WE'RE HAVING A BAD DAY AND IT'D BE A BIG HELP IF YOU PUT DOWN YOUR...
YOU'RE GONNA GET US ARRESTED, MAN.
YOU SAW THAT GUY COMING ON TO ME...
...FANCY... WALKIE-TALKIE?

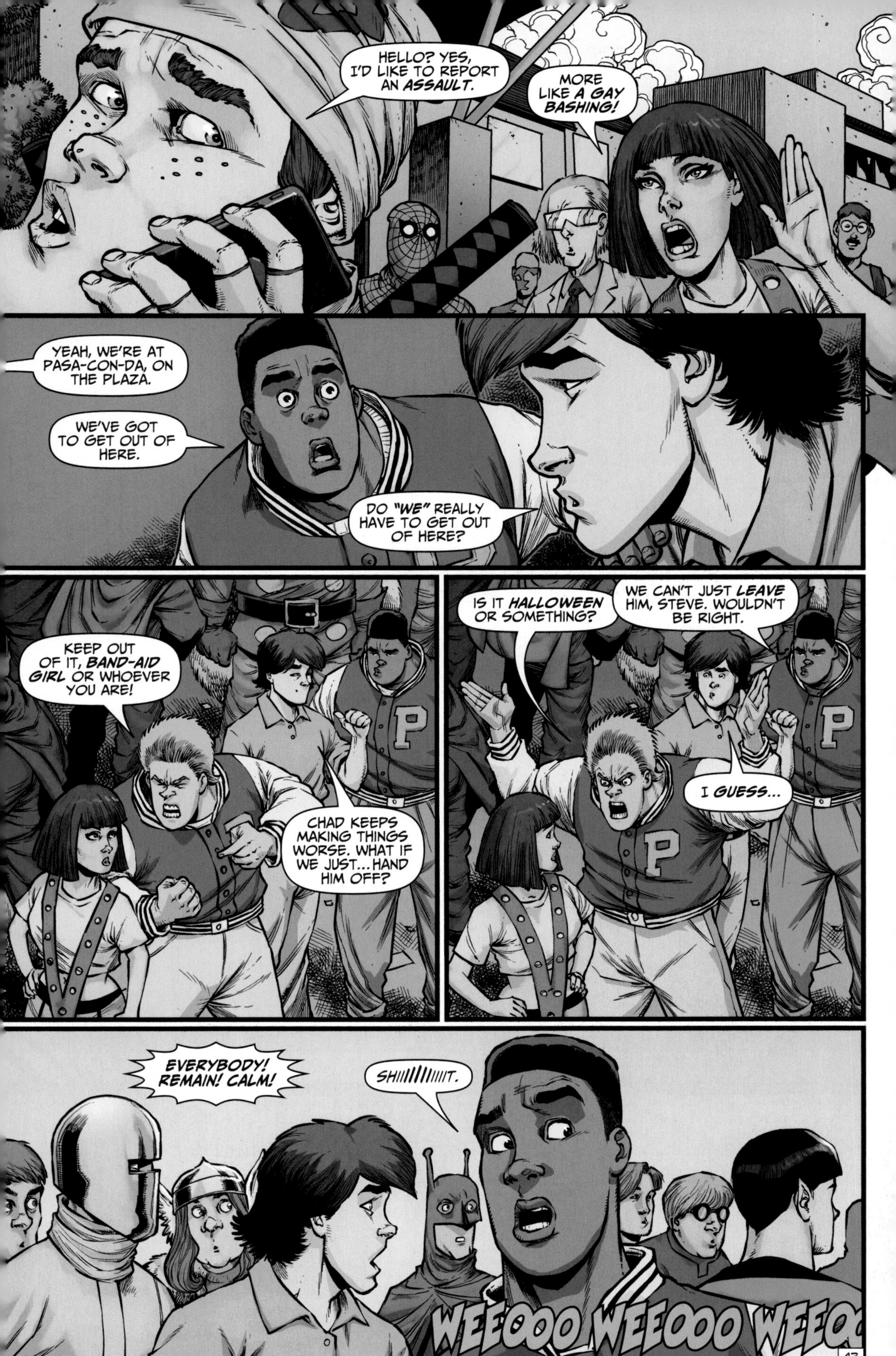
HELLO? YES, I'D LIKE TO REPORT AN ASSAULT.
MORE LIKE A GAY BASHING!
YEAH, WE'RE AT PASA-CON-DA, ON THE PLAZA.
WE'VE GOT TO GET OUT OF HERE.
DO "WE" REALLY HAVE TO GET OUT OF HERE?
KEEP OUT OF IT, BAND-AID GIRL OR WHOEVER YOU ARE!
CHAD KEEPS MAKING THINGS WORSE. WHAT IF WE JUST...HAND HIM OFF?
IS IT HALLOWEEN OR SOMETHING?
WE CAN'T JUST LEAVE HIM, STEVE. WOULDN'T BE RIGHT.
I GUESS...
EVERYBODY! REMAIN! CALM!
SHIIIIIIIIT.
WEEOOO WEEOOO WEEO

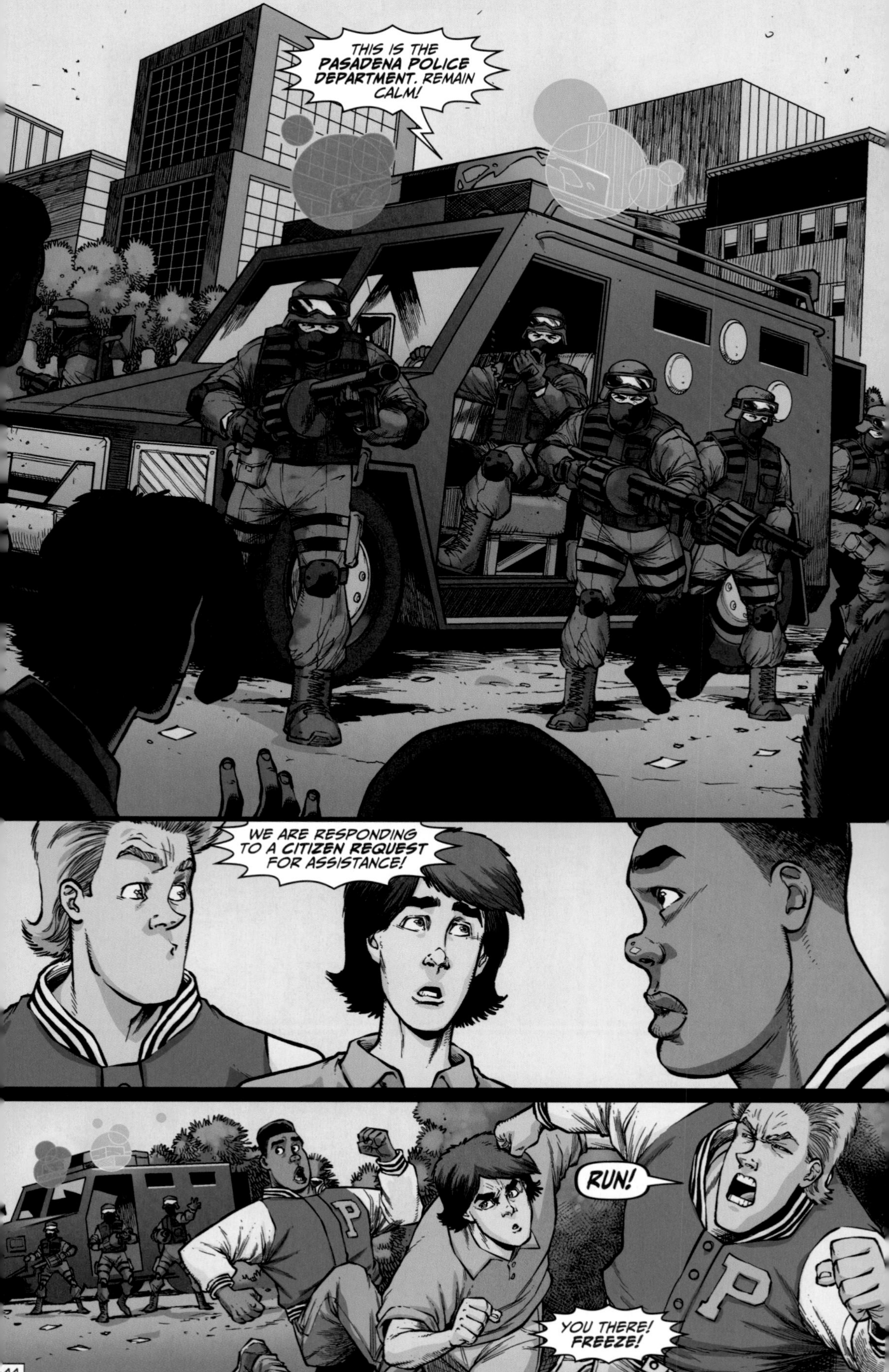
THIS IS THE PASADENA POLICE DEPARTMENT. REMAIN CALM!
WE ARE RESPONDING TO A CITIZEN REQUEST FOR ASSISTANCE!
RUN!
YOU THERE! FREEZE!

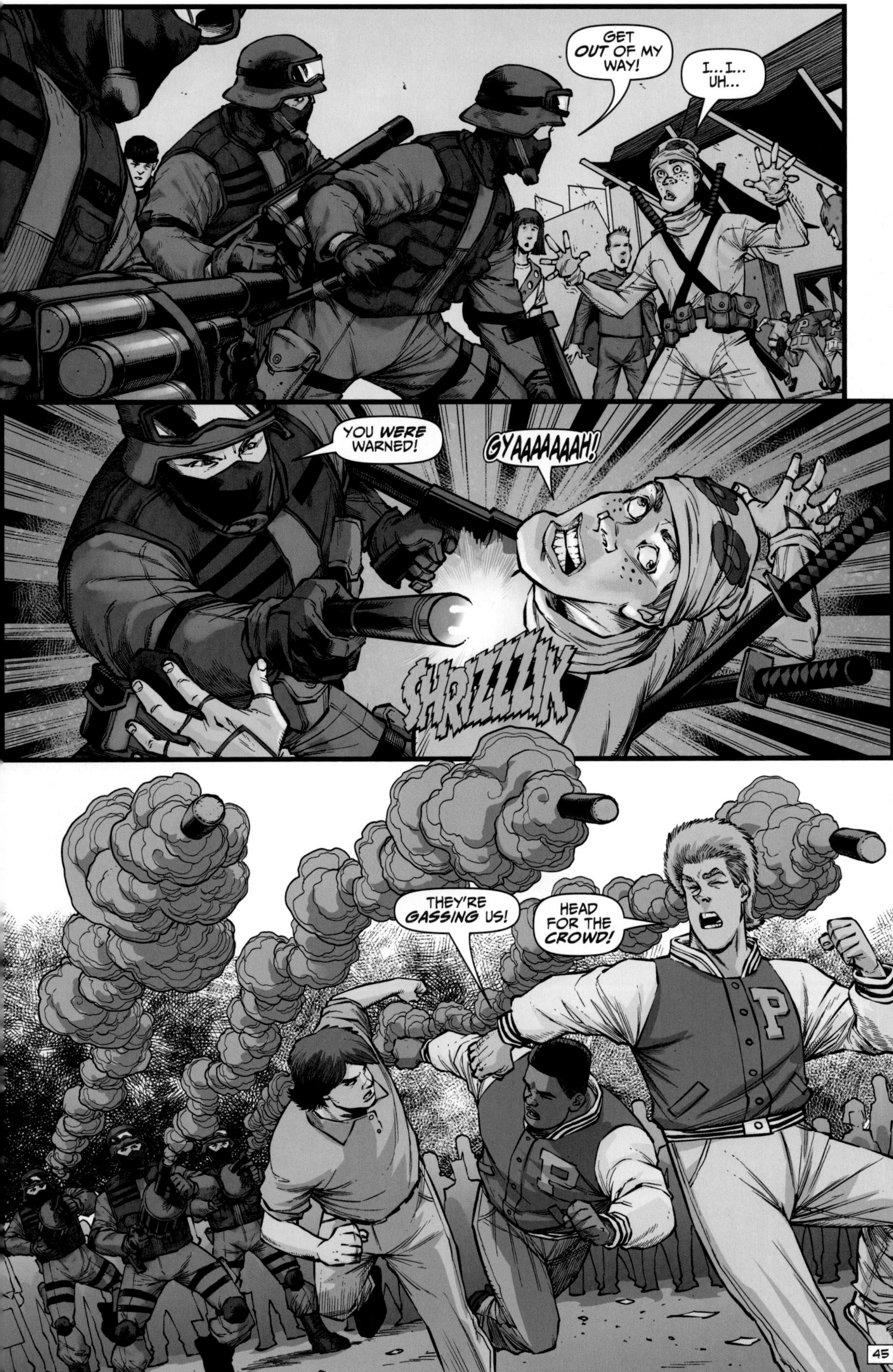
GET OUT OF MY WAY!
I... I... UH...
YOU WERE WARNED!
GYAAAAAAAH!
SHRIZZZK
THEY'RE GASSING US!
HEAD FOR THE CROWD!

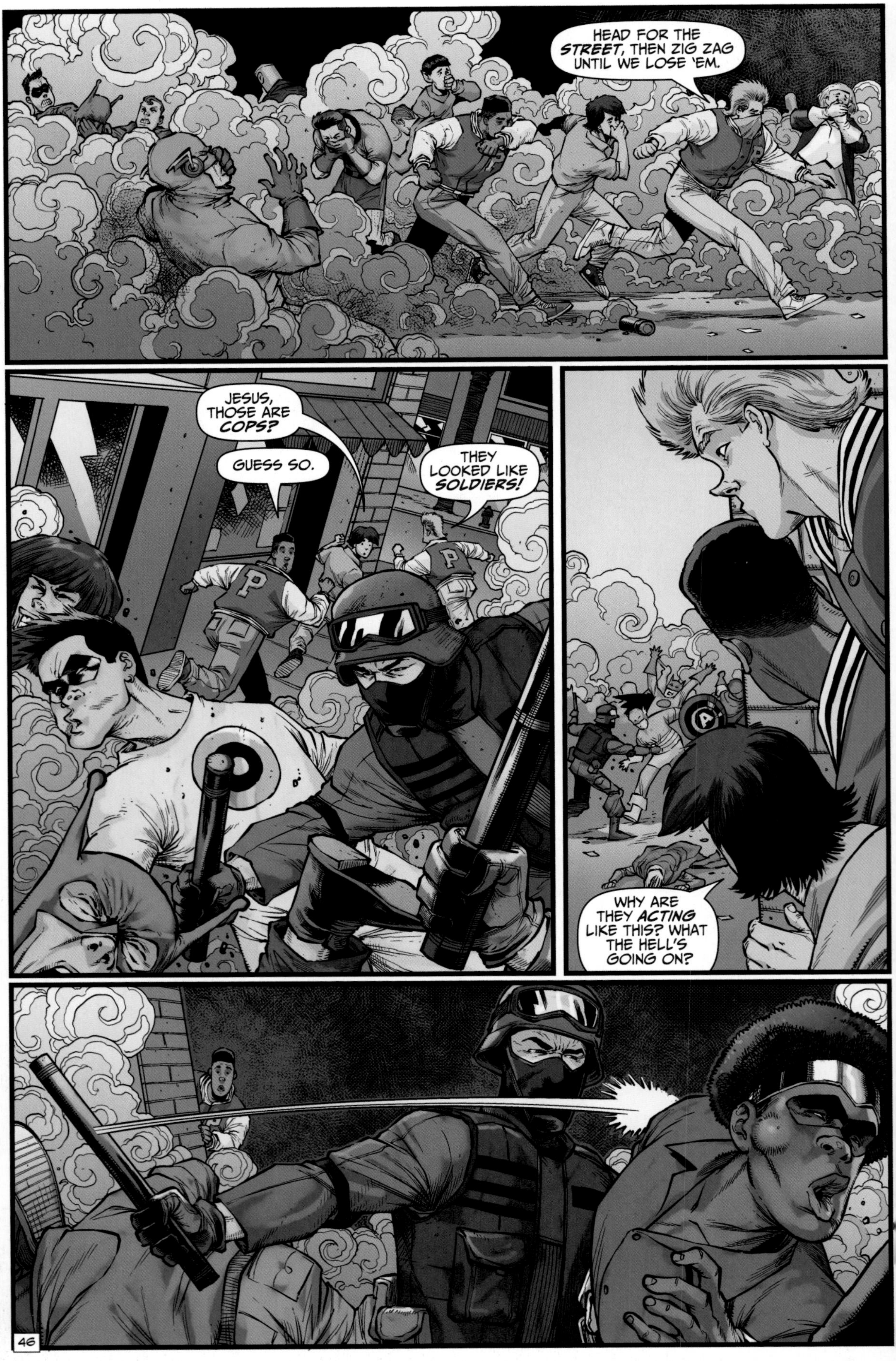
HEAD FOR THE STREET, THEN ZIG ZAG UNTIL WE LOSE 'EM.
JESUS, THOSE ARE COPS?
GUESS SO.
THEY LOOKED LIKE SOLDIERS!
WHY ARE THEY ACTING LIKE THIS? WHAT THE HELL'S GOING ON?

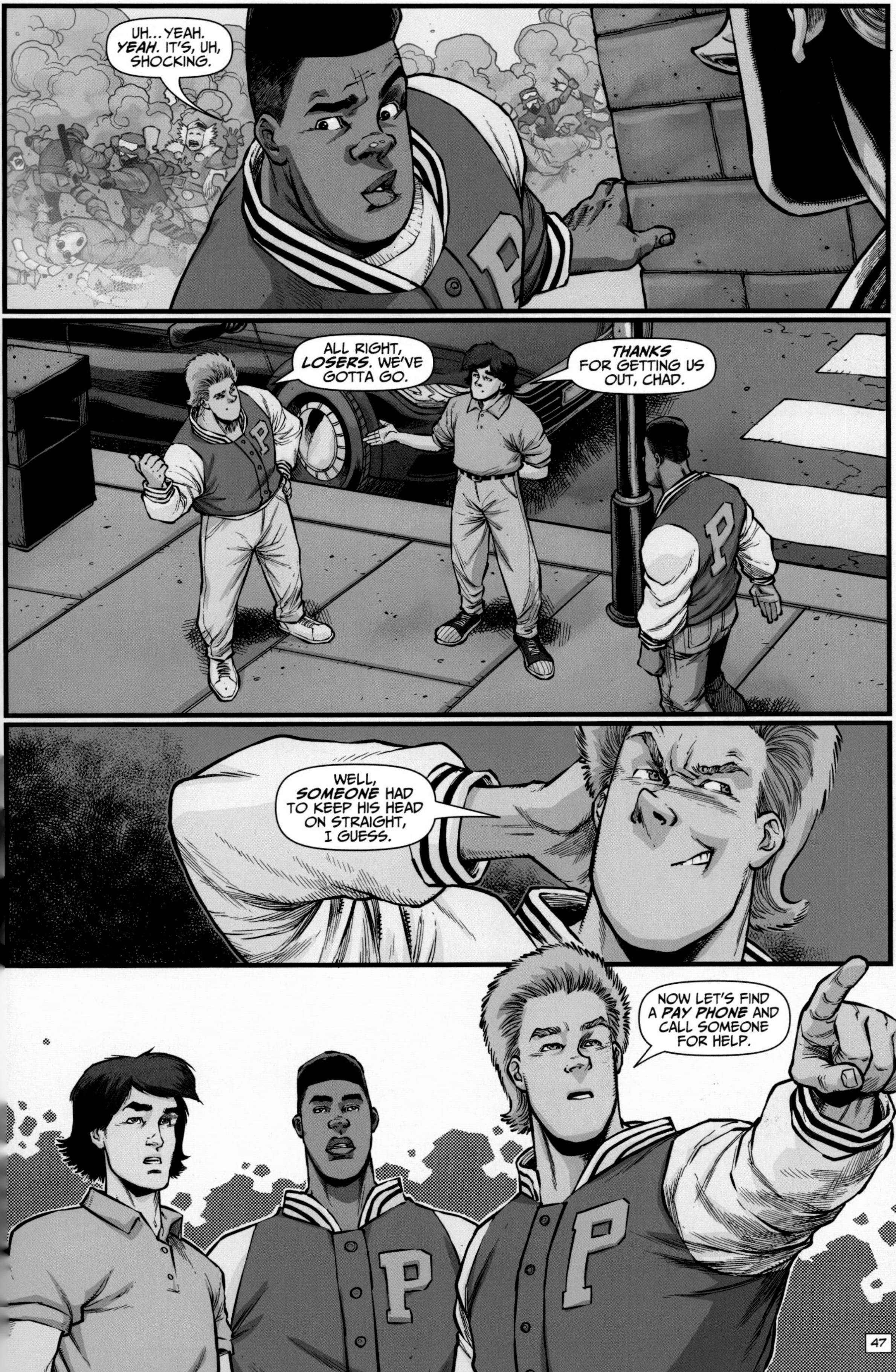
UH... YEAH. YEAH. IT'S, UH, SHOCKING.
ALL RIGHT, LOSERS. WE'VE GOTTA GO.
THANKS FOR GETTING US OUT, CHAD.
WELL, SOMEONE HAD TO KEEP HIS HEAD ON STRAIGHT, I GUESS.
NOW LET'S FIND A PAY PHONE AND CALL SOMEONE FOR HELP.

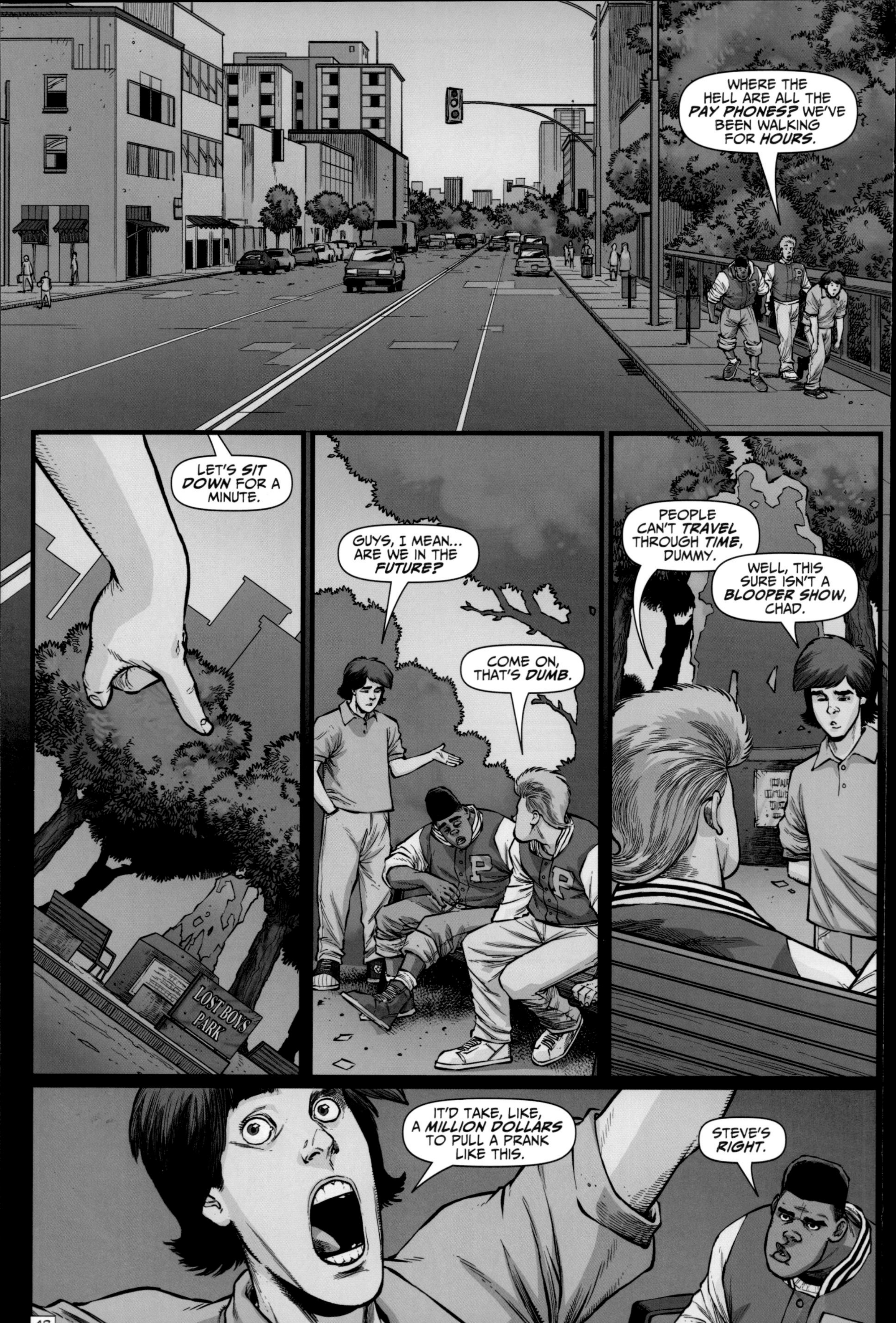
WHERE THE HELL ARE ALL THE PAY PHONES? WE'VE BEEN WALKING FOR HOURS.
LET'S SIT DOWN FOR A MINUTE.
LOST BOYS PARK
GUYS, I MEAN... ARE WE IN THE FUTURE?
COME ON, THAT'S DUMB.
PEOPLE CAN'T TRAVEL THROUGH TIME, DUMMY.
WELL, THIS SURE ISN'T A BLOOPER SHOW, CHAD.
IT'D TAKE, LIKE, A MILLION DOLLARS TO PULL A PRANK LIKE THIS.
STEVE'S RIGHT.

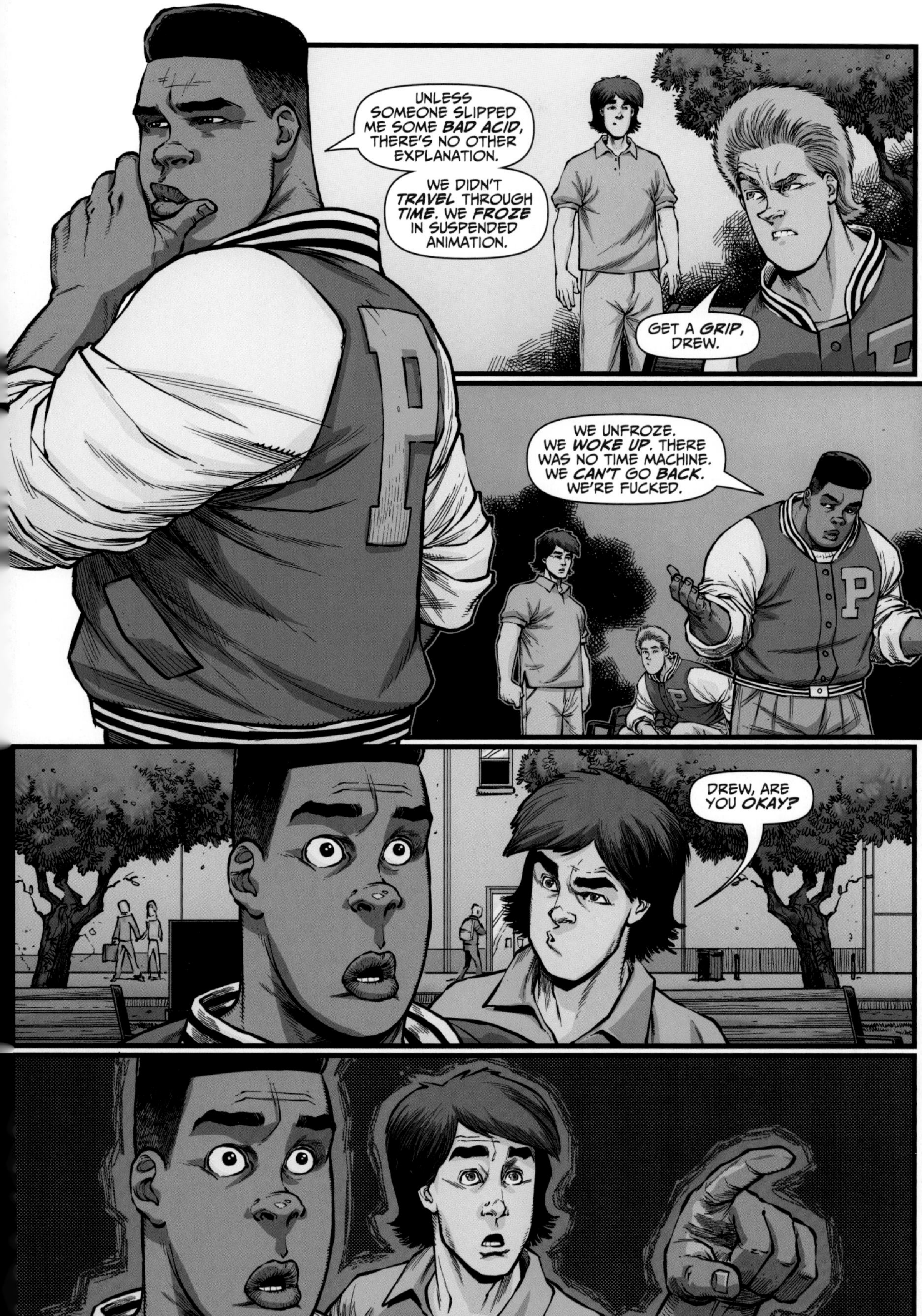
UNLESS SOMEONE SLIPPED ME SOME BAD ACID, THERE'S NO OTHER EXPLANATION.
WE DIDN'T TRAVEL THROUGH TIME. WE FROZE IN SUSPENDED ANIMATION.
GET A GRIP, DREW.
WE UNFROZE. WE WOKE UP. THERE WAS NO TIME MACHINE. WE CAN'T GO BACK. WE'RE FUCKED.
DREW, ARE YOU OKAY?

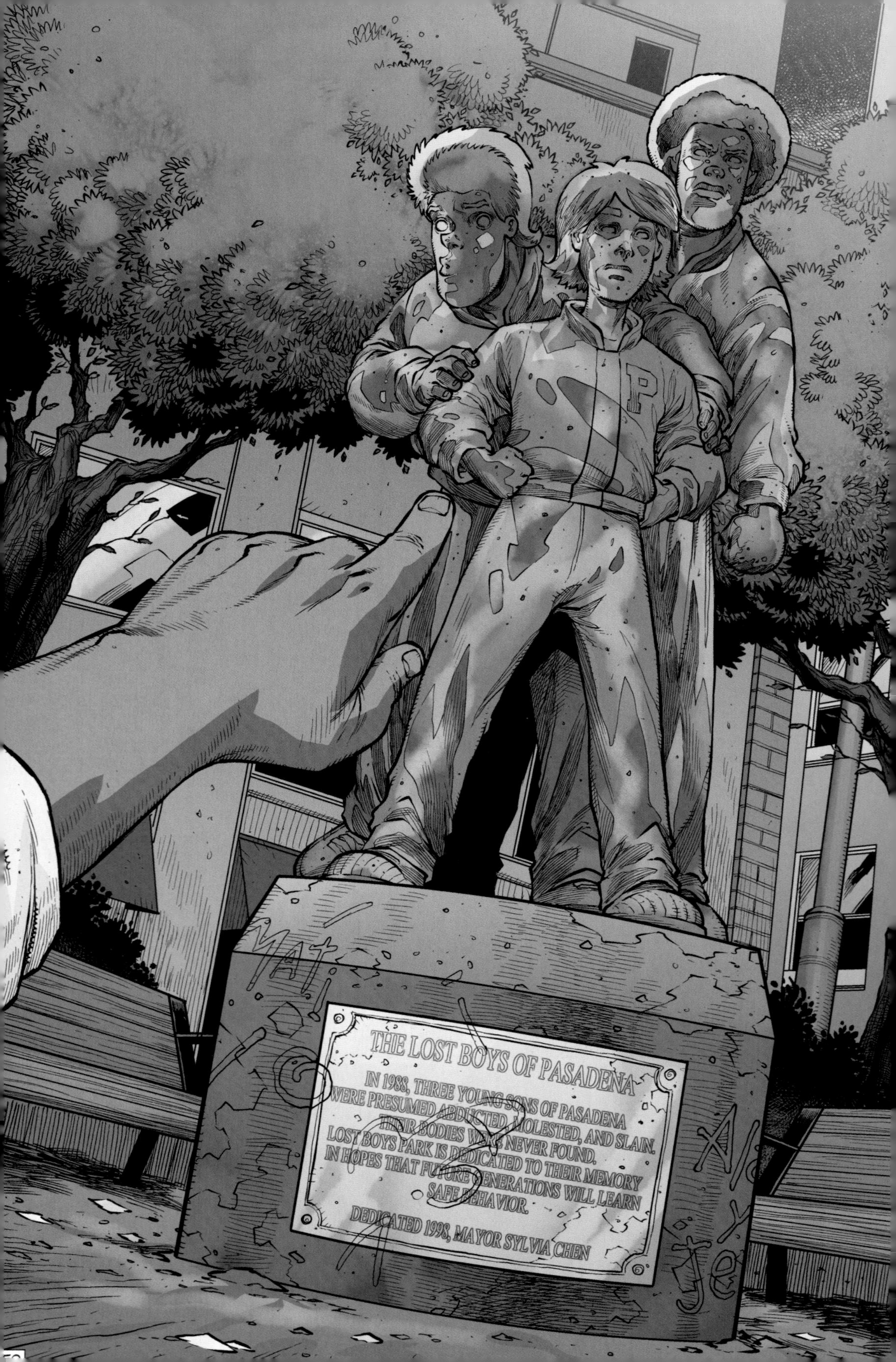
THE LOST BOYS OF PASADENA
IN 1988, THREE YOUNG SONS OF PASADENA
WERE PRESUMED ABDUCTED, MOLESTED, AND SLAIN.
THEIR BODIES WERE NEVER FOUND.
LOST BOYS PARK IS DEDICATED TO THEIR MEMORY
IN HOPES THAT FUTURE GENERATIONS WILL LEARN
SAFE BEHAVIOR.
DEDICATED 1998, MAYOR SYLVIA CHEN

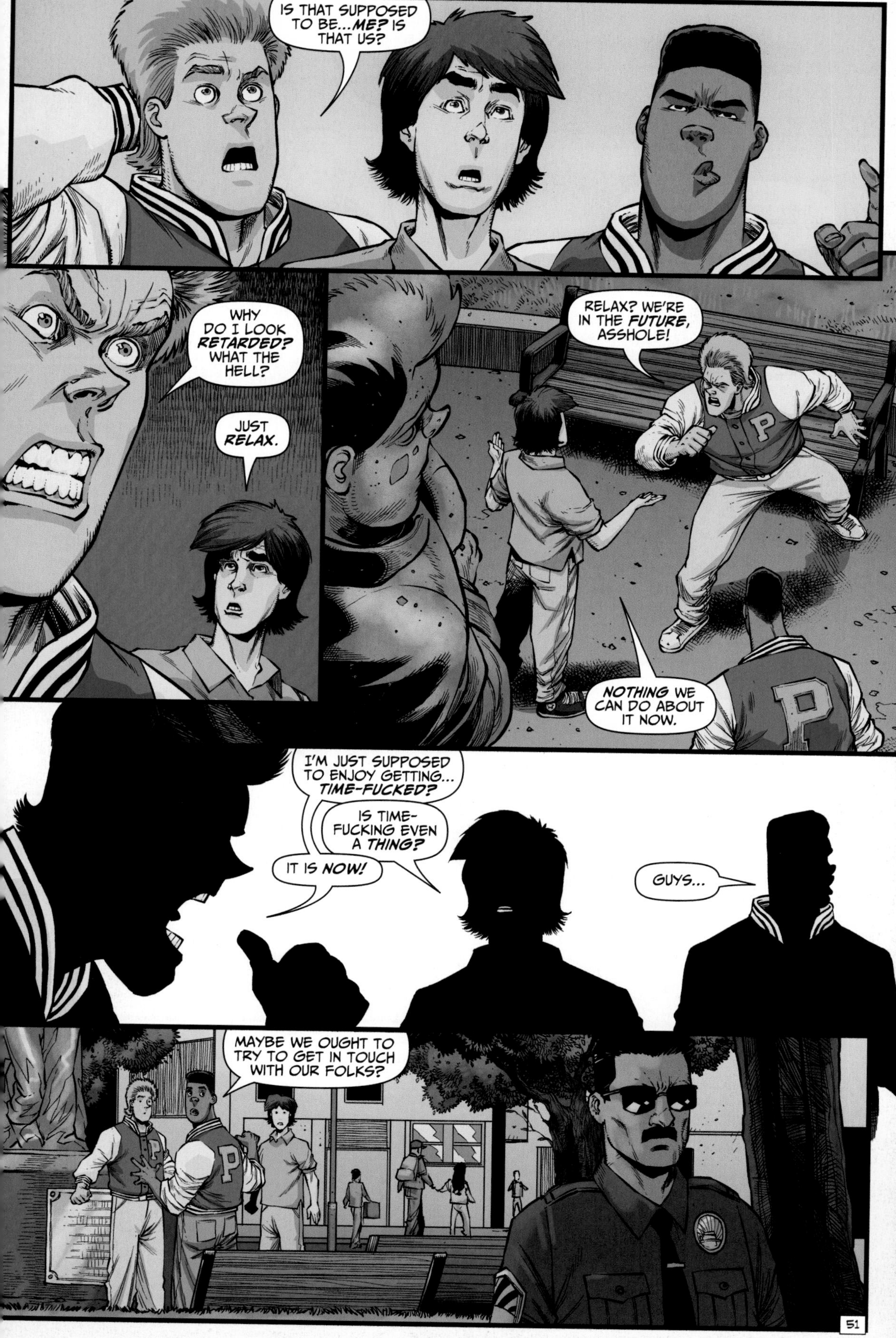
IS THAT SUPPOSED TO BE...ME? IS THAT US?
WHY DO I LOOK RETARDED? WHAT THE HELL?
JUST RELAX.
RELAX? WE'RE IN THE FUTURE, ASSHOLE!
NOTHING WE CAN DO ABOUT IT NOW.
I'M JUST SUPPOSED TO ENJOY GETTING... TIME-FUCKED?
IS TIME-FUCKING EVEN A THING?
IT IS NOW!
GUYS...
MAYBE WE OUGHT TO TRY TO GET IN TOUCH WITH OUR FOLKS?

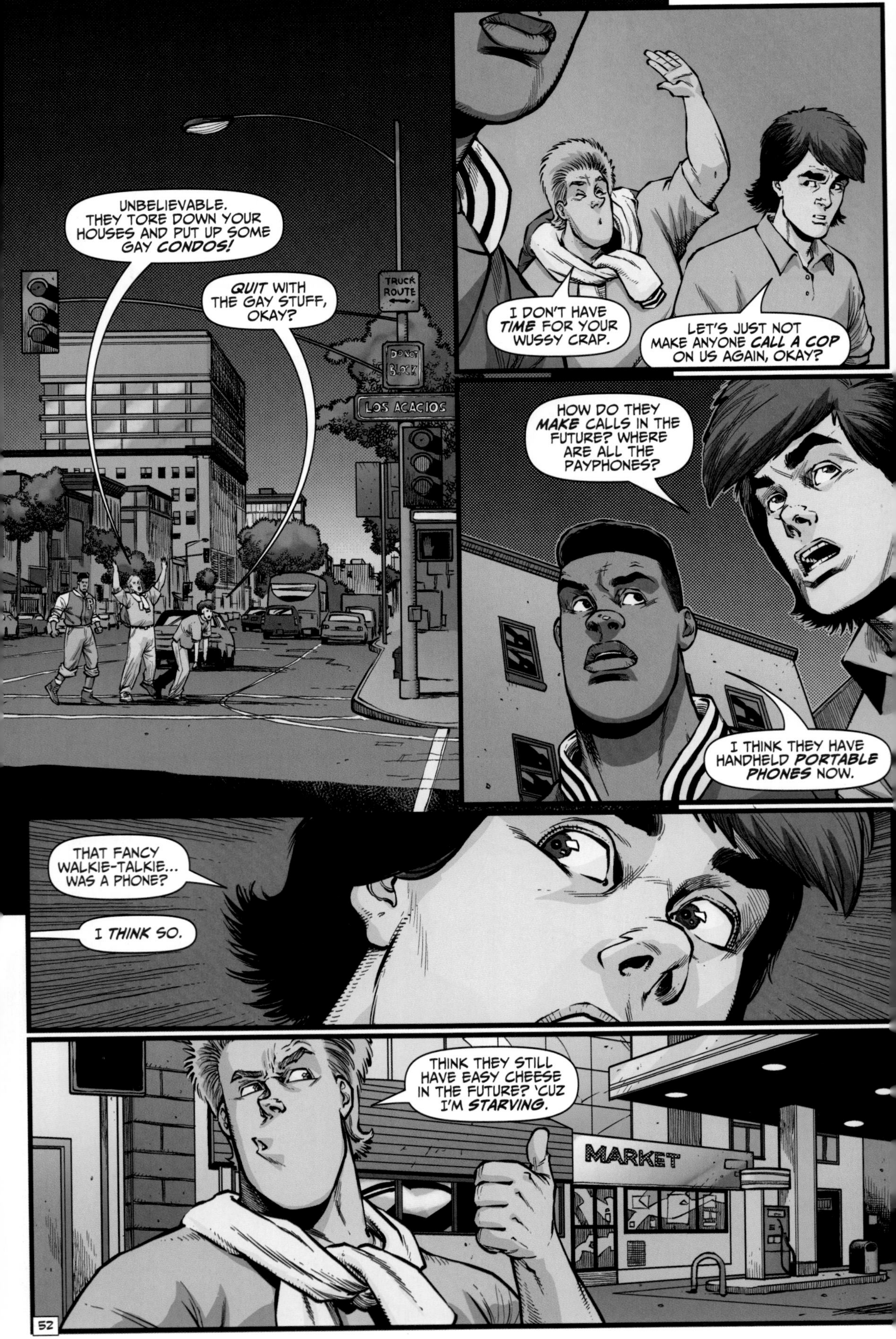
UNBELIEVABLE. THEY TORE DOWN YOUR HOUSES AND PUT UP SOME GAY CONDOS!
QUIT WITH THE GAY STUFF, OKAY?
TRUCK ROUTE
DO NOT BLOCK
LOS ACACIOS
I DON'T HAVE TIME FOR YOUR WUSSY CRAP.
LET'S JUST NOT MAKE ANYONE CALL A COP ON US AGAIN, OKAY?
HOW DO THEY MAKE CALLS IN THE FUTURE? WHERE ARE ALL THE PAYPHONES?
I THINK THEY HAVE HANDHELD PORTABLE PHONES NOW.
THAT FANCY WALKIE-TALKIE... WAS A PHONE?
I THINK SO.
THINK THEY STILL HAVE EASY CHEESE IN THE FUTURE? 'CUZ I'M STARVING.
MARKET

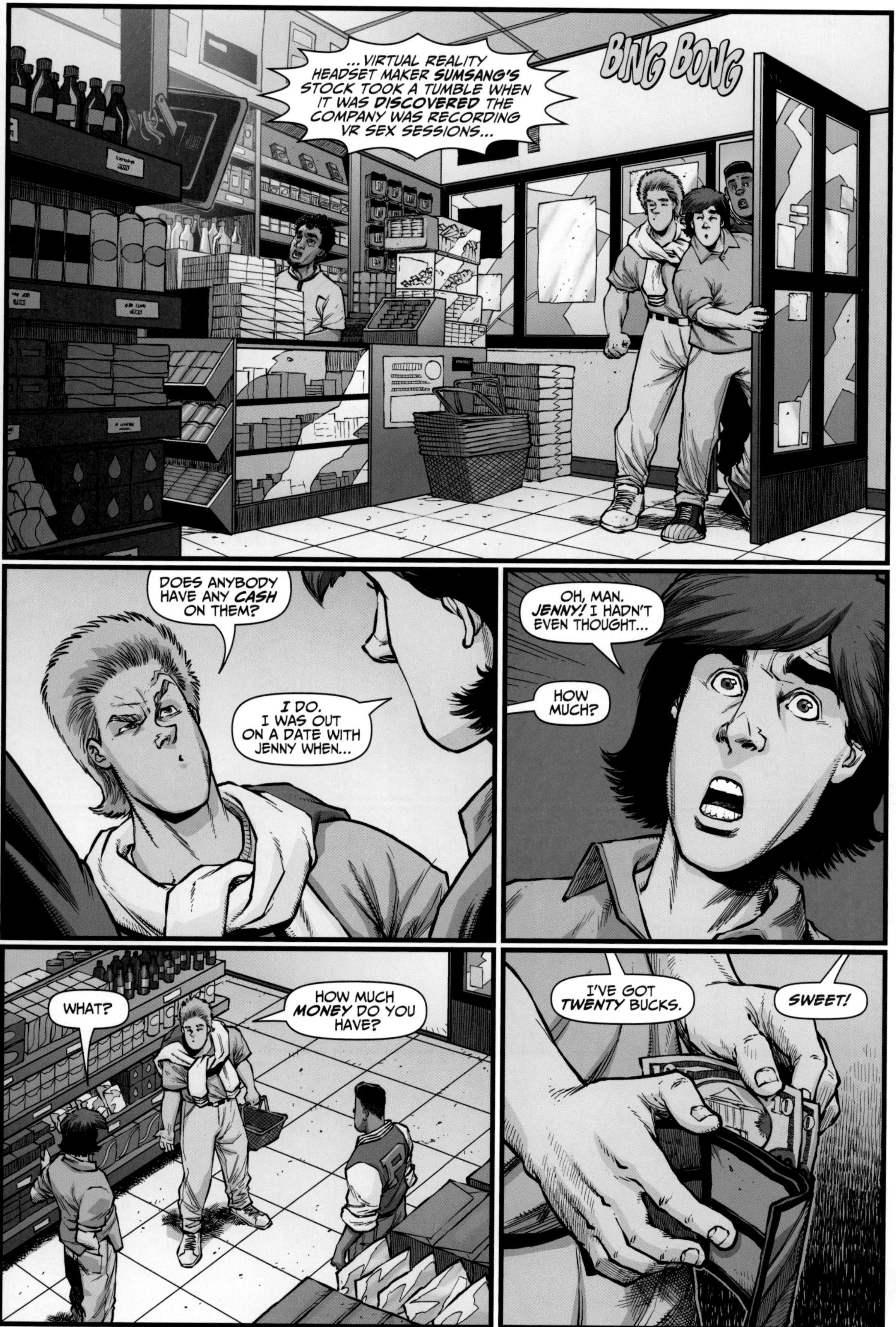
...VIRTUAL REALITY HEADSET MAKER SUMSANG'S STOCK TOOK A TUMBLE WHEN IT WAS DISCOVERED THE COMPANY WAS RECORDING VR SEX SESSIONS...
BING BONG
DOES ANYBODY HAVE ANY CASH ON THEM?
I DO. I WAS OUT ON A DATE WITH JENNY WHEN...
OH, MAN. JENNY! I HADN'T EVEN THOUGHT...
HOW MUCH?
WHAT?
HOW MUCH MONEY DO YOU HAVE?
I'VE GOT TWENTY BUCKS.
SWEET!

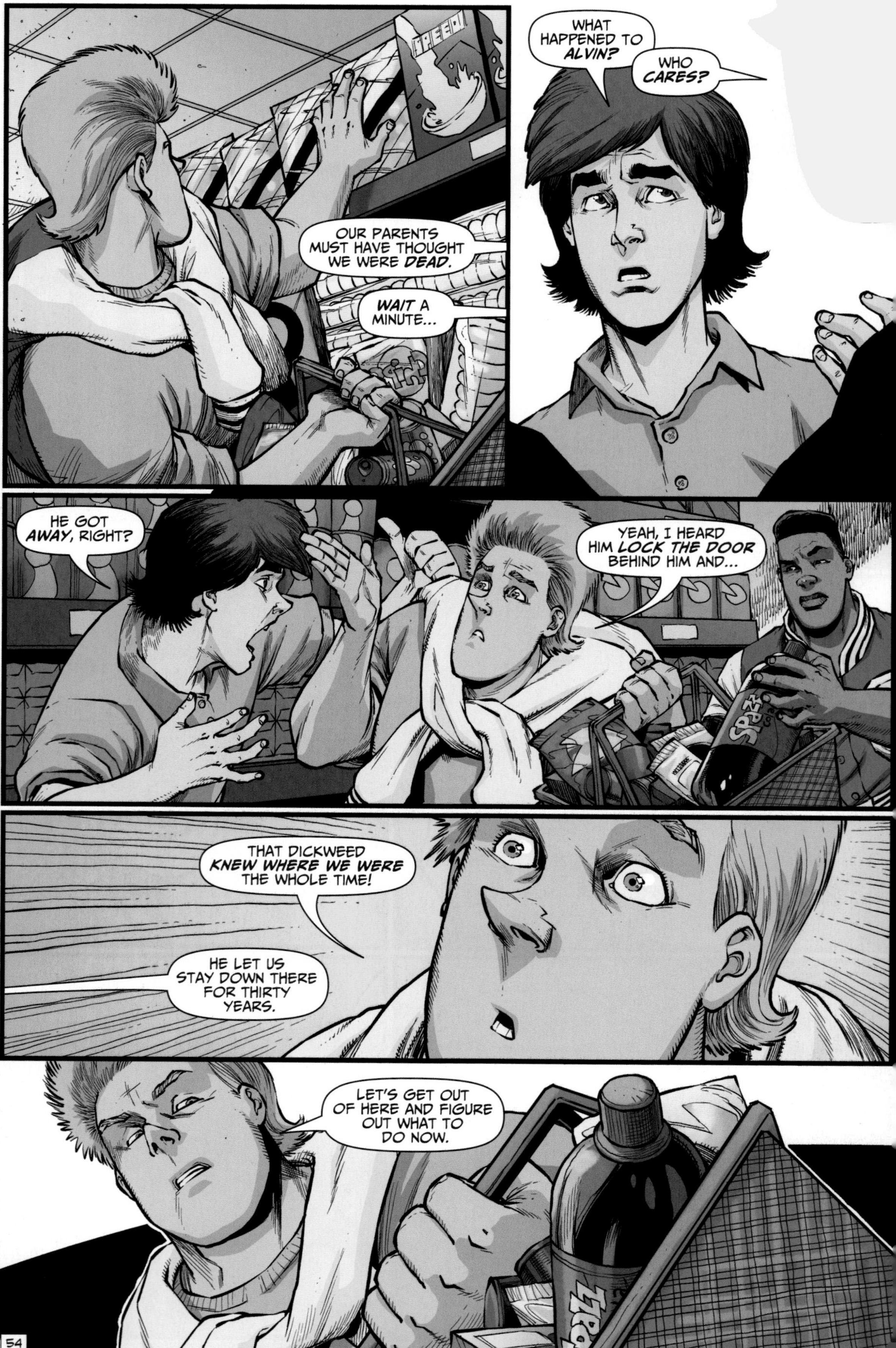
WHAT HAPPENED TO ALVIN?
WHO CARES?
OUR PARENTS MUST HAVE THOUGHT WE WERE DEAD.
WAIT A MINUTE...
HE GOT AWAY, RIGHT?
YEAH, I HEARD HIM LOCK THE DOOR BEHIND HIM AND...
THAT DICKWEED KNEW WHERE WE WERE THE WHOLE TIME!
HE LET US STAY DOWN THERE FOR THIRTY YEARS.
LET'S GET OUT OF HERE AND FIGURE OUT WHAT TO DO NOW.

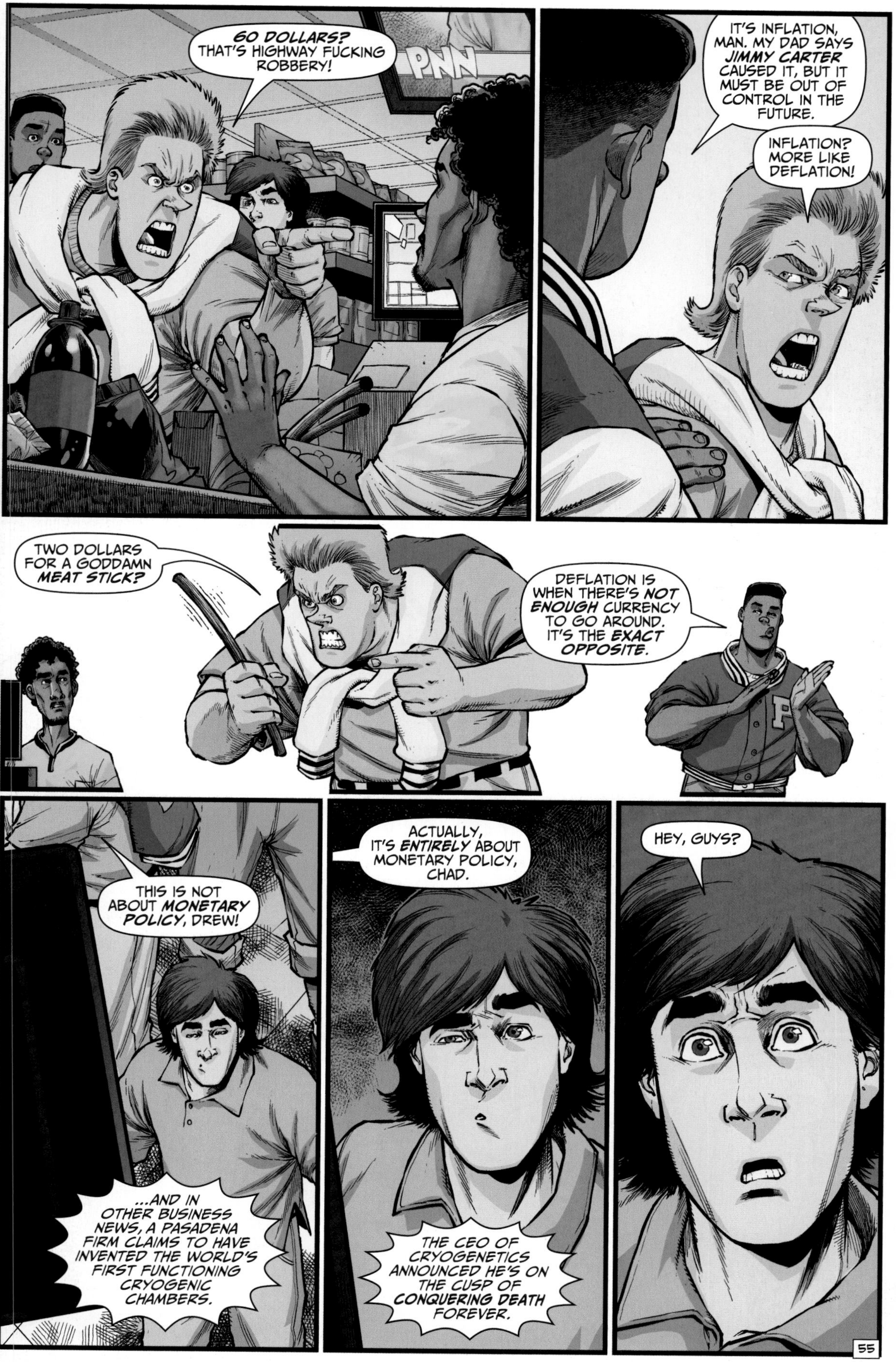

GO DOLLARS? THAT'S HIGHWAY FUCKING ROBBERY!
PNN
IT'S INFLATION, MAN. MY DAD SAYS JIMMY CARTER CAUSED IT, BUT IT MUST BE OUT OF CONTROL IN THE FUTURE.
INFLATION? MORE LIKE DEFLATION!
TWO DOLLARS FOR A GODDAMN MEAT STICK?
DEFLATION IS WHEN THERE'S NOT ENOUGH CURRENCY TO GO AROUND. IT'S THE EXACT OPPOSITE.
THIS IS NOT ABOUT MONETARY POLICY, DREW!
...AND IN OTHER BUSINESS NEWS, A PASADENA FIRM CLAIMS TO HAVE INVENTED THE WORLD'S FIRST FUNCTIONING CRYOGENIC CHAMBERS.
ACTUALLY, IT'S ENTIRELY ABOUT MONETARY POLICY, CHAD.
THE CEO OF CRYOGENETICS ANNOUNCED HE'S ON THE CUSP OF CONQUERING DEATH FOREVER.
HEY, GUYS?

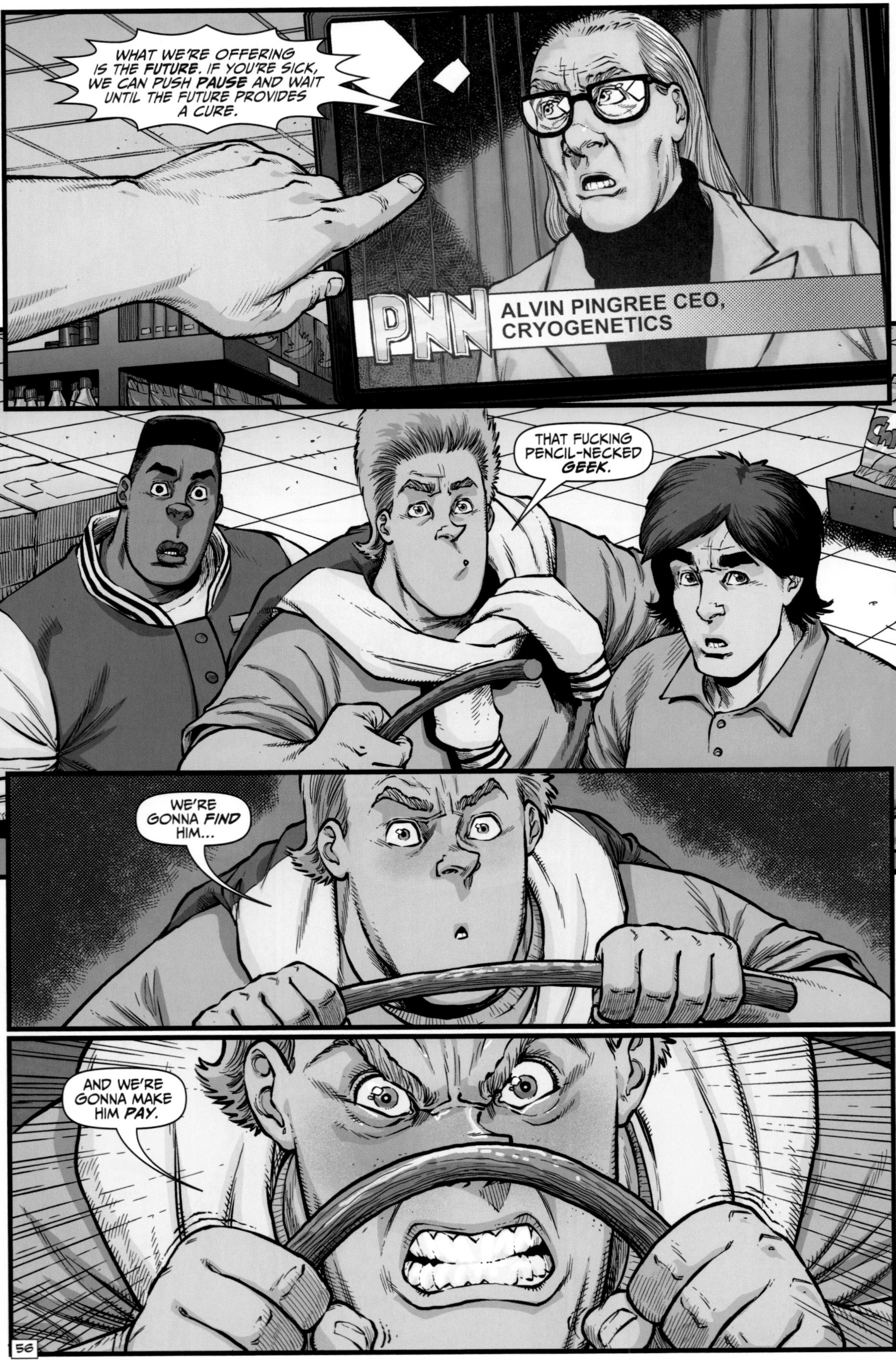
WHAT WE'RE OFFERING IS THE FUTURE. IF YOU'RE SICK, WE CAN PUSH PAUSE AND WAIT UNTIL THE FUTURE PROVIDES A CURE.
PNN
ALVIN PINGREE CEO, CRYOGENETICS
THAT FUCKING PENCIL-NECKED GEEK.
WE'RE GONNA FIND HIM...
AND WE'RE GONNA MAKE HIM PAY.

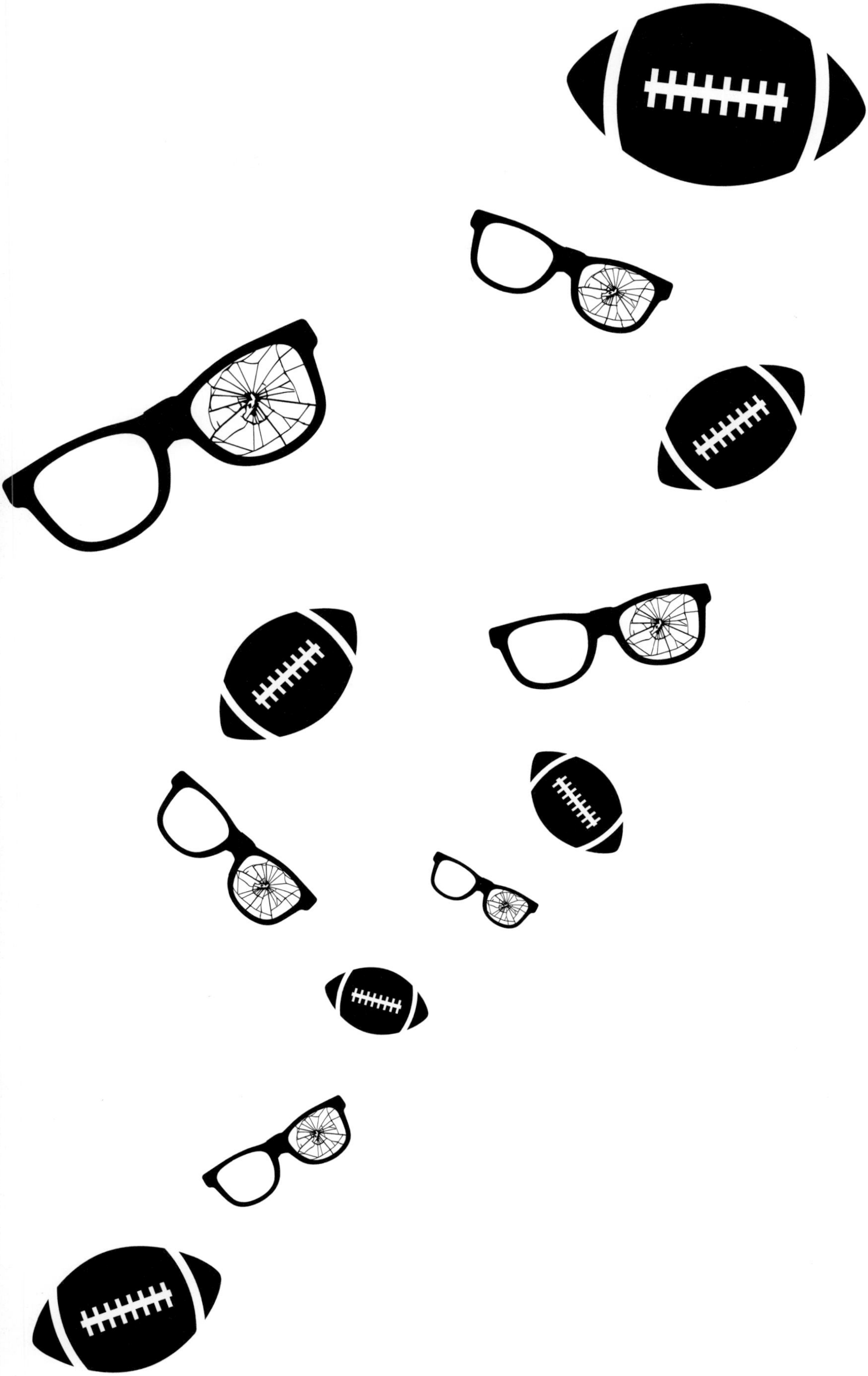

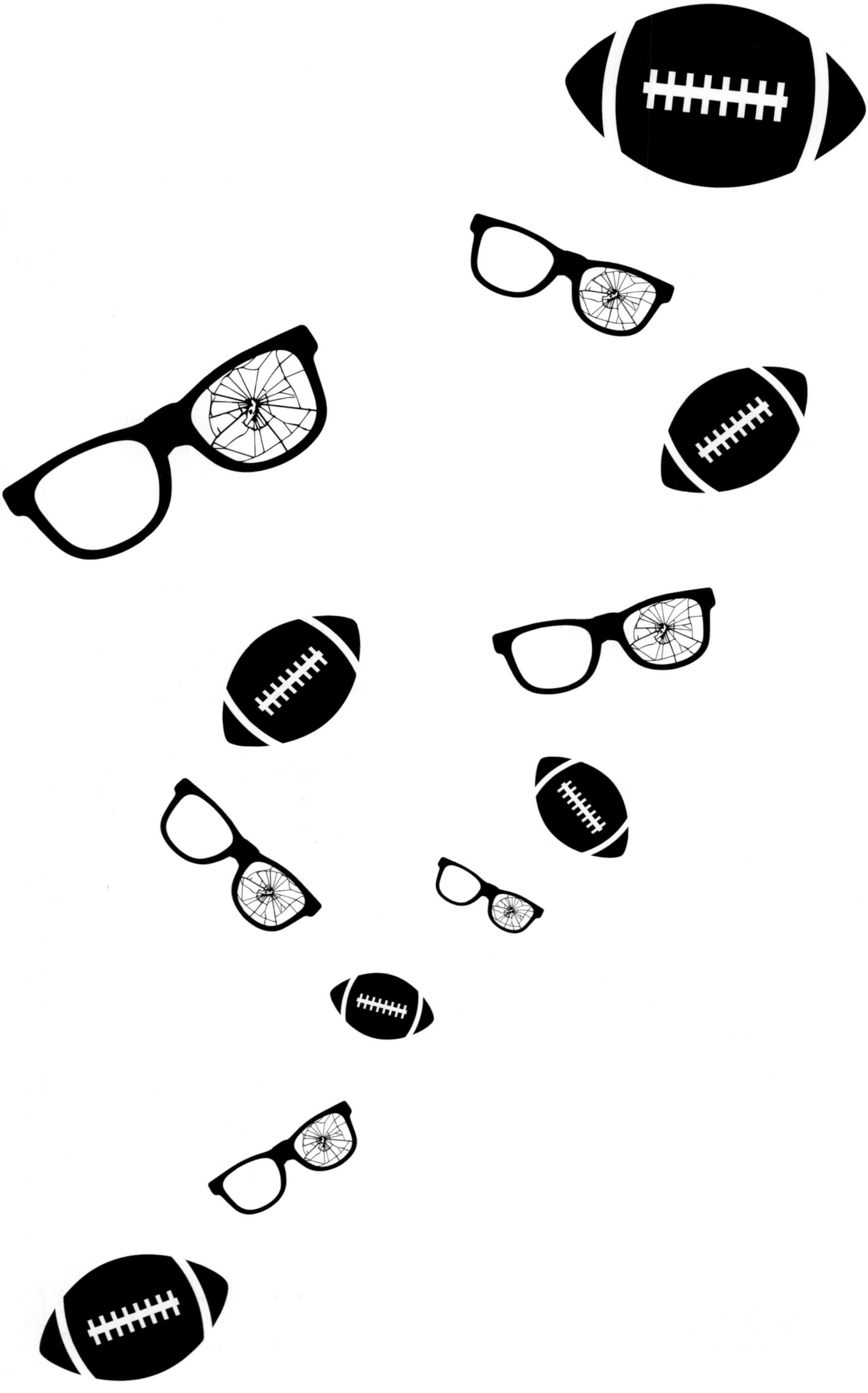

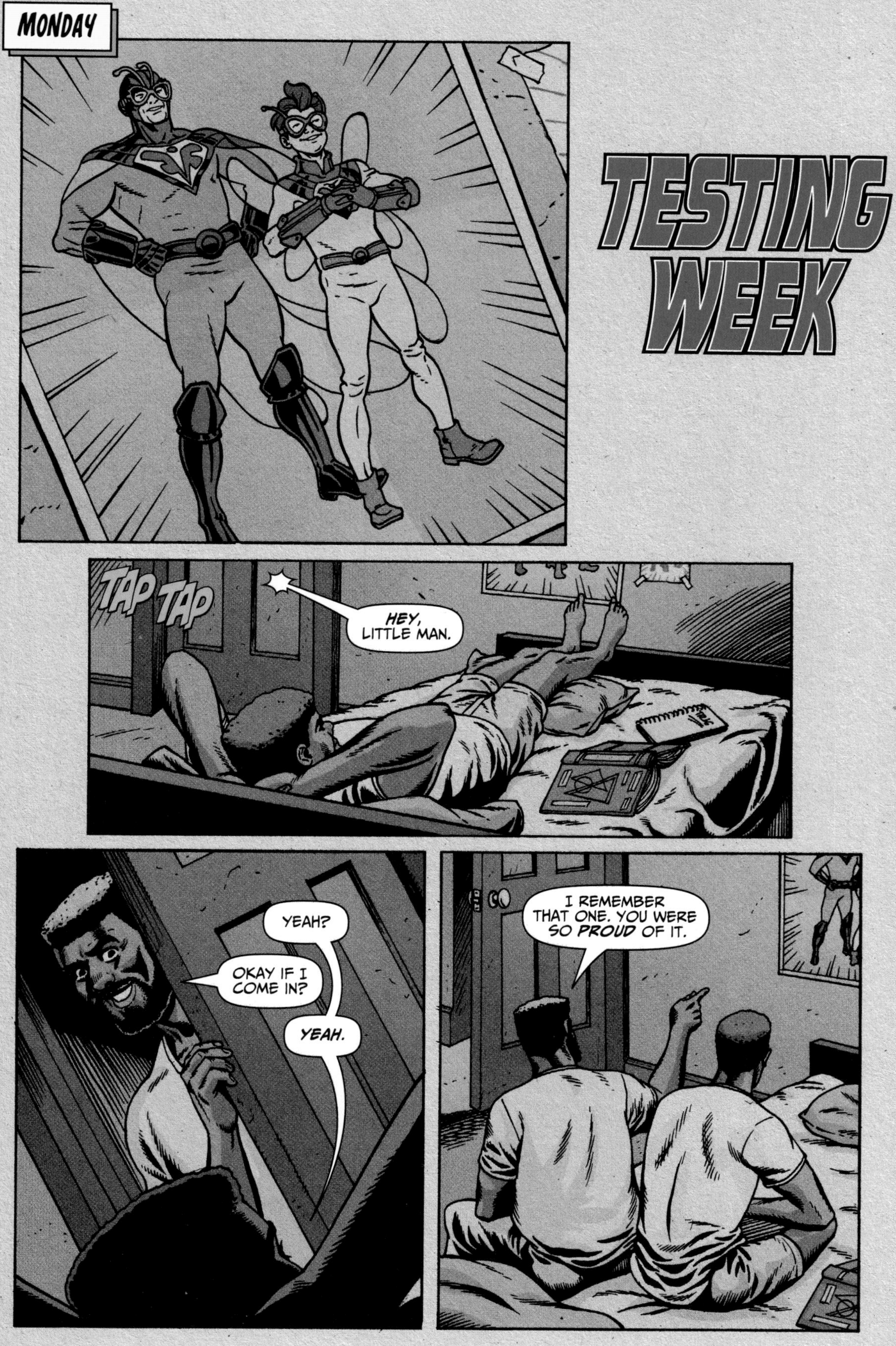
MONDAY
TESTING WEEK
TAP TAP
HEY, LITTLE MAN.
YEAH?
OKAY IF I COME IN?
YEAH.
I REMEMBER THAT ONE. YOU WERE SO PROUD OF IT.

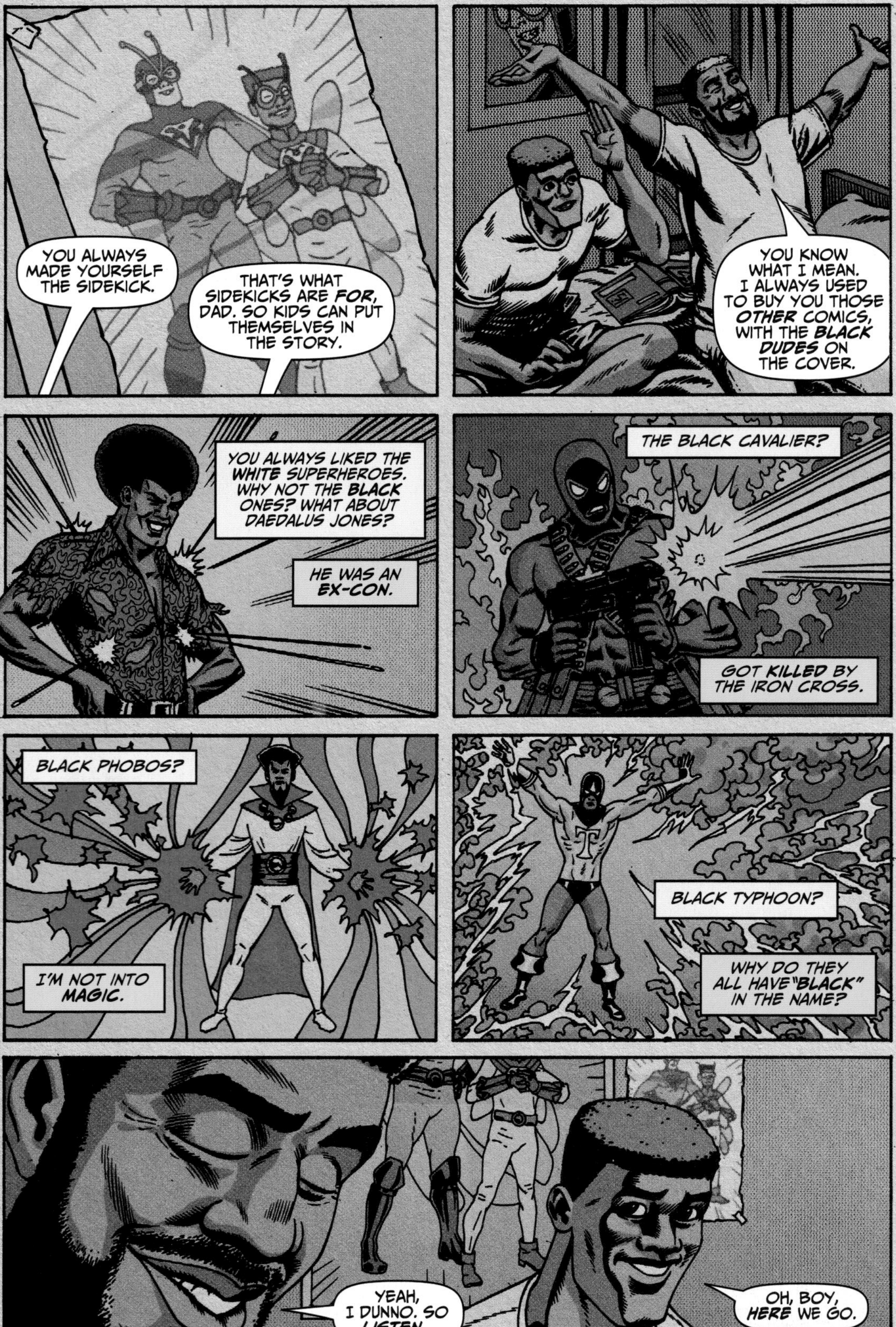
YOU ALWAYS MADE YOURSELF THE SIDEKICK.
THAT'S WHAT SIDEKICKS ARE FOR, DAD. SO KIDS CAN PUT THEMSELVES IN THE STORY.
YOU KNOW WHAT I MEAN. I ALWAYS USED TO BUY YOU THOSE OTHER COMICS, WITH THE BLACK DUDES ON THE COVER.
YOU ALWAYS LIKED THE WHITE SUPERHEROES. WHY NOT THE BLACK ONES? WHAT ABOUT DAEDALUS JONES?
HE WAS AN EX-CON.
THE BLACK CAVALIER?
GOT KILLED BY THE IRON CROSS.
BLACK PHOBOS?
I'M NOT INTO MAGIC.
BLACK TYPHOON?
WHY DO THEY ALL HAVE "BLACK" IN THE NAME?
YEAH, I DUNNO. SO LISTEN...
OH, BOY, HERE WE GO.

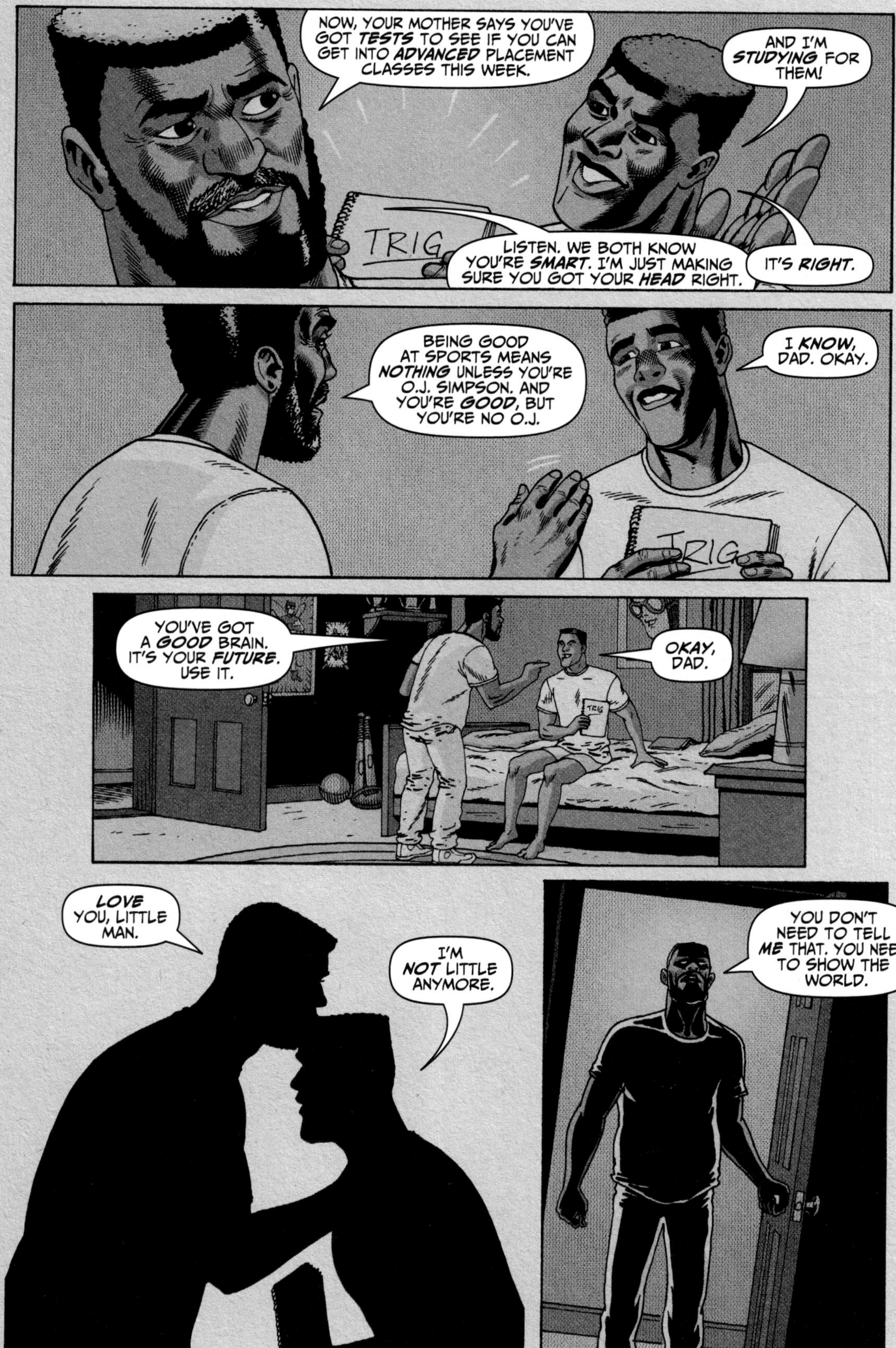
NOW, YOUR MOTHER SAYS YOU'VE GOT TESTS TO SEE IF YOU CAN GET INTO ADVANCED PLACEMENT CLASSES THIS WEEK.
AND I'M STUDYING FOR THEM!
TRIG
LISTEN. WE BOTH KNOW YOU'RE SMART. I'M JUST MAKING SURE YOU GOT YOUR HEAD RIGHT.
IT'S RIGHT.
BEING GOOD AT SPORTS MEANS NOTHING UNLESS YOU'RE O.J. SIMPSON. AND YOU'RE GOOD, BUT YOU'RE NO O.J.
I KNOW, DAD. OKAY.
TRIG
YOU'VE GOT A GOOD BRAIN. IT'S YOUR FUTURE. USE IT.
OKAY, DAD.
LOVE YOU, LITTLE MAN.
I'M NOT LITTLE ANYMORE.
YOU DON'T NEED TO TELL ME THAT. YOU NEED TO SHOW THE WORLD.

TUESDAY

ADVANCED PLACEMENT TRIG

NO CALCULATORS

WEDNESDAY

...a paragraph composed of at least five sentences, please identify at least one symbol in classic American literature that you believe is still true today.

In Nathaniel Hawthorne's "The Scarlet Letter," the embroidered "A" on Hester Prynne's clothing represents unrealistic community expectations. You can still see those expectations on the cover of the "National Enquirer" in the superman's...

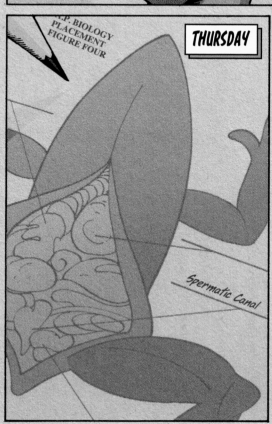

A.P. BIOLOGY
PLACEMENT
FIGURE FOUR

Spermatic Canal

THURSDAY

FRIDAY

SO DREW, WE GOT YOUR TEST RESULTS.

GUIDANCE COUNSELOR

YOU DID VERY WELL— *ESPECIALLY* ON THE TRIG EXAM! *FINE* WORK.

THANKS, MS. GREER.

JOHNSON, DREW

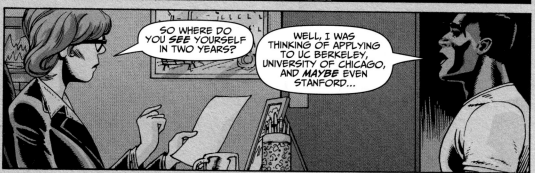

SO WHERE DO YOU *SEE* YOURSELF IN TWO YEARS?

WELL, I WAS THINKING OF APPLYING TO UC BERKELEY, UNIVERSITY OF CHICAGO, AND *MAYBE* EVEN STANFORD...

OH, MY. THAT'S CERTAINLY... *ASPIRATIONAL* OF YOU.

BUT MY *GRADES* ARE GOOD...

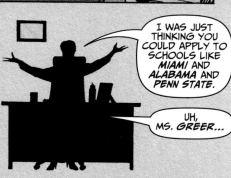

I WAS JUST THINKING YOU COULD APPLY TO SCHOOLS LIKE *MIAMI* AND *ALABAMA* AND *PENN STATE.*

UH, *MS. GREER...*

THOSE ARE, LIKE, THE *BEST* FOOTBALL SCHOOLS IN THE COUNTRY. THAT'S NOT REALLY WHAT I...

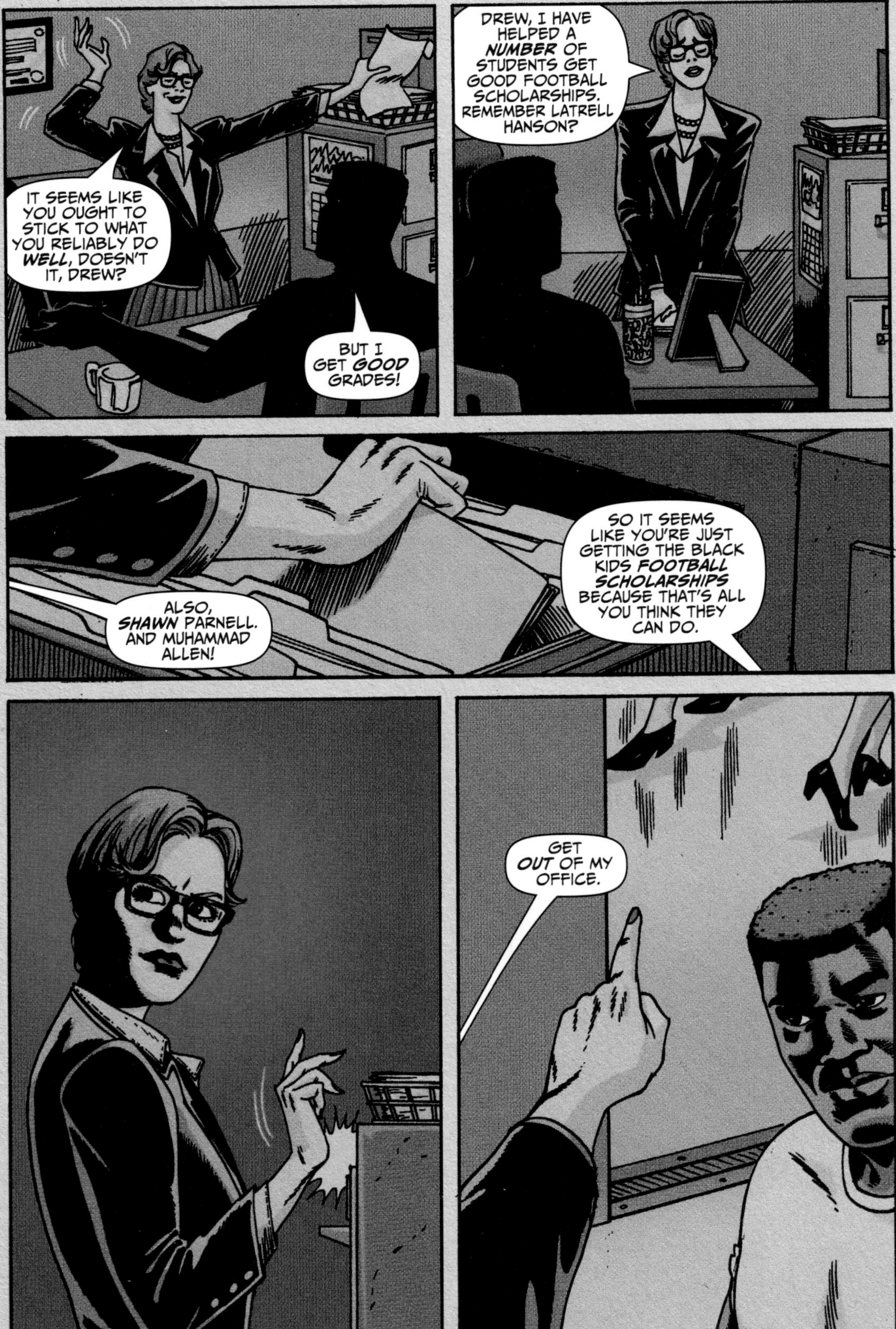
IT SEEMS LIKE YOU OUGHT TO STICK TO WHAT YOU RELIABLY DO WELL, DOESN'T IT, DREW?
BUT I GET GOOD GRADES!
DREW, I HAVE HELPED A NUMBER OF STUDENTS GET GOOD FOOTBALL SCHOLARSHIPS. REMEMBER LATRELL HANSON?
ALSO, SHAWN PARNELL. AND MUHAMMAD ALLEN!
SO IT SEEMS LIKE YOU'RE JUST GETTING THE BLACK KIDS FOOTBALL SCHOLARSHIPS BECAUSE THAT'S ALL YOU THINK THEY CAN DO.
GET OUT OF MY OFFICE.

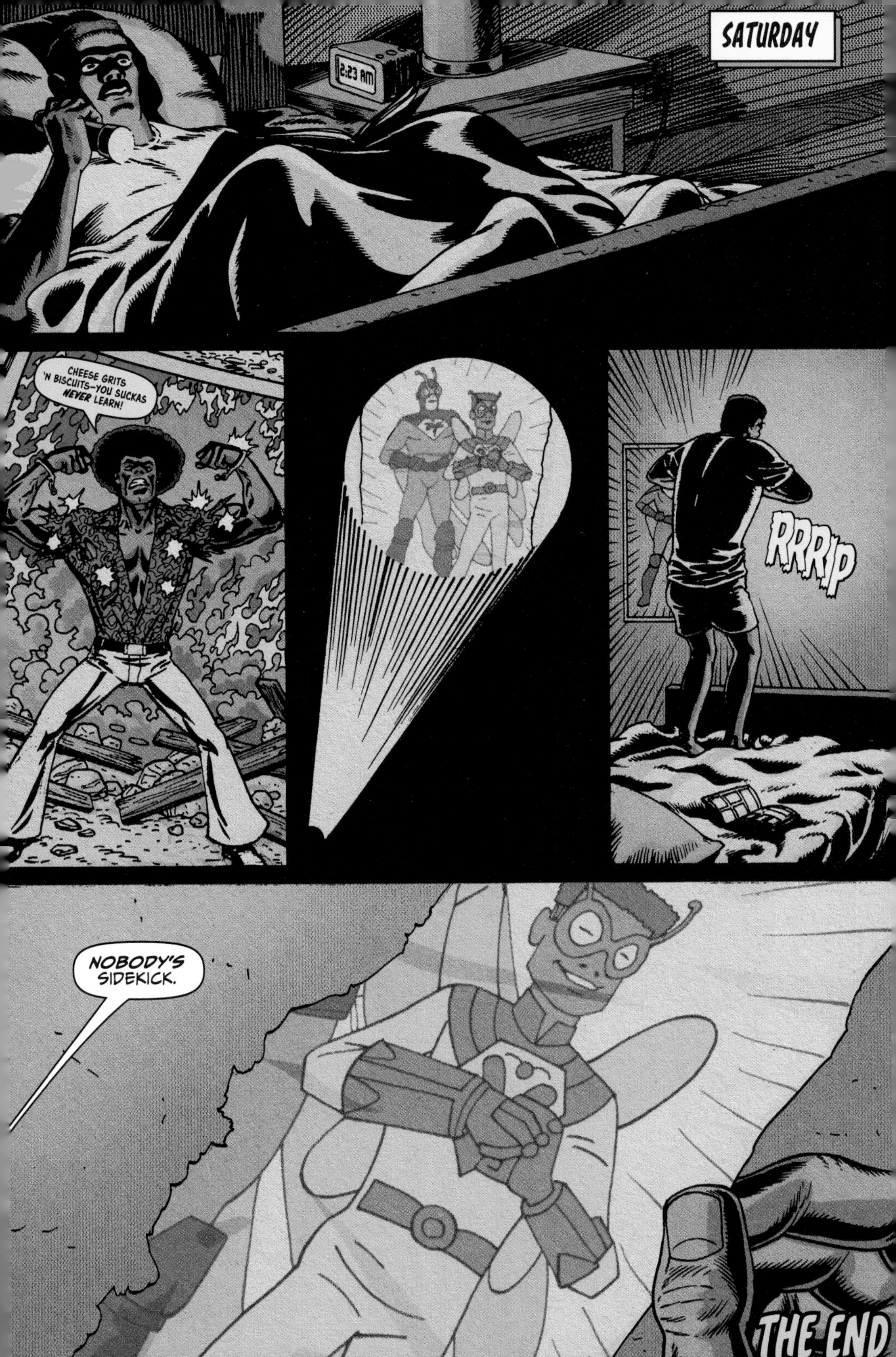
SATURDAY
2:23 AM
CHEESE GRITS 'N BISCUITS—YOU SUCKAS NEVER LEARN!
RRRIP
NOBODY'S SIDEKICK.
THE END

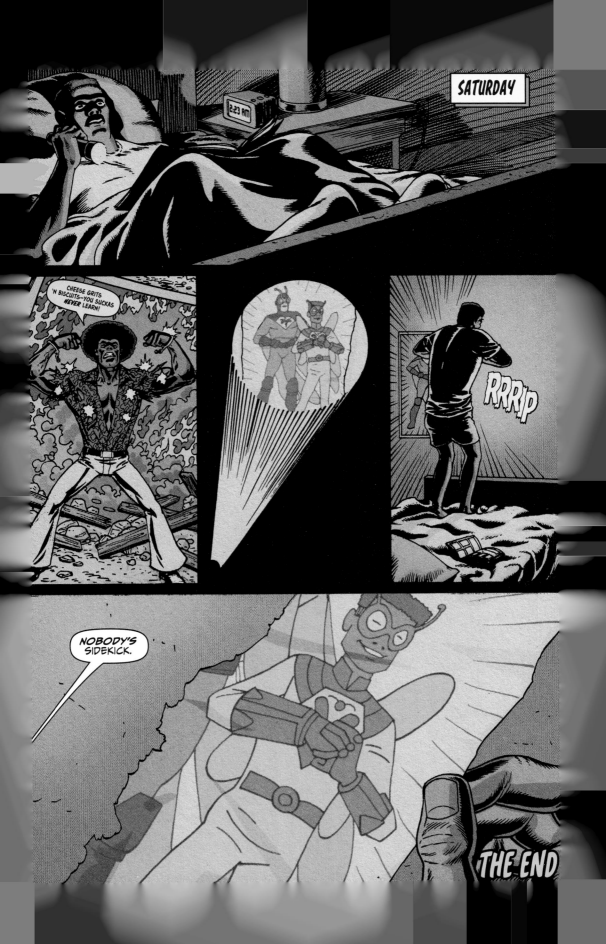

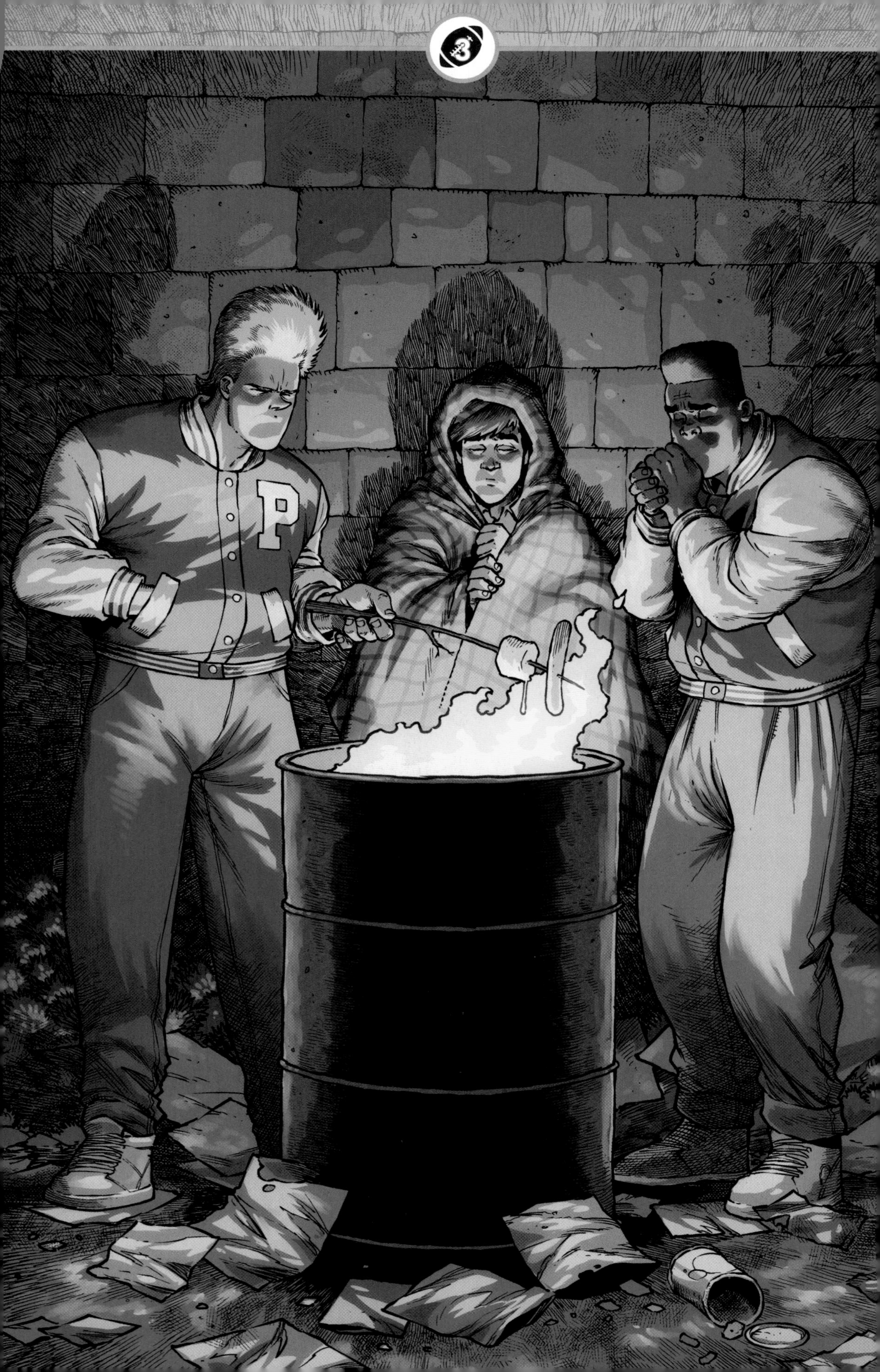

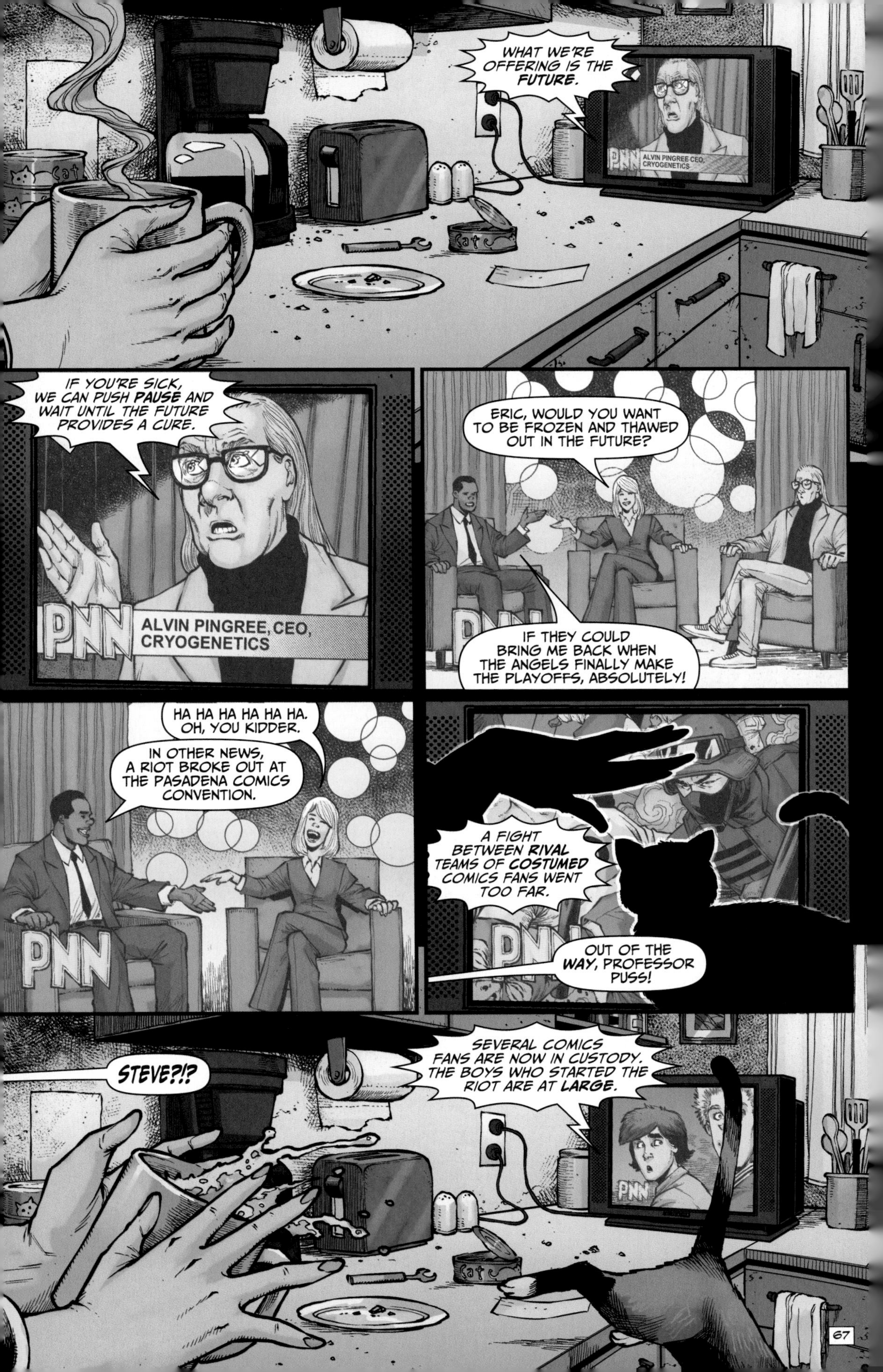
WHAT WE'RE OFFERING IS THE FUTURE.
PNN ALVIN PINGREE CEO, CRYOGENETICS
IF YOU'RE SICK, WE CAN PUSH PAUSE AND WAIT UNTIL THE FUTURE PROVIDES A CURE.
PNN ALVIN PINGREE, CEO, CRYOGENETICS
ERIC, WOULD YOU WANT TO BE FROZEN AND THAWED OUT IN THE FUTURE?
IF THEY COULD BRING ME BACK WHEN THE ANGELS FINALLY MAKE THE PLAYOFFS, ABSOLUTELY!
HA HA HA HA HA HA. OH, YOU KIDDER.
IN OTHER NEWS, A RIOT BROKE OUT AT THE PASADENA COMICS CONVENTION.
PNN
A FIGHT BETWEEN RIVAL TEAMS OF COSTUMED COMICS FANS WENT TOO FAR.
OUT OF THE WAY, PROFESSOR PUSS!
STEVE?!?
SEVERAL COMICS FANS ARE NOW IN CUSTODY. THE BOYS WHO STARTED THE RIOT ARE AT LARGE.
PNN

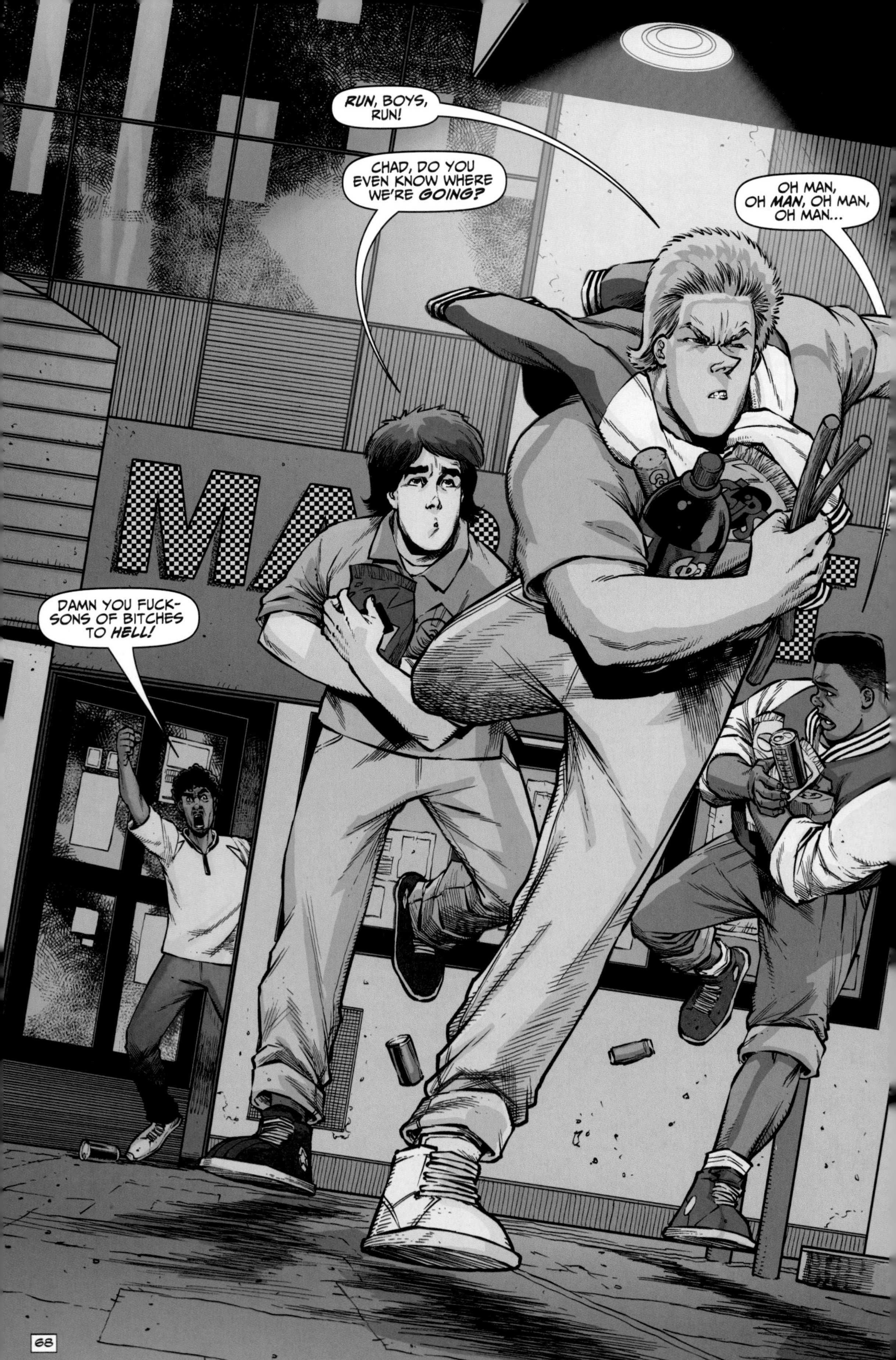
RUN, BOYS, RUN!
CHAD, DO YOU EVEN KNOW WHERE WE'RE GOING?
OH MAN, OH MAN, OH MAN, OH MAN...
DAMN YOU FUCK-SONS OF BITCHES TO HELL!

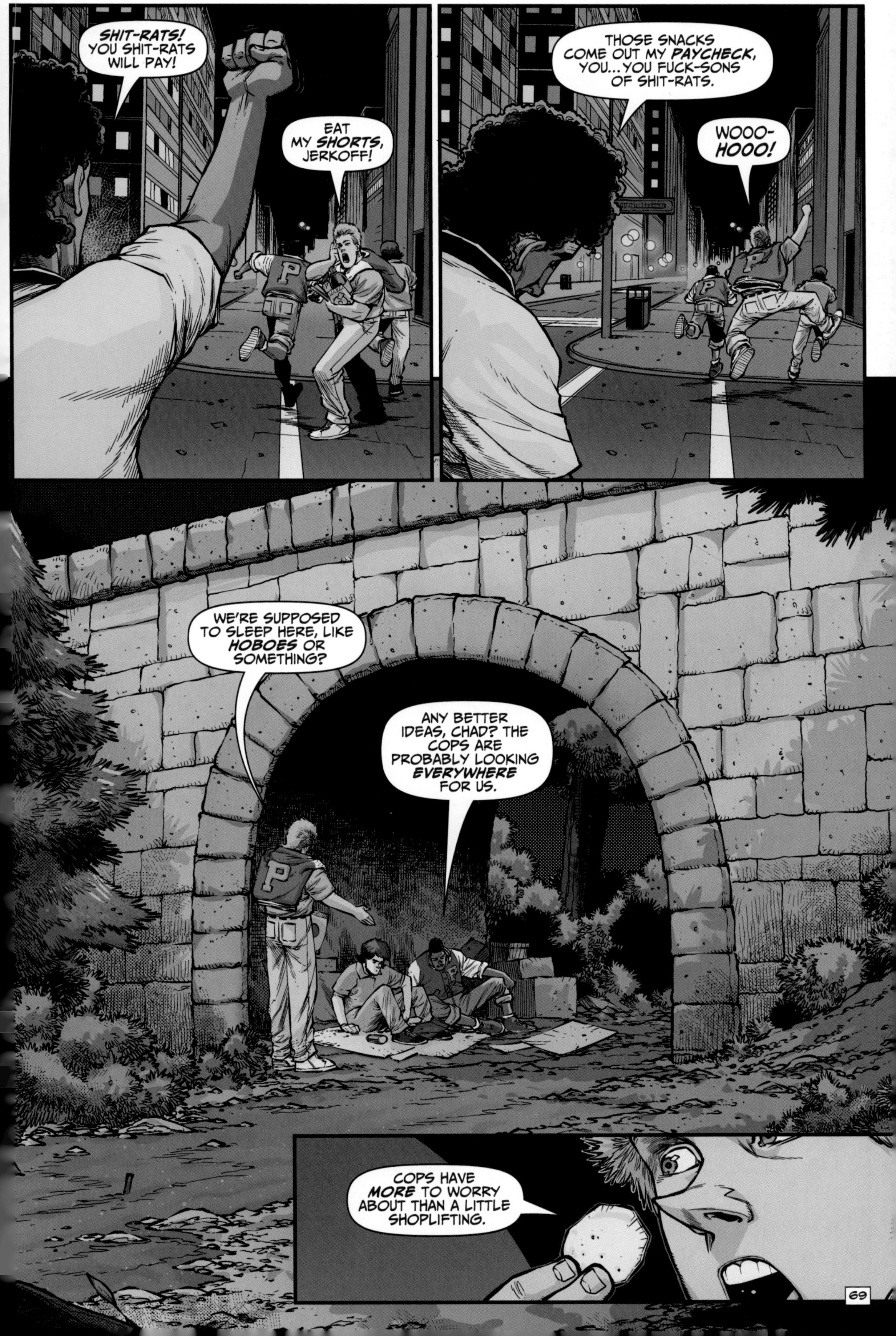

SHIT-RATS! YOU SHIT-RATS WILL PAY!
EAT MY SHORTS, JERKOFF!
THOSE SNACKS COME OUT MY PAYCHECK, YOU...YOU FUCK-SONS OF SHIT-RATS.
WOOO-HOOO!
WE'RE SUPPOSED TO SLEEP HERE, LIKE HOBOES OR SOMETHING?
ANY BETTER IDEAS, CHAD? THE COPS ARE PROBABLY LOOKING EVERYWHERE FOR US.
COPS HAVE MORE TO WORRY ABOUT THAN A LITTLE SHOPLIFTING.

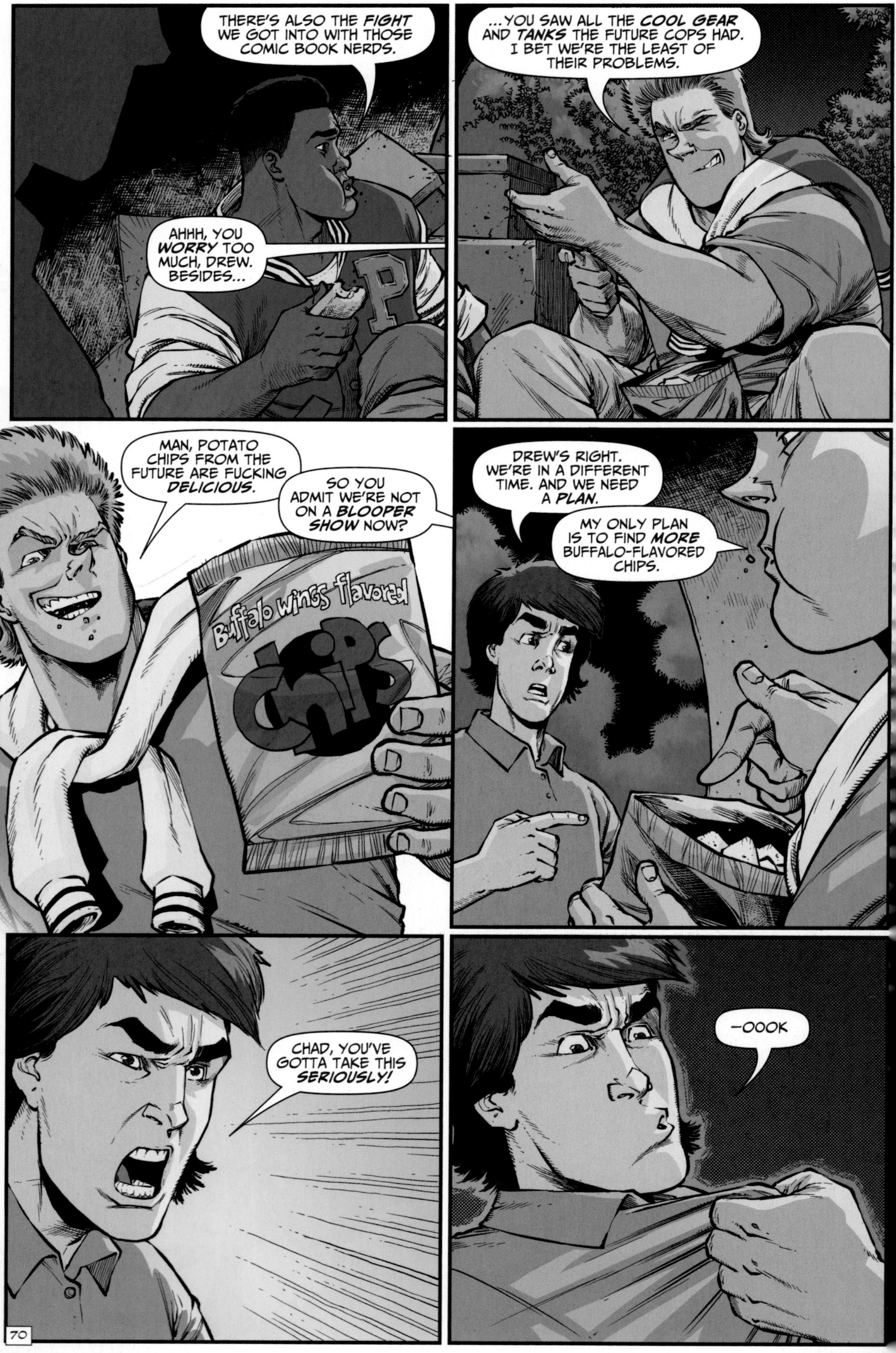
THERE'S ALSO THE FIGHT WE GOT INTO WITH THOSE COMIC BOOK NERDS.
AHHH, YOU WORRY TOO MUCH, DREW. BESIDES...
...YOU SAW ALL THE COOL GEAR AND TANKS THE FUTURE COPS HAD. I BET WE'RE THE LEAST OF THEIR PROBLEMS.
MAN, POTATO CHIPS FROM THE FUTURE ARE FUCKING DELICIOUS.
SO YOU ADMIT WE'RE NOT ON A BLOOPER SHOW NOW?
Buffalo wings flavored
Chips
DREW'S RIGHT. WE'RE IN A DIFFERENT TIME. AND WE NEED A PLAN.
MY ONLY PLAN IS TO FIND MORE BUFFALO-FLAVORED CHIPS.
CHAD, YOU'VE GOTTA TAKE THIS SERIOUSLY!
—OOOK

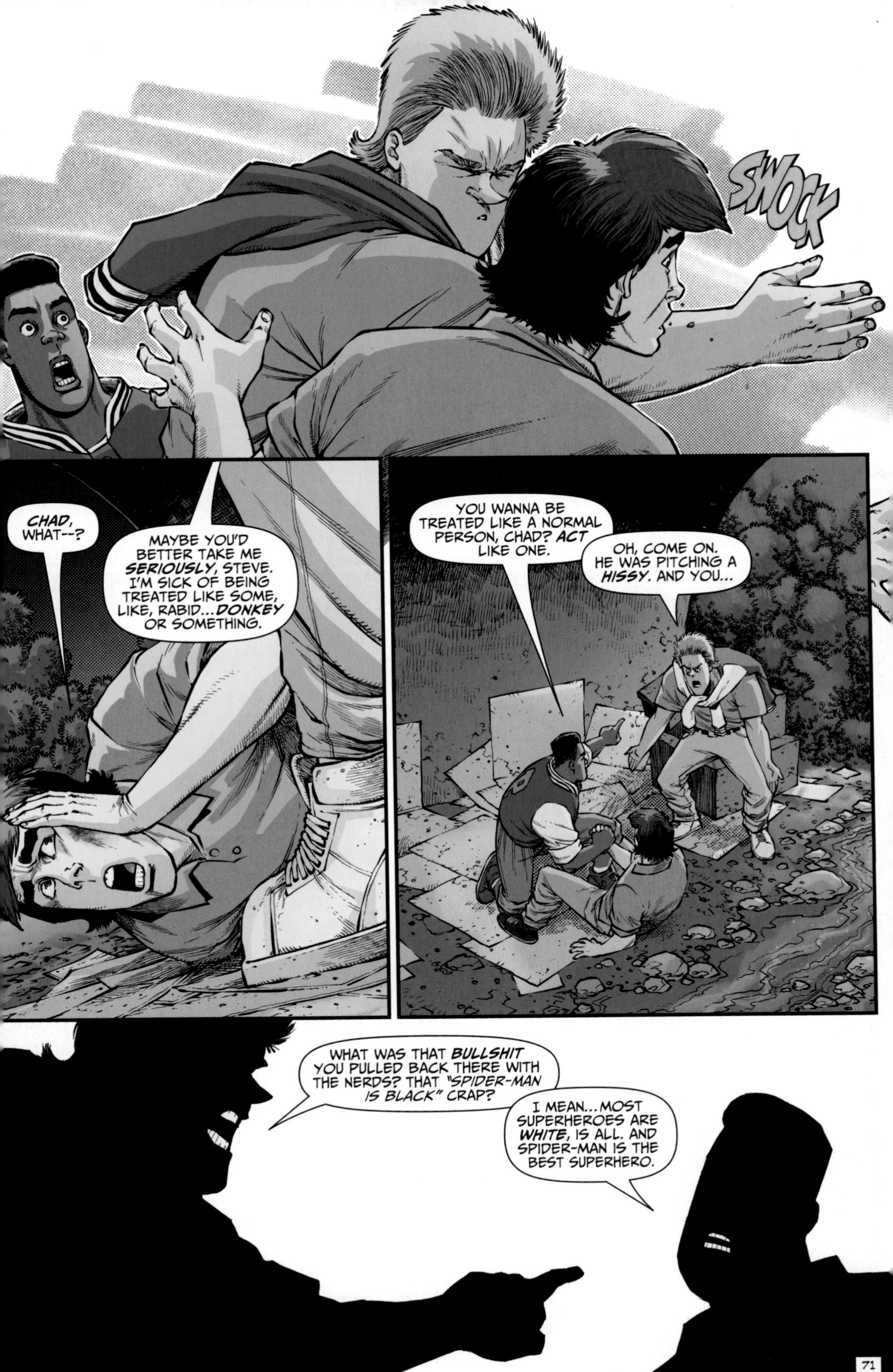
SWOCK
CHAD, WHAT--?
MAYBE YOU'D BETTER TAKE ME SERIOUSLY, STEVE. I'M SICK OF BEING TREATED LIKE SOME, LIKE, RABID...DONKEY OR SOMETHING.
YOU WANNA BE TREATED LIKE A NORMAL PERSON, CHAD? ACT LIKE ONE.
OH, COME ON. HE WAS PITCHING A HISSY. AND YOU...
WHAT WAS THAT BULLSHIT YOU PULLED BACK THERE WITH THE NERDS? THAT "SPIDER-MAN IS BLACK" CRAP?
I MEAN...MOST SUPERHEROES ARE WHITE, IS ALL. AND SPIDER-MAN IS THE BEST SUPERHERO.

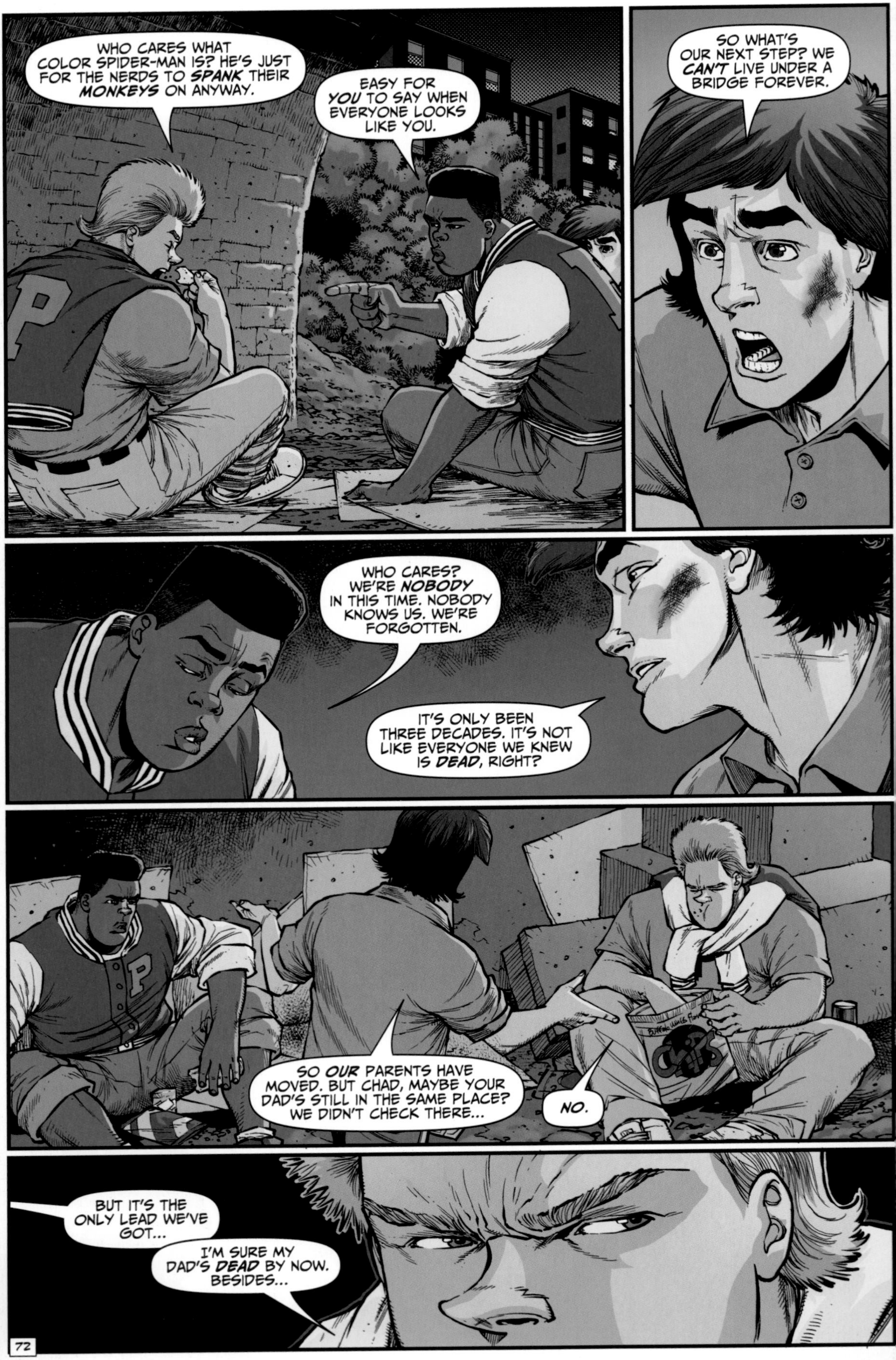
WHO CARES WHAT COLOR SPIDER-MAN IS? HE'S JUST FOR THE NERDS TO SPANK THEIR MONKEYS ON ANYWAY.
EASY FOR YOU TO SAY WHEN EVERYONE LOOKS LIKE YOU.
SO WHAT'S OUR NEXT STEP? WE CAN'T LIVE UNDER A BRIDGE FOREVER.
WHO CARES? WE'RE NOBODY IN THIS TIME. NOBODY KNOWS US. WE'RE FORGOTTEN.
IT'S ONLY BEEN THREE DECADES. IT'S NOT LIKE EVERYONE WE KNEW IS DEAD, RIGHT?
SO OUR PARENTS HAVE MOVED. BUT CHAD, MAYBE YOUR DAD'S STILL IN THE SAME PLACE? WE DIDN'T CHECK THERE...
NO.
BUT IT'S THE ONLY LEAD WE'VE GOT...
I'M SURE MY DAD'S DEAD BY NOW. BESIDES...

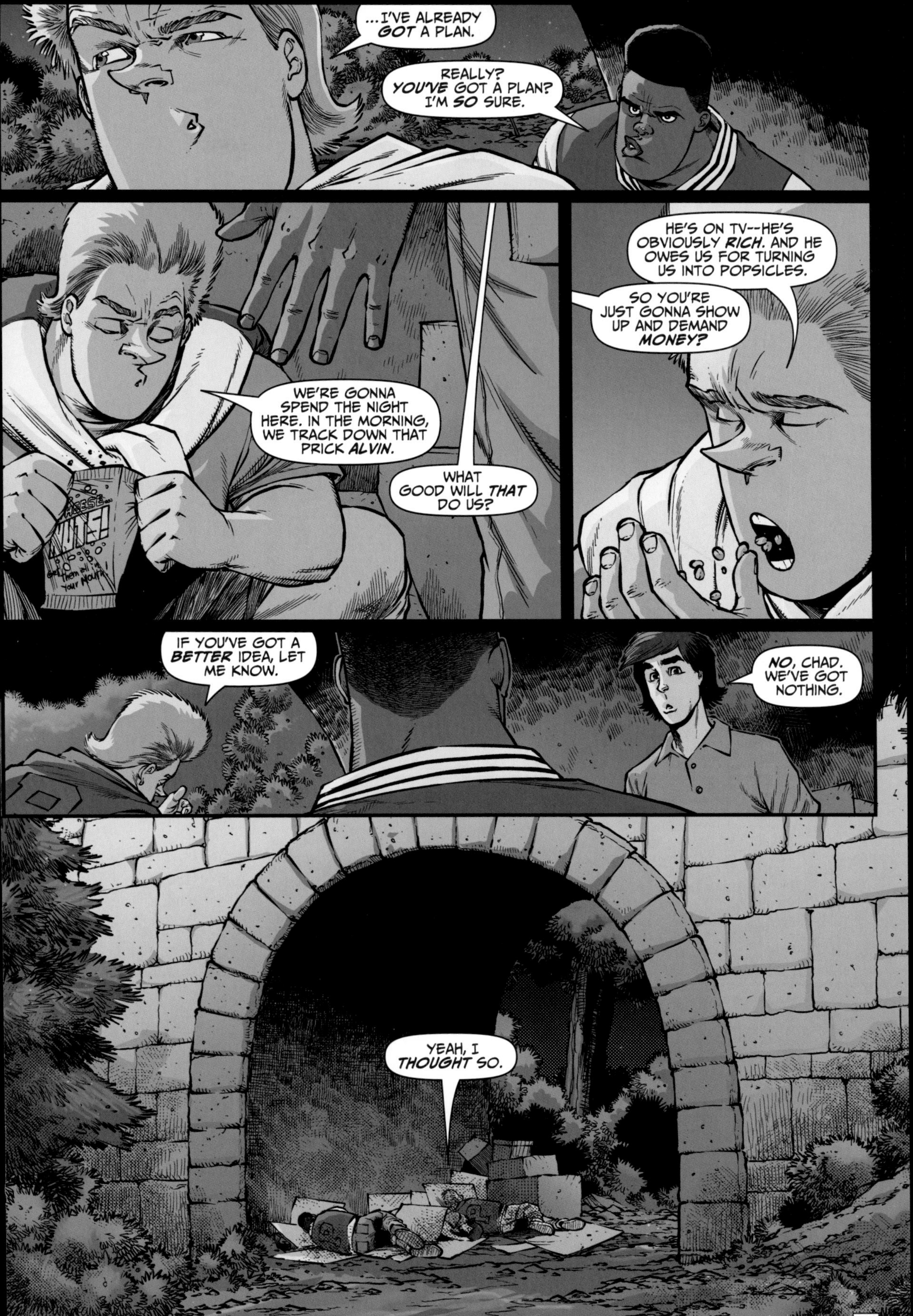
...I'VE ALREADY *GOT* A PLAN.
REALLY? *YOU'VE* GOT A PLAN? I'M *SO* SURE.
WE'RE GONNA SPEND THE NIGHT HERE. IN THE MORNING, WE TRACK DOWN THAT PRICK *ALVIN*.
WHAT GOOD WILL *THAT* DO US?
HE'S ON TV--HE'S OBVIOUSLY *RICH*. AND HE OWES US FOR TURNING US INTO POPSICLES.
SO YOU'RE JUST GONNA SHOW UP AND DEMAND *MONEY?*
IF YOU'VE GOT A *BETTER* IDEA, LET ME KNOW.
NO, CHAD. WE'VE GOT NOTHING.
YEAH, I *THOUGHT* SO.

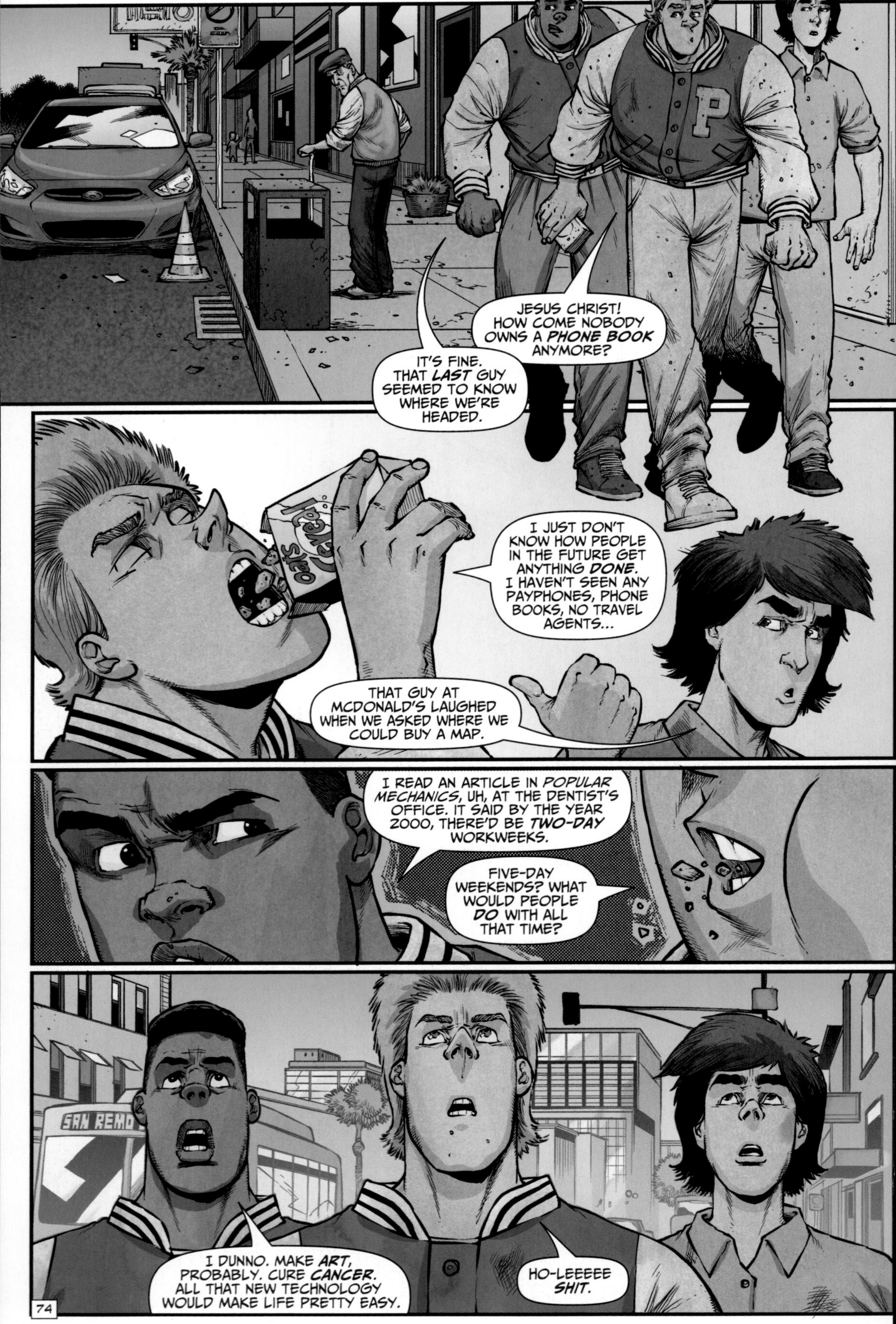
JESUS CHRIST! HOW COME NOBODY OWNS A *PHONE BOOK* ANYMORE?
IT'S FINE. THAT *LAST* GUY SEEMED TO KNOW WHERE WE'RE HEADED.
I JUST DON'T KNOW HOW PEOPLE IN THE FUTURE GET ANYTHING *DONE*. I HAVEN'T SEEN ANY PAYPHONES, PHONE BOOKS, NO TRAVEL AGENTS...
THAT GUY AT MCDONALD'S LAUGHED WHEN WE ASKED WHERE WE COULD BUY A MAP.
I READ AN ARTICLE IN *POPULAR MECHANICS*, UH, AT THE DENTIST'S OFFICE. IT SAID BY THE YEAR 2000, THERE'D BE *TWO-DAY* WORKWEEKS.
FIVE-DAY WEEKENDS? WHAT WOULD PEOPLE *DO* WITH ALL THAT TIME?
SAN REMO
I DUNNO. MAKE *ART*, PROBABLY. CURE *CANCER*. ALL THAT NEW TECHNOLOGY WOULD MAKE LIFE PRETTY EASY.
HO-LEEEEE *SHIT*.

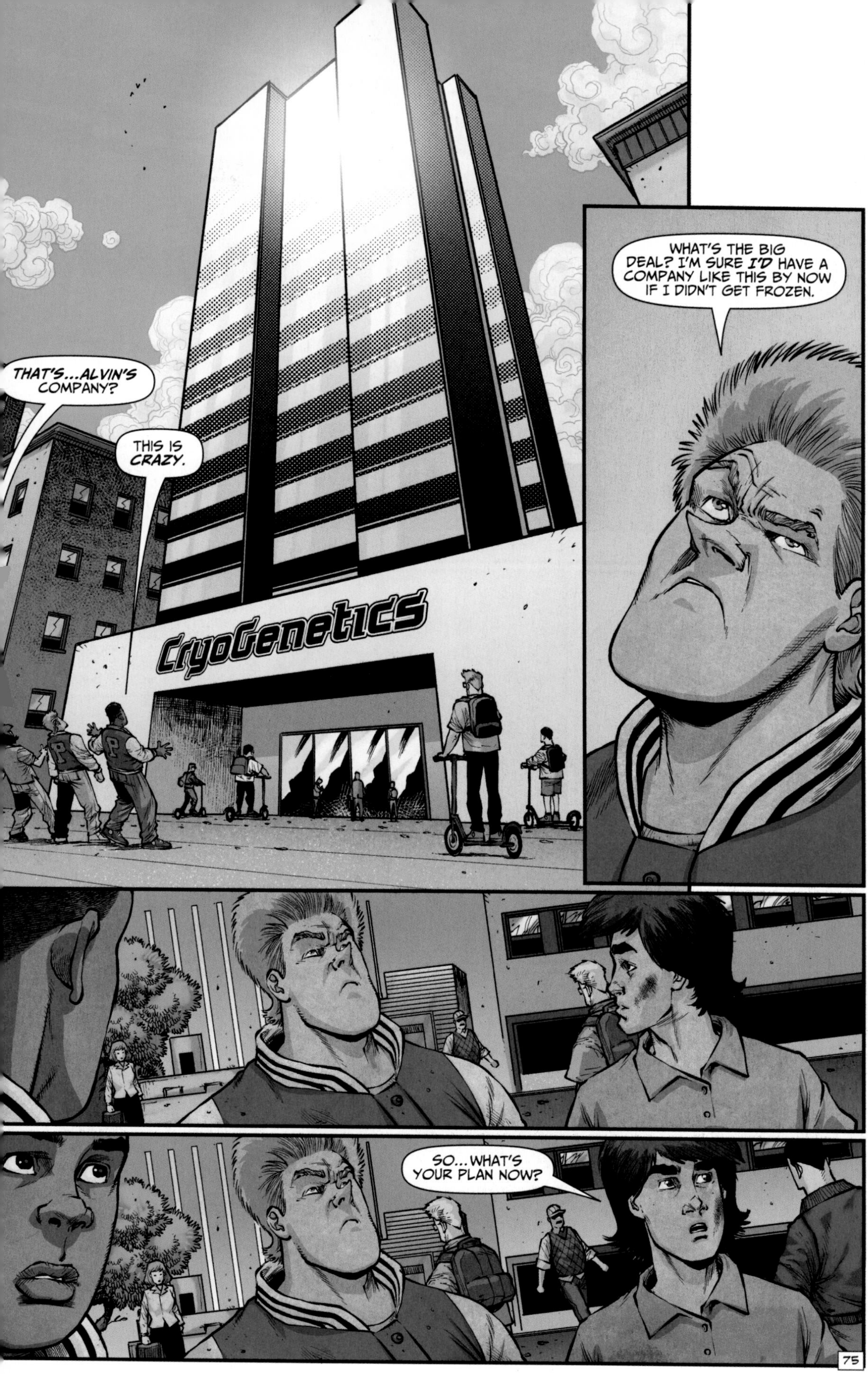
CryoGenetics
THAT'S...ALVIN'S COMPANY?
THIS IS CRAZY.
WHAT'S THE BIG DEAL? I'M SURE I'D HAVE A COMPANY LIKE THIS BY NOW IF I DIDN'T GET FROZEN.
SO...WHAT'S YOUR PLAN NOW?

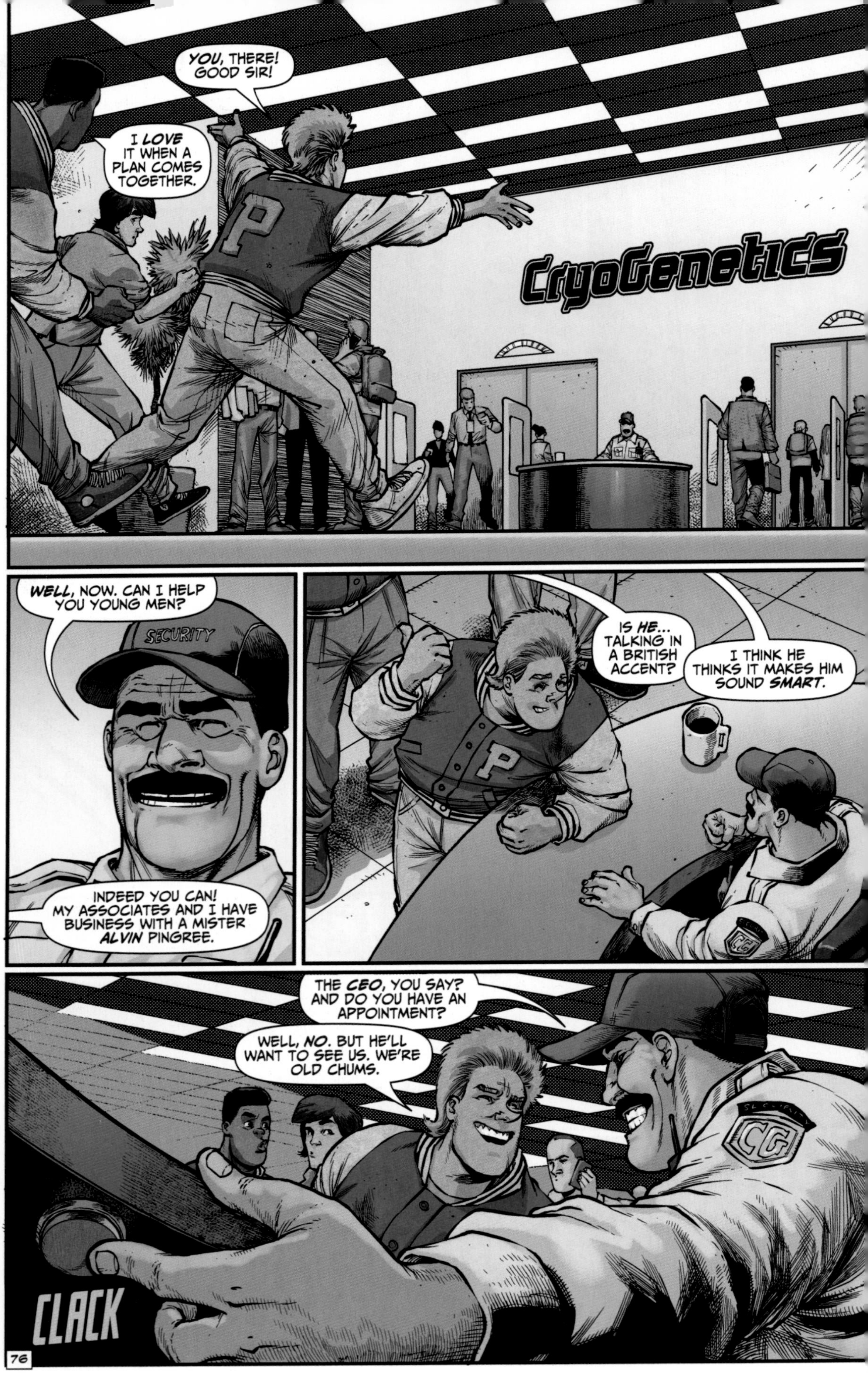
YOU, THERE! GOOD SIR!
I LOVE IT WHEN A PLAN COMES TOGETHER.
CryoGenetics
WELL, NOW. CAN I HELP YOU YOUNG MEN?
SECURITY
INDEED YOU CAN! MY ASSOCIATES AND I HAVE BUSINESS WITH A MISTER ALVIN PINGREE.
IS HE... TALKING IN A BRITISH ACCENT?
I THINK HE THINKS IT MAKES HIM SOUND SMART.
THE CEO, YOU SAY? AND DO YOU HAVE AN APPOINTMENT?
WELL, NO. BUT HE'LL WANT TO SEE US. WE'RE OLD CHUMS.
CLACK

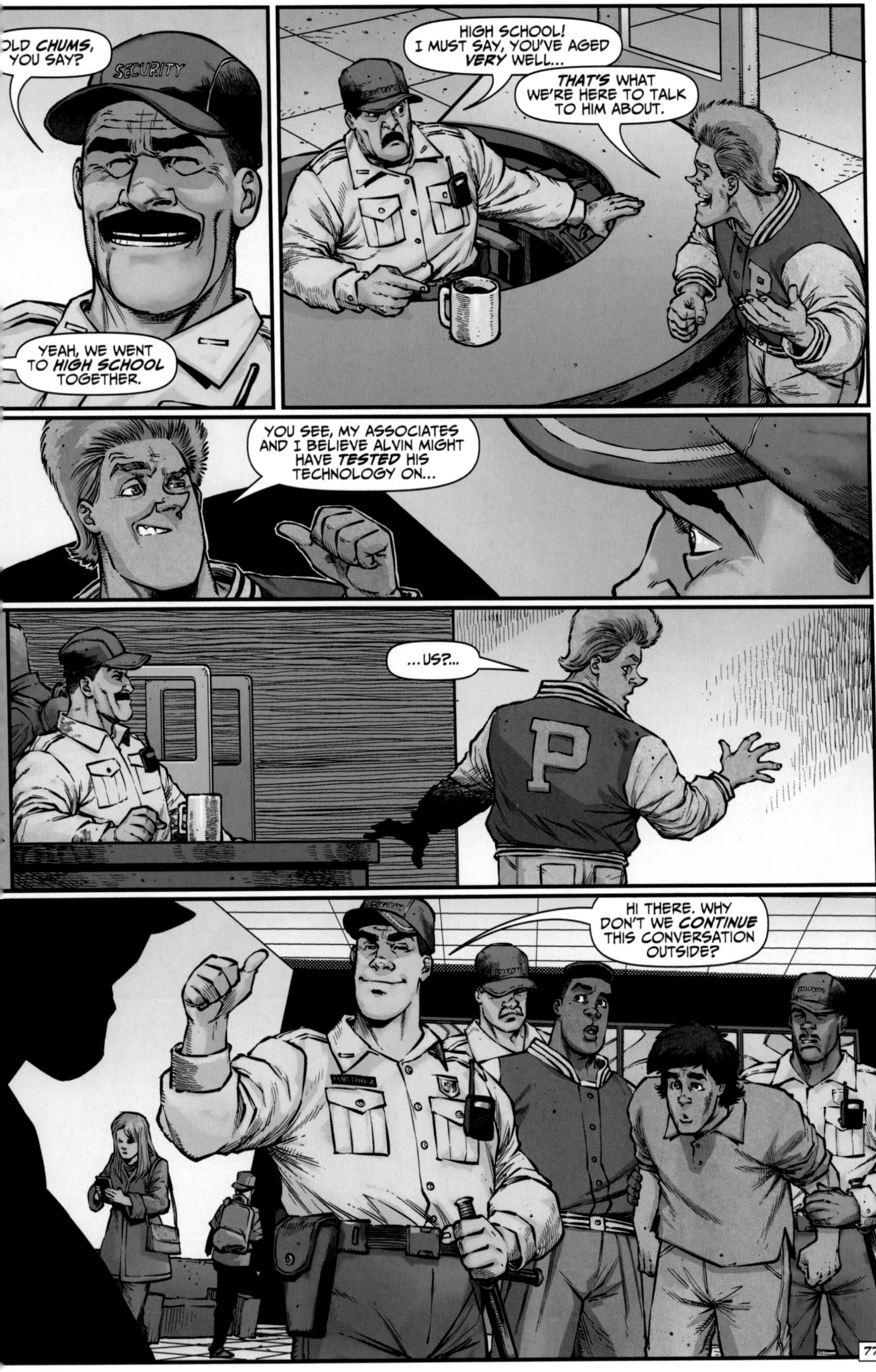

OLD CHUMS, YOU SAY?
YEAH, WE WENT TO HIGH SCHOOL TOGETHER.
HIGH SCHOOL! I MUST SAY, YOU'VE AGED VERY WELL...
THAT'S WHAT WE'RE HERE TO TALK TO HIM ABOUT.
YOU SEE, MY ASSOCIATES AND I BELIEVE ALVIN MIGHT HAVE TESTED HIS TECHNOLOGY ON...
...US?...
HI THERE. WHY DON'T WE CONTINUE THIS CONVERSATION OUTSIDE?

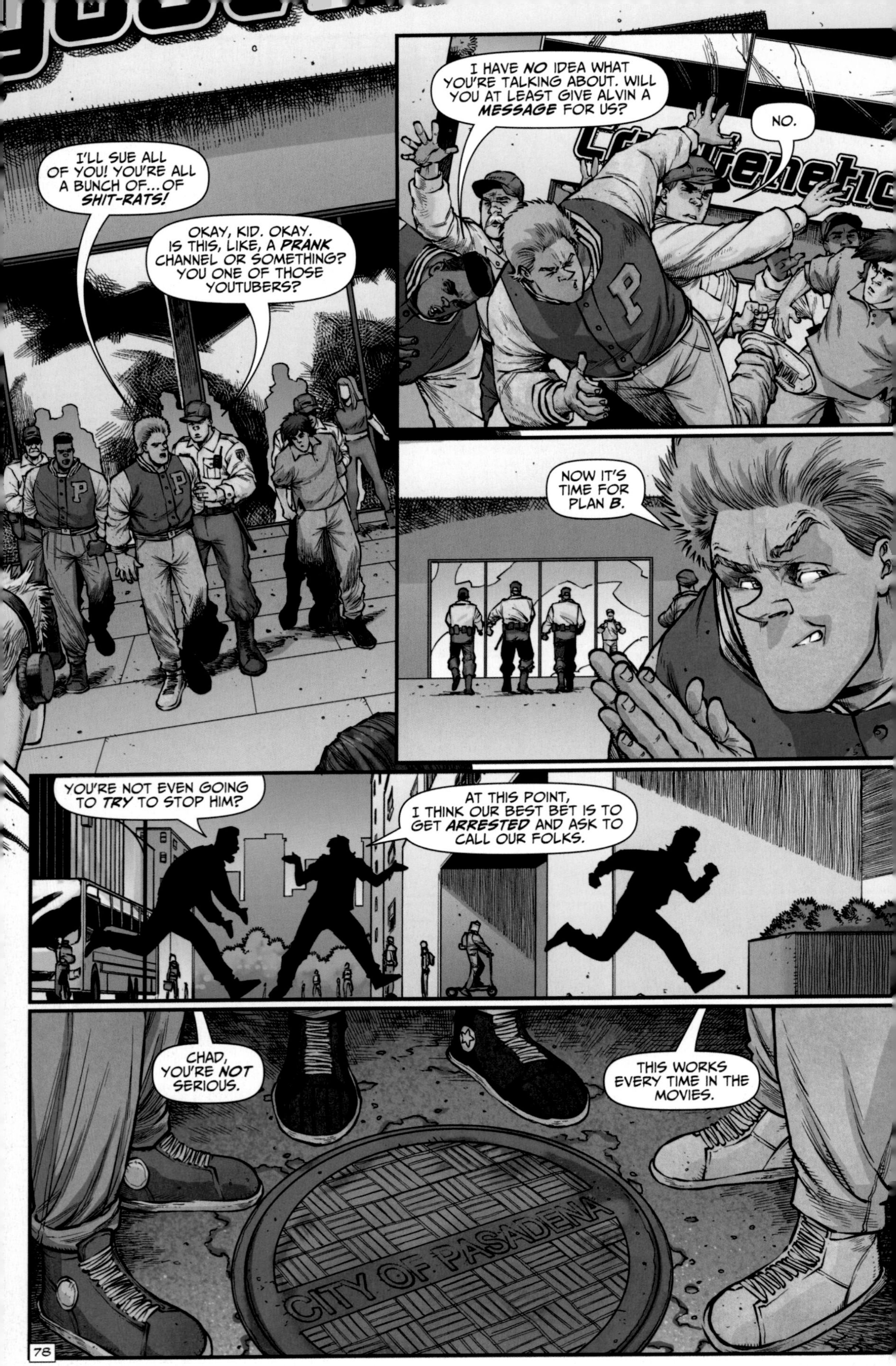
I'LL SUE ALL OF YOU! YOU'RE ALL A BUNCH OF...OF SHIT-RATS!
OKAY, KID. OKAY. IS THIS, LIKE, A PRANK CHANNEL OR SOMETHING? YOU ONE OF THOSE YOUTUBERS?
I HAVE NO IDEA WHAT YOU'RE TALKING ABOUT. WILL YOU AT LEAST GIVE ALVIN A MESSAGE FOR US?
NO.
NOW IT'S TIME FOR PLAN B.
YOU'RE NOT EVEN GOING TO TRY TO STOP HIM?
AT THIS POINT, I THINK OUR BEST BET IS TO GET ARRESTED AND ASK TO CALL OUR FOLKS.
CHAD, YOU'RE NOT SERIOUS.
THIS WORKS EVERY TIME IN THE MOVIES.
CITY OF PASADENA

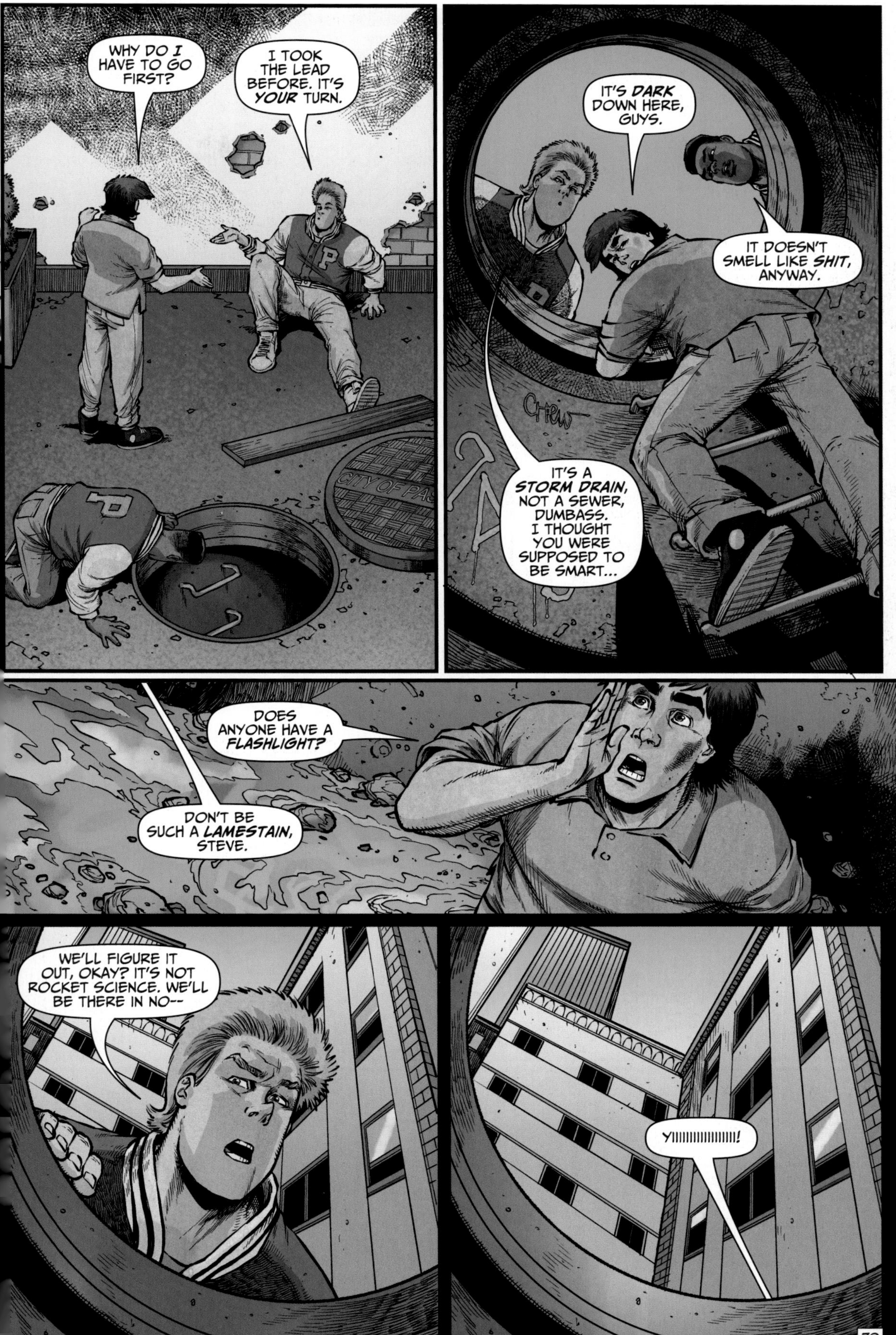

WHY DO *I* HAVE TO GO FIRST?
I TOOK THE LEAD BEFORE. IT'S *YOUR* TURN.
CITY OF PAS
IT'S *DARK* DOWN HERE, GUYS.
IT DOESN'T SMELL LIKE *SHIT*, ANYWAY.
IT'S A *STORM DRAIN*, NOT A SEWER, DUMBASS. I THOUGHT YOU WERE SUPPOSED TO BE SMART...
DOES ANYONE HAVE A *FLASHLIGHT?*
DON'T BE SUCH A *LAMESTAIN*, STEVE.
WE'LL FIGURE IT OUT, OKAY? IT'S NOT ROCKET SCIENCE. WE'LL BE THERE IN NO--
YIIIIIIIIIIIIIIII!

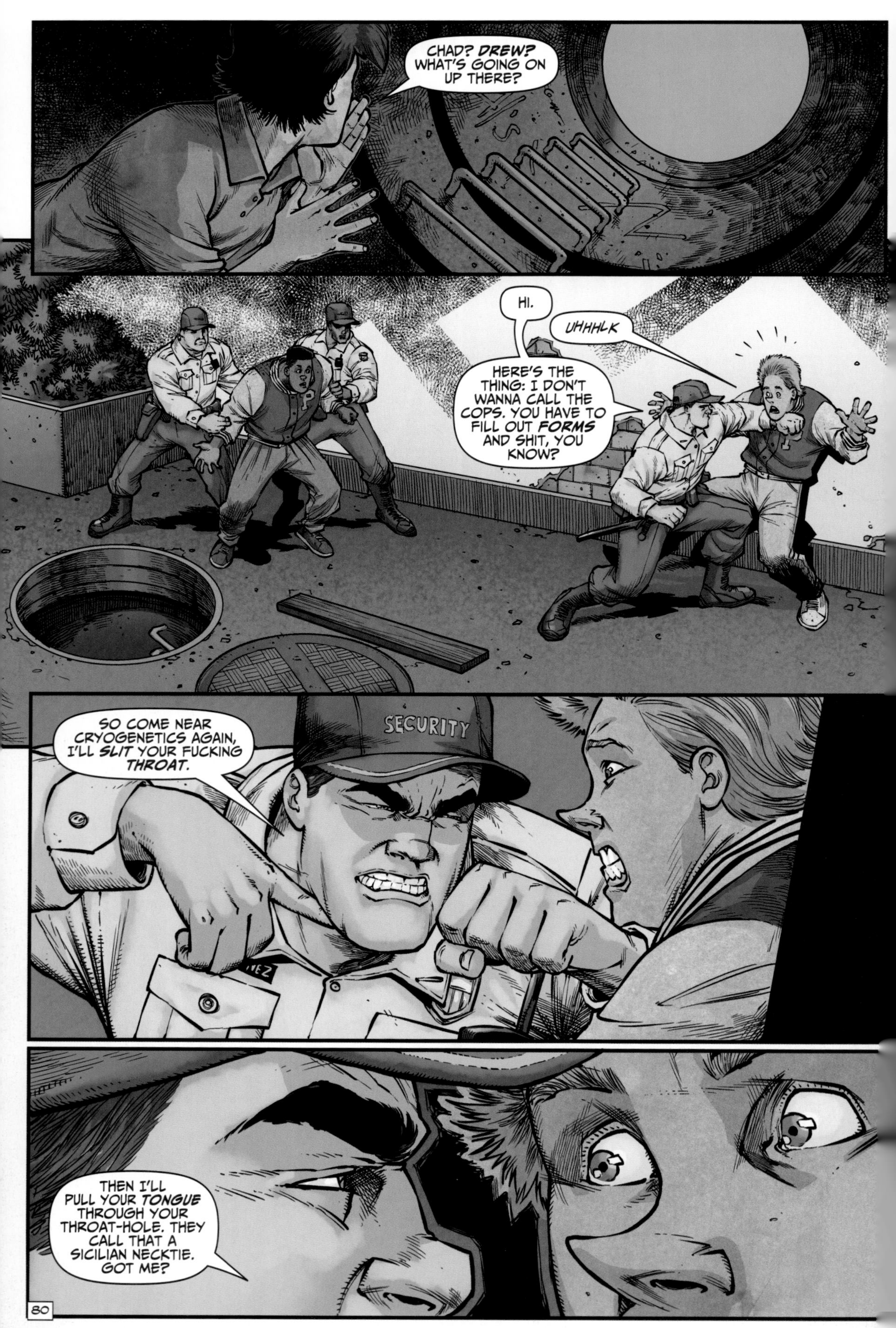
CHAD? DREW? WHAT'S GOING ON UP THERE?
HI.
UHHHLK
HERE'S THE THING: I DON'T WANNA CALL THE COPS. YOU HAVE TO FILL OUT FORMS AND SHIT, YOU KNOW?
SECURITY
SO COME NEAR CRYOGENETICS AGAIN, I'LL SLIT YOUR FUCKING THROAT.
THEN I'LL PULL YOUR TONGUE THROUGH YOUR THROAT-HOLE. THEY CALL THAT A SICILIAN NECKTIE. GOT ME?

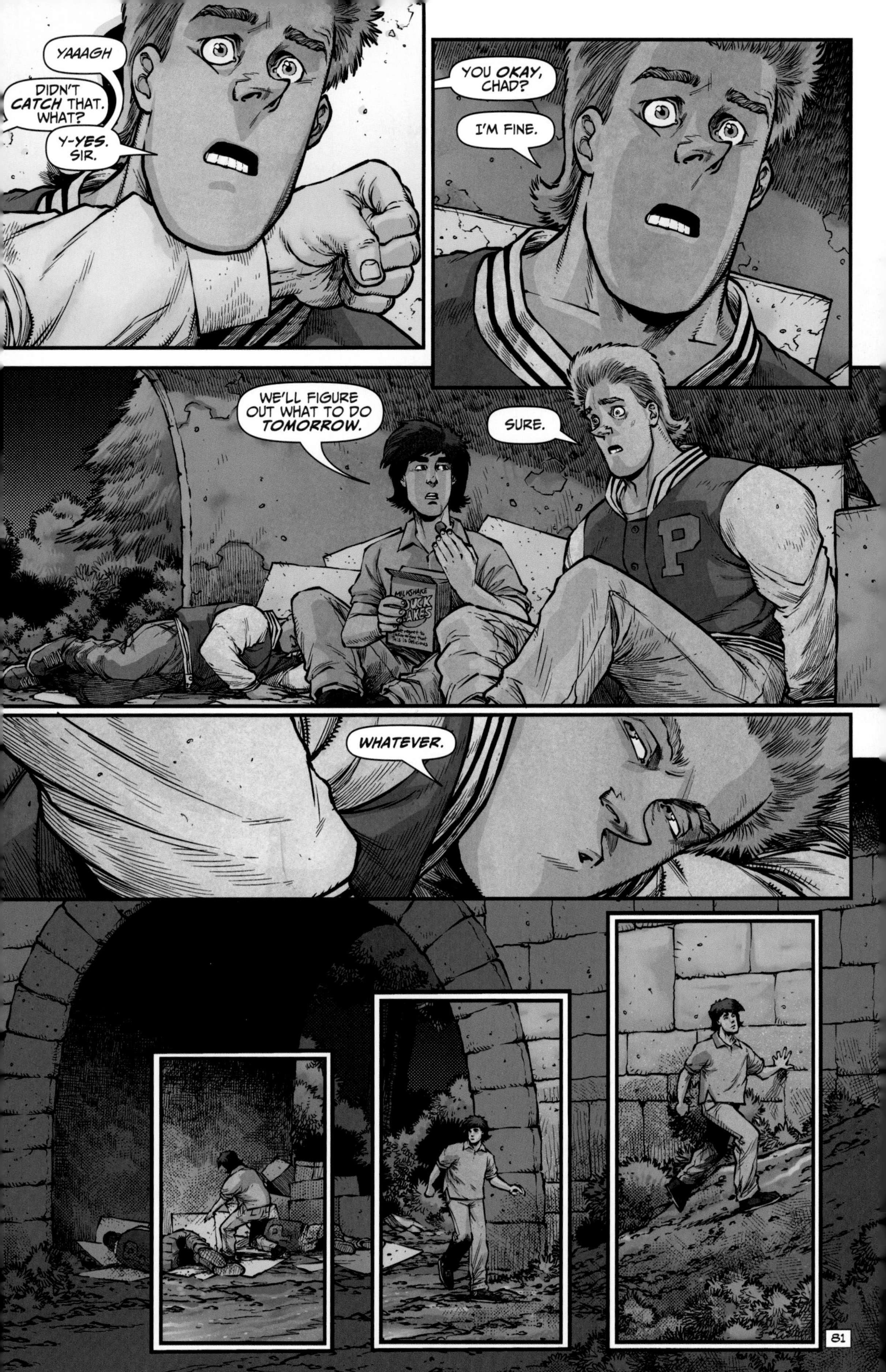
YAAAGH
DIDN'T CATCH THAT. WHAT?
Y-YES. SIR.
YOU OKAY, CHAD?
I'M FINE.
WE'LL FIGURE OUT WHAT TO DO TOMORROW.
SURE.
MILKSHAKE DUCK CAKES
WHATEVER.

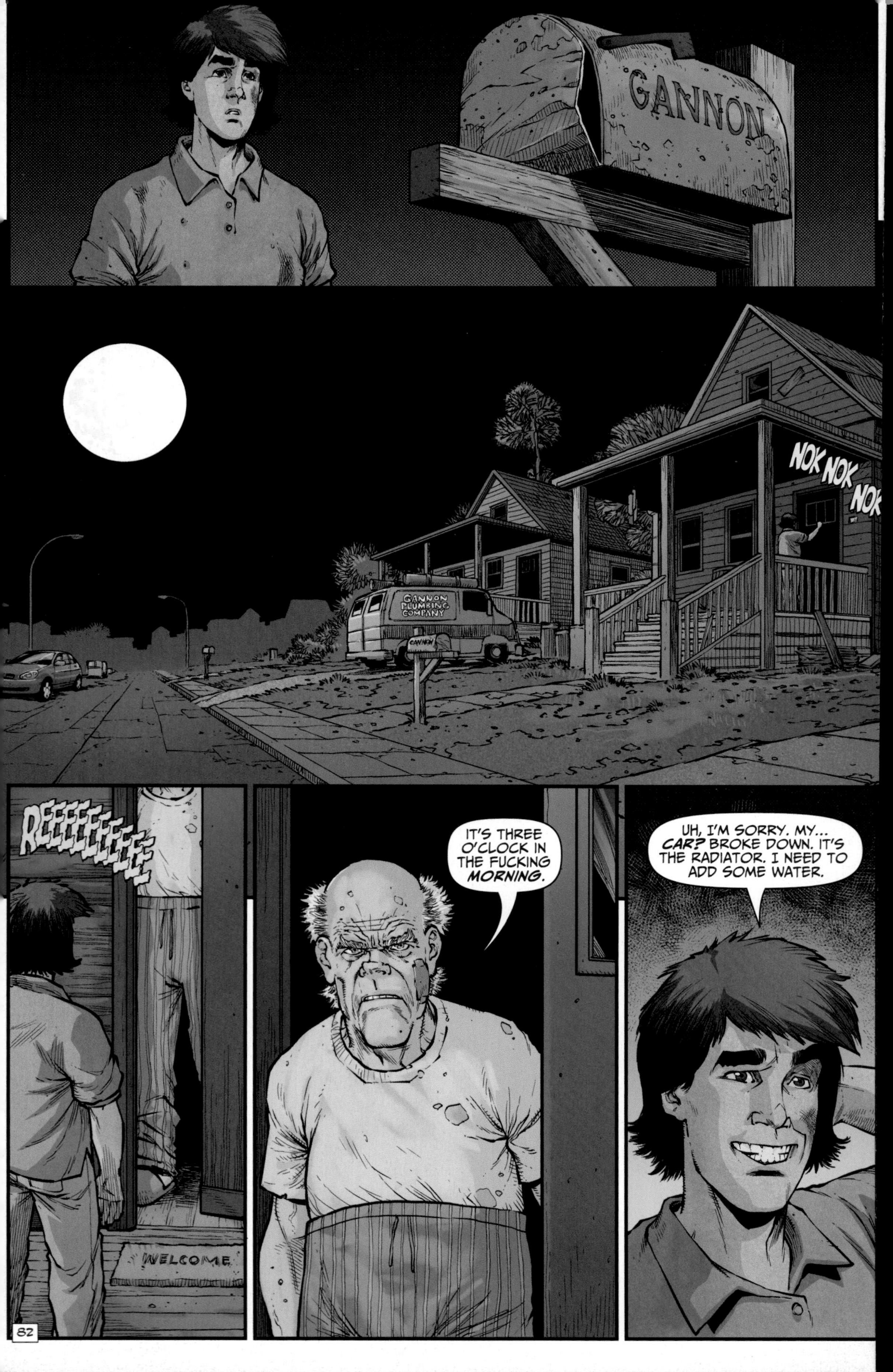
GANNON
GANNON PLUMBING COMPANY
GANNON
NOK NOK NOK
REEEEEEEEEE
WELCOME
IT'S THREE O'CLOCK IN THE FUCKING *MORNING*.
UH, I'M SORRY. MY... *CAR?* BROKE DOWN. IT'S THE RADIATOR. I NEED TO ADD SOME WATER.

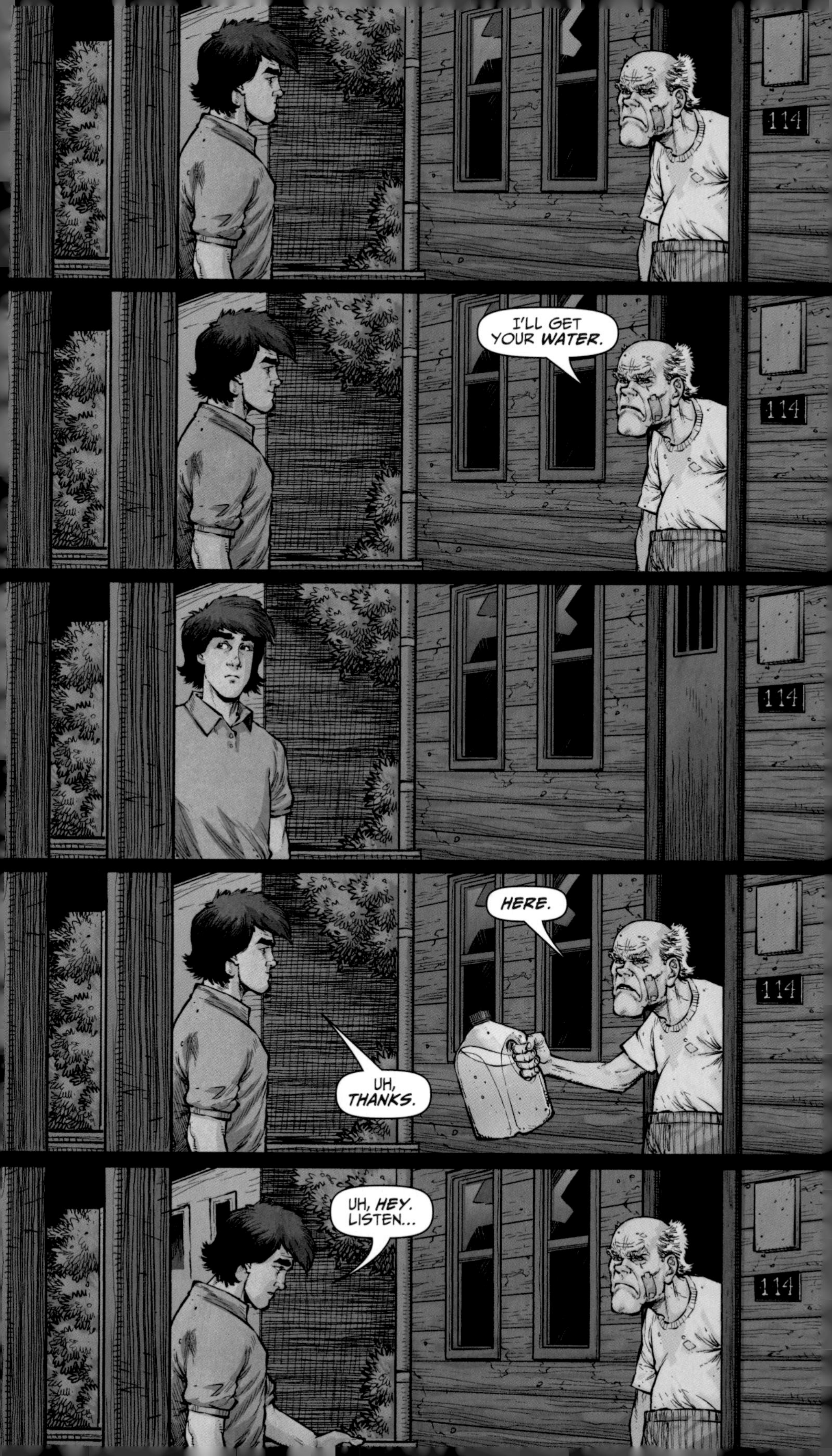
114
I'LL GET YOUR WATER.
114
114
HERE.
UH, THANKS.
114
UH, HEY. LISTEN...
114

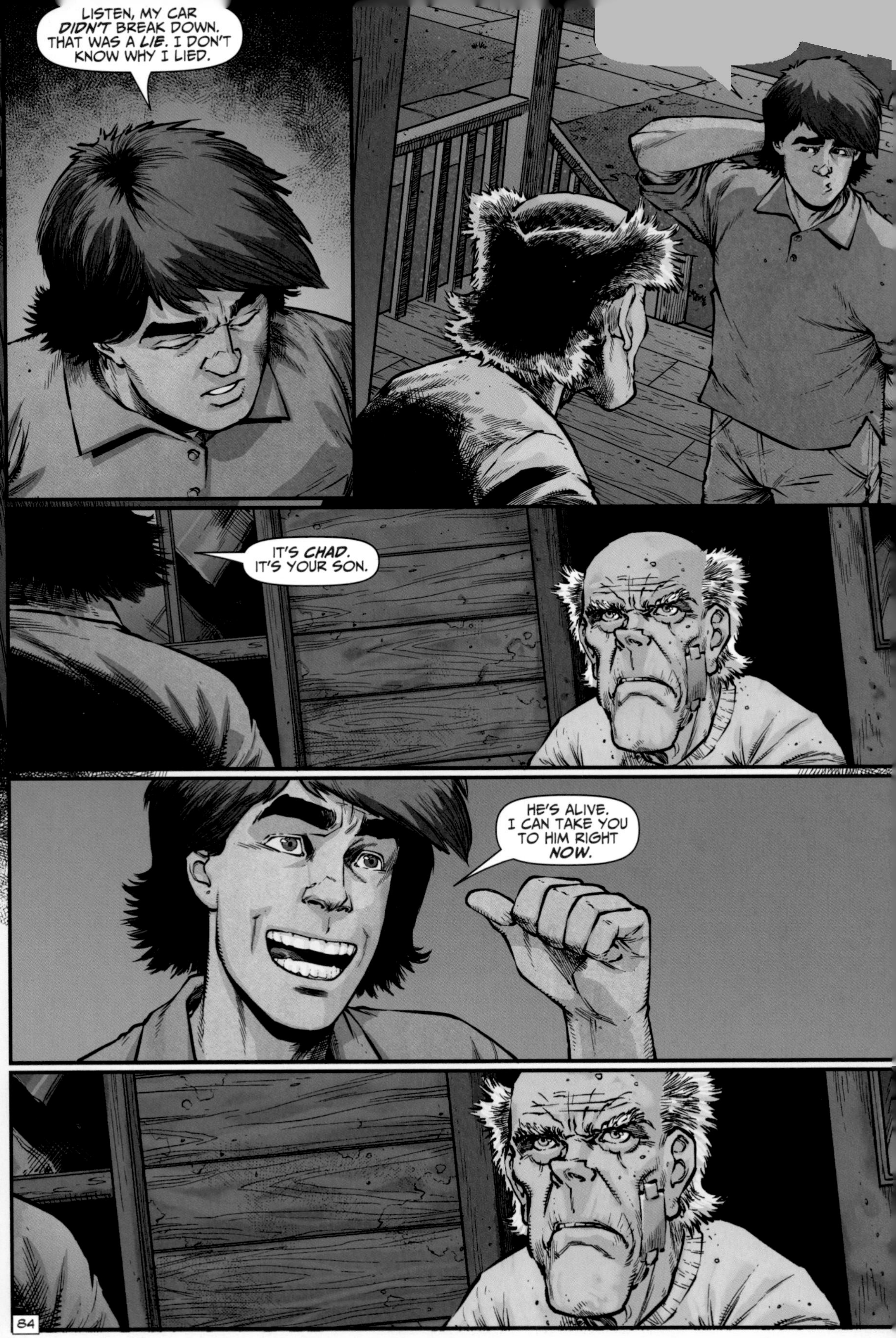

LISTEN, MY CAR *DIDN'T* BREAK DOWN. THAT WAS A *LIE*. I DON'T KNOW WHY I LIED.
IT'S *CHAD*. IT'S YOUR SON.
HE'S ALIVE. I CAN TAKE YOU TO HIM RIGHT *NOW*.

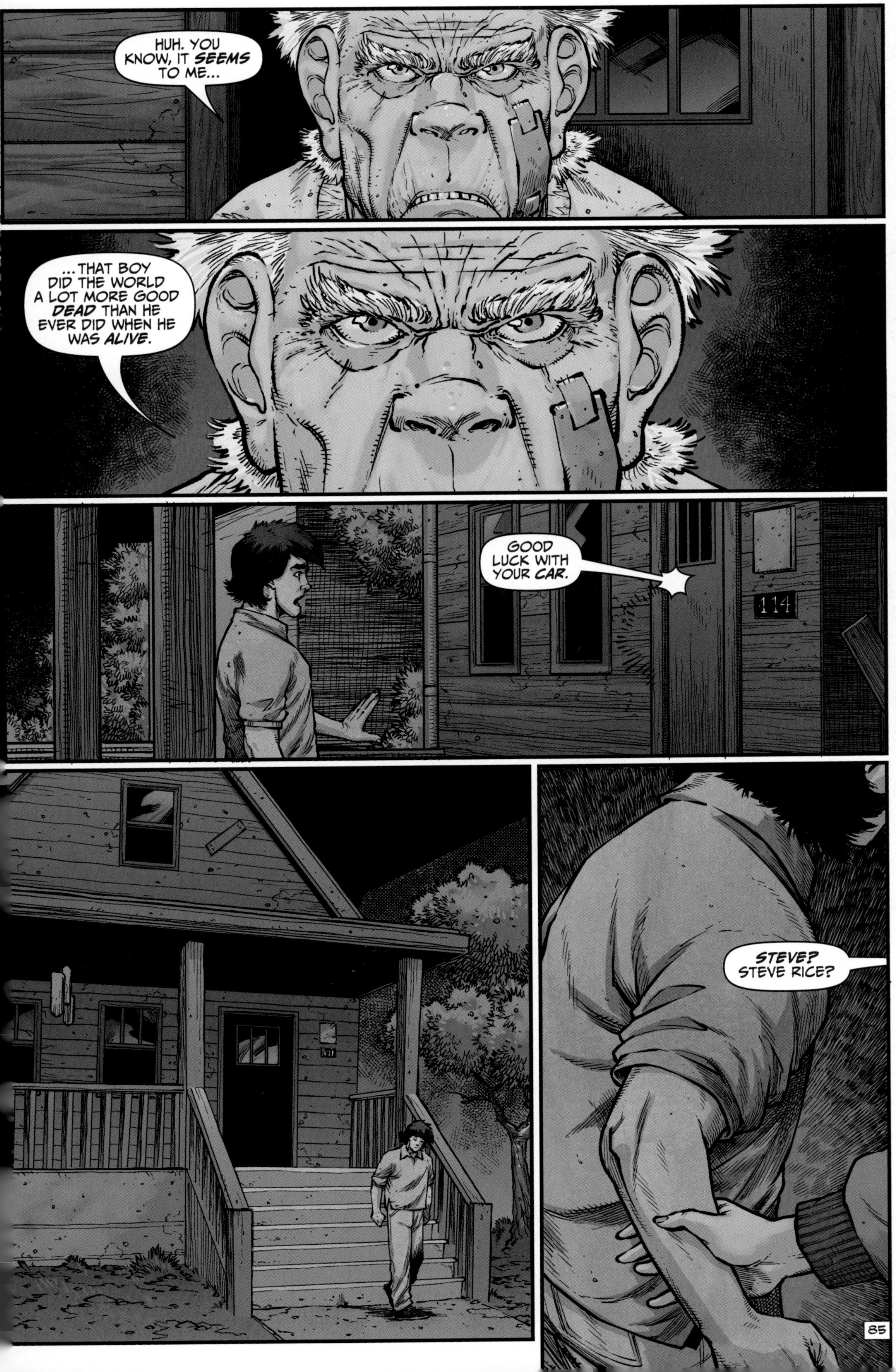
HUH. YOU KNOW, IT SEEMS TO ME...
...THAT BOY DID THE WORLD A LOT MORE GOOD DEAD THAN HE EVER DID WHEN HE WAS ALIVE.
GOOD LUCK WITH YOUR CAR.
114
STEVE? STEVE RICE?

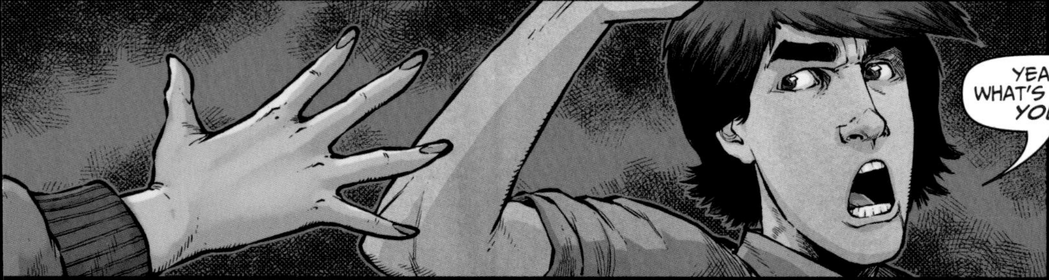
YEAH? WHAT'S IT TO *YOU?*

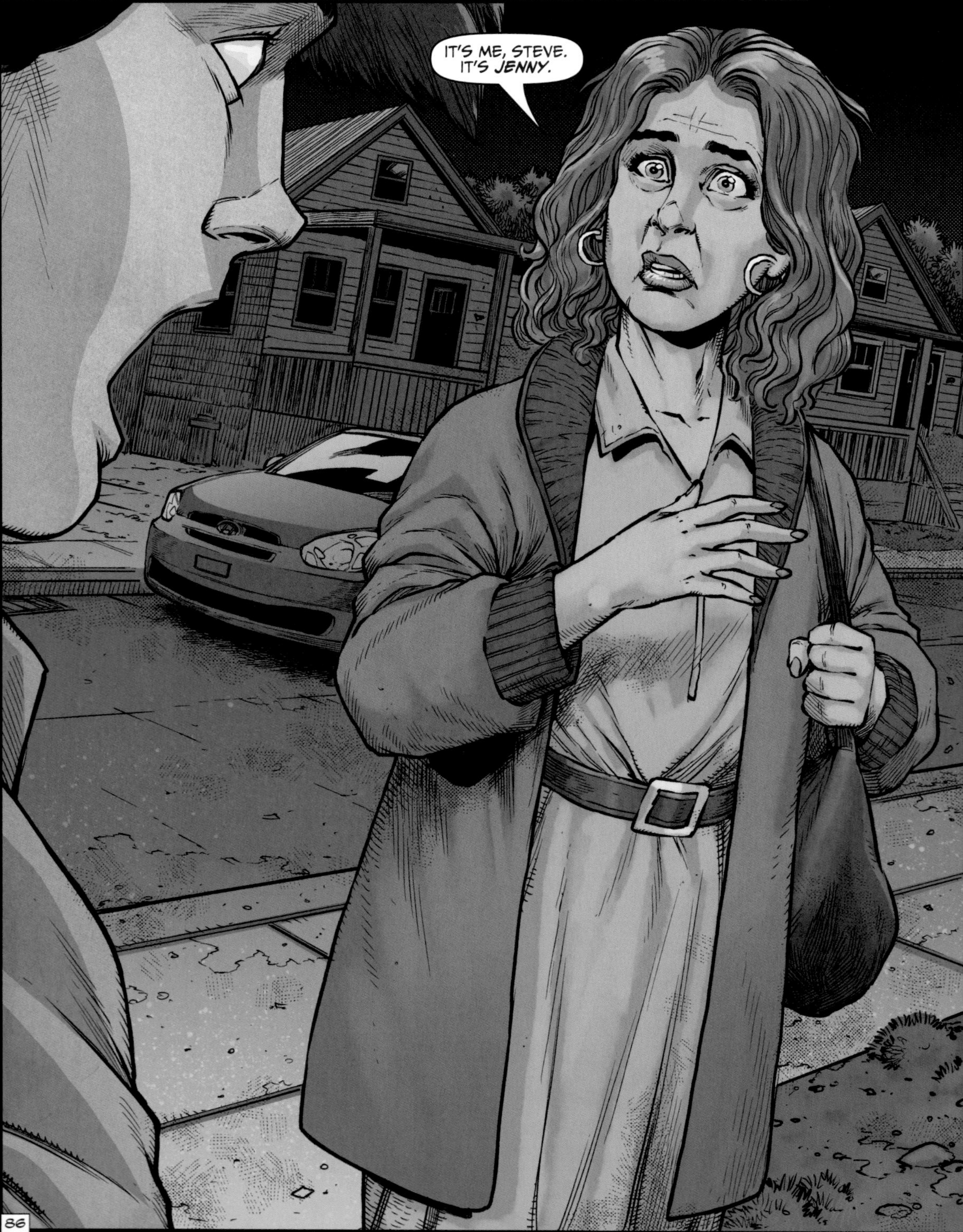
IT'S ME, STEVE. IT'S *JENNY*.

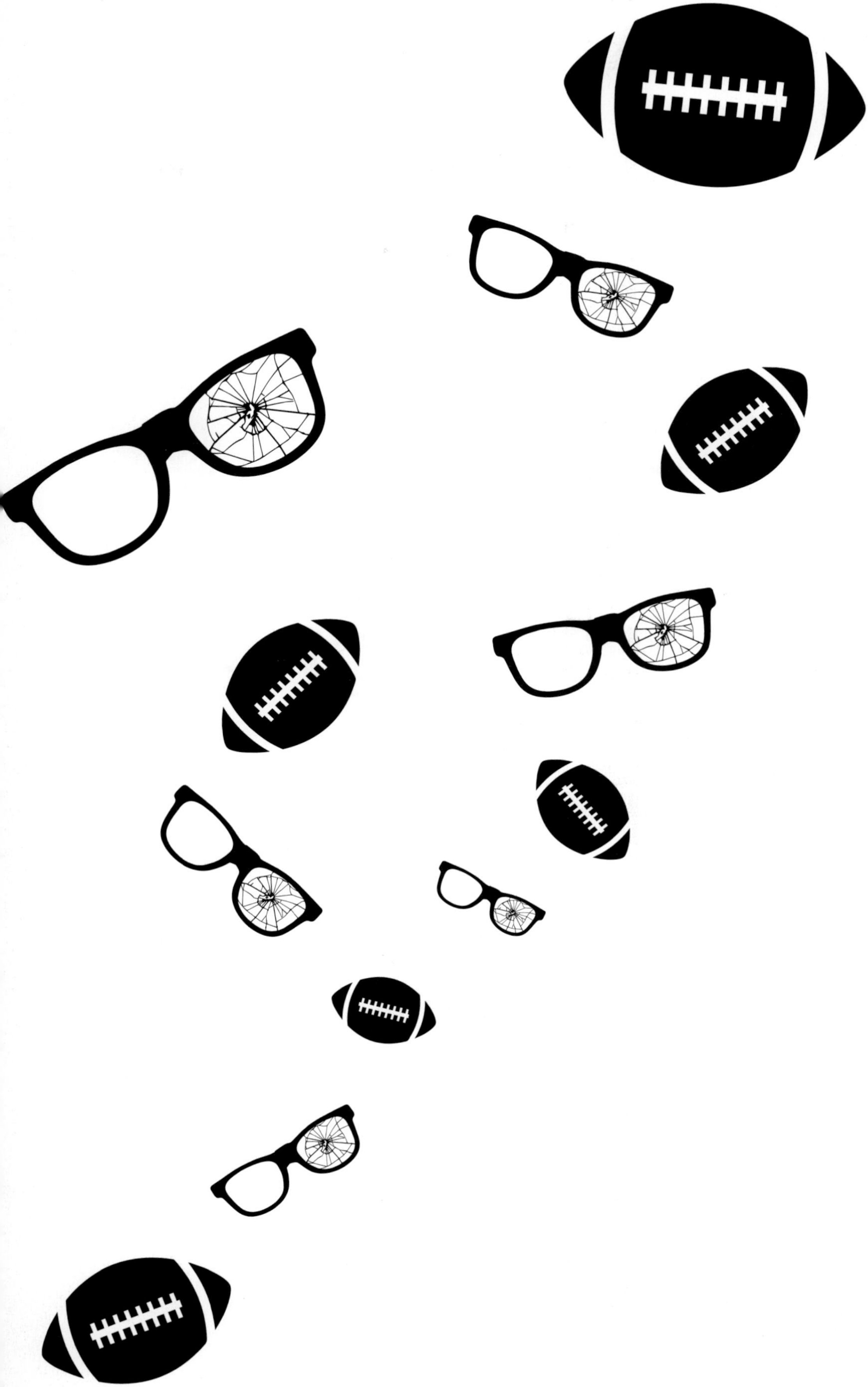

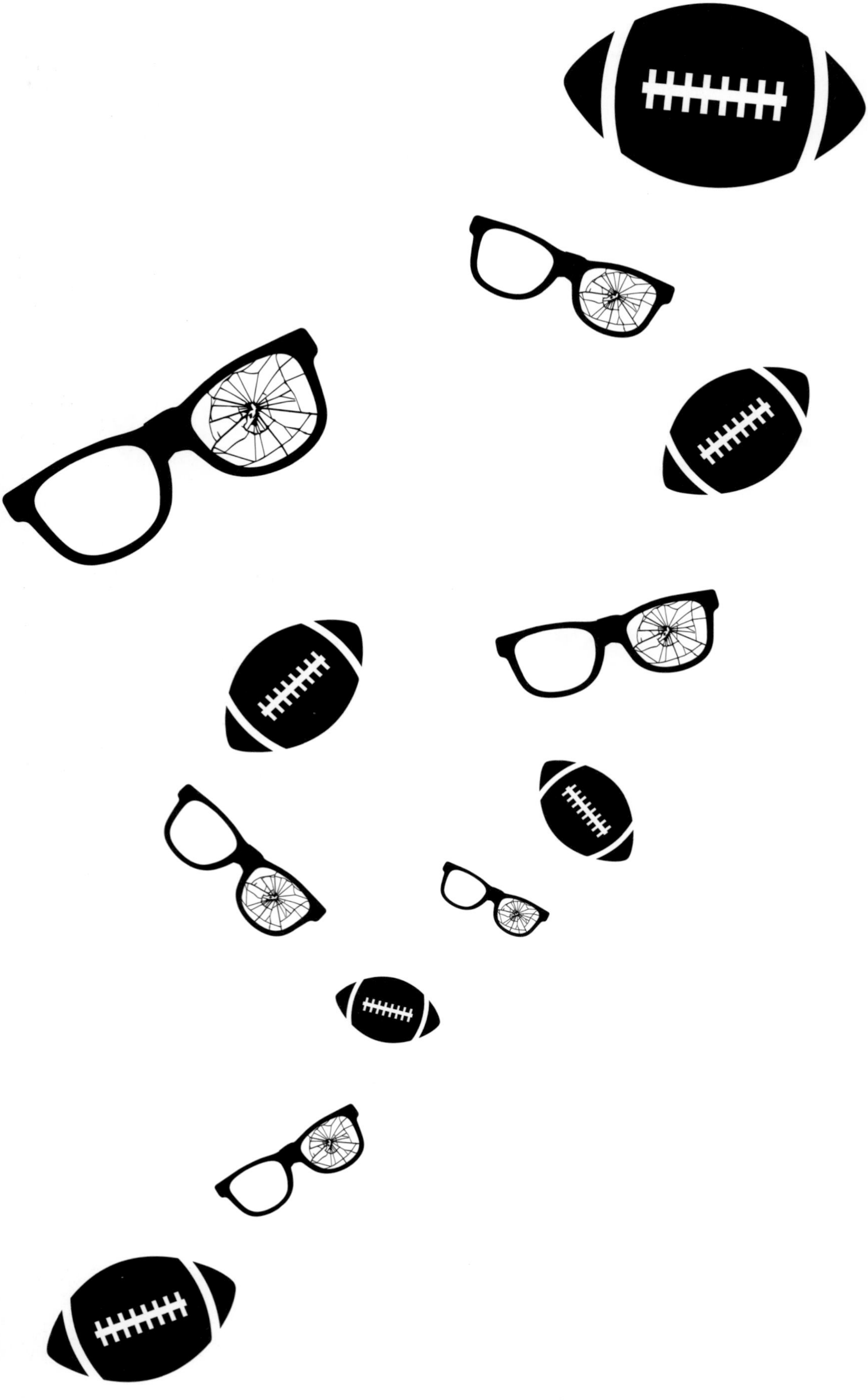

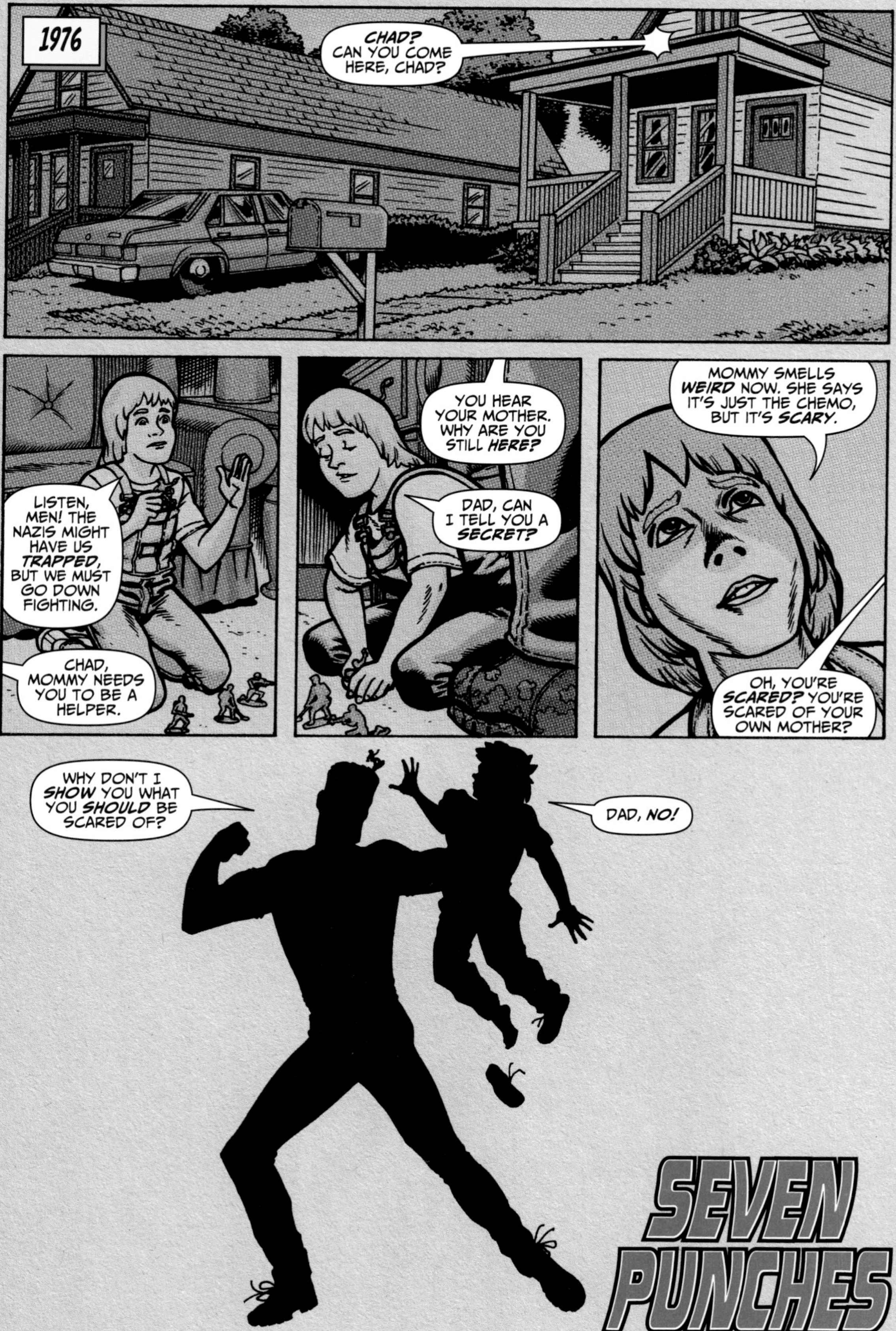
1976
CHAD? CAN YOU COME HERE, CHAD?
LISTEN, MEN! THE NAZIS MIGHT HAVE US TRAPPED, BUT WE MUST GO DOWN FIGHTING.
CHAD, MOMMY NEEDS YOU TO BE A HELPER.
YOU HEAR YOUR MOTHER. WHY ARE YOU STILL HERE?
DAD, CAN I TELL YOU A SECRET?
MOMMY SMELLS WEIRD NOW. SHE SAYS IT'S JUST THE CHEMO, BUT IT'S SCARY.
OH, YOU'RE SCARED? YOU'RE SCARED OF YOUR OWN MOTHER?
WHY DON'T I SHOW YOU WHAT YOU SHOULD BE SCARED OF?
DAD, NO!
SEVEN PUNCHES

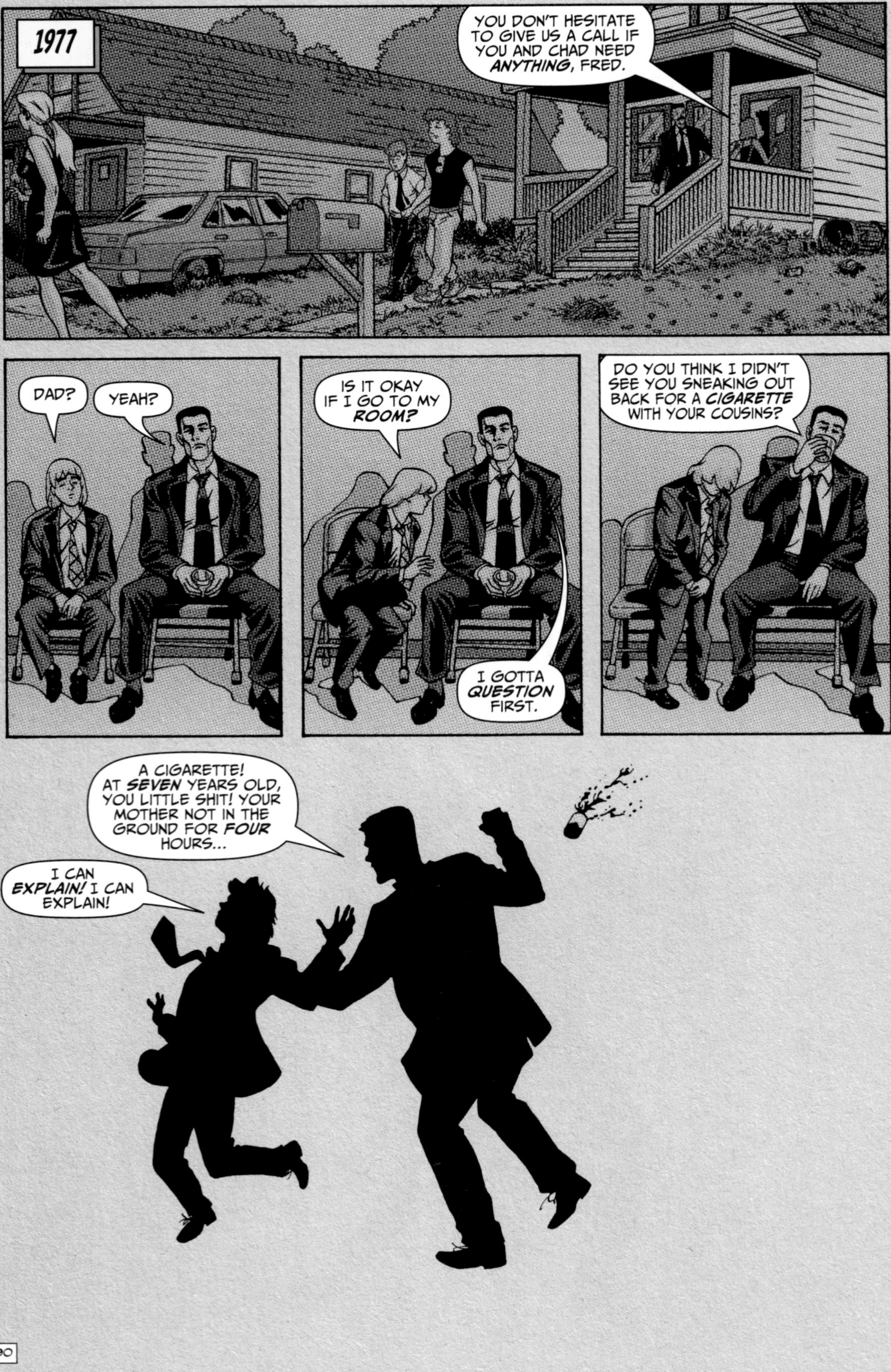
1977
YOU DON'T HESITATE TO GIVE US A CALL IF YOU AND CHAD NEED *ANYTHING*, FRED.
DAD?
YEAH?
IS IT OKAY IF I GO TO MY *ROOM?*
I GOTTA *QUESTION* FIRST.
DO YOU THINK I DIDN'T SEE YOU SNEAKING OUT BACK FOR A *CIGARETTE* WITH YOUR COUSINS?
A CIGARETTE! AT *SEVEN* YEARS OLD, YOU LITTLE SHIT! YOUR MOTHER NOT IN THE GROUND FOR *FOUR* HOURS...
I CAN *EXPLAIN!* I CAN EXPLAIN!

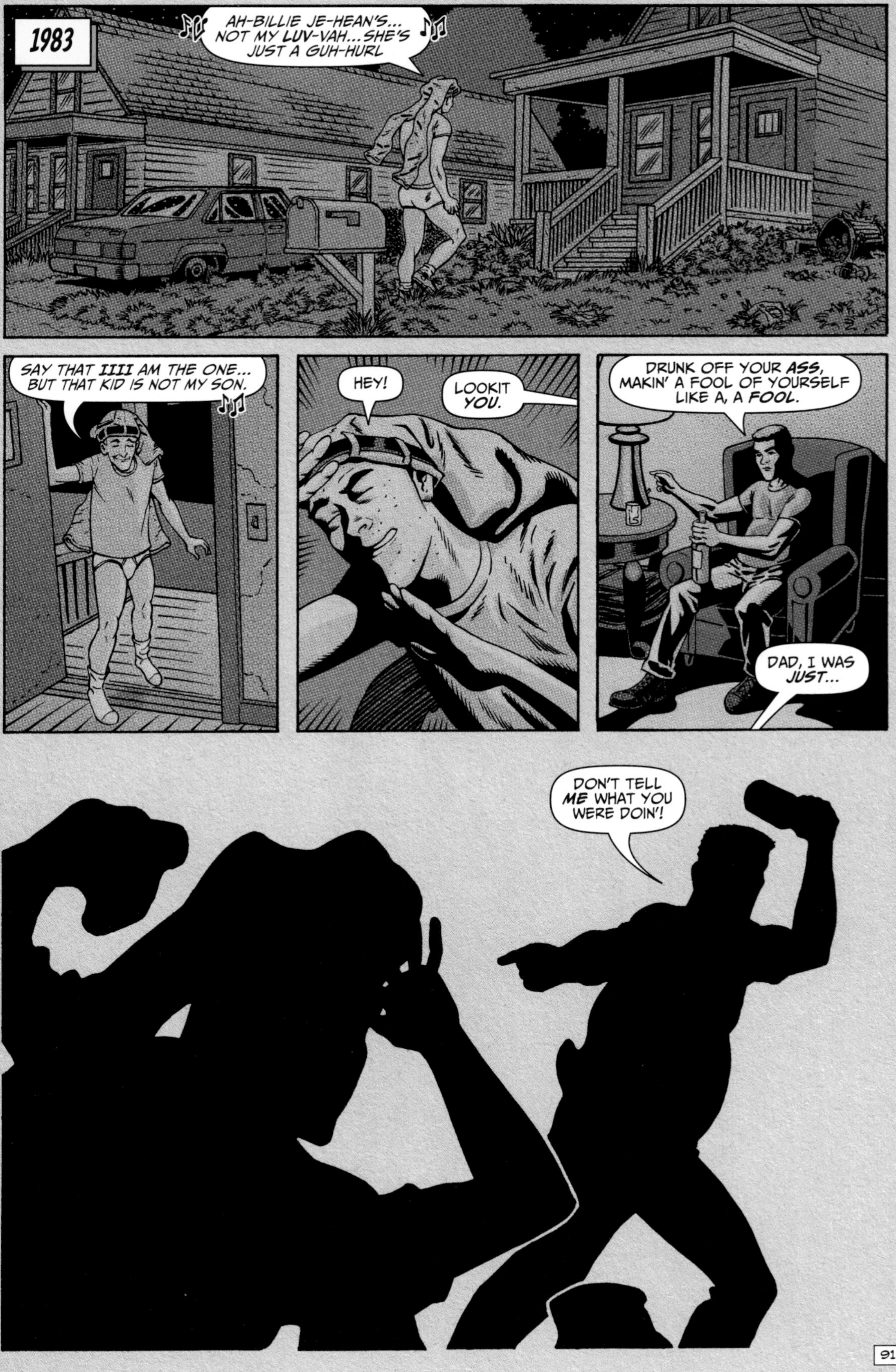
1983
AH-BILLIE JE-HEAN'S... NOT MY LUV-VAH... SHE'S JUST A GUH-HURL
SAY THAT IIII AM THE ONE... BUT THAT KID IS NOT MY SON.
HEY!
LOOKIT YOU.
DRUNK OFF YOUR ASS, MAKIN' A FOOL OF YOURSELF LIKE A, A FOOL.
DAD, I WAS JUST...
DON'T TELL ME WHAT YOU WERE DOIN'!

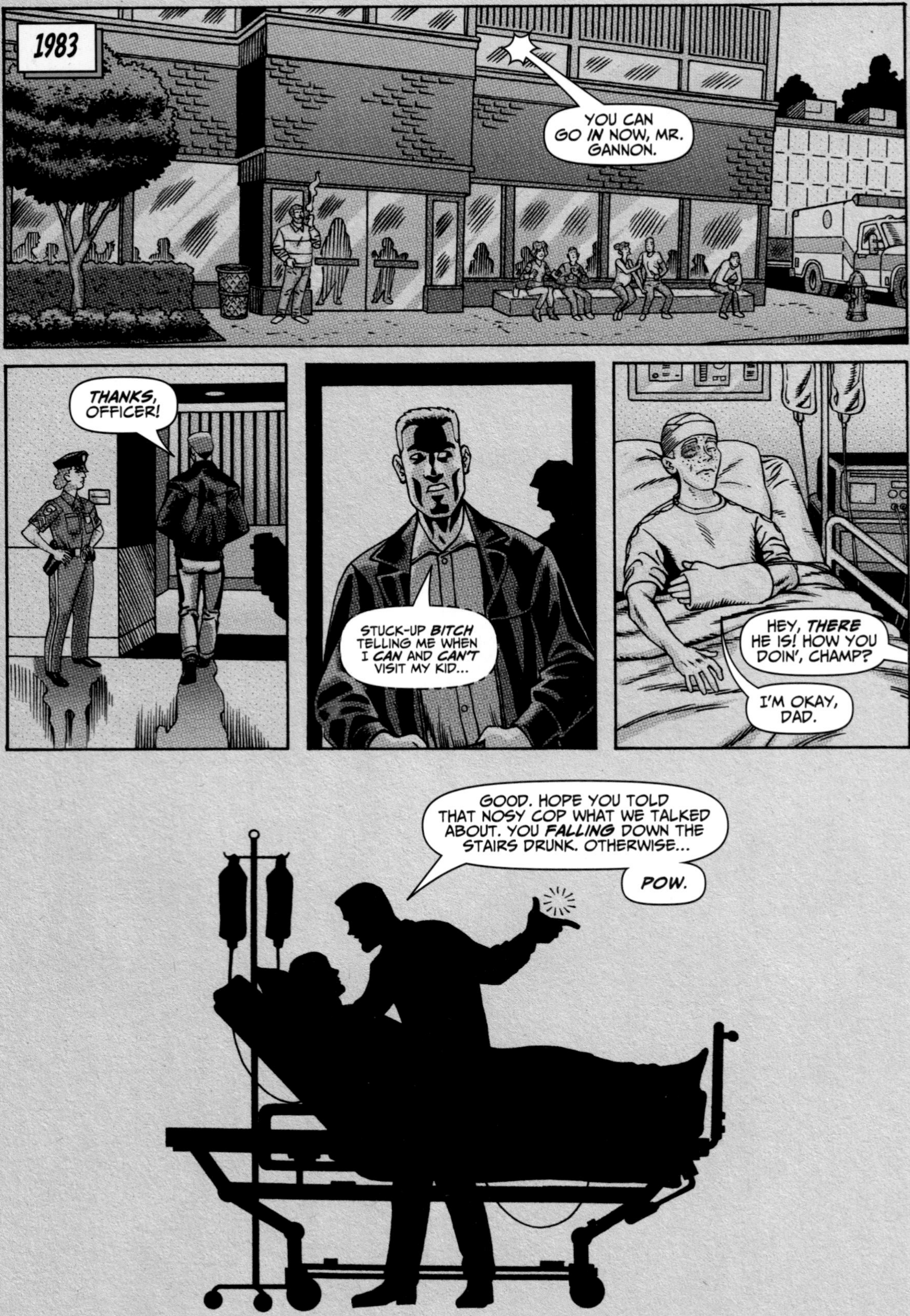
1983
YOU CAN GO IN NOW, MR. GANNON.
THANKS, OFFICER!
STUCK-UP BITCH TELLING ME WHEN I CAN AND CAN'T VISIT MY KID...
HEY, THERE HE IS! HOW YOU DOIN', CHAMP?
I'M OKAY, DAD.
GOOD. HOPE YOU TOLD THAT NOSY COP WHAT WE TALKED ABOUT. YOU FALLING DOWN THE STAIRS DRUNK. OTHERWISE...
POW.

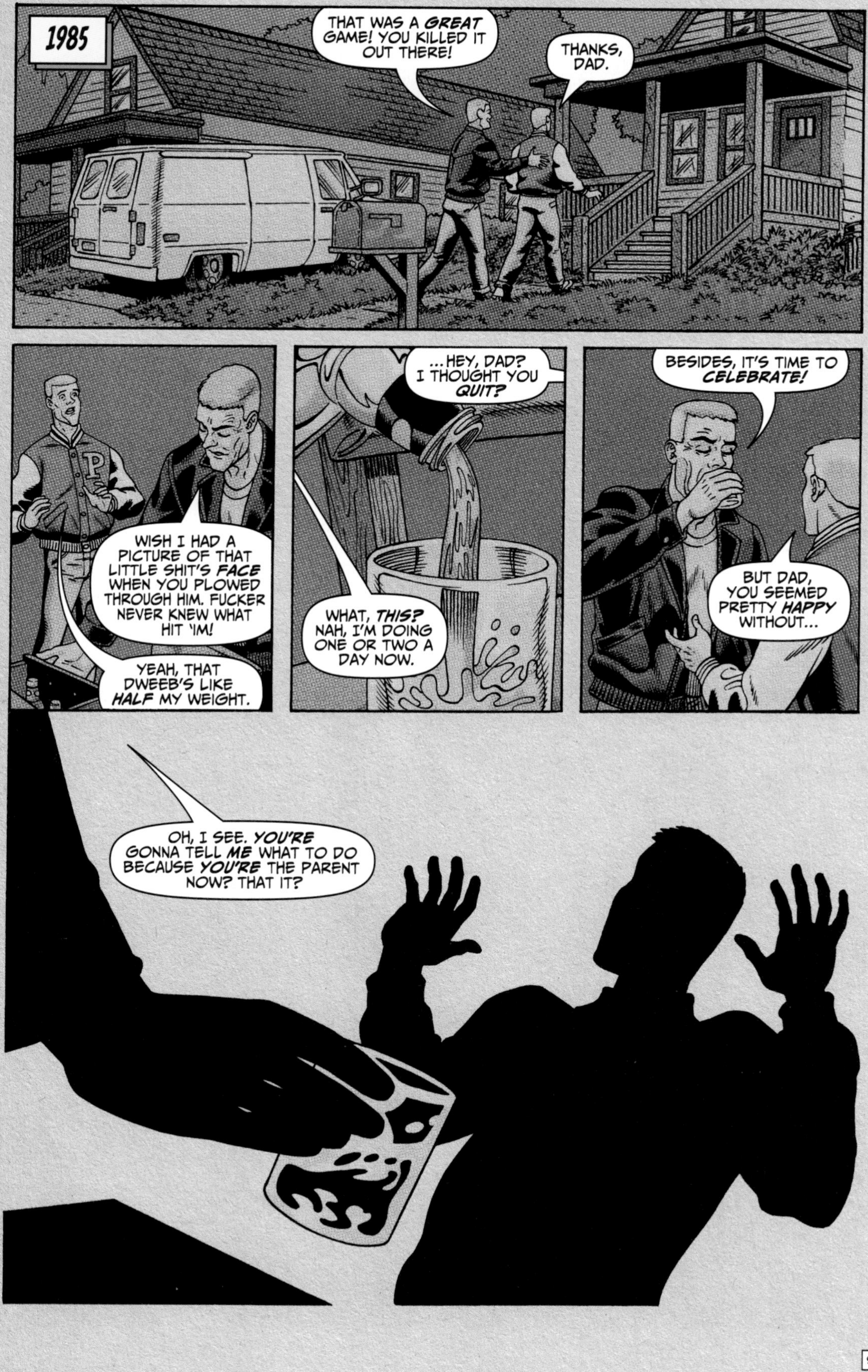
1985
THAT WAS A GREAT GAME! YOU KILLED IT OUT THERE!
THANKS, DAD.
WISH I HAD A PICTURE OF THAT LITTLE SHIT'S FACE WHEN YOU PLOWED THROUGH HIM. FUCKER NEVER KNEW WHAT HIT 'IM!
YEAH, THAT DWEEB'S LIKE HALF MY WEIGHT.
...HEY, DAD? I THOUGHT YOU QUIT?
WHAT, THIS? NAH, I'M DOING ONE OR TWO A DAY NOW.
BESIDES, IT'S TIME TO CELEBRATE!
BUT DAD, YOU SEEMED PRETTY HAPPY WITHOUT...
OH, I SEE. YOU'RE GONNA TELL ME WHAT TO DO BECAUSE YOU'RE THE PARENT NOW? THAT IT?

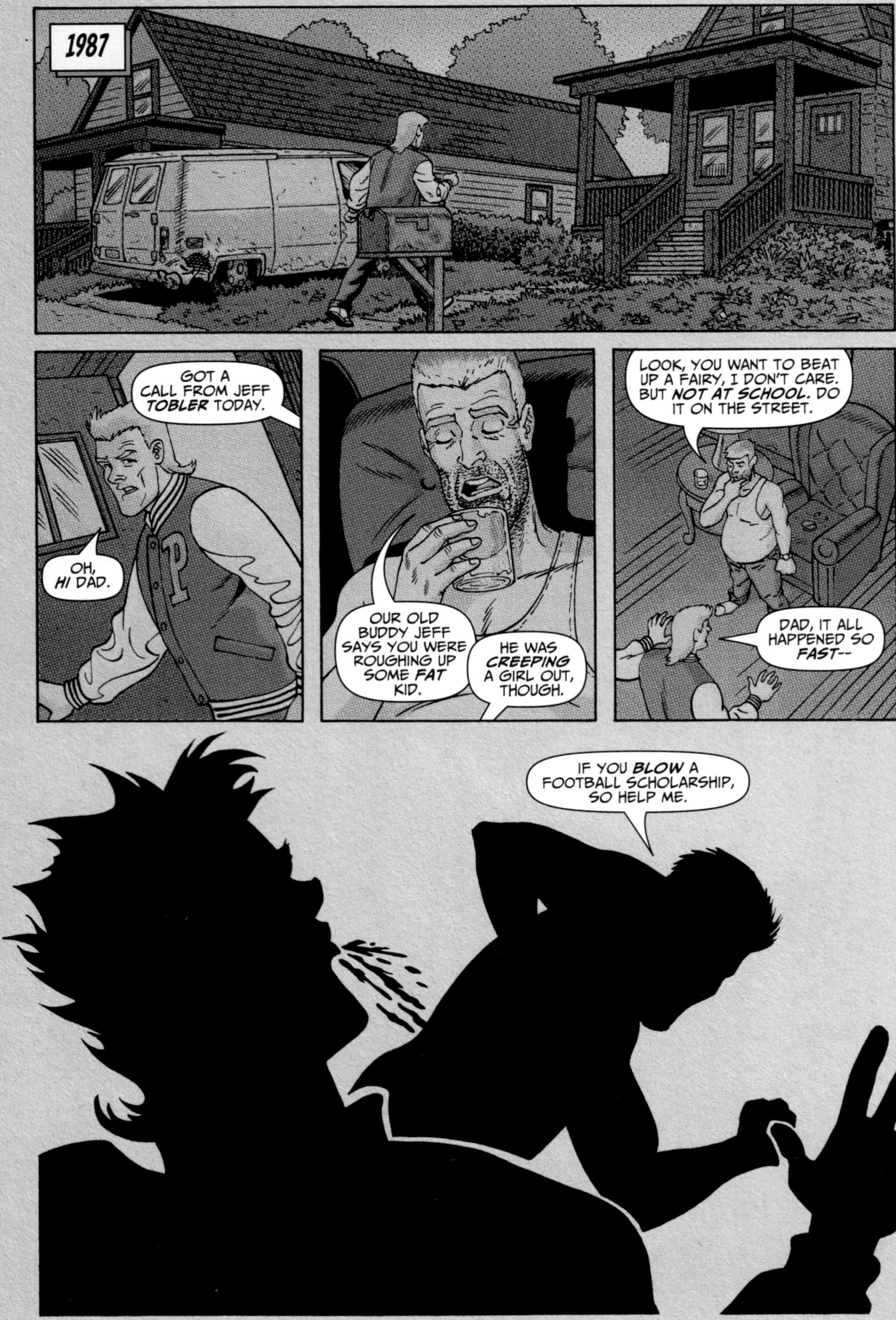
1987
GOT A CALL FROM JEFF TOBLER TODAY.
OH, HI DAD.
OUR OLD BUDDY JEFF SAYS YOU WERE ROUGHING UP SOME FAT KID.
HE WAS CREEPING A GIRL OUT, THOUGH.
LOOK, YOU WANT TO BEAT UP A FAIRY, I DON'T CARE. BUT NOT AT SCHOOL. DO IT ON THE STREET.
DAD, IT ALL HAPPENED SO FAST--
IF YOU BLOW A FOOTBALL SCHOLARSHIP, SO HELP ME.

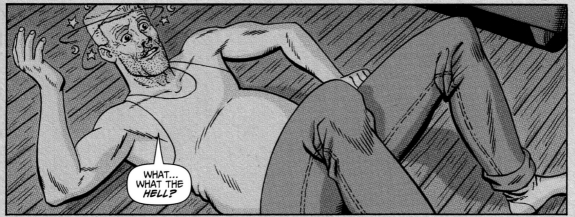
WHAT... WHAT THE *HELL?*

MAYBE THINGS ARE GOING TO BE *DIFFERENT* AROUND HERE NOW.

NOW YOU *WAIT* A MINUTE--

THE END

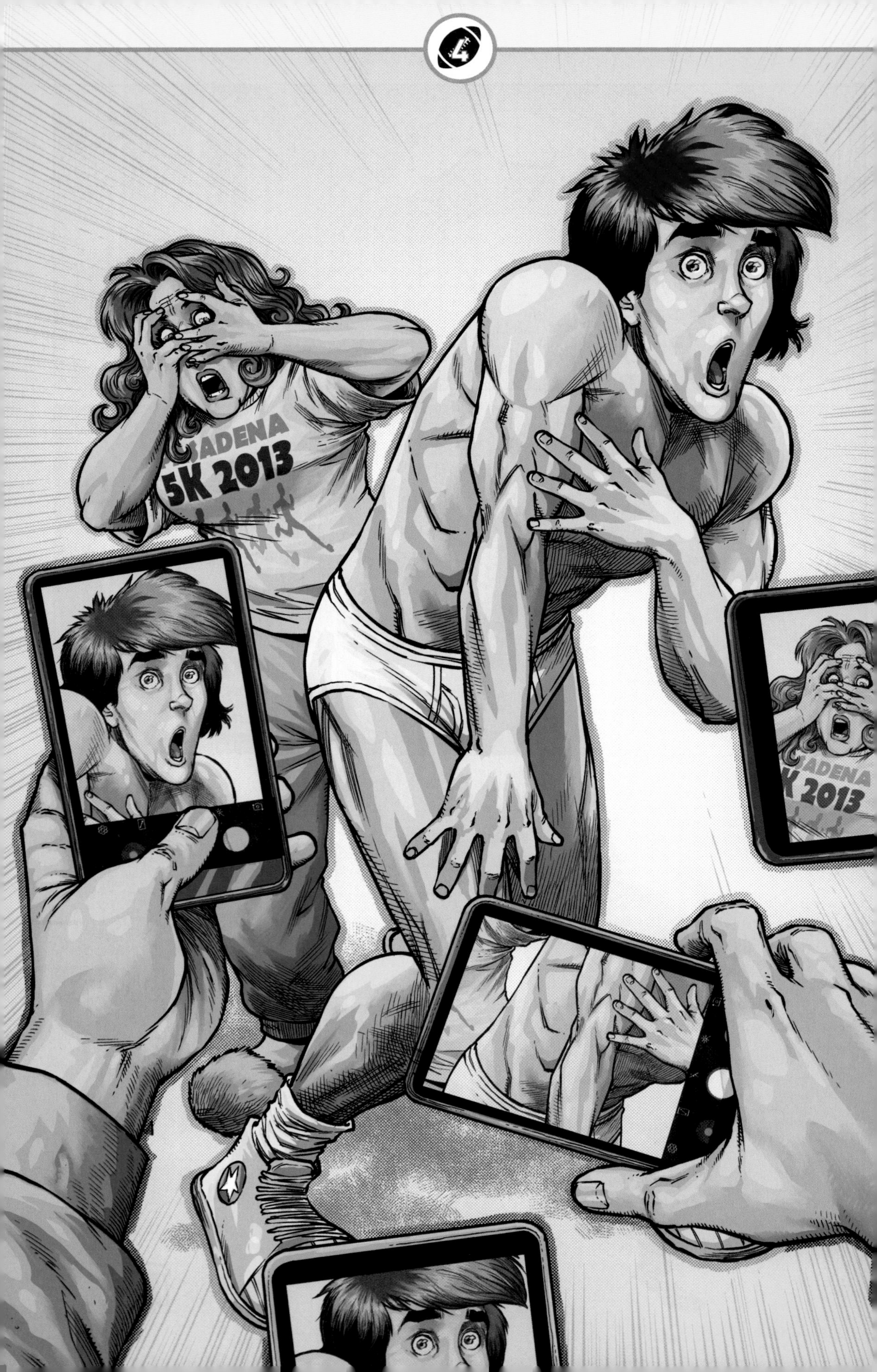
4
SADENA
5K 2013

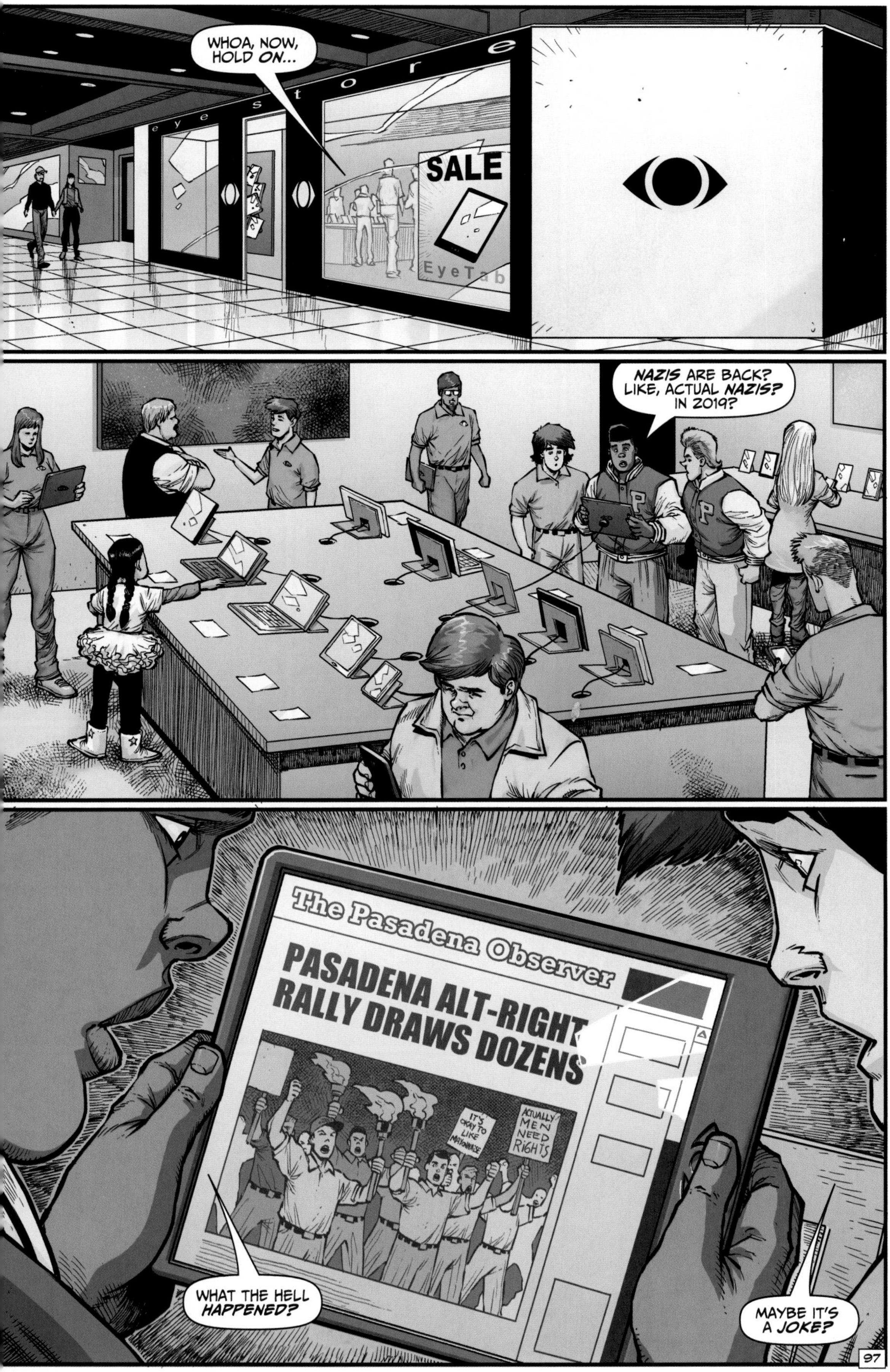
eye store
SALE
EyeTab
WHOA, NOW, HOLD ON...
NAZIS ARE BACK? LIKE, ACTUAL NAZIS? IN 2019?
The Pasadena Observer
PASADENA ALT-RIGHT RALLY DRAWS DOZENS
IT'S OKAY TO LIKE MAYONNAISE
ACTUALLY MEN NEED RIGHTS
WHAT THE HELL HAPPENED?
MAYBE IT'S A JOKE?

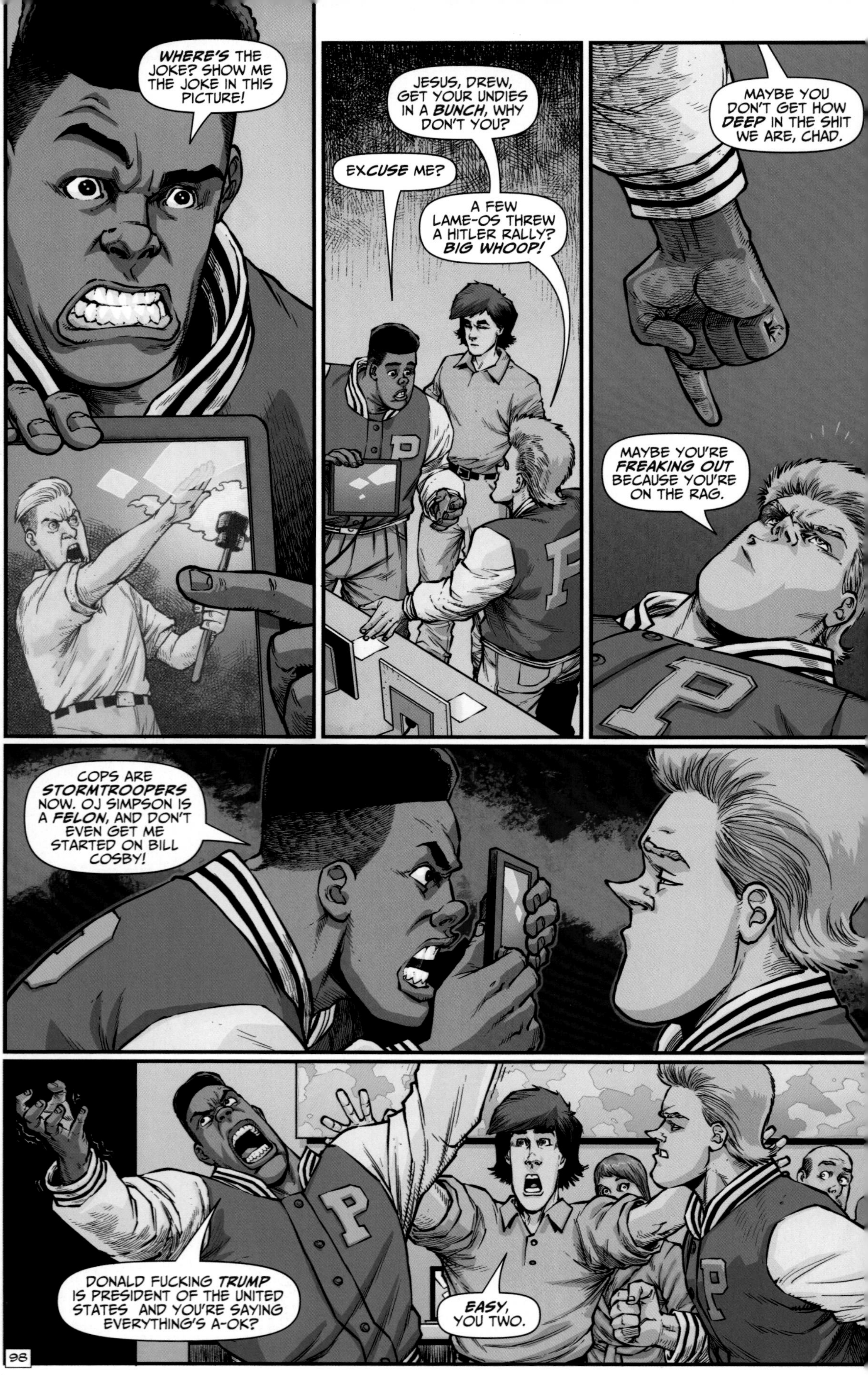
WHERE'S THE JOKE? SHOW ME THE JOKE IN THIS PICTURE!
JESUS, DREW, GET YOUR UNDIES IN A BUNCH, WHY DON'T YOU?
EXCUSE ME?
A FEW LAME-OS THREW A HITLER RALLY? BIG WHOOP!
MAYBE YOU DON'T GET HOW DEEP IN THE SHIT WE ARE, CHAD.
MAYBE YOU'RE FREAKING OUT BECAUSE YOU'RE ON THE RAG.
COPS ARE STORMTROOPERS NOW. OJ SIMPSON IS A FELON, AND DON'T EVEN GET ME STARTED ON BILL COSBY!
DONALD FUCKING TRUMP IS PRESIDENT OF THE UNITED STATES AND YOU'RE SAYING EVERYTHING'S A-OK?
EASY, YOU TWO.

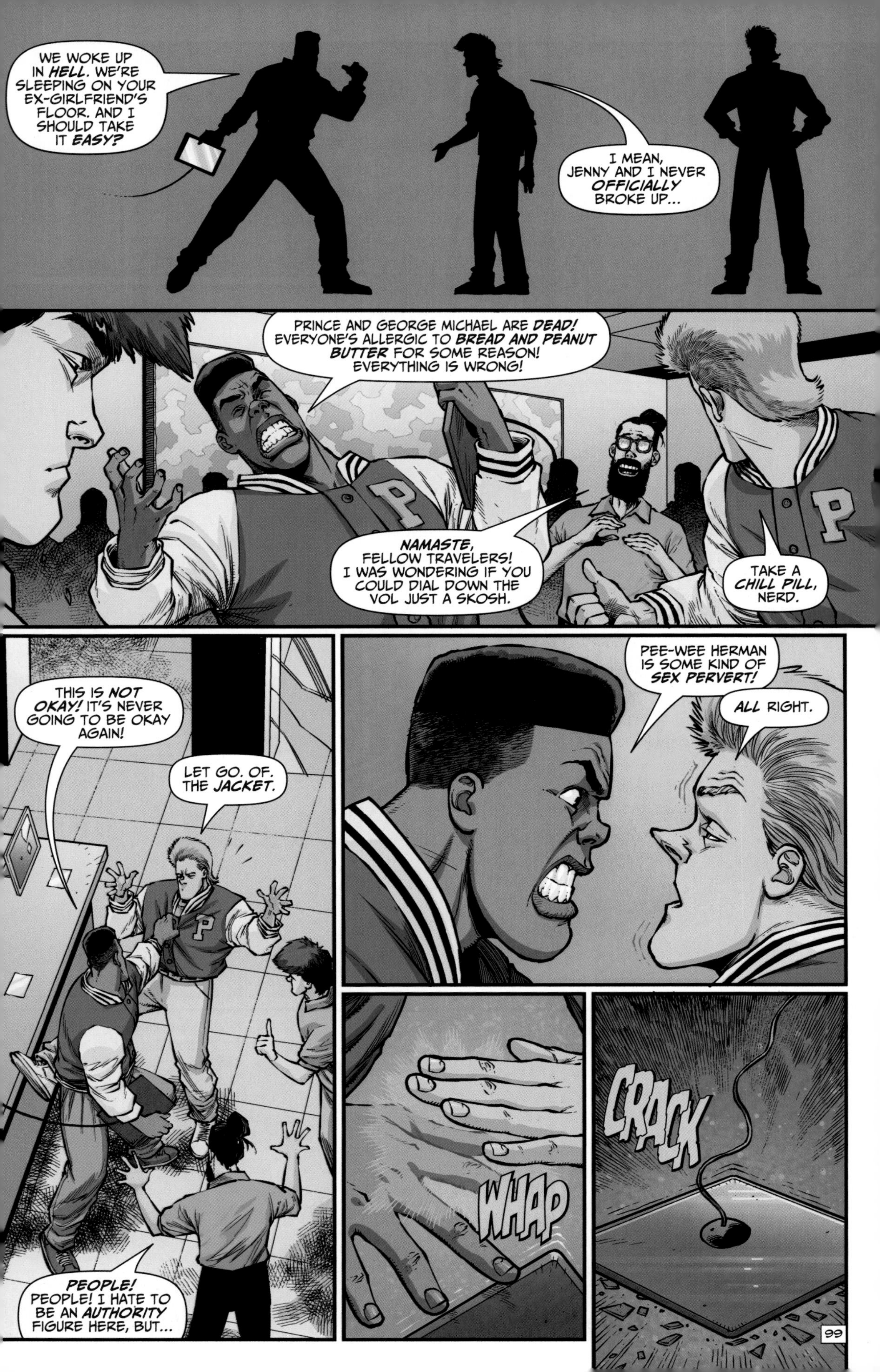
WE WOKE UP IN HELL. WE'RE SLEEPING ON YOUR EX-GIRLFRIEND'S FLOOR. AND I SHOULD TAKE IT EASY?
I MEAN, JENNY AND I NEVER OFFICIALLY BROKE UP...
PRINCE AND GEORGE MICHAEL ARE DEAD! EVERYONE'S ALLERGIC TO BREAD AND PEANUT BUTTER FOR SOME REASON! EVERYTHING IS WRONG!
NAMASTE, FELLOW TRAVELERS! I WAS WONDERING IF YOU COULD DIAL DOWN THE VOL JUST A SKOSH.
TAKE A CHILL PILL, NERD.
THIS IS NOT OKAY! IT'S NEVER GOING TO BE OKAY AGAIN!
LET GO. OF. THE JACKET.
PEOPLE! PEOPLE! I HATE TO BE AN AUTHORITY FIGURE HERE, BUT...
PEE-WEE HERMAN IS SOME KIND OF SEX PERVERT!
ALL RIGHT.
WHAP
CRACK

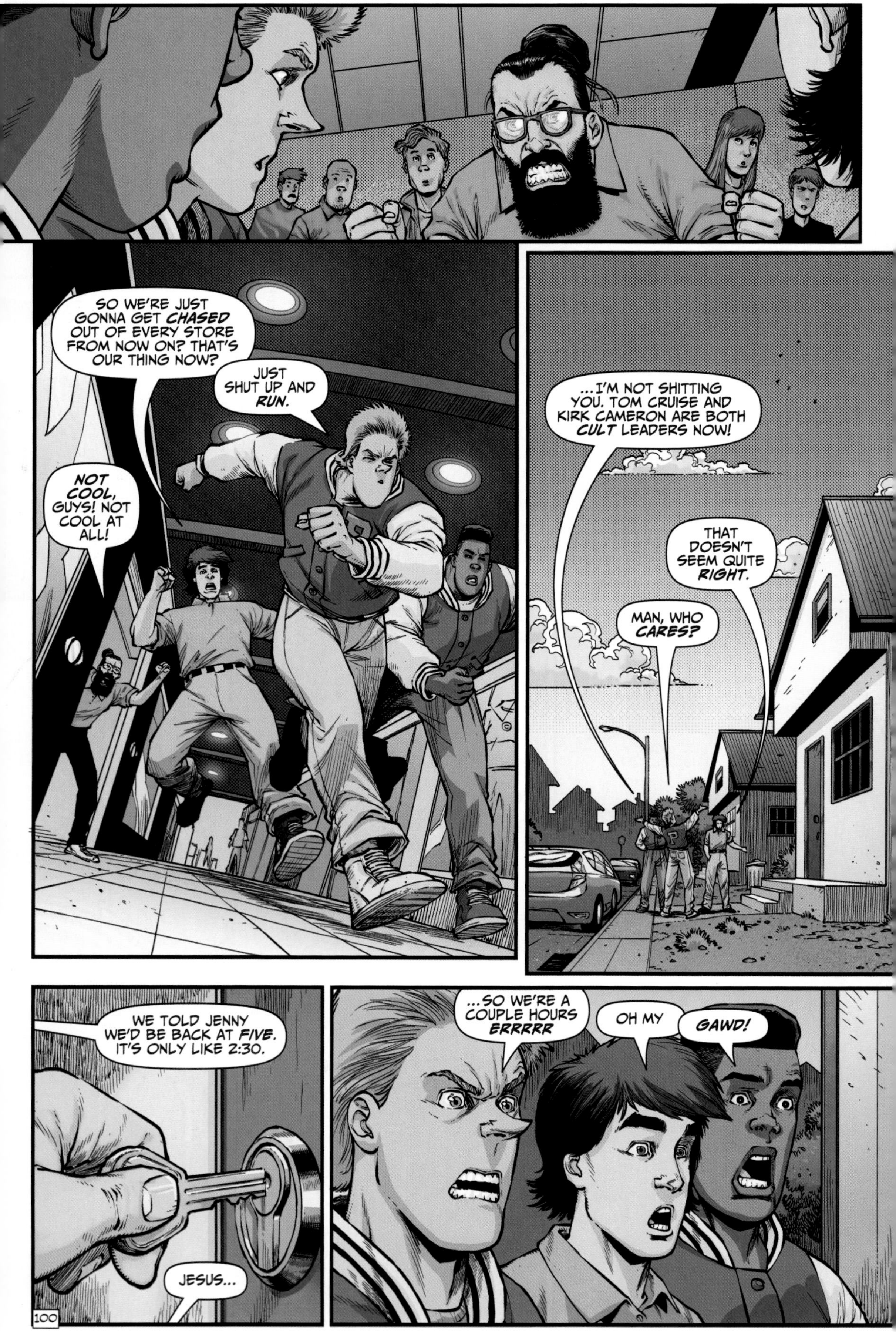
SO WE'RE JUST GONNA GET CHASED OUT OF EVERY STORE FROM NOW ON? THAT'S OUR THING NOW?
JUST SHUT UP AND RUN.
NOT COOL, GUYS! NOT COOL AT ALL!
...I'M NOT SHITTING YOU. TOM CRUISE AND KIRK CAMERON ARE BOTH CULT LEADERS NOW!
THAT DOESN'T SEEM QUITE RIGHT.
MAN, WHO CARES?
WE TOLD JENNY WE'D BE BACK AT FIVE. IT'S ONLY LIKE 2:30.
JESUS...
...SO WE'RE A COUPLE HOURS ERRRRR
OH MY
GAWD!

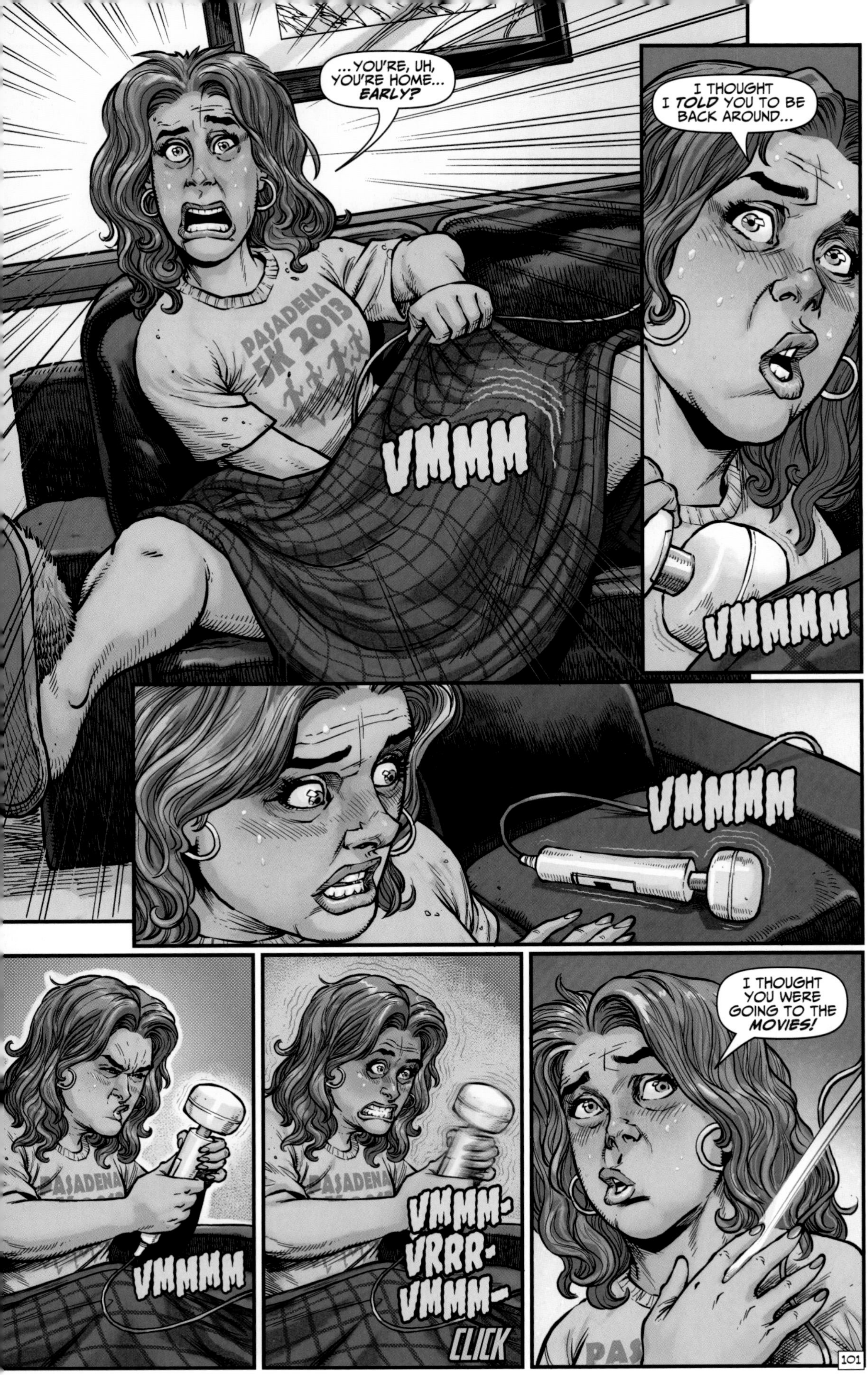
...YOU'RE, UH, YOU'RE HOME... *EARLY?*
PASADENA 5K 2013
VMMM
I THOUGHT I *TOLD* YOU TO BE BACK AROUND...
VMMMM
VMMMM
PASADENA
VMMMM
PASADENA
VMMM-
VRRR-
VMMM-
CLICK
I THOUGHT YOU WERE GOING TO THE *MOVIES!*

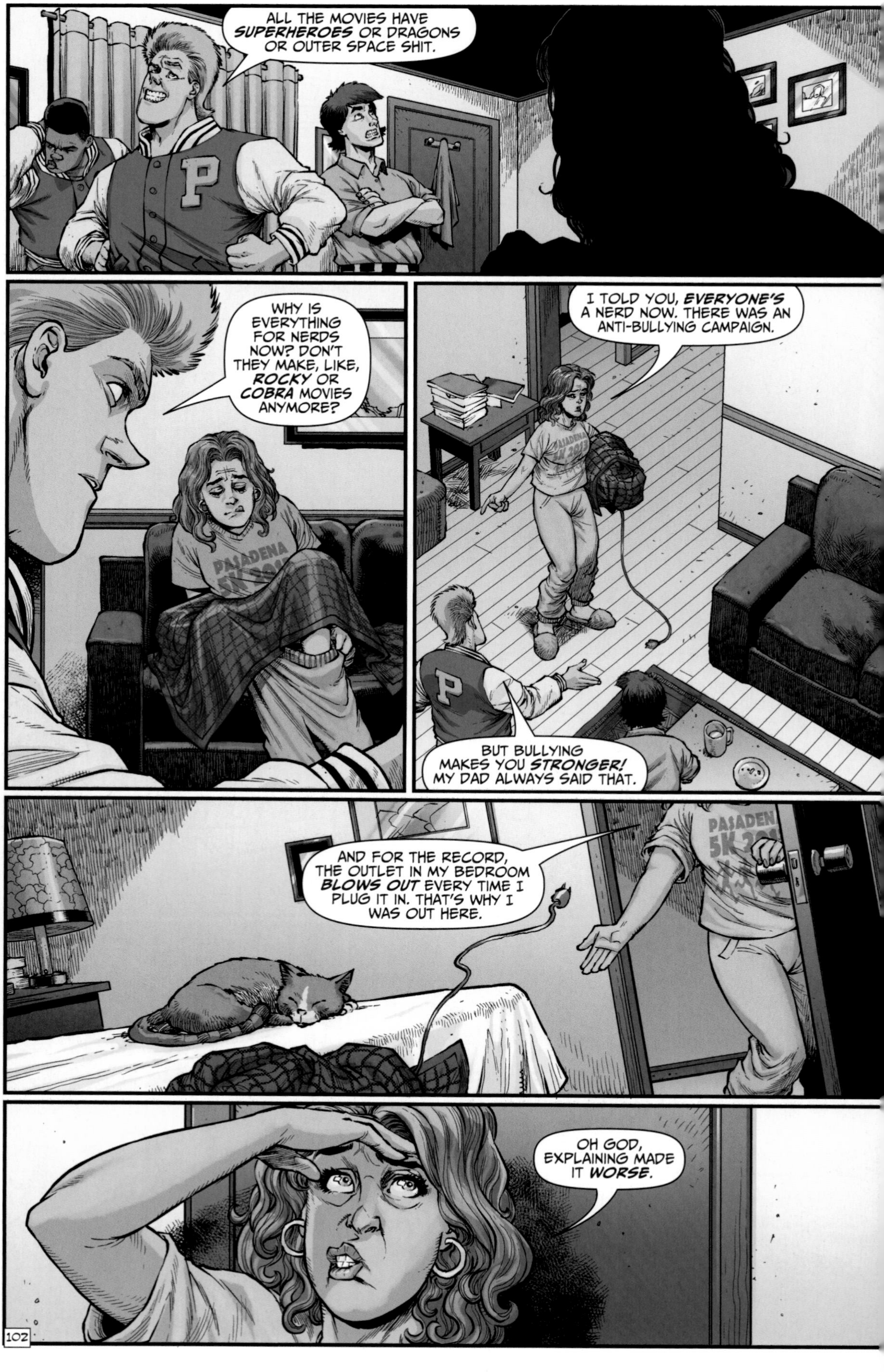
ALL THE MOVIES HAVE SUPERHEROES OR DRAGONS OR OUTER SPACE SHIT.
WHY IS EVERYTHING FOR NERDS NOW? DON'T THEY MAKE, LIKE, ROCKY OR COBRA MOVIES ANYMORE?
I TOLD YOU, EVERYONE'S A NERD NOW. THERE WAS AN ANTI-BULLYING CAMPAIGN.
BUT BULLYING MAKES YOU STRONGER! MY DAD ALWAYS SAID THAT.
AND FOR THE RECORD, THE OUTLET IN MY BEDROOM BLOWS OUT EVERY TIME I PLUG IT IN. THAT'S WHY I WAS OUT HERE.
OH GOD, EXPLAINING MADE IT WORSE.

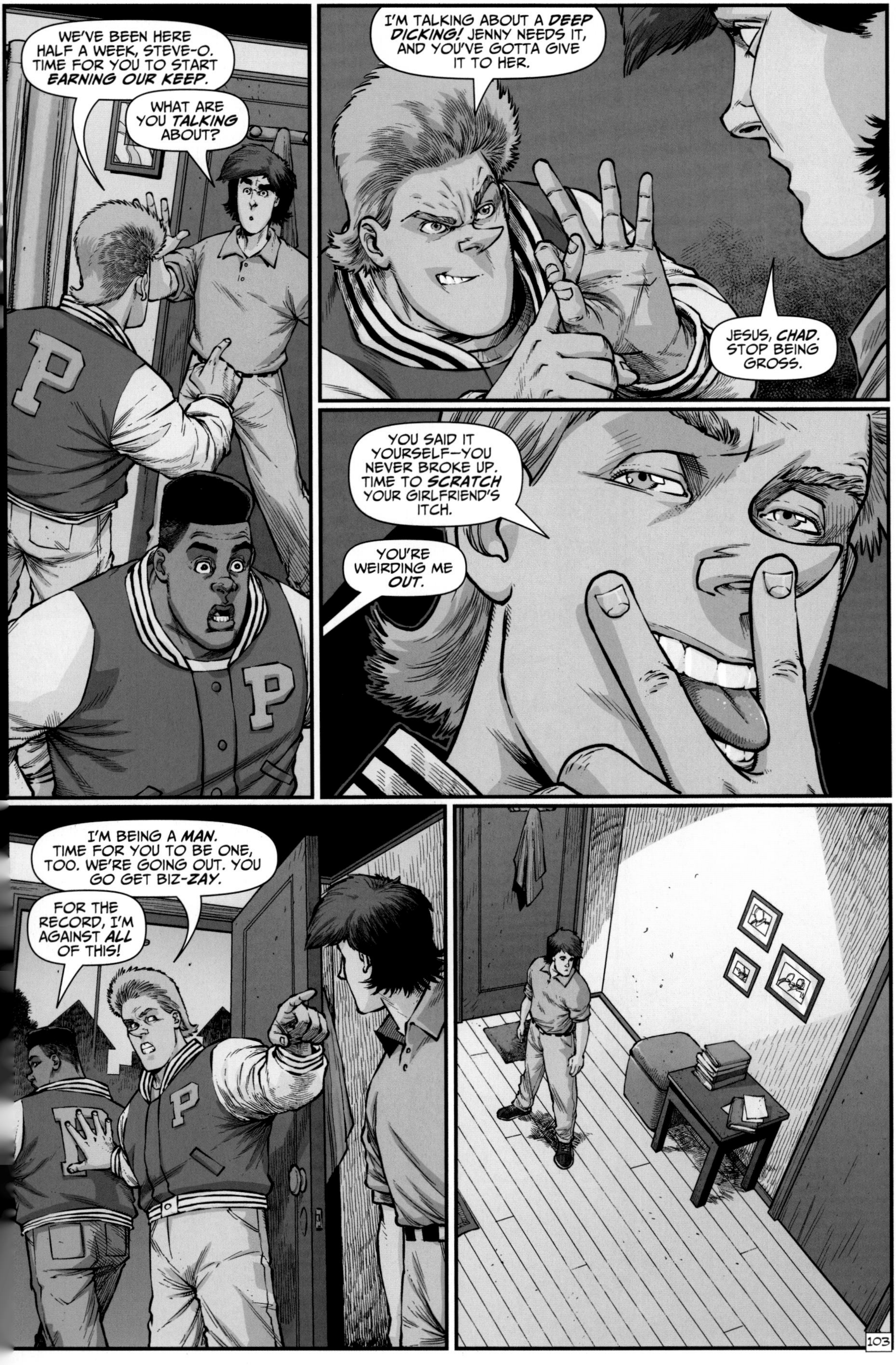
WE'VE BEEN HERE HALF A WEEK, STEVE-O. TIME FOR YOU TO START EARNING OUR KEEP.
WHAT ARE YOU TALKING ABOUT?
I'M TALKING ABOUT A DEEP DICKING! JENNY NEEDS IT, AND YOU'VE GOTTA GIVE IT TO HER.
JESUS, CHAD. STOP BEING GROSS.
YOU SAID IT YOURSELF—YOU NEVER BROKE UP. TIME TO SCRATCH YOUR GIRLFRIEND'S ITCH.
YOU'RE WEIRDING ME OUT.
I'M BEING A MAN. TIME FOR YOU TO BE ONE, TOO. WE'RE GOING OUT. YOU GO GET BIZ-ZAY.
FOR THE RECORD, I'M AGAINST ALL OF THIS!

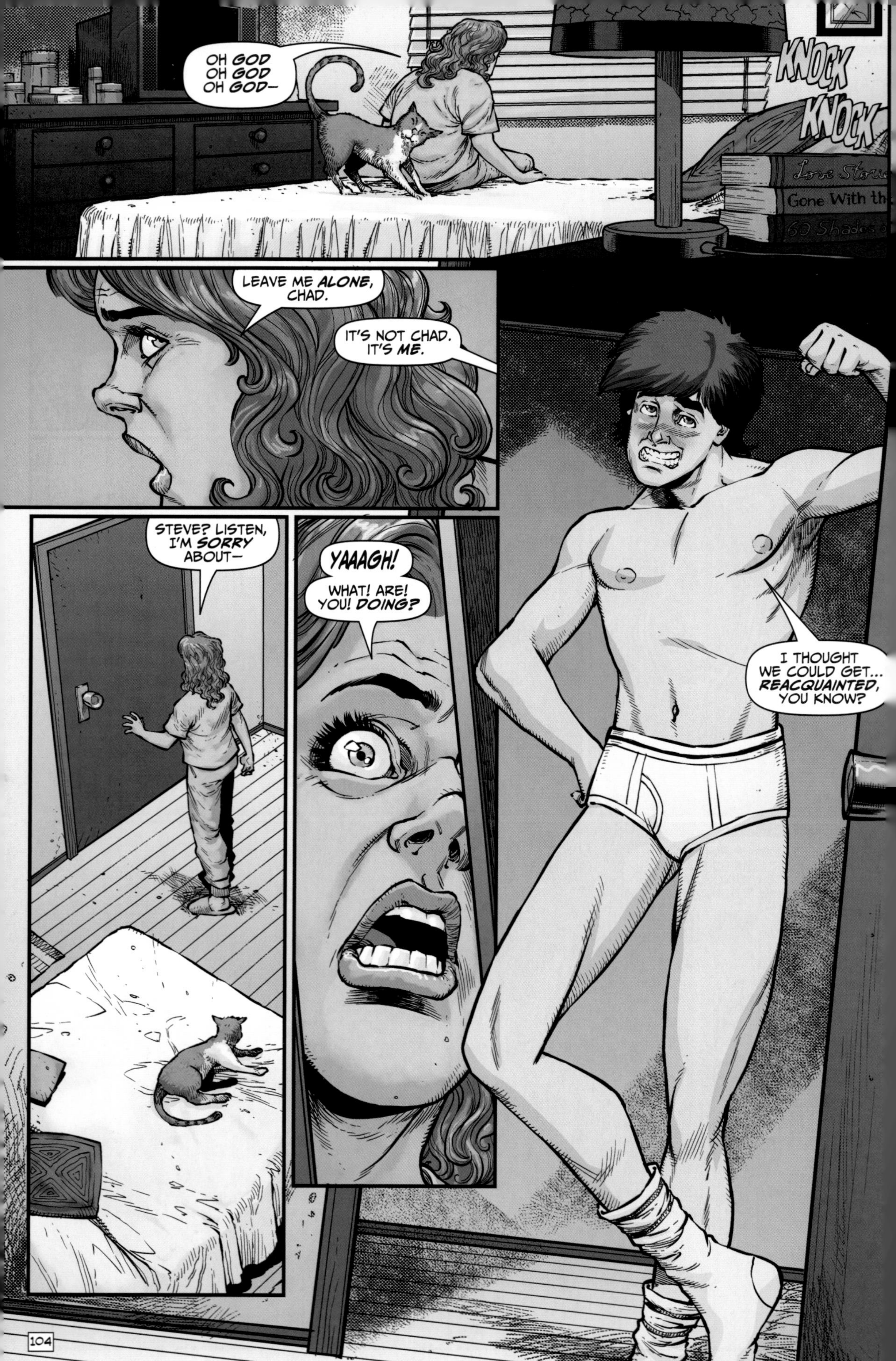

OH GOD OH GOD OH GOD—
KNOCK
KNOCK
Love Stories
Gone With the
60 Shades of
LEAVE ME ALONE, CHAD.
IT'S NOT CHAD. IT'S ME.
STEVE? LISTEN, I'M SORRY ABOUT—
YAAAGH!
WHAT! ARE! YOU! DOING?
I THOUGHT WE COULD GET... REACQUAINTED, YOU KNOW?

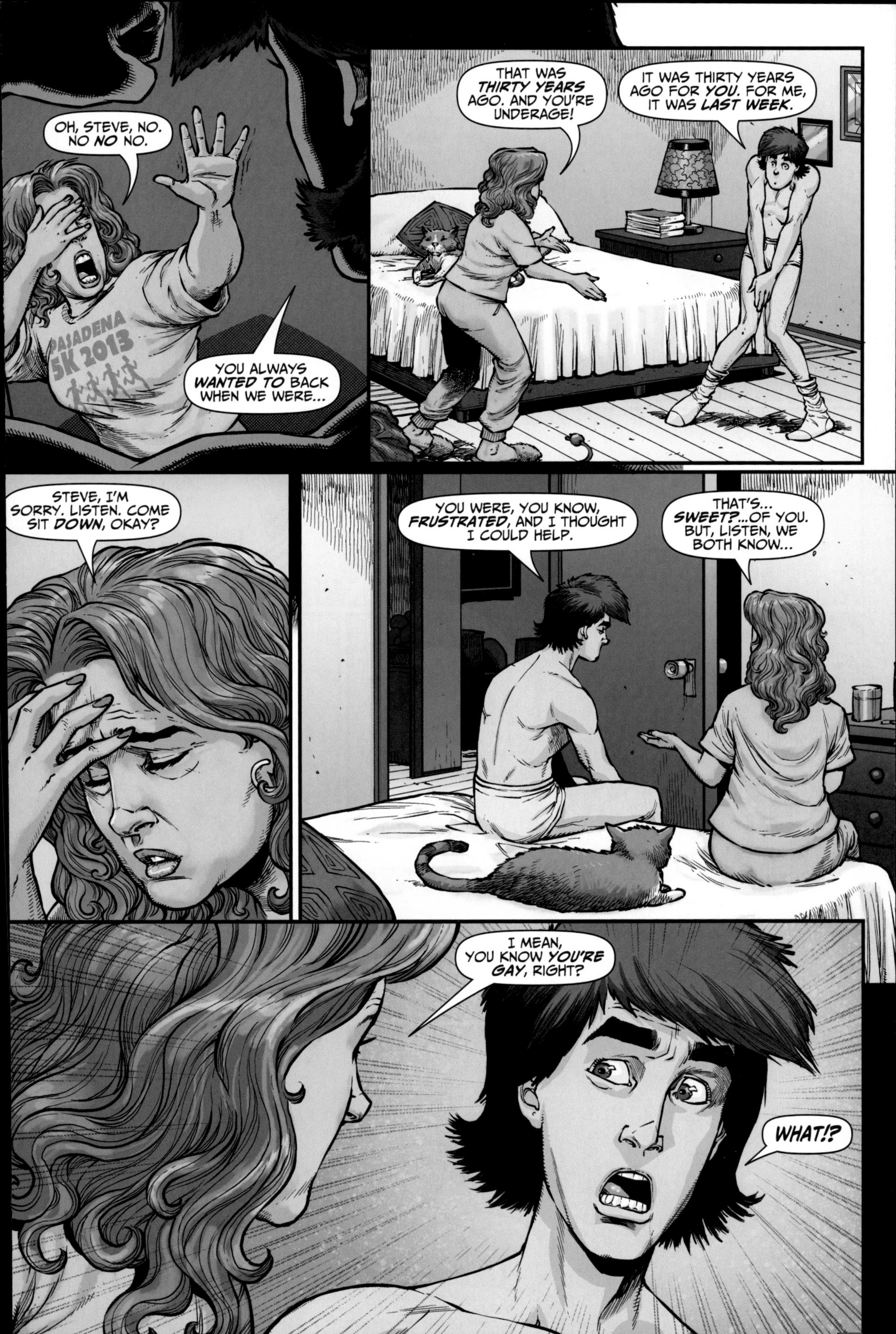
OH, STEVE, NO. NO *NO* NO.
YOU ALWAYS *WANTED TO* BACK WHEN WE WERE...
PASADENA 5K 2013
THAT WAS *THIRTY YEARS* AGO. AND YOU'RE UNDERAGE!
IT WAS THIRTY YEARS AGO FOR *YOU*. FOR ME, IT WAS *LAST WEEK*.
STEVE, I'M SORRY. LISTEN. COME SIT *DOWN*, OKAY?
YOU WERE, YOU KNOW, *FRUSTRATED*, AND I THOUGHT I COULD HELP.
THAT'S... *SWEET?*...OF YOU. BUT, LISTEN, WE BOTH KNOW...
I MEAN, YOU KNOW *YOU'RE GAY*, RIGHT?
WHAT!?

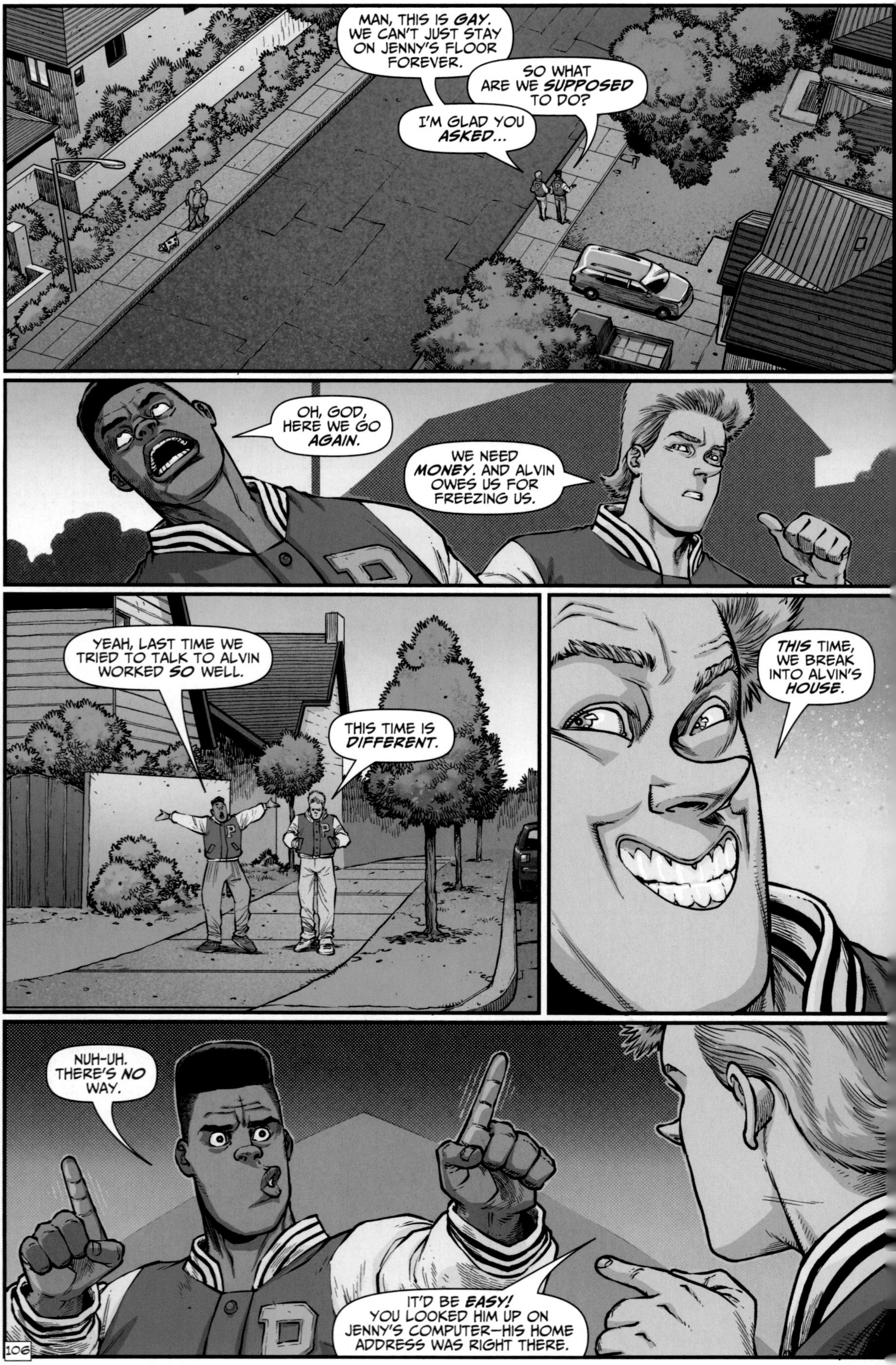
MAN, THIS IS GAY. WE CAN'T JUST STAY ON JENNY'S FLOOR FOREVER.
SO WHAT ARE WE SUPPOSED TO DO?
I'M GLAD YOU ASKED...
OH, GOD, HERE WE GO AGAIN.
WE NEED MONEY. AND ALVIN OWES US FOR FREEZING US.
YEAH, LAST TIME WE TRIED TO TALK TO ALVIN WORKED SO WELL.
THIS TIME IS DIFFERENT.
THIS TIME, WE BREAK INTO ALVIN'S HOUSE.
NUH-UH. THERE'S NO WAY.
IT'D BE EASY! YOU LOOKED HIM UP ON JENNY'S COMPUTER—HIS HOME ADDRESS WAS RIGHT THERE.

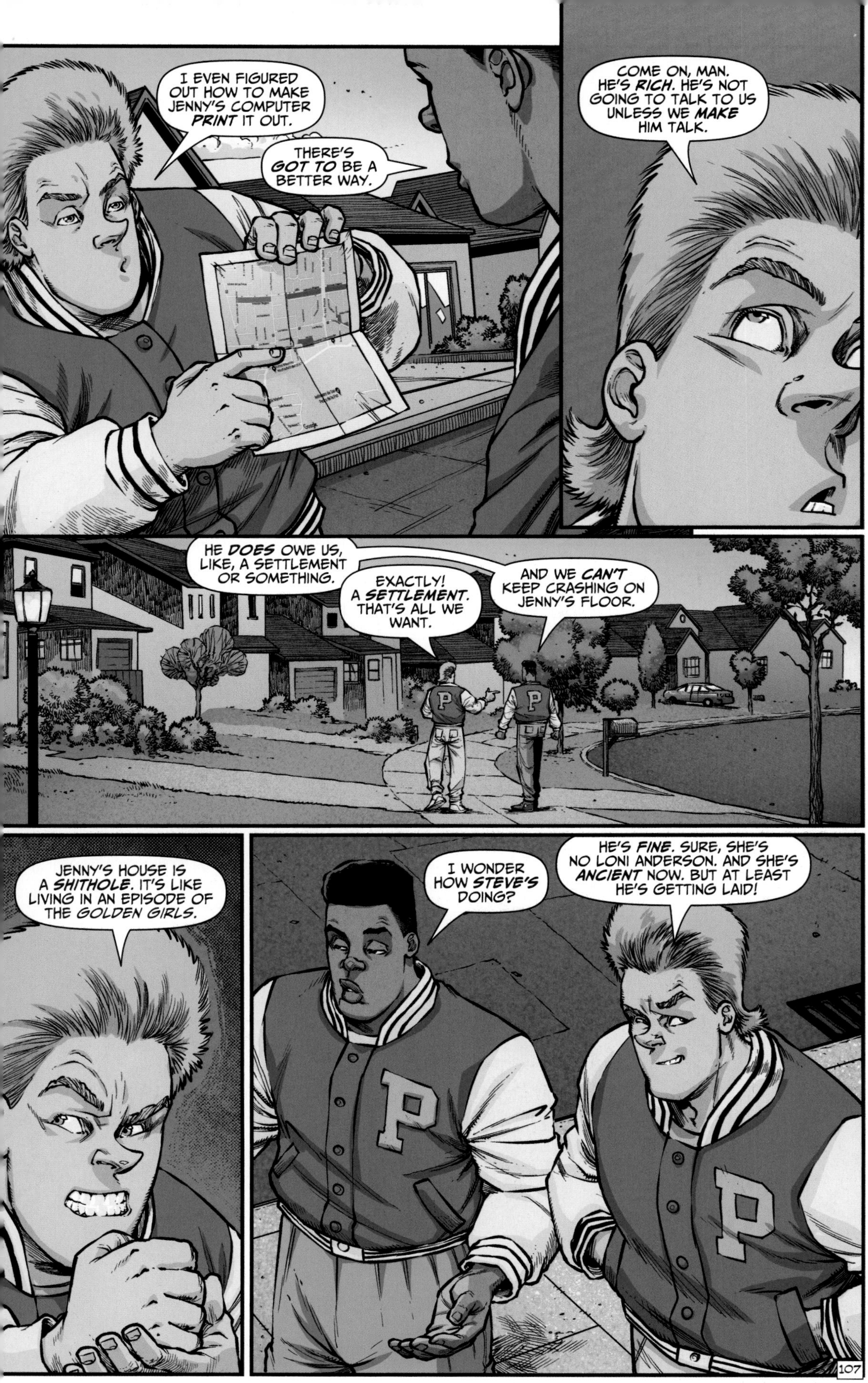
I EVEN FIGURED OUT HOW TO MAKE JENNY'S COMPUTER PRINT IT OUT.
THERE'S GOT TO BE A BETTER WAY.
COME ON, MAN. HE'S RICH. HE'S NOT GOING TO TALK TO US UNLESS WE MAKE HIM TALK.
HE DOES OWE US, LIKE, A SETTLEMENT OR SOMETHING.
EXACTLY! A SETTLEMENT. THAT'S ALL WE WANT.
AND WE CAN'T KEEP CRASHING ON JENNY'S FLOOR.
JENNY'S HOUSE IS A SHITHOLE. IT'S LIKE LIVING IN AN EPISODE OF THE GOLDEN GIRLS.
I WONDER HOW STEVE'S DOING?
HE'S FINE. SURE, SHE'S NO LONI ANDERSON. AND SHE'S ANCIENT NOW. BUT AT LEAST HE'S GETTING LAID!

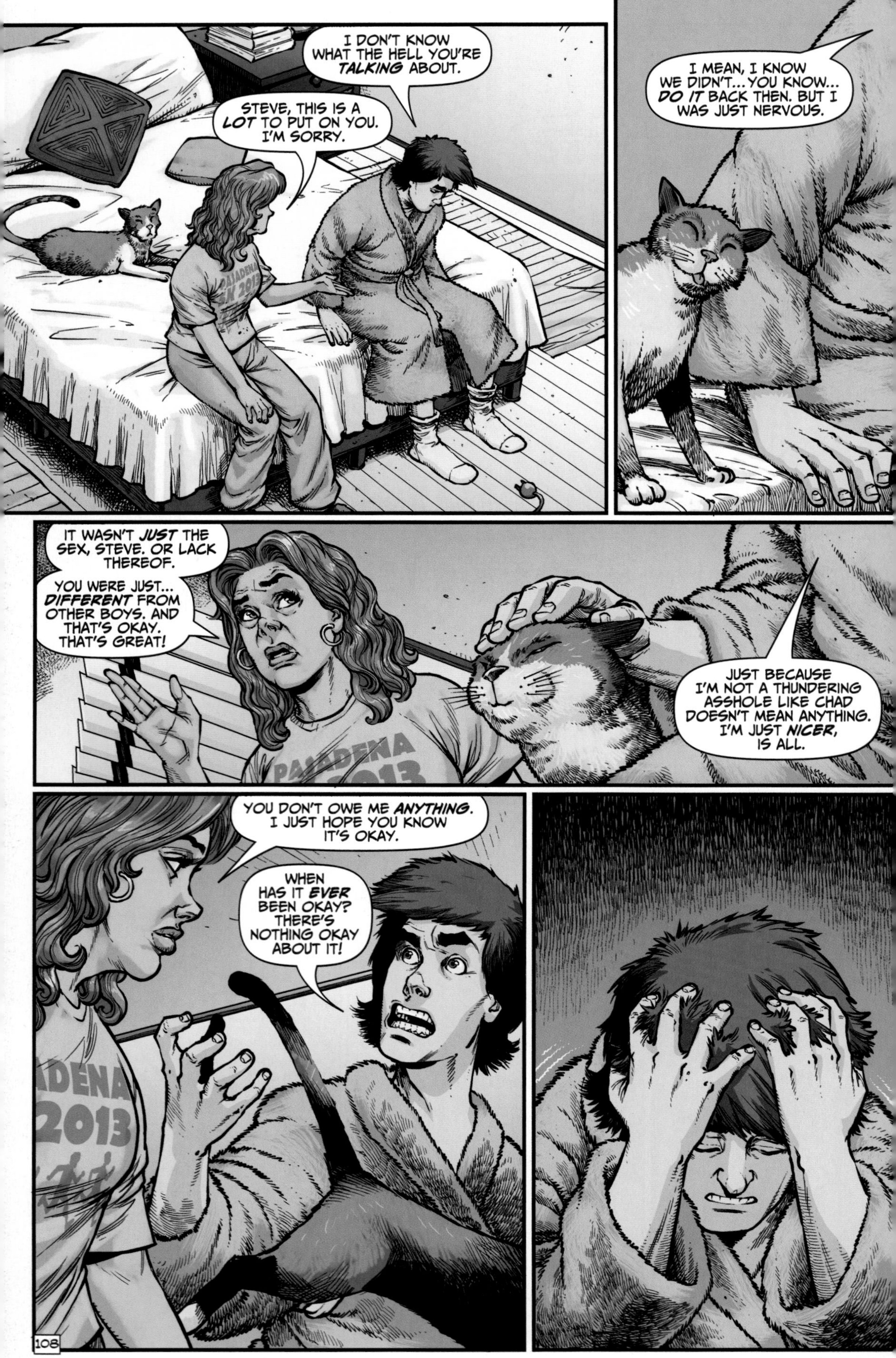
I DON'T KNOW WHAT THE HELL YOU'RE *TALKING* ABOUT.
STEVE, THIS IS A *LOT* TO PUT ON YOU. I'M SORRY.
I MEAN, I KNOW WE DIDN'T...YOU KNOW... *DO IT* BACK THEN. BUT I WAS JUST NERVOUS.
IT WASN'T *JUST* THE SEX, STEVE. OR LACK THEREOF.
YOU WERE JUST... *DIFFERENT* FROM OTHER BOYS. AND THAT'S OKAY. THAT'S GREAT!
JUST BECAUSE I'M NOT A THUNDERING ASSHOLE LIKE CHAD DOESN'T MEAN ANYTHING. I'M JUST *NICER,* IS ALL.
YOU DON'T OWE ME *ANYTHING*. I JUST HOPE YOU KNOW IT'S OKAY.
WHEN HAS IT *EVER* BEEN OKAY? THERE'S NOTHING OKAY ABOUT IT!
PASADENA 2013

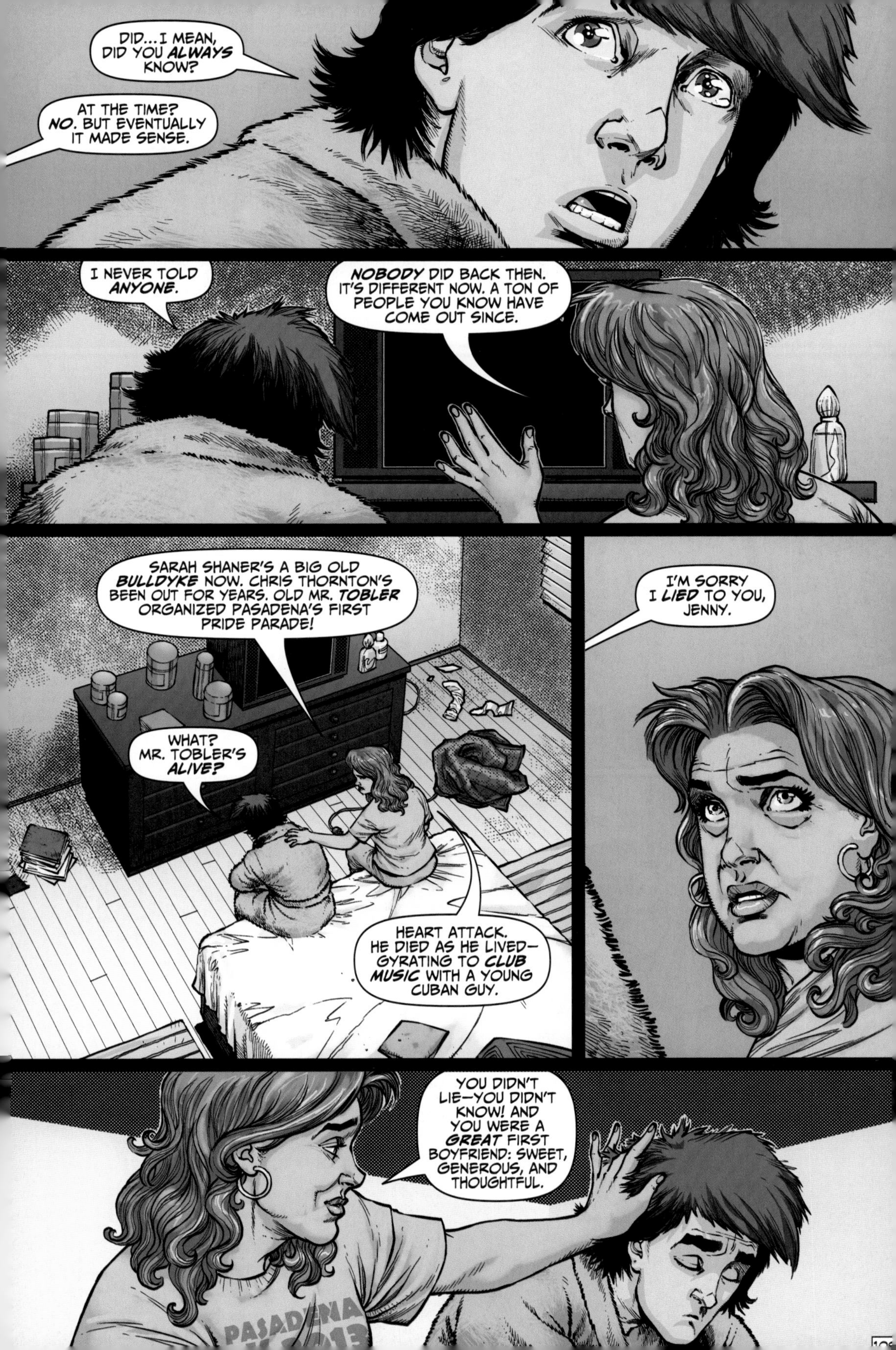
DID... I MEAN, DID YOU *ALWAYS* KNOW?
AT THE TIME? *NO*. BUT EVENTUALLY IT MADE SENSE.
I NEVER TOLD *ANYONE*.
NOBODY DID BACK THEN. IT'S DIFFERENT NOW. A TON OF PEOPLE YOU KNOW HAVE COME OUT SINCE.
SARAH SHANER'S A BIG OLD *BULLDYKE* NOW. CHRIS THORNTON'S BEEN OUT FOR YEARS. OLD MR. *TOBLER* ORGANIZED PASADENA'S FIRST PRIDE PARADE!
WHAT? MR. TOBLER'S *ALIVE?*
HEART ATTACK. HE DIED AS HE LIVED— GYRATING TO *CLUB MUSIC* WITH A YOUNG CUBAN GUY.
I'M SORRY I *LIED* TO YOU, JENNY.
YOU DIDN'T LIE—YOU DIDN'T KNOW! AND YOU WERE A *GREAT* FIRST BOYFRIEND: SWEET, GENEROUS, AND THOUGHTFUL.
PASADENA

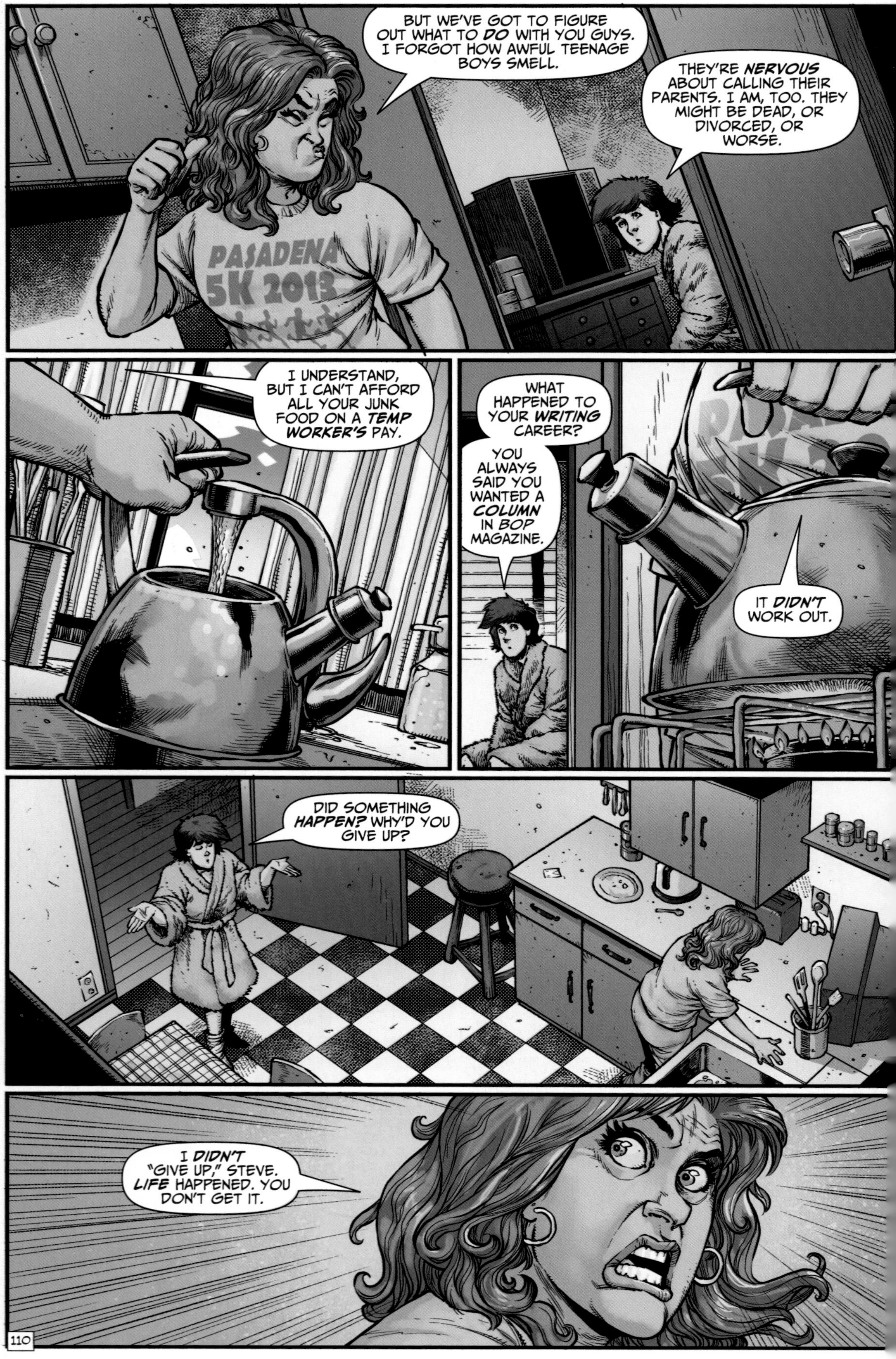
BUT WE'VE GOT TO FIGURE OUT WHAT TO *DO* WITH YOU GUYS. I FORGOT HOW AWFUL TEENAGE BOYS SMELL.
THEY'RE *NERVOUS* ABOUT CALLING THEIR PARENTS. I AM, TOO. THEY MIGHT BE DEAD, OR DIVORCED, OR WORSE.
PASADENA 5K 2013
I UNDERSTAND, BUT I CAN'T AFFORD ALL YOUR JUNK FOOD ON A *TEMP WORKER'S* PAY.
WHAT HAPPENED TO YOUR *WRITING* CAREER?
YOU ALWAYS SAID YOU WANTED A *COLUMN* IN *BOP* MAGAZINE.
IT *DIDN'T* WORK OUT.
DID SOMETHING *HAPPEN?* WHY'D YOU GIVE UP?
I *DIDN'T* "GIVE UP," STEVE. *LIFE* HAPPENED. YOU DON'T GET IT.

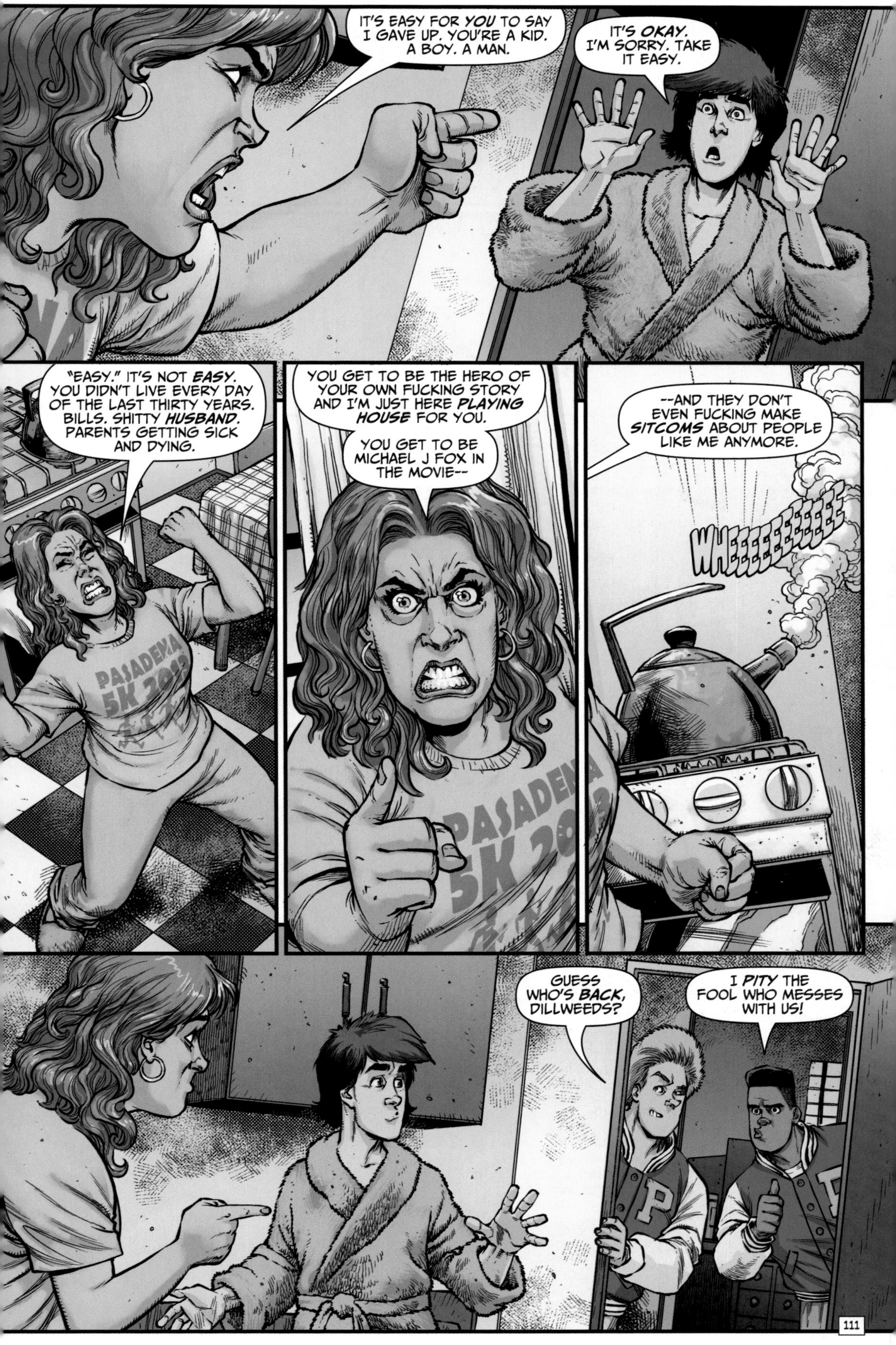
IT'S EASY FOR *YOU* TO SAY I GAVE UP. YOU'RE A KID. A BOY. A MAN.
IT'S *OKAY*. I'M SORRY. TAKE IT EASY.
"EASY." IT'S NOT *EASY*. YOU DIDN'T LIVE EVERY DAY OF THE LAST THIRTY YEARS. BILLS. SHITTY *HUSBAND*. PARENTS GETTING SICK AND DYING.
PASADENA 5K 2012
YOU GET TO BE THE HERO OF YOUR OWN FUCKING STORY AND I'M JUST HERE *PLAYING HOUSE* FOR YOU.
YOU GET TO BE MICHAEL J FOX IN THE MOVIE--
--AND THEY DON'T EVEN FUCKING MAKE *SITCOMS* ABOUT PEOPLE LIKE ME ANYMORE.
WHEEEEEEEEEEE
GUESS WHO'S *BACK*, DILLWEEDS?
I *PITY* THE FOOL WHO MESSES WITH US!

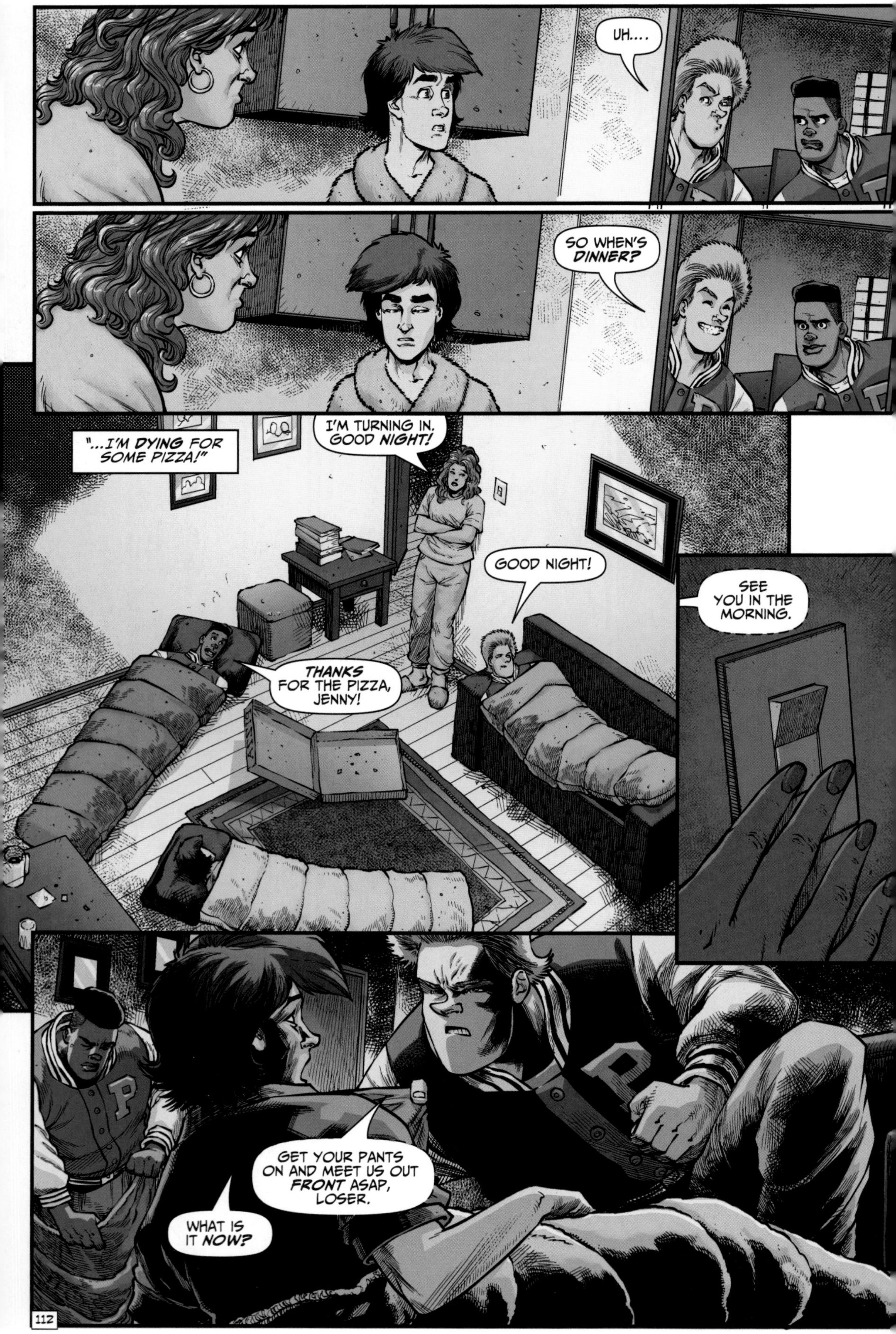
UH....
SO WHEN'S DINNER?
"...I'M DYING FOR SOME PIZZA!"
I'M TURNING IN. GOOD NIGHT!
GOOD NIGHT!
THANKS FOR THE PIZZA, JENNY!
SEE YOU IN THE MORNING.
GET YOUR PANTS ON AND MEET US OUT FRONT ASAP, LOSER.
WHAT IS IT NOW?

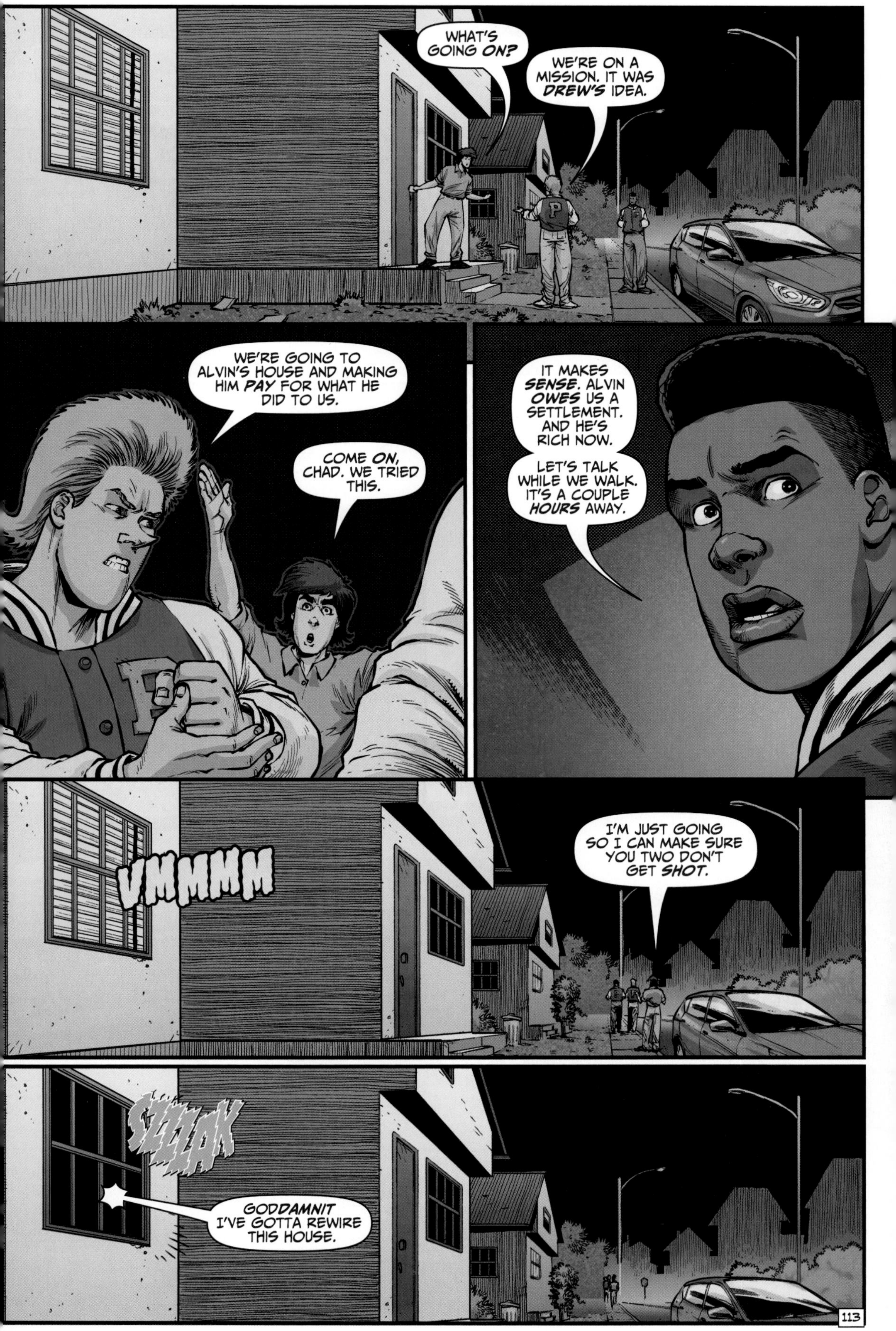
WHAT'S GOING ON?
WE'RE ON A MISSION. IT WAS DREW'S IDEA.
WE'RE GOING TO ALVIN'S HOUSE AND MAKING HIM PAY FOR WHAT HE DID TO US.
COME ON, CHAD. WE TRIED THIS.
IT MAKES SENSE. ALVIN OWES US A SETTLEMENT. AND HE'S RICH NOW.
LET'S TALK WHILE WE WALK. IT'S A COUPLE HOURS AWAY.
VMMMM
I'M JUST GOING SO I CAN MAKE SURE YOU TWO DON'T GET SHOT.
SZZZAK
GODDAMNIT I'VE GOTTA REWIRE THIS HOUSE.

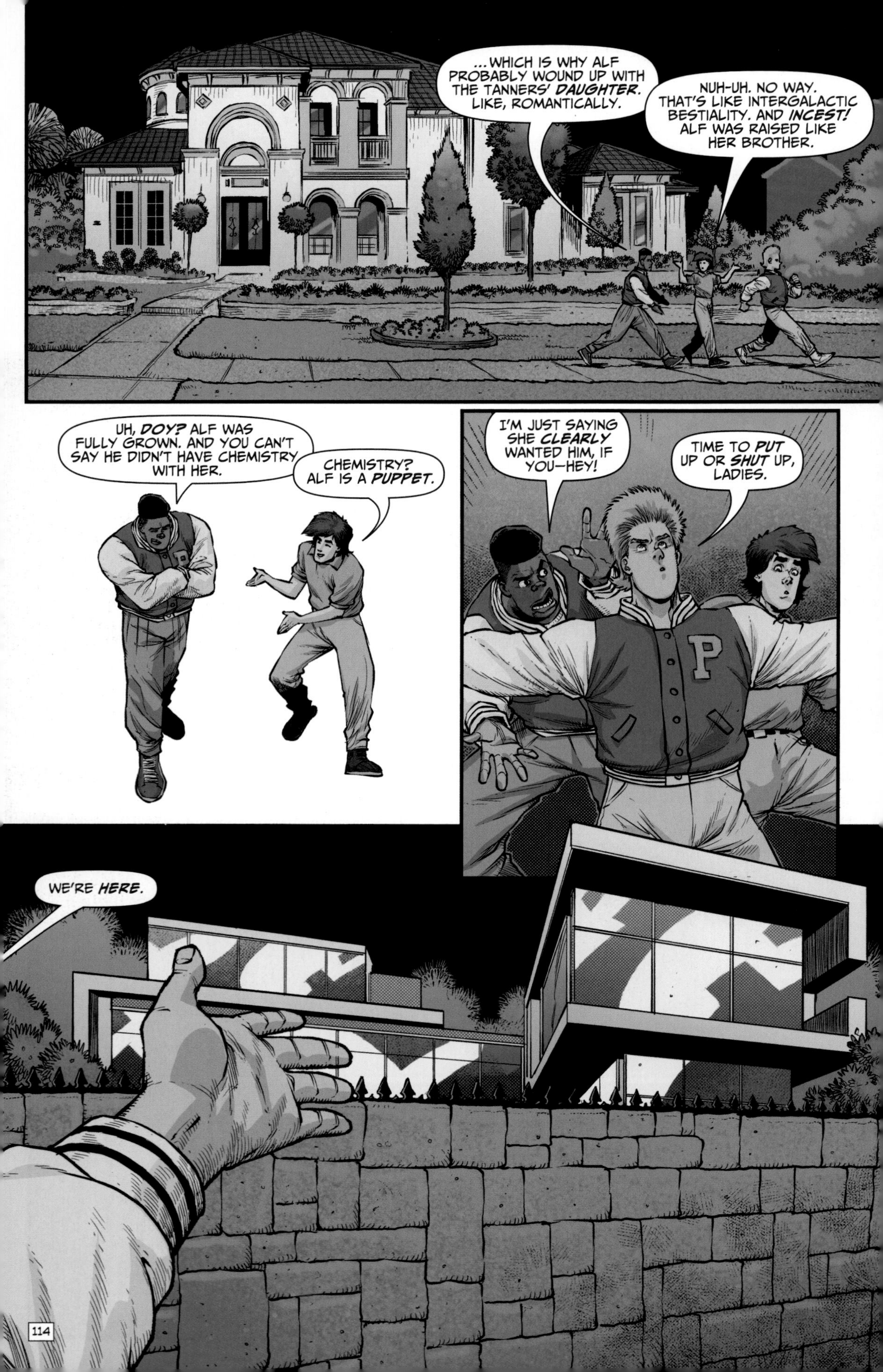
...WHICH IS WHY ALF PROBABLY WOUND UP WITH THE TANNERS' *DAUGHTER*. LIKE, ROMANTICALLY.
NUH-UH. NO WAY. THAT'S LIKE INTERGALACTIC BESTIALITY. AND *INCEST!* ALF WAS RAISED LIKE HER BROTHER.
UH, *DOY?* ALF WAS FULLY GROWN. AND YOU CAN'T SAY HE DIDN'T HAVE CHEMISTRY WITH HER.
CHEMISTRY? ALF IS A *PUPPET*.
I'M JUST SAYING SHE *CLEARLY* WANTED HIM, IF YOU—HEY!
TIME TO *PUT* UP OR *SHUT* UP, LADIES.
WE'RE *HERE*.

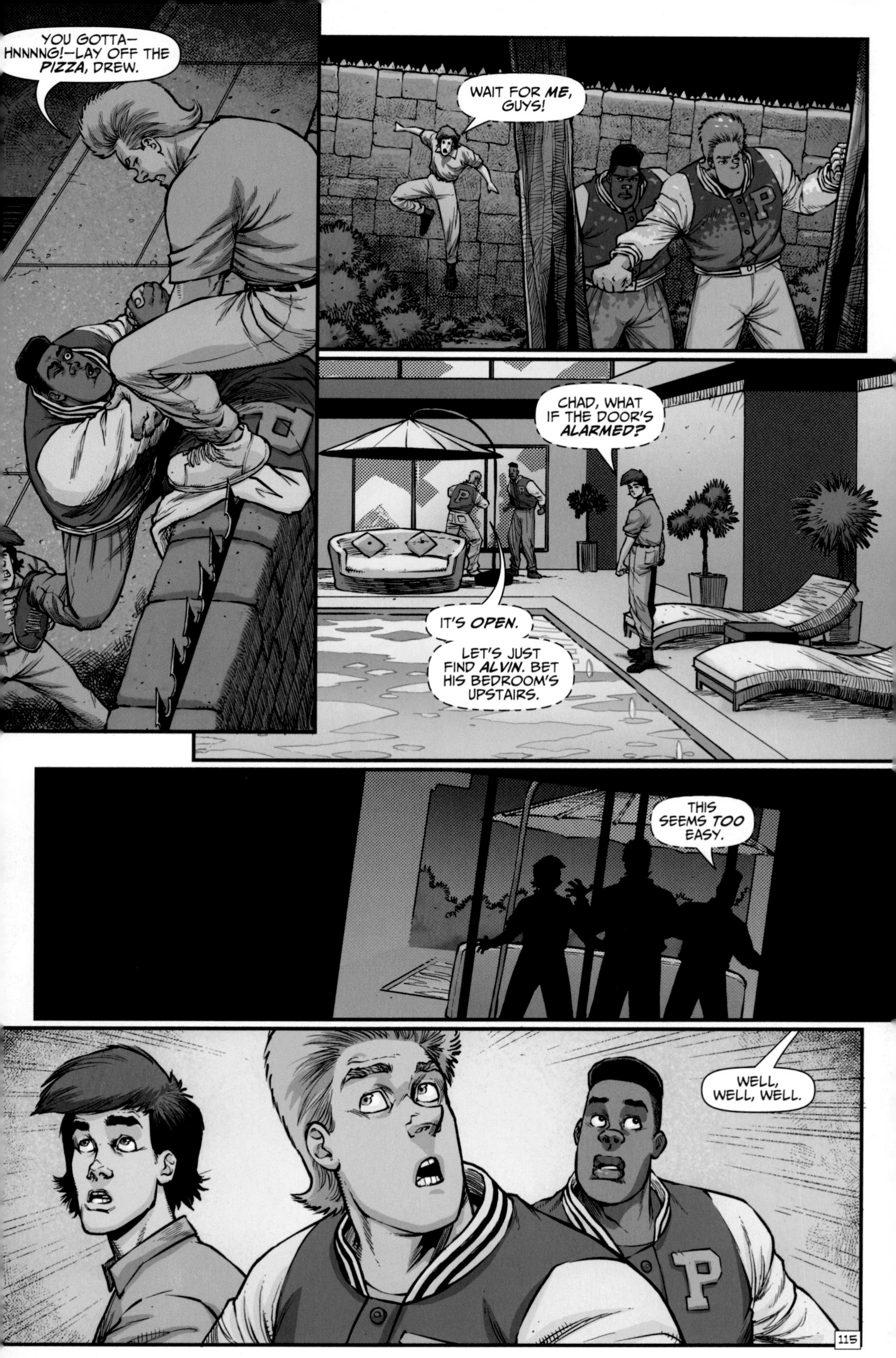
YOU GOTTA—HNNNNG!—LAY OFF THE PIZZA, DREW.
WAIT FOR ME, GUYS!
CHAD, WHAT IF THE DOOR'S ALARMED?
IT'S OPEN.
LET'S JUST FIND ALVIN. BET HIS BEDROOM'S UPSTAIRS.
THIS SEEMS TOO EASY.
WELL, WELL, WELL.

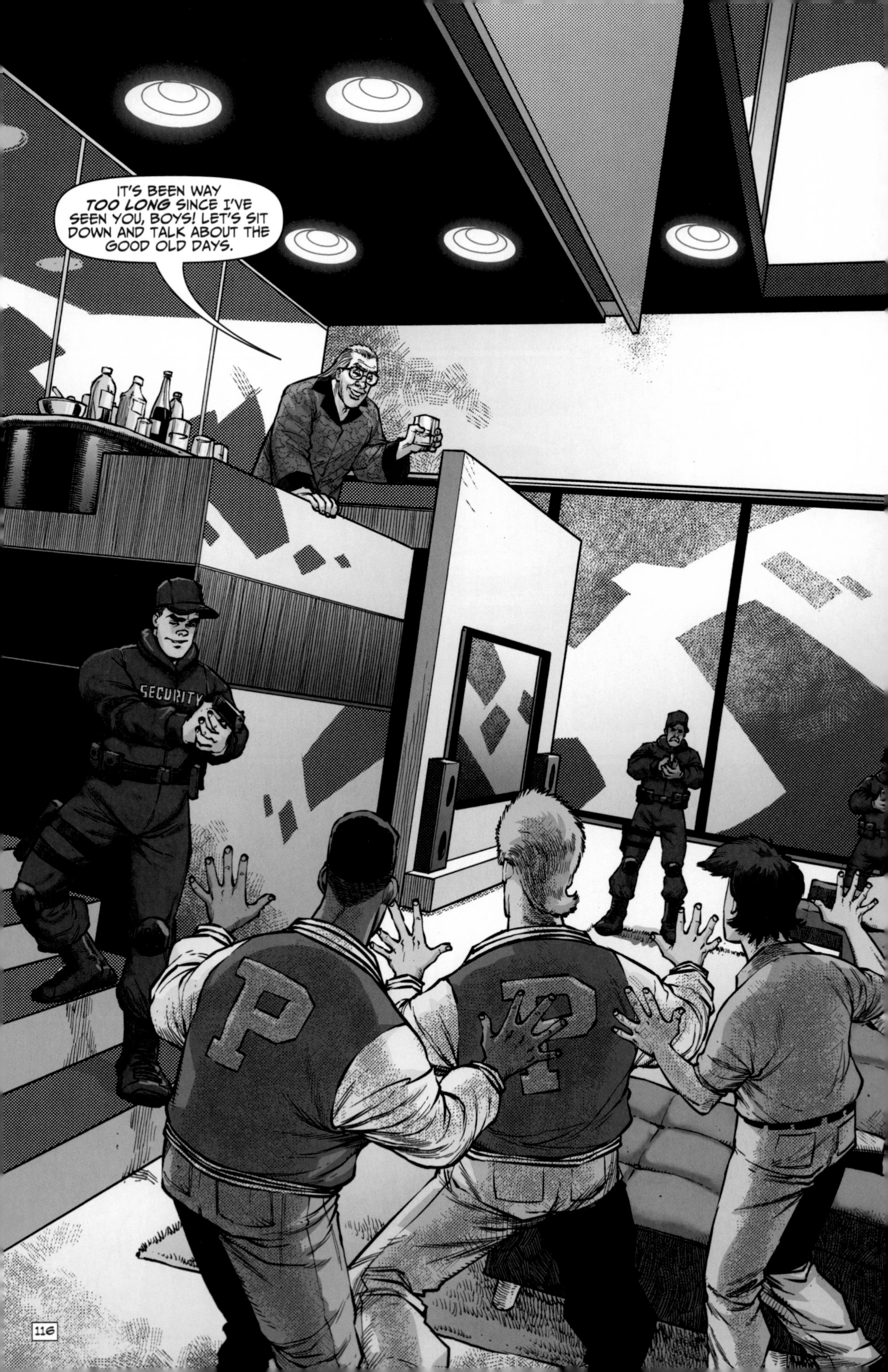
IT'S BEEN WAY *TOO LONG* SINCE I'VE SEEN YOU, BOYS! LET'S SIT DOWN AND TALK ABOUT THE GOOD OLD DAYS.
SECURITY

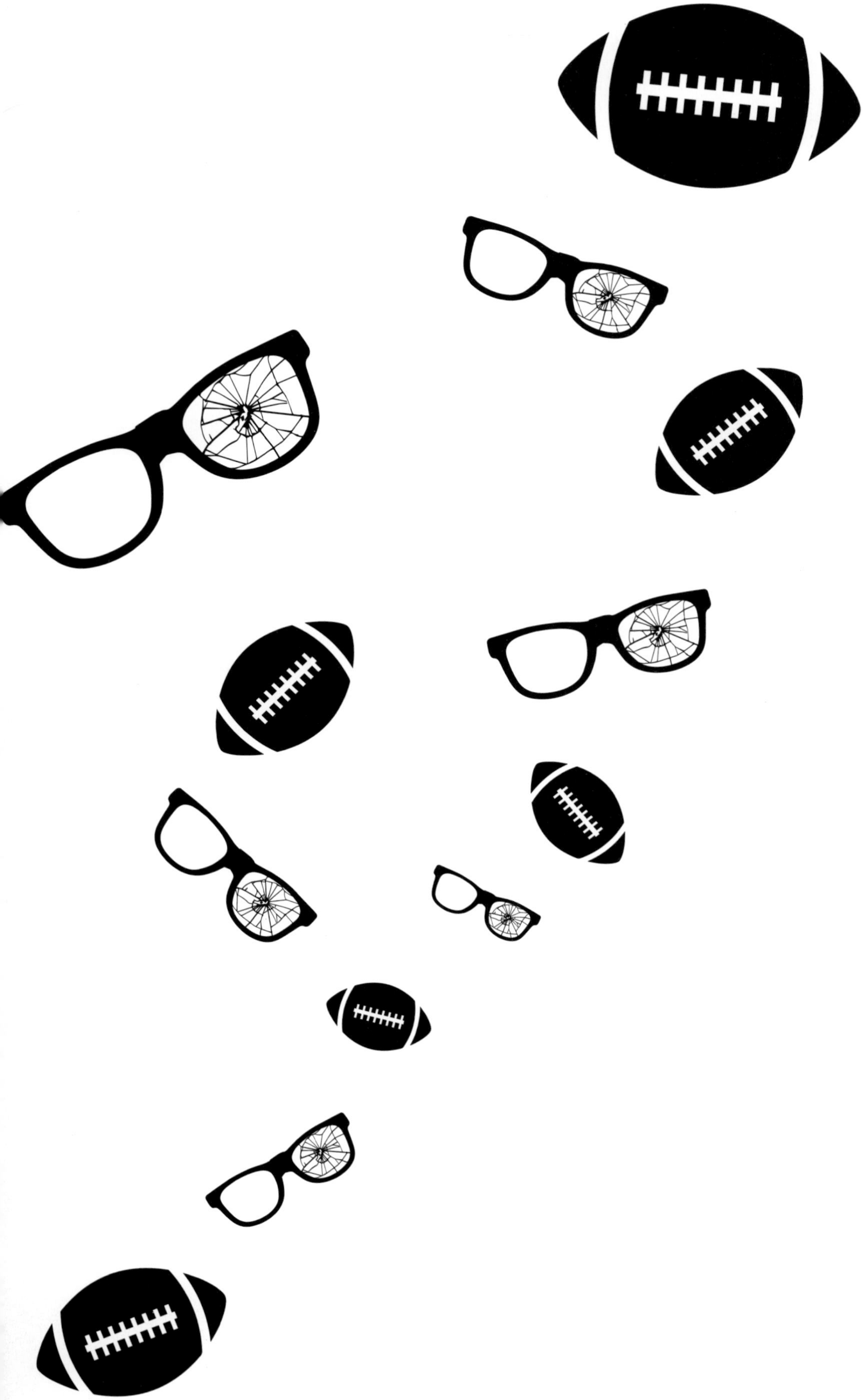

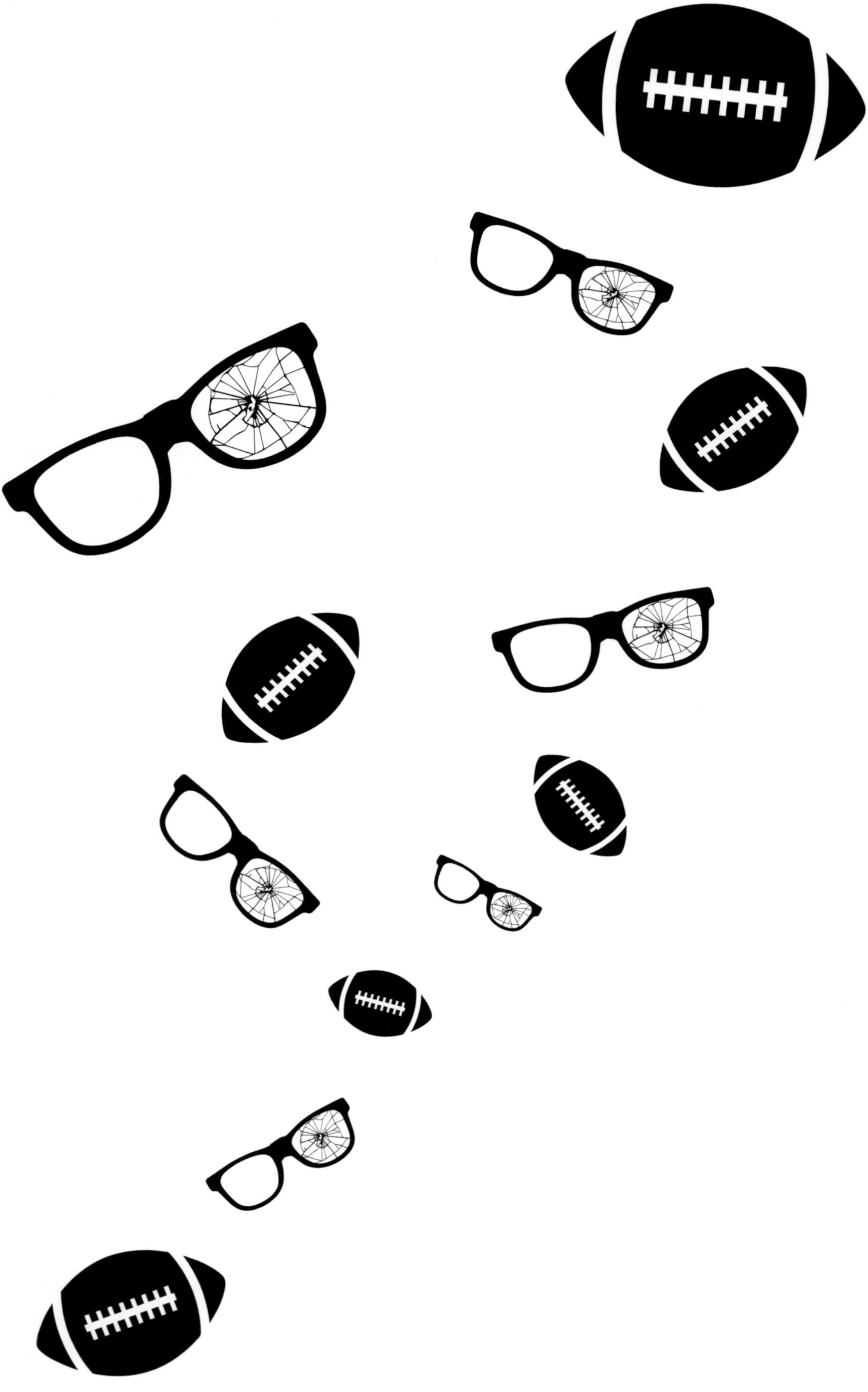

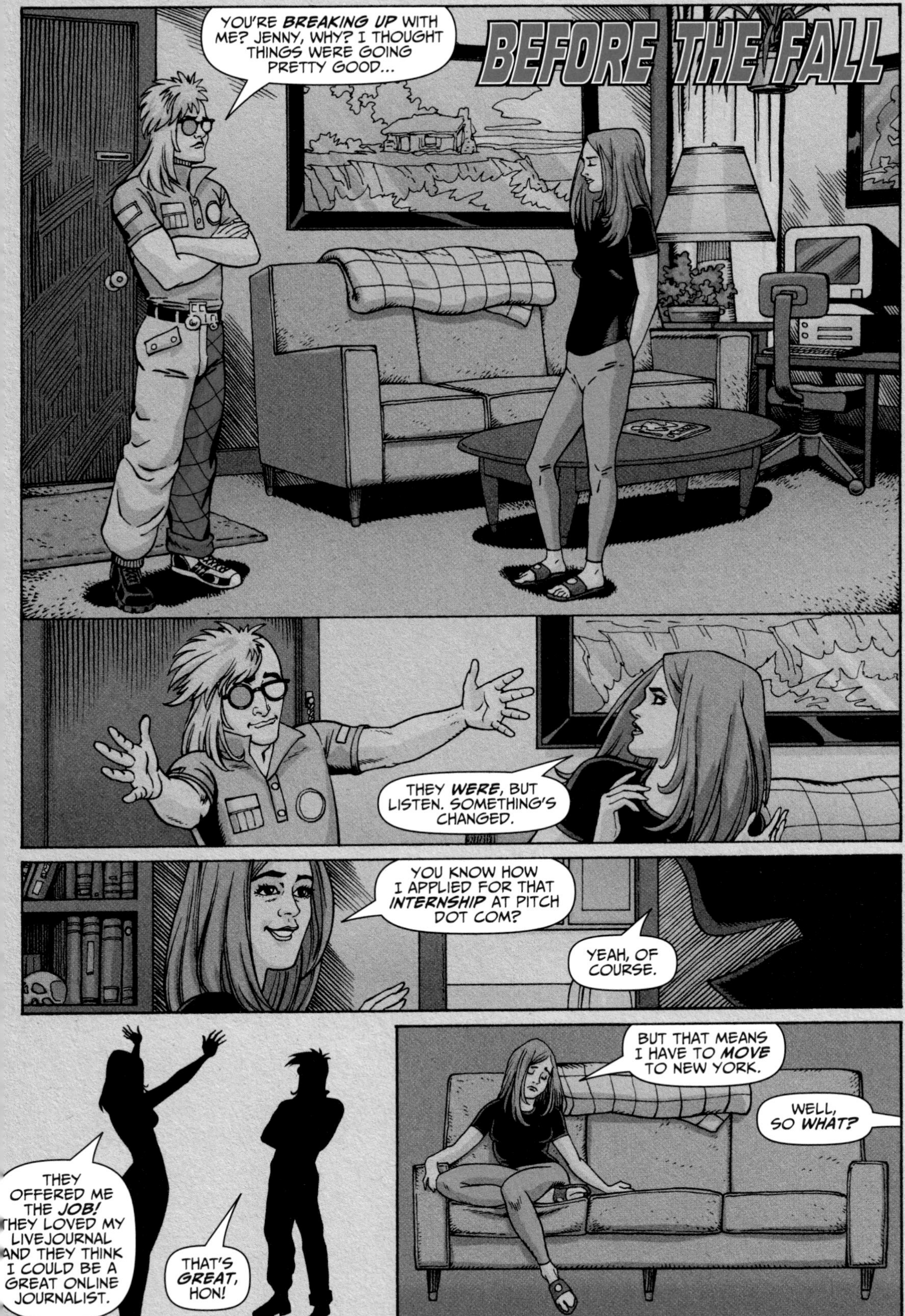

BEFORE THE FALL
YOU'RE BREAKING UP WITH ME? JENNY, WHY? I THOUGHT THINGS WERE GOING PRETTY GOOD...
THEY WERE, BUT LISTEN. SOMETHING'S CHANGED.
YOU KNOW HOW I APPLIED FOR THAT INTERNSHIP AT PITCH DOT COM?
YEAH, OF COURSE.
THEY OFFERED ME THE JOB! THEY LOVED MY LIVEJOURNAL AND THEY THINK I COULD BE A GREAT ONLINE JOURNALIST.
THAT'S GREAT, HON!
BUT THAT MEANS I HAVE TO MOVE TO NEW YORK.
WELL, SO WHAT?

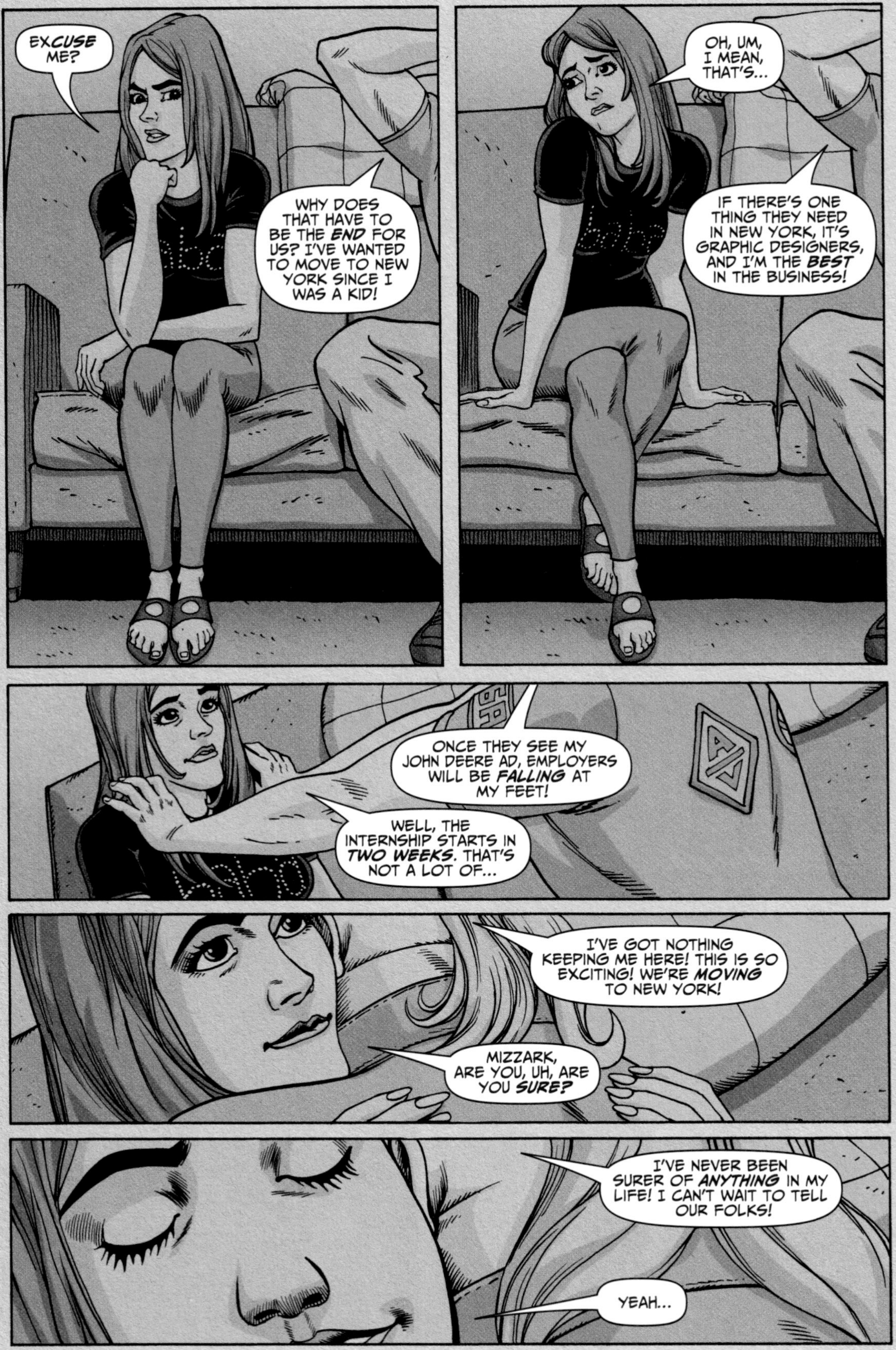
EXCUSE ME?
WHY DOES THAT HAVE TO BE THE END FOR US? I'VE WANTED TO MOVE TO NEW YORK SINCE I WAS A KID!
OH, UM, I MEAN, THAT'S...
IF THERE'S ONE THING THEY NEED IN NEW YORK, IT'S GRAPHIC DESIGNERS, AND I'M THE BEST IN THE BUSINESS!
ONCE THEY SEE MY JOHN DEERE AD, EMPLOYERS WILL BE FALLING AT MY FEET!
WELL, THE INTERNSHIP STARTS IN TWO WEEKS. THAT'S NOT A LOT OF...
I'VE GOT NOTHING KEEPING ME HERE! THIS IS SO EXCITING! WE'RE MOVING TO NEW YORK!
MIZZARK, ARE YOU, UH, ARE YOU SURE?
I'VE NEVER BEEN SURER OF ANYTHING IN MY LIFE! I CAN'T WAIT TO TELL OUR FOLKS!
YEAH...

...THE LOOK ON MY MOM'S FACE WILL BE *PRICELESS.*

THERE SHE IS!

HI, MOM.

OH, *HELLO,* MAZURPHY.

IT'S ACTUALLY *'MIZZARK.'*

RIGHT! BECAUSE YOUR NAME IS REALLY *'MARK.'* I FORGOT.

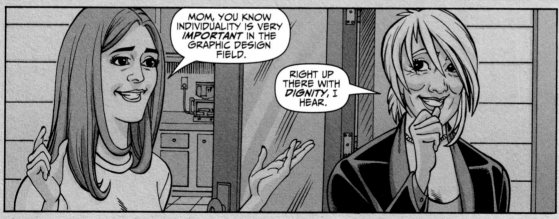

MOM, YOU KNOW INDIVIDUALITY IS VERY *IMPORTANT* IN THE GRAPHIC DESIGN FIELD.

RIGHT UP THERE WITH *DIGNITY,* I HEAR.

MMM, DO I SMELL LASAGNA? CAN'T *WAIT* TO DIG IN!

LOTS OF ARTISTS RENAME THEMSELVES. PRINCE, MADONNA...

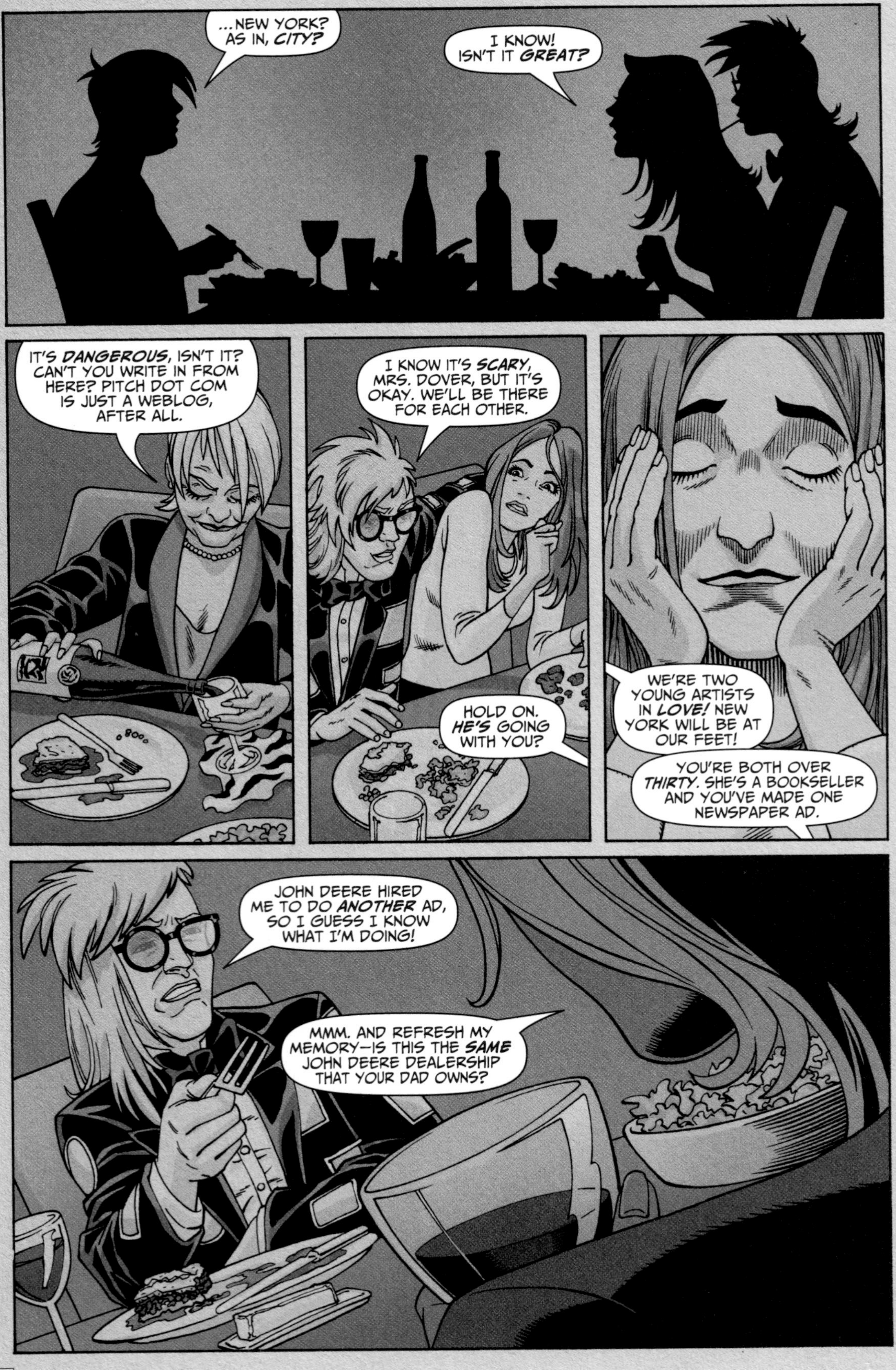
...NEW YORK? AS IN, *CITY?*
I KNOW! ISN'T IT *GREAT?*
IT'S *DANGEROUS,* ISN'T IT? CAN'T YOU WRITE IN FROM HERE? PITCH DOT COM IS JUST A WEBLOG, AFTER ALL.
I KNOW IT'S *SCARY,* MRS. DOVER, BUT IT'S OKAY. WE'LL BE THERE FOR EACH OTHER.
HOLD ON. *HE'S* GOING WITH YOU?
WE'RE TWO YOUNG ARTISTS IN *LOVE!* NEW YORK WILL BE AT OUR FEET!
YOU'RE BOTH OVER *THIRTY.* SHE'S A BOOKSELLER AND YOU'VE MADE ONE NEWSPAPER AD.
JOHN DEERE HIRED ME TO DO *ANOTHER* AD, SO I GUESS I KNOW WHAT I'M DOING!
MMM. AND REFRESH MY MEMORY—IS THIS THE *SAME* JOHN DEERE DEALERSHIP THAT YOUR DAD OWNS?

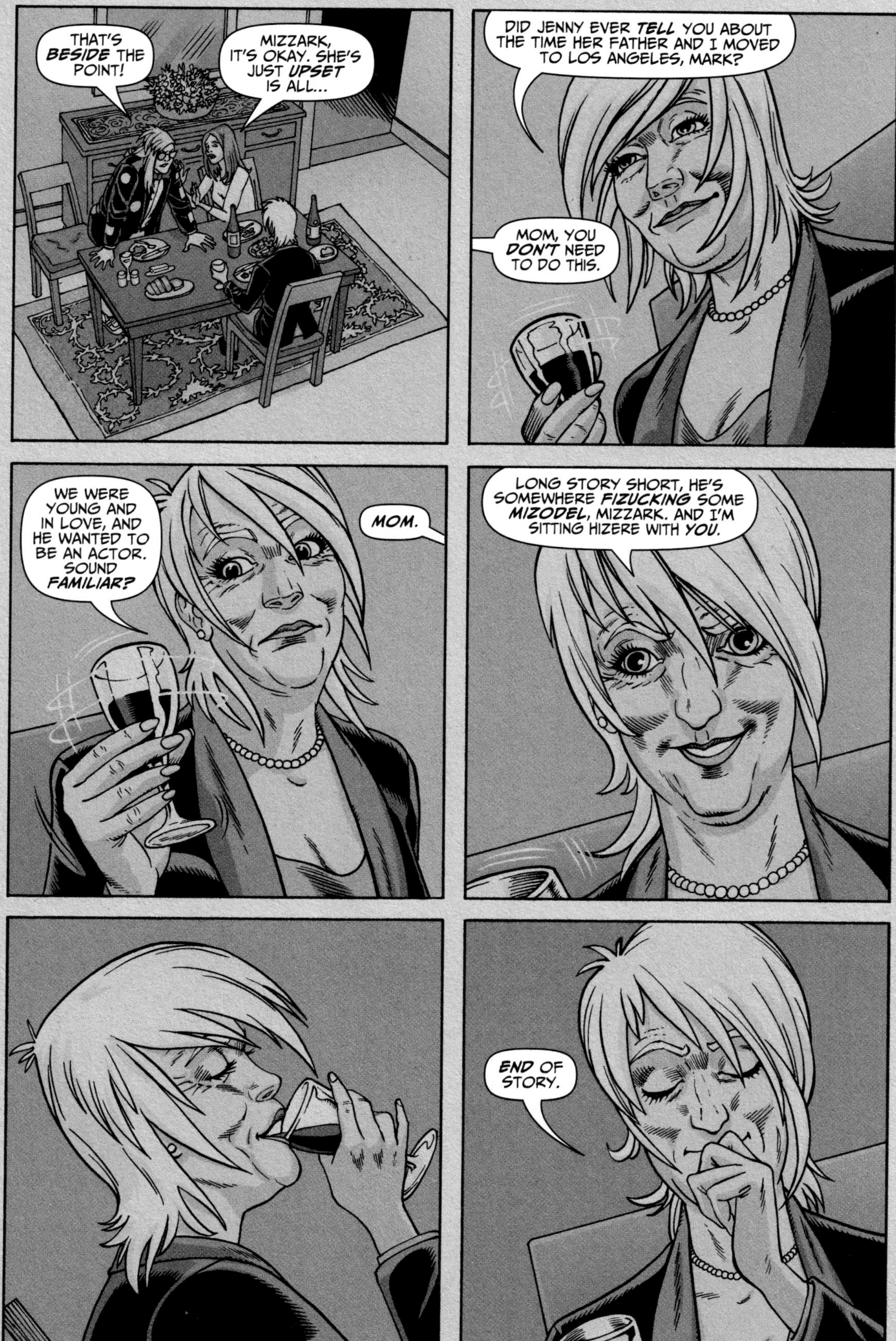
THAT'S *BESIDE* THE POINT!
MIZZARK, IT'S OKAY. SHE'S JUST *UPSET* IS ALL...
DID JENNY EVER *TELL* YOU ABOUT THE TIME HER FATHER AND I MOVED TO LOS ANGELES, MARK?
MOM, YOU *DON'T* NEED TO DO THIS.
WE WERE YOUNG AND IN LOVE, AND HE WANTED TO BE AN ACTOR. SOUND *FAMILIAR?*
MOM.
LONG STORY SHORT, HE'S SOMEWHERE *FIZUCKING* SOME *MIZODEL*, MIZZARK. AND I'M SITTING HIZERE WITH *YOU*.
END OF STORY.

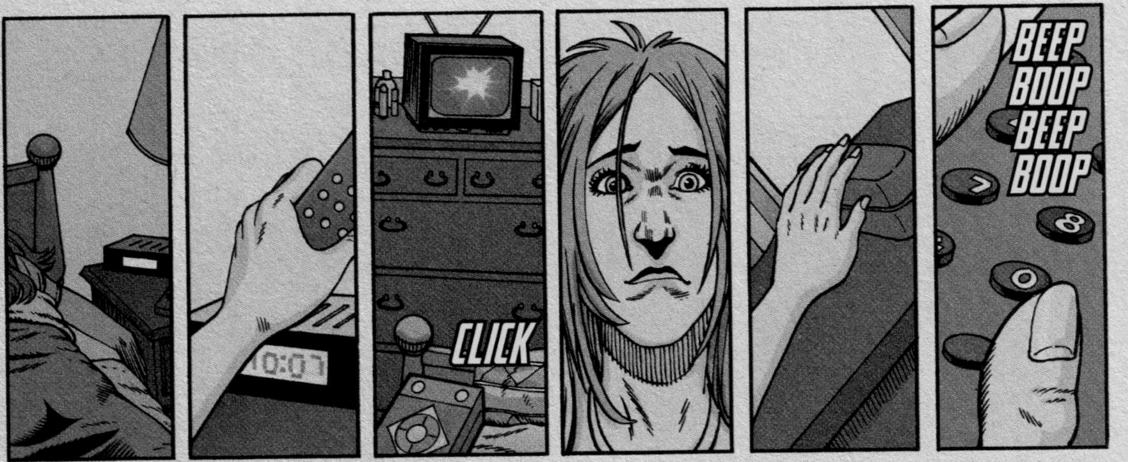
CLICK
BEEP
BOOP
BEEP
BOOP

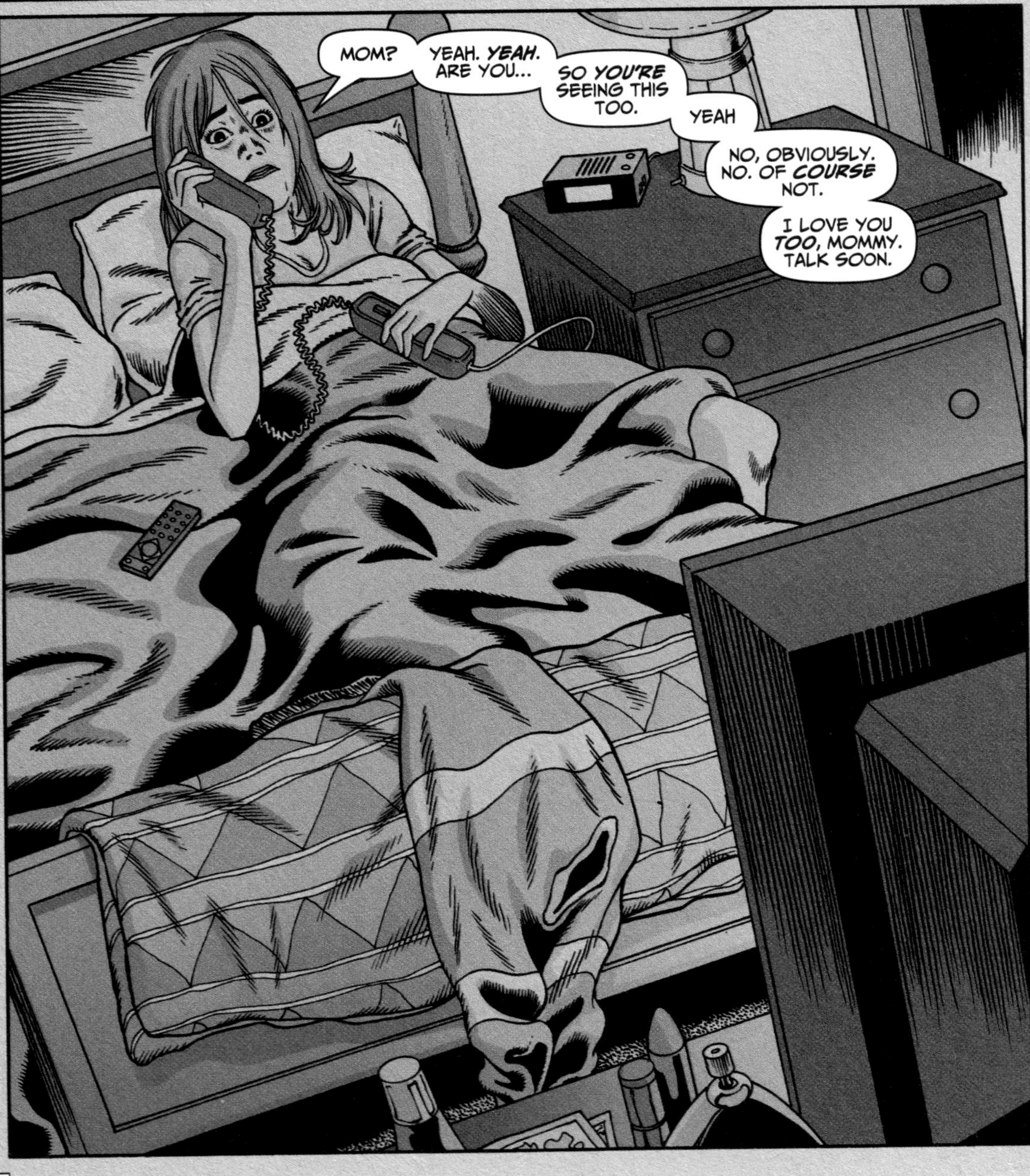
MOM?
YEAH. *YEAH.* ARE YOU...
SO *YOU'RE* SEEING THIS TOO.
YEAH
NO, OBVIOUSLY. NO. OF *COURSE* NOT.
I LOVE YOU *TOO*, MOMMY. TALK SOON.

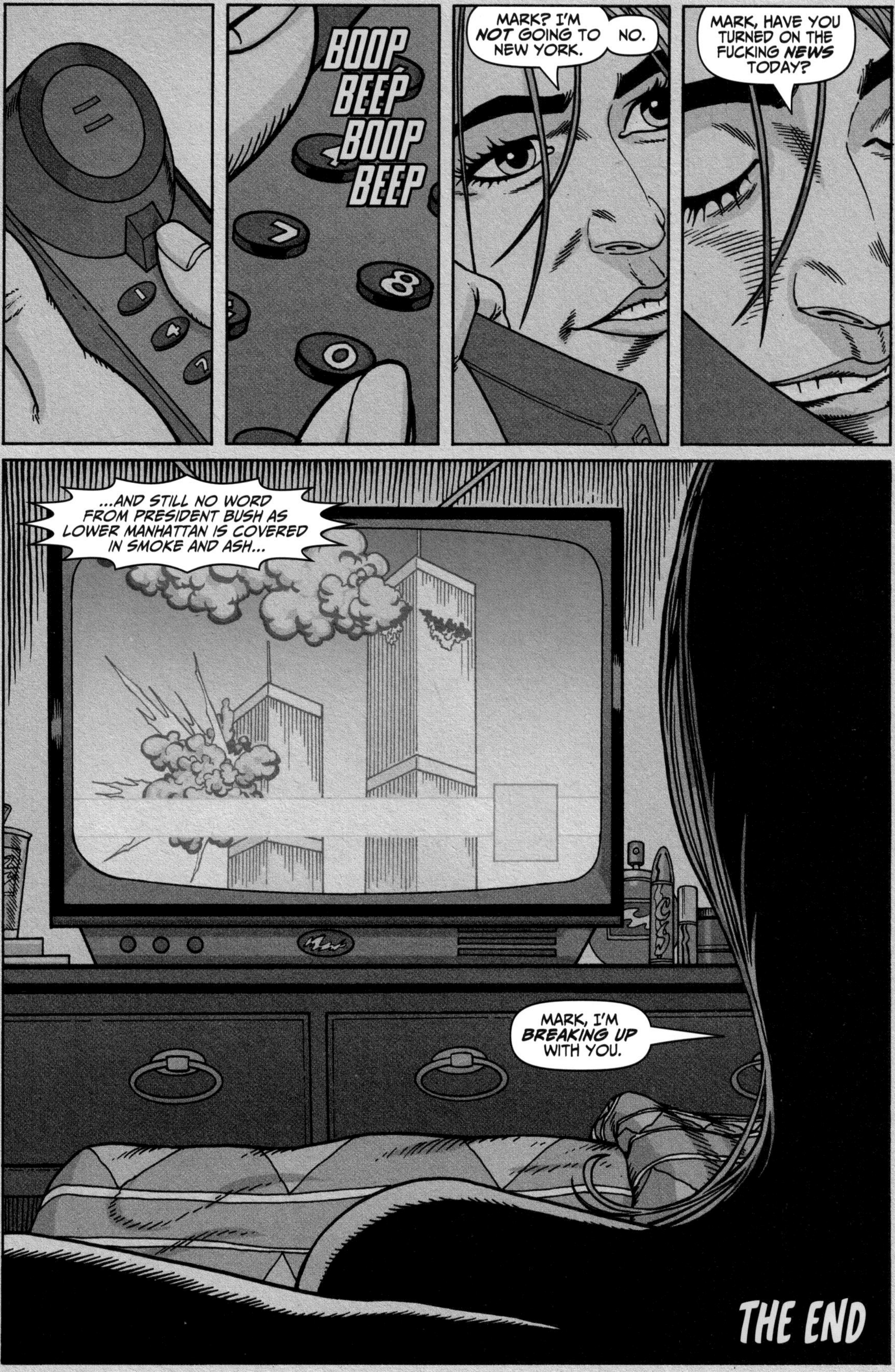
BOOP BEEP BOOP BEEP
MARK? I'M NOT GOING TO NEW YORK.
NO.
MARK, HAVE YOU TURNED ON THE FUCKING NEWS TODAY?
...AND STILL NO WORD FROM PRESIDENT BUSH AS LOWER MANHATTAN IS COVERED IN SMOKE AND ASH...
MARK, I'M BREAKING UP WITH YOU.
THE END

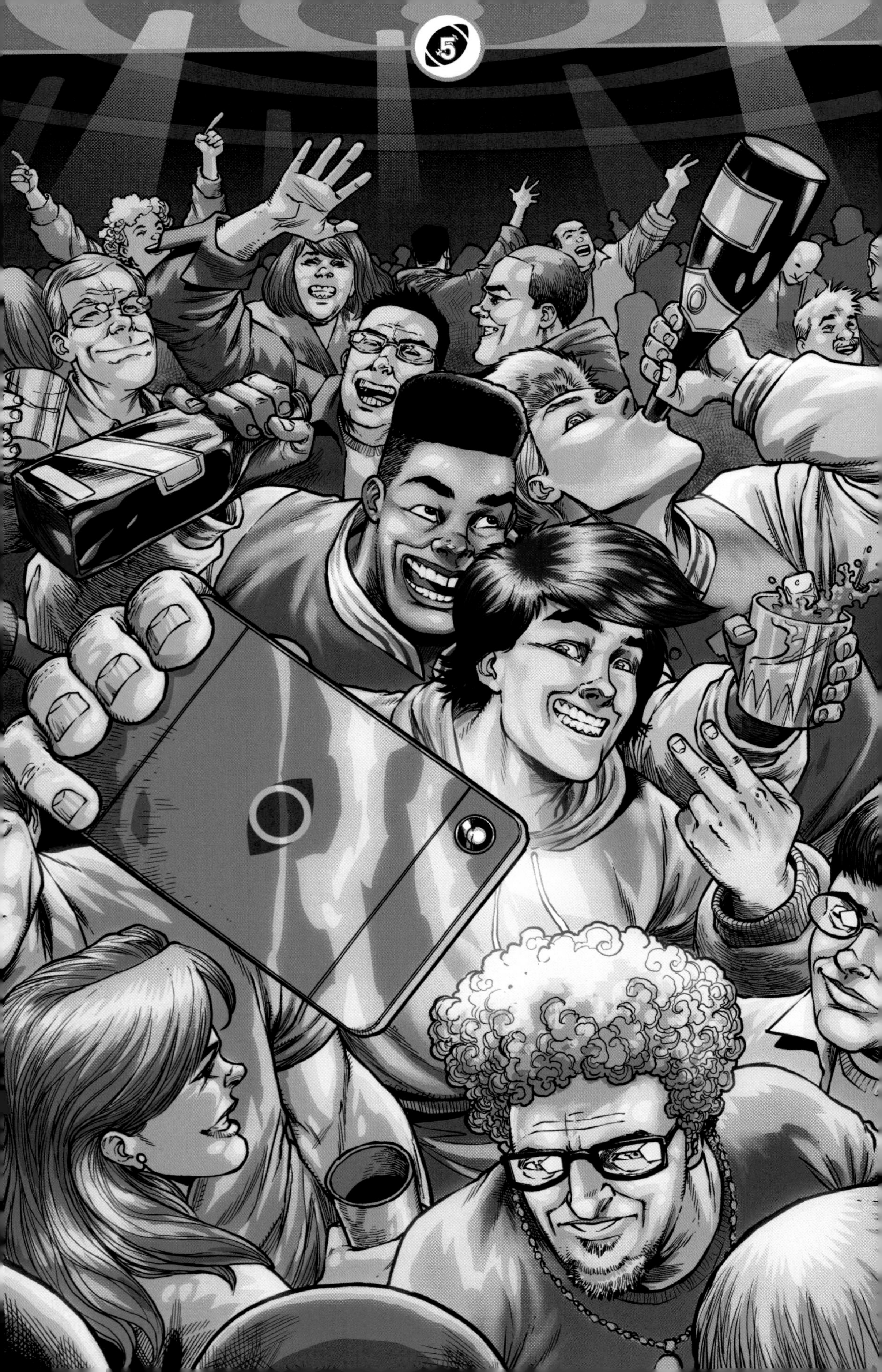
5

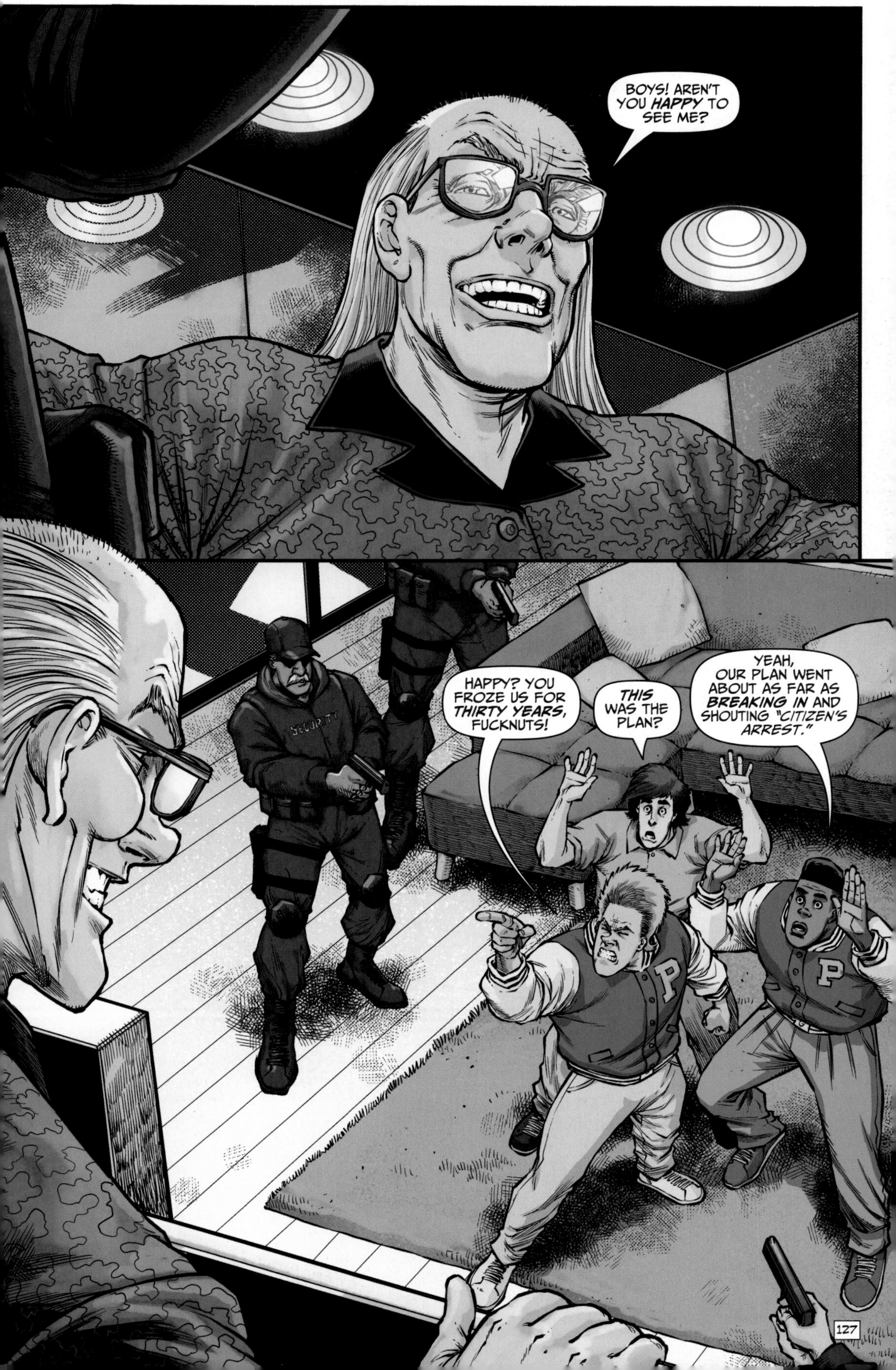
BOYS! AREN'T YOU HAPPY TO SEE ME?
SECURITY
HAPPY? YOU FROZE US FOR THIRTY YEARS, FUCKNUTS!
THIS WAS THE PLAN?
YEAH, OUR PLAN WENT ABOUT AS FAR AS BREAKING IN AND SHOUTING "CITIZEN'S ARREST."

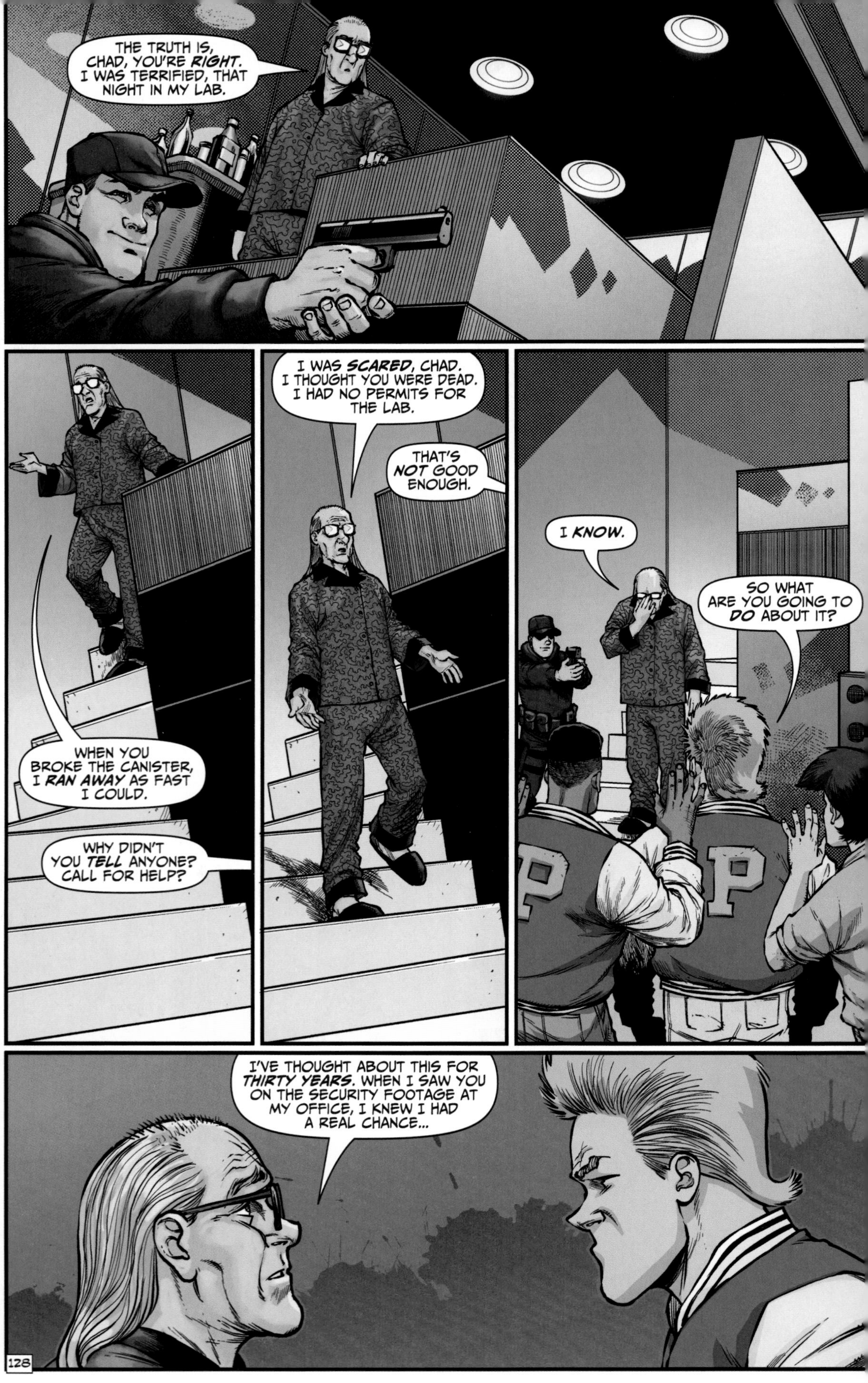
THE TRUTH IS, CHAD, YOU'RE RIGHT. I WAS TERRIFIED, THAT NIGHT IN MY LAB.
WHEN YOU BROKE THE CANISTER, I RAN AWAY AS FAST I COULD.
WHY DIDN'T YOU TELL ANYONE? CALL FOR HELP?
I WAS SCARED, CHAD. I THOUGHT YOU WERE DEAD. I HAD NO PERMITS FOR THE LAB.
THAT'S NOT GOOD ENOUGH.
I KNOW.
SO WHAT ARE YOU GOING TO DO ABOUT IT?
I'VE THOUGHT ABOUT THIS FOR THIRTY YEARS. WHEN I SAW YOU ON THE SECURITY FOOTAGE AT MY OFFICE, I KNEW I HAD A REAL CHANCE...

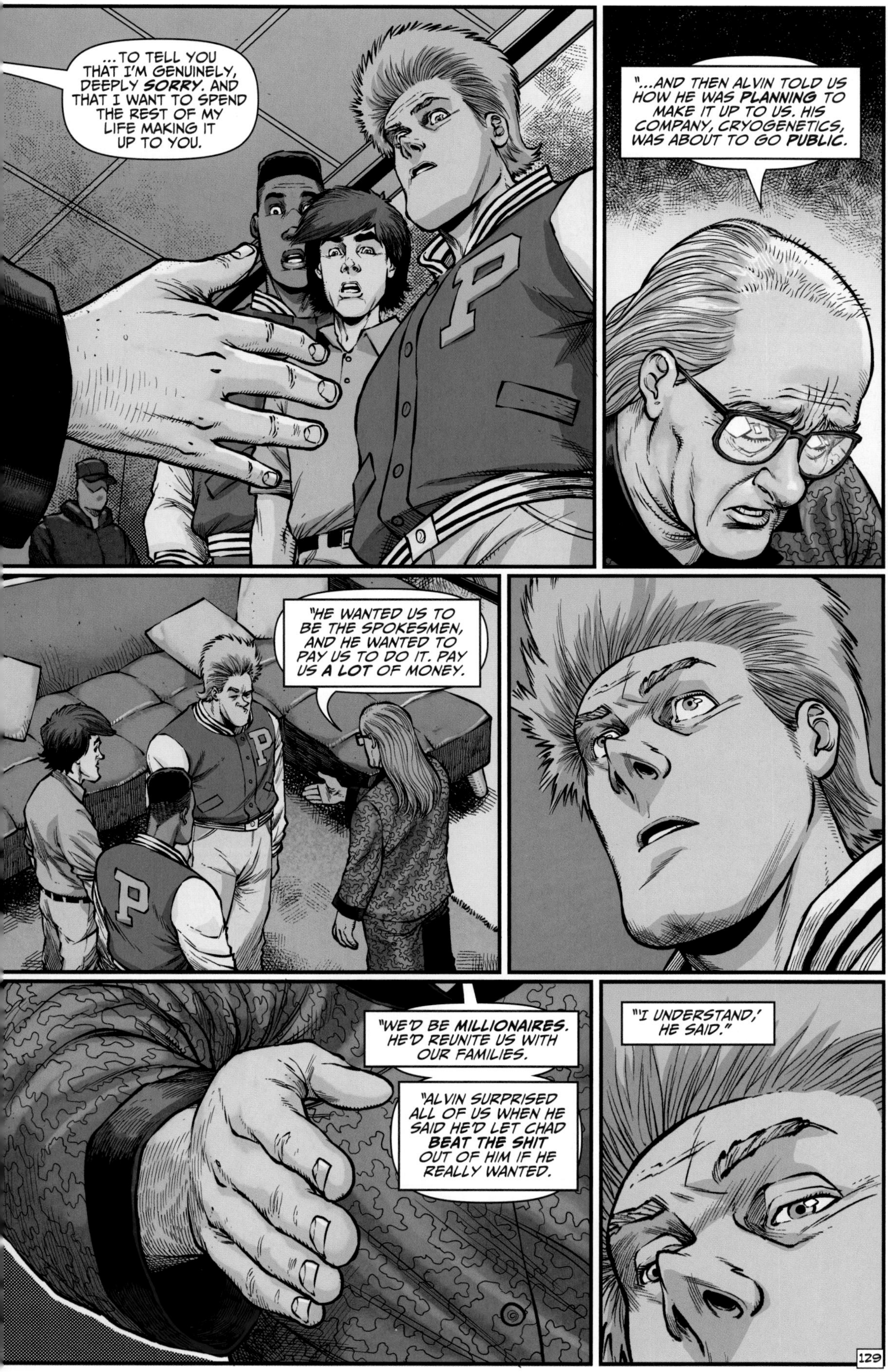
...TO TELL YOU THAT I'M GENUINELY, DEEPLY SORRY. AND THAT I WANT TO SPEND THE REST OF MY LIFE MAKING IT UP TO YOU.
"...AND THEN ALVIN TOLD US HOW HE WAS PLANNING TO MAKE IT UP TO US. HIS COMPANY, CRYOGENETICS, WAS ABOUT TO GO PUBLIC.
"HE WANTED US TO BE THE SPOKESMEN, AND HE WANTED TO PAY US TO DO IT. PAY US A LOT OF MONEY.
"WE'D BE MILLIONAIRES. HE'D REUNITE US WITH OUR FAMILIES.
"ALVIN SURPRISED ALL OF US WHEN HE SAID HE'D LET CHAD BEAT THE SHIT OUT OF HIM IF HE REALLY WANTED.
"'I UNDERSTAND,' HE SAID."

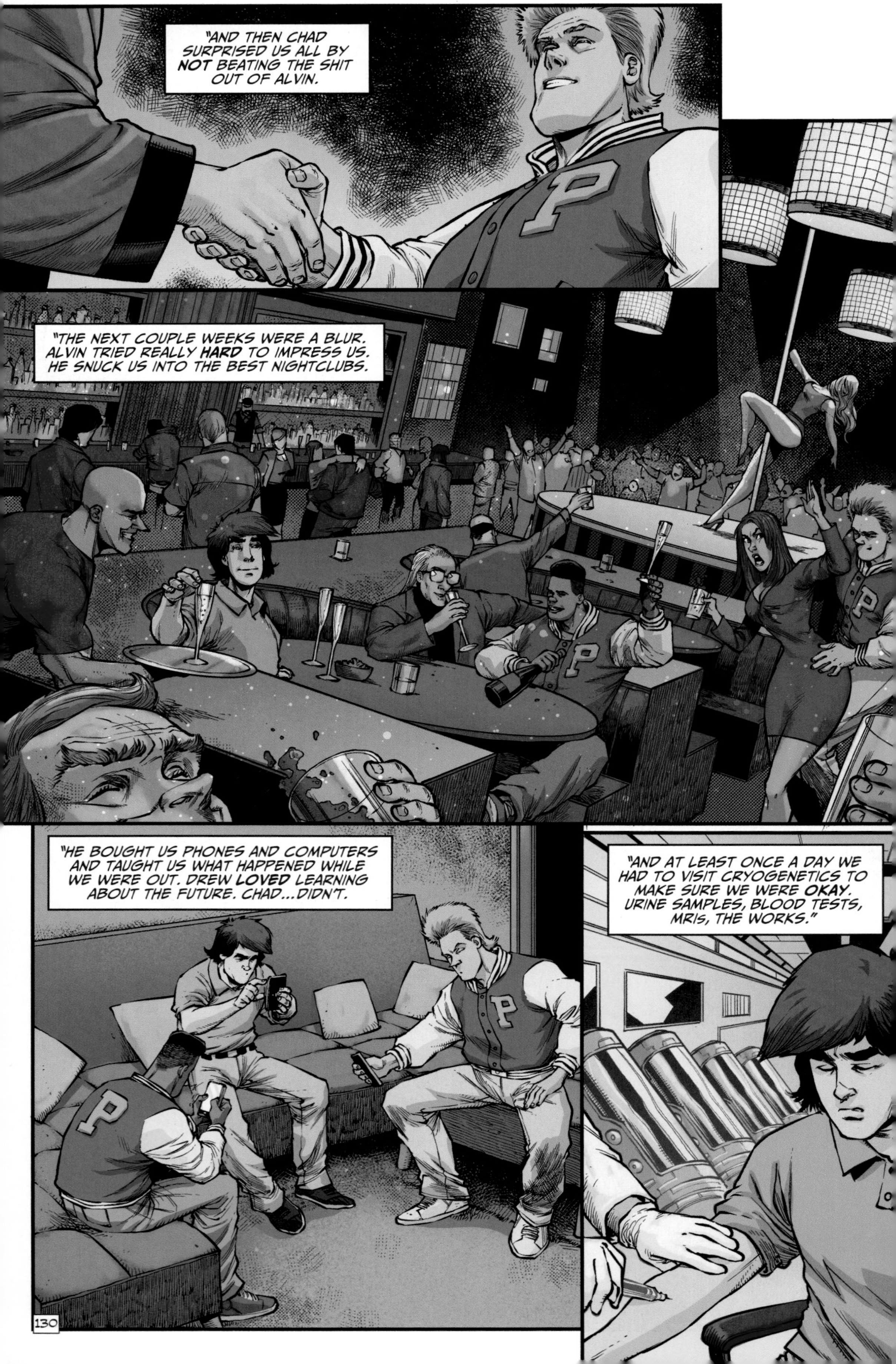
"AND THEN CHAD SURPRISED US ALL BY NOT BEATING THE SHIT OUT OF ALVIN.
"THE NEXT COUPLE WEEKS WERE A BLUR. ALVIN TRIED REALLY HARD TO IMPRESS US. HE SNUCK US INTO THE BEST NIGHTCLUBS.
"HE BOUGHT US PHONES AND COMPUTERS AND TAUGHT US WHAT HAPPENED WHILE WE WERE OUT. DREW LOVED LEARNING ABOUT THE FUTURE. CHAD...DIDN'T.
"AND AT LEAST ONCE A DAY WE HAD TO VISIT CRYOGENETICS TO MAKE SURE WE WERE OKAY. URINE SAMPLES, BLOOD TESTS, MRIS, THE WORKS."

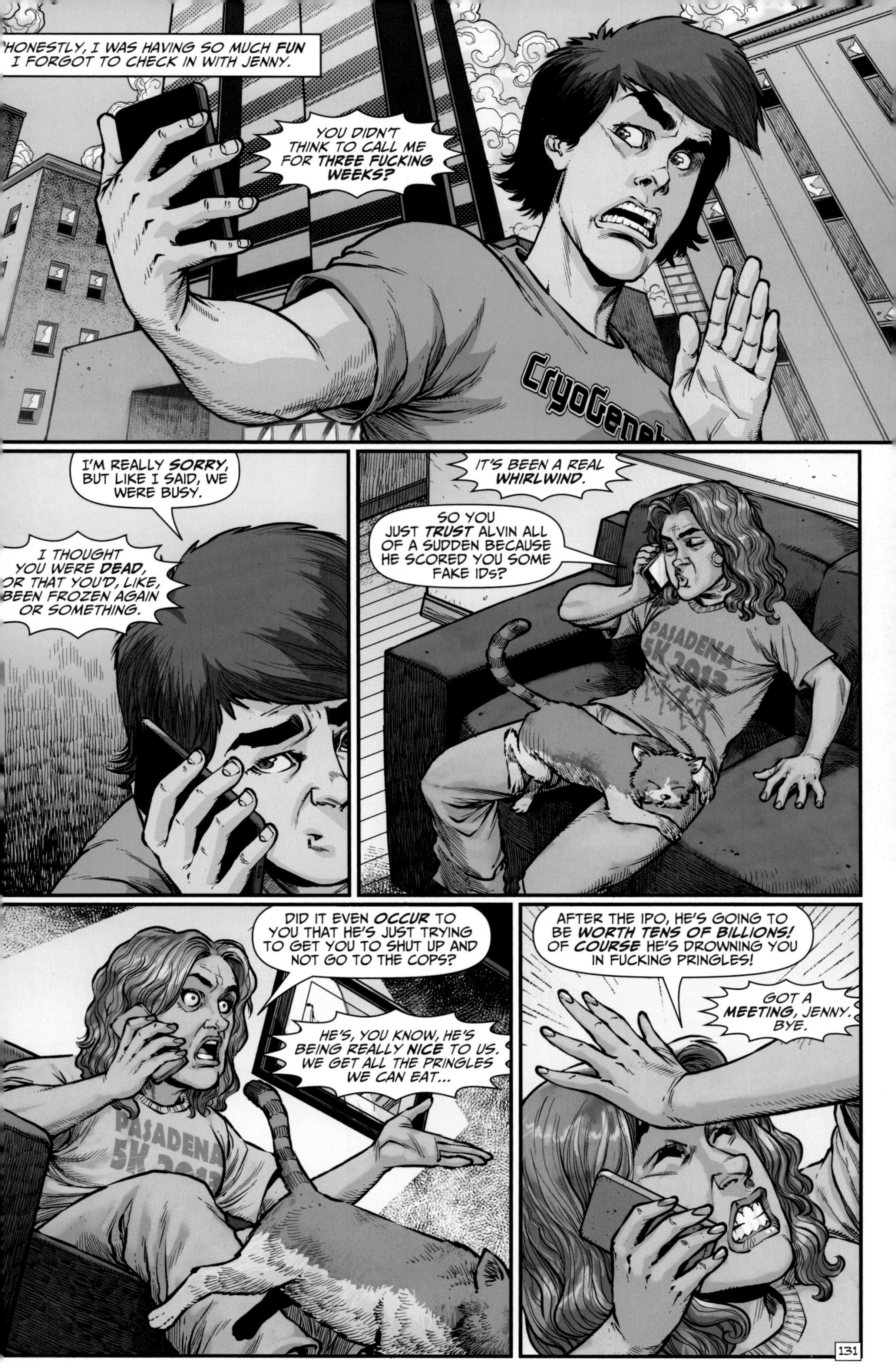
HONESTLY, I WAS HAVING SO MUCH FUN I FORGOT TO CHECK IN WITH JENNY.
YOU DIDN'T THINK TO CALL ME FOR THREE FUCKING WEEKS?
CryoGenet
I'M REALLY SORRY, BUT LIKE I SAID, WE WERE BUSY.
I THOUGHT YOU WERE DEAD, OR THAT YOU'D, LIKE, BEEN FROZEN AGAIN OR SOMETHING.
IT'S BEEN A REAL WHIRLWIND.
SO YOU JUST TRUST ALVIN ALL OF A SUDDEN BECAUSE HE SCORED YOU SOME FAKE IDS?
PASADENA 5K 2013
DID IT EVEN OCCUR TO YOU THAT HE'S JUST TRYING TO GET YOU TO SHUT UP AND NOT GO TO THE COPS?
HE'S, YOU KNOW, HE'S BEING REALLY NICE TO US. WE GET ALL THE PRINGLES WE CAN EAT...
AFTER THE IPO, HE'S GOING TO BE WORTH TENS OF BILLIONS! OF COURSE HE'S DROWNING YOU IN FUCKING PRINGLES!
GOT A MEETING, JENNY. BYE.

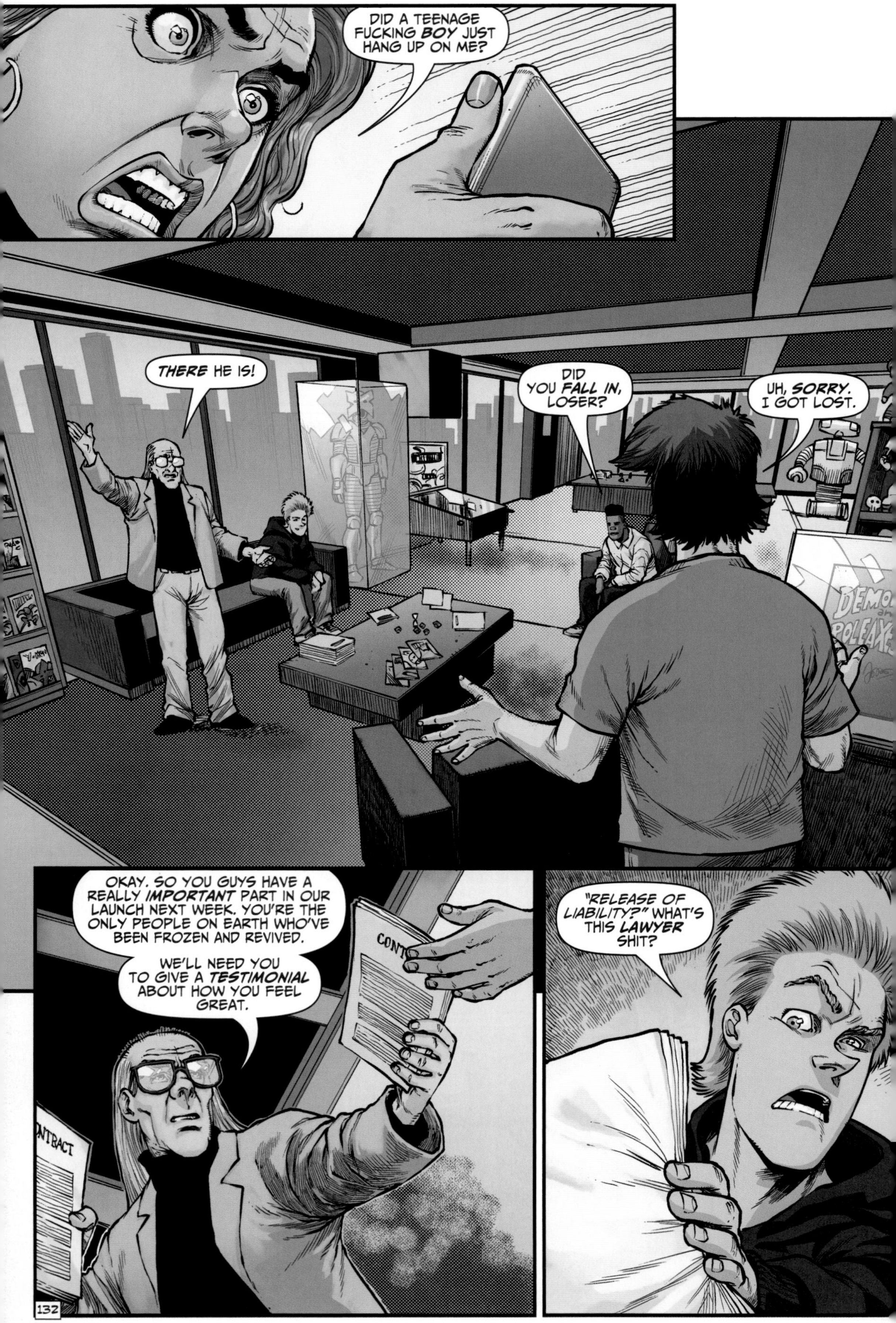
DID A TEENAGE FUCKING BOY JUST HANG UP ON ME?
THERE HE IS!
DID YOU FALL IN, LOSER?
UH, SORRY. I GOT LOST.
OKAY. SO YOU GUYS HAVE A REALLY IMPORTANT PART IN OUR LAUNCH NEXT WEEK. YOU'RE THE ONLY PEOPLE ON EARTH WHO'VE BEEN FROZEN AND REVIVED.
WE'LL NEED YOU TO GIVE A TESTIMONIAL ABOUT HOW YOU FEEL GREAT.
"RELEASE OF LIABILITY?" WHAT'S THIS LAWYER SHIT?

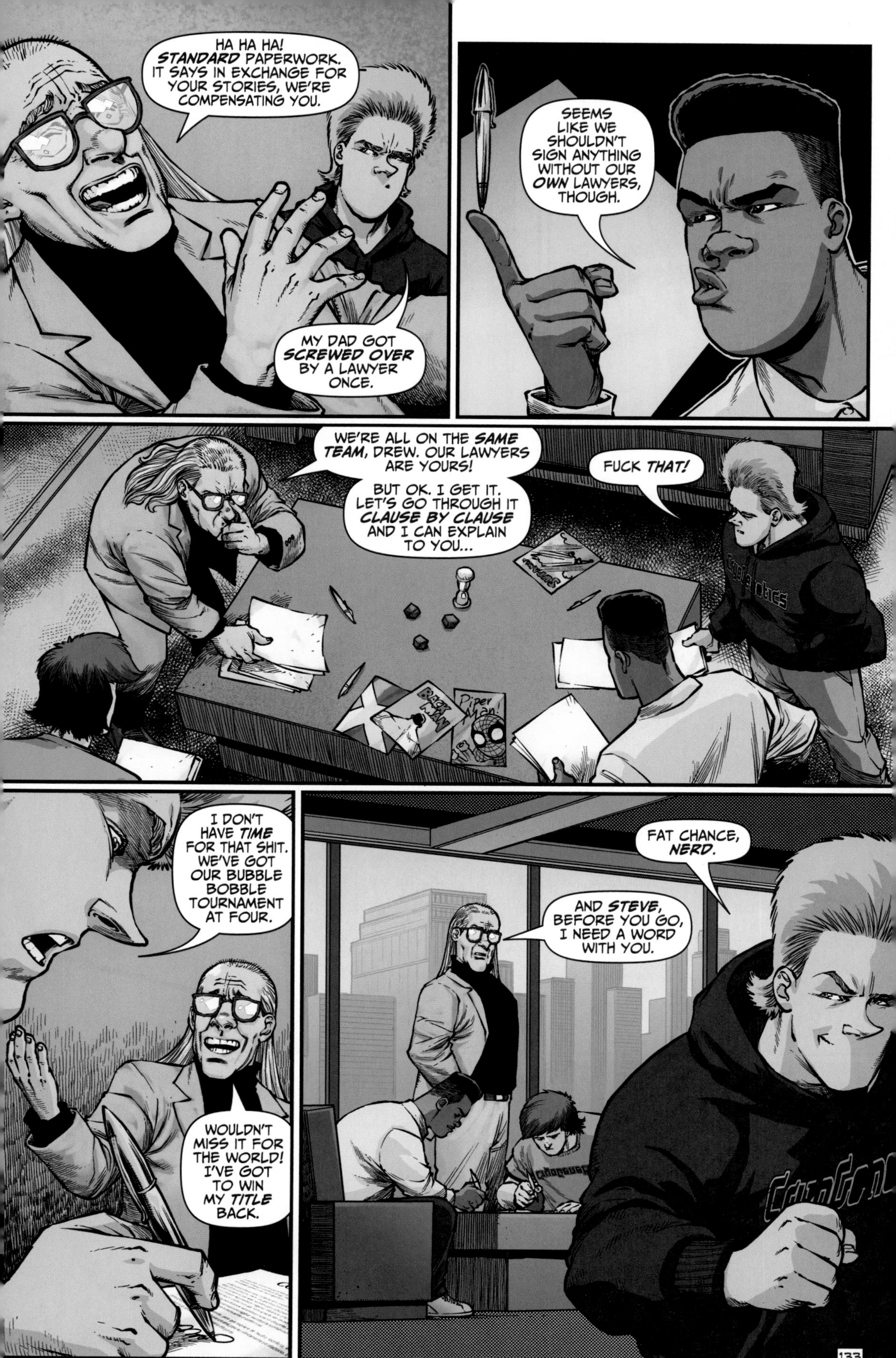

HA HA HA! STANDARD PAPERWORK. IT SAYS IN EXCHANGE FOR YOUR STORIES, WE'RE COMPENSATING YOU.
MY DAD GOT SCREWED OVER BY A LAWYER ONCE.
SEEMS LIKE WE SHOULDN'T SIGN ANYTHING WITHOUT OUR OWN LAWYERS, THOUGH.
WE'RE ALL ON THE SAME TEAM, DREW. OUR LAWYERS ARE YOURS!
BUT OK. I GET IT. LET'S GO THROUGH IT CLAUSE BY CLAUSE AND I CAN EXPLAIN TO YOU...
FUCK THAT!
Piper Man!
I DON'T HAVE TIME FOR THAT SHIT. WE'VE GOT OUR BUBBLE BOBBLE TOURNAMENT AT FOUR.
WOULDN'T MISS IT FOR THE WORLD! I'VE GOT TO WIN MY TITLE BACK.
FAT CHANCE, NERD.
AND STEVE, BEFORE YOU GO, I NEED A WORD WITH YOU.

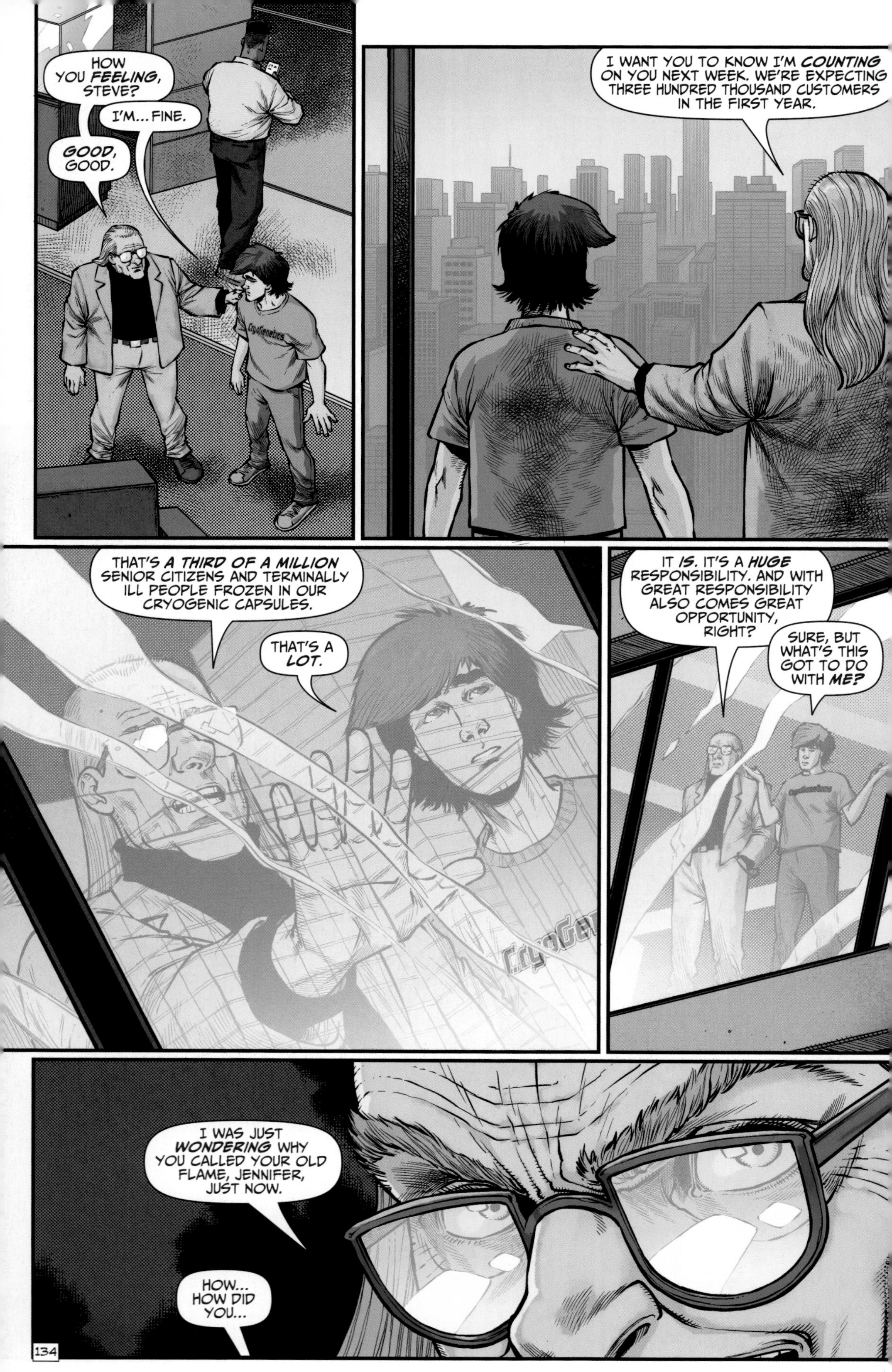
HOW YOU FEELING, STEVE?
I'M... FINE.
GOOD, GOOD.
I WANT YOU TO KNOW I'M COUNTING ON YOU NEXT WEEK. WE'RE EXPECTING THREE HUNDRED THOUSAND CUSTOMERS IN THE FIRST YEAR.
THAT'S A THIRD OF A MILLION SENIOR CITIZENS AND TERMINALLY ILL PEOPLE FROZEN IN OUR CRYOGENIC CAPSULES.
THAT'S A LOT.
IT IS. IT'S A HUGE RESPONSIBILITY. AND WITH GREAT RESPONSIBILITY ALSO COMES GREAT OPPORTUNITY, RIGHT?
SURE, BUT WHAT'S THIS GOT TO DO WITH ME?
I WAS JUST WONDERING WHY YOU CALLED YOUR OLD FLAME, JENNIFER, JUST NOW.
HOW... HOW DID YOU...

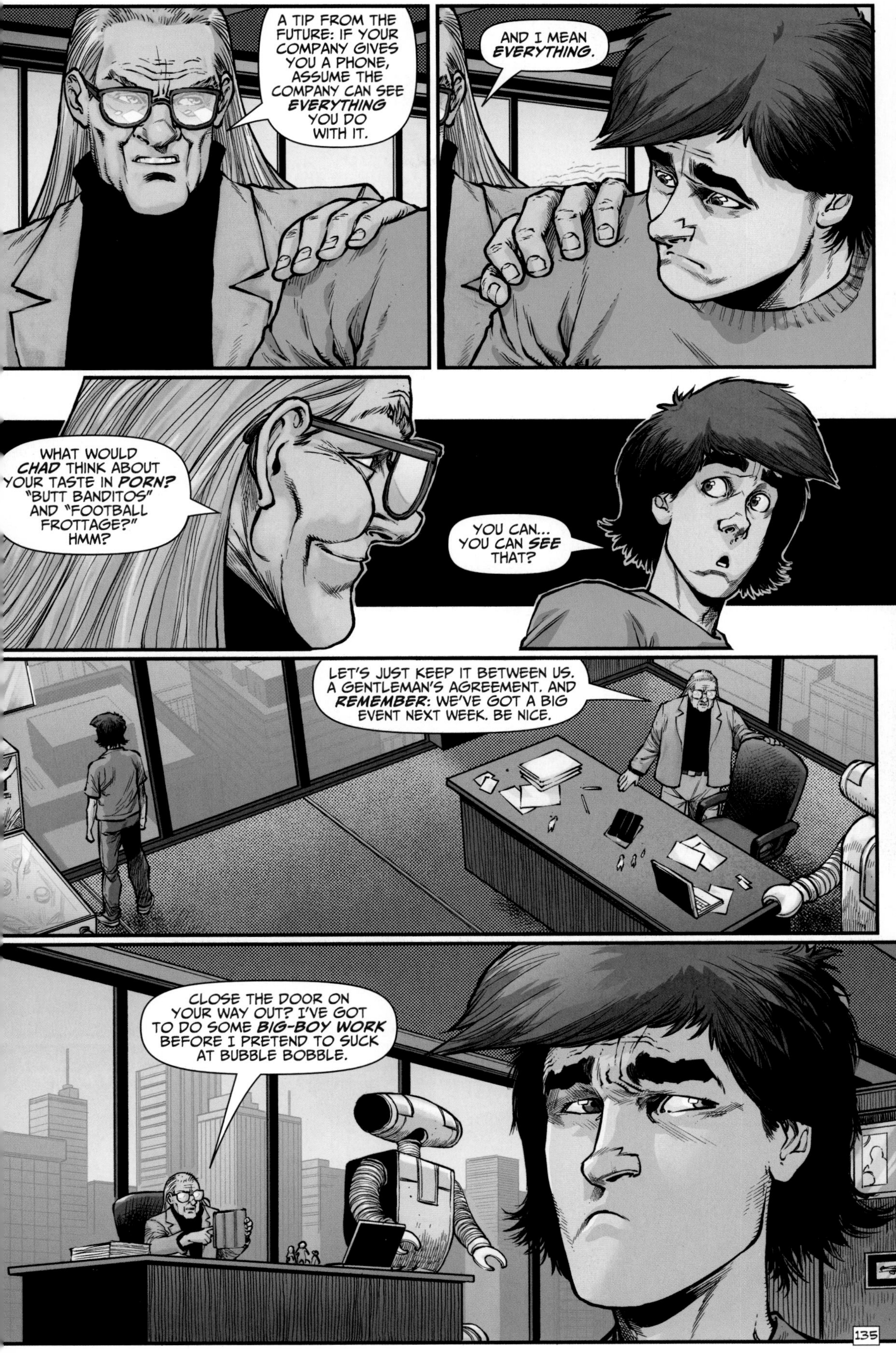
A TIP FROM THE FUTURE: IF YOUR COMPANY GIVES YOU A PHONE, ASSUME THE COMPANY CAN SEE *EVERYTHING* YOU DO WITH IT.
AND I MEAN *EVERYTHING*.
WHAT WOULD *CHAD* THINK ABOUT YOUR TASTE IN *PORN?* "BUTT BANDITOS" AND "FOOTBALL FROTTAGE?" HMM?
YOU CAN... YOU CAN *SEE* THAT?
LET'S JUST KEEP IT BETWEEN US. A GENTLEMAN'S AGREEMENT. AND *REMEMBER*: WE'VE GOT A BIG EVENT NEXT WEEK. BE NICE.
CLOSE THE DOOR ON YOUR WAY OUT? I'VE GOT TO DO SOME *BIG-BOY WORK* BEFORE I PRETEND TO SUCK AT BUBBLE BOBBLE.

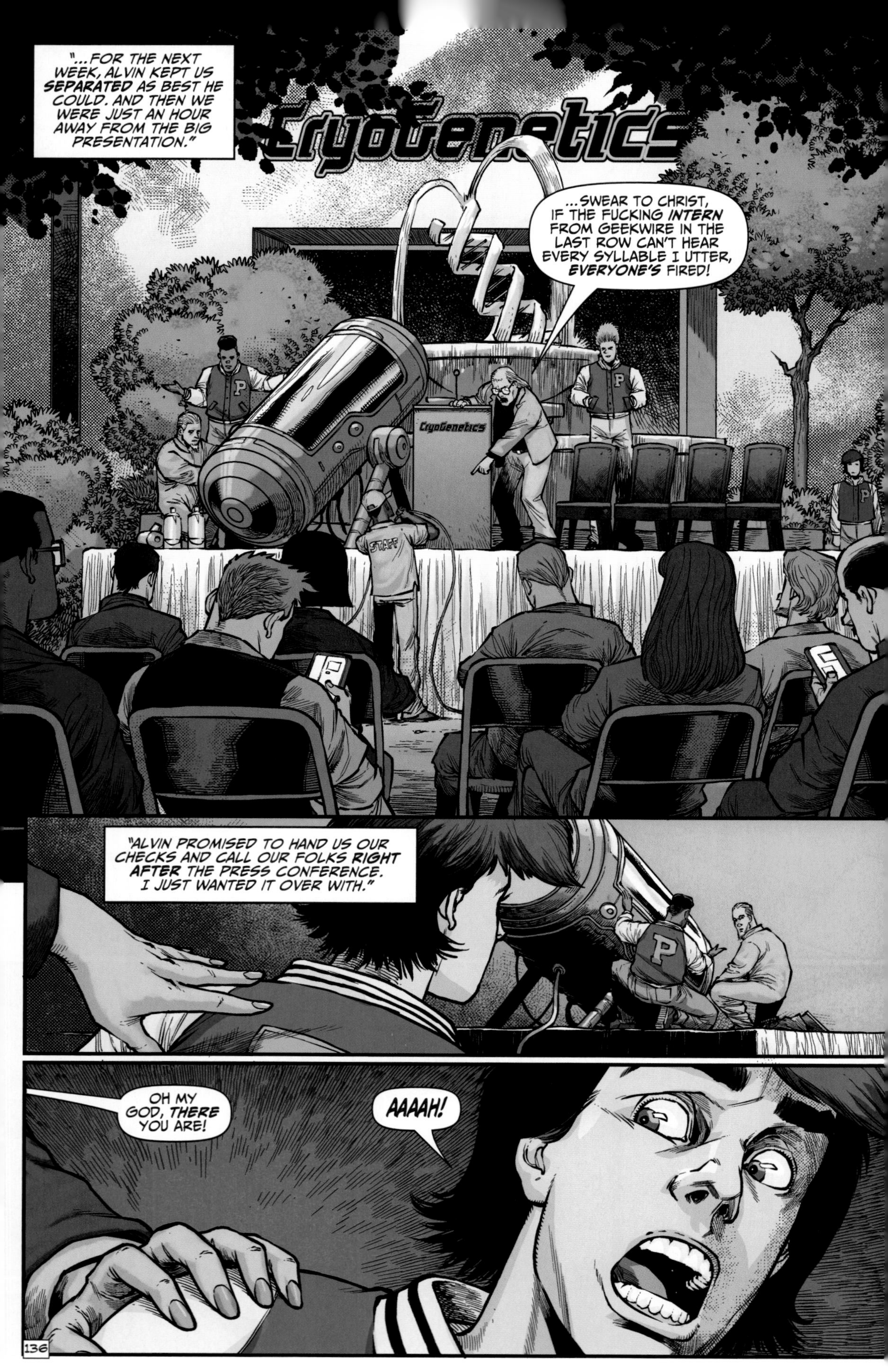
"...FOR THE NEXT WEEK, ALVIN KEPT US SEPARATED AS BEST HE COULD. AND THEN WE WERE JUST AN HOUR AWAY FROM THE BIG PRESENTATION."
CryoGenetics
...SWEAR TO CHRIST, IF THE FUCKING INTERN FROM GEEKWIRE IN THE LAST ROW CAN'T HEAR EVERY SYLLABLE I UTTER, EVERYONE'S FIRED!
CryoGenetics
STAFF
"ALVIN PROMISED TO HAND US OUR CHECKS AND CALL OUR FOLKS RIGHT AFTER THE PRESS CONFERENCE. I JUST WANTED IT OVER WITH."
OH MY GOD, THERE YOU ARE!
AAAAH!

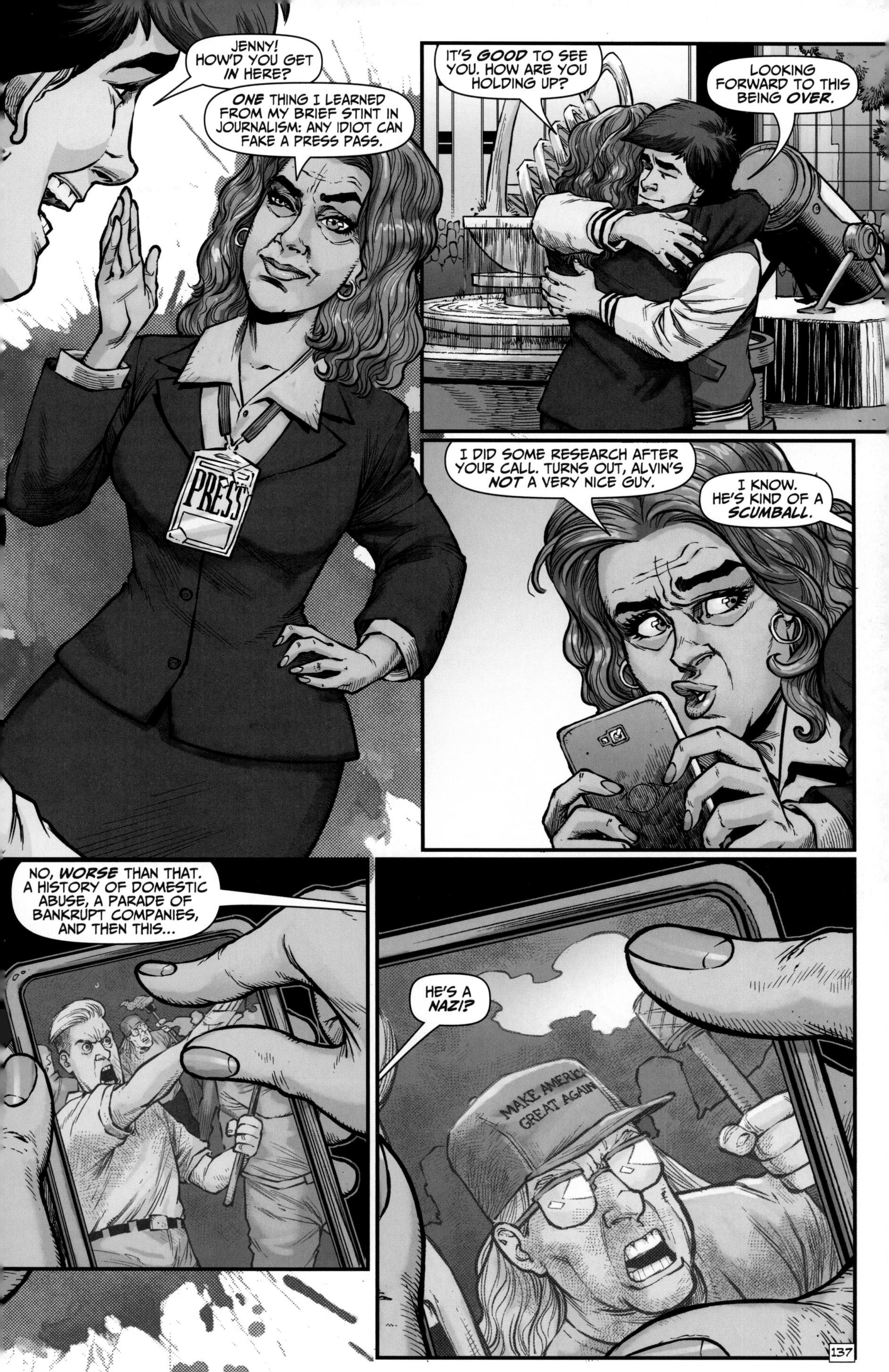

JENNY! HOW'D YOU GET IN HERE?
ONE THING I LEARNED FROM MY BRIEF STINT IN JOURNALISM: ANY IDIOT CAN FAKE A PRESS PASS.
PRESS
IT'S GOOD TO SEE YOU. HOW ARE YOU HOLDING UP?
LOOKING FORWARD TO THIS BEING OVER.
I DID SOME RESEARCH AFTER YOUR CALL. TURNS OUT, ALVIN'S NOT A VERY NICE GUY.
I KNOW. HE'S KIND OF A SCUMBALL.
NO, WORSE THAN THAT. A HISTORY OF DOMESTIC ABUSE, A PARADE OF BANKRUPT COMPANIES, AND THEN THIS...
HE'S A NAZI?
MAKE AMERICA GREAT AGAIN

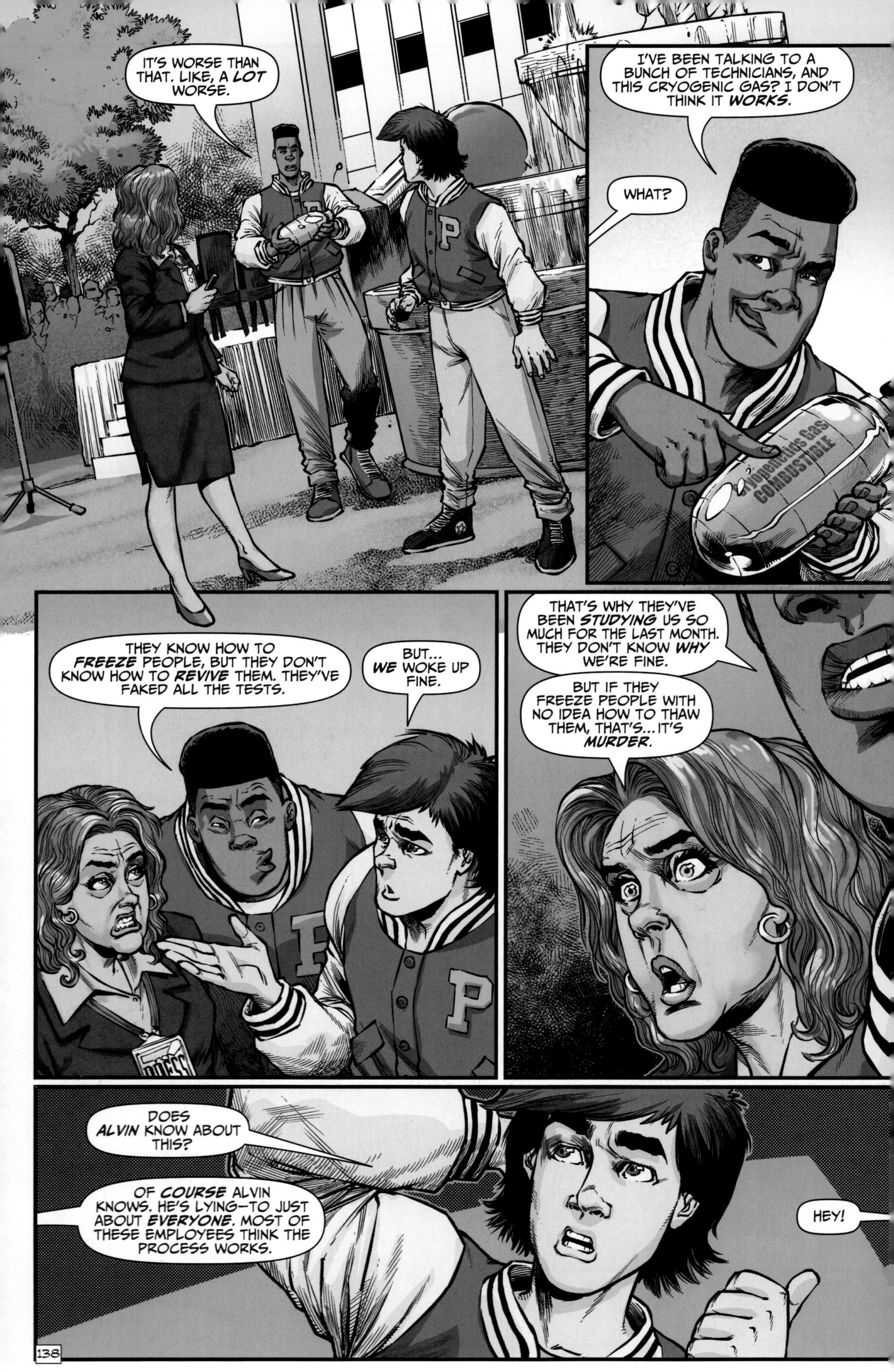
IT'S WORSE THAN THAT. LIKE, A LOT WORSE.
I'VE BEEN TALKING TO A BUNCH OF TECHNICIANS, AND THIS CRYOGENIC GAS? I DON'T THINK IT WORKS.
WHAT?
Cryogenics Gas
COMBUSTIBLE
THEY KNOW HOW TO FREEZE PEOPLE, BUT THEY DON'T KNOW HOW TO REVIVE THEM. THEY'VE FAKED ALL THE TESTS.
BUT... WE WOKE UP FINE.
THAT'S WHY THEY'VE BEEN STUDYING US SO MUCH FOR THE LAST MONTH. THEY DON'T KNOW WHY WE'RE FINE.
BUT IF THEY FREEZE PEOPLE WITH NO IDEA HOW TO THAW THEM, THAT'S... IT'S MURDER.
DOES ALVIN KNOW ABOUT THIS?
OF COURSE ALVIN KNOWS. HE'S LYING—TO JUST ABOUT EVERYONE. MOST OF THESE EMPLOYEES THINK THE PROCESS WORKS.
HEY!

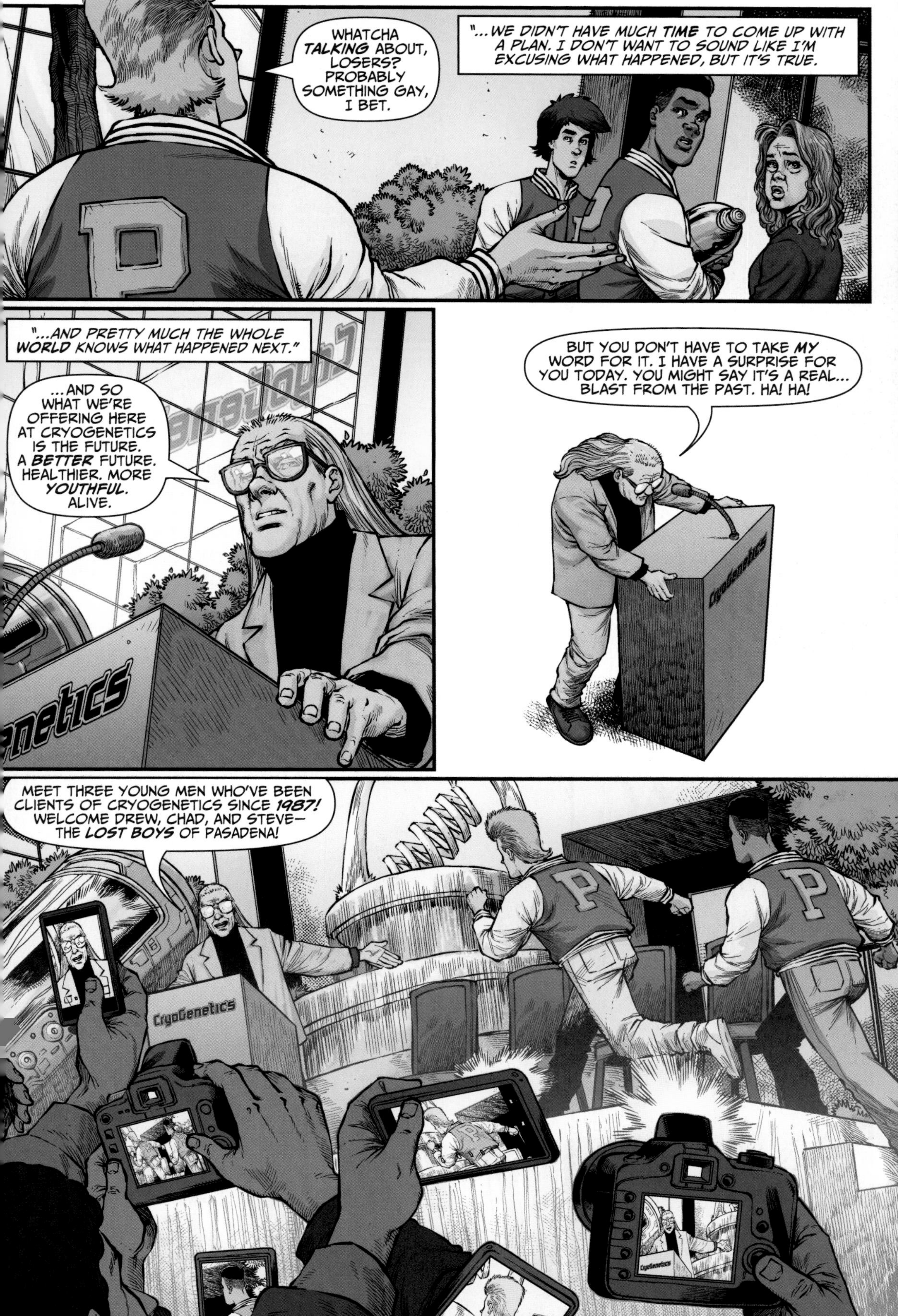
WHATCHA TALKING ABOUT, LOSERS? PROBABLY SOMETHING GAY, I BET.
"...WE DIDN'T HAVE MUCH TIME TO COME UP WITH A PLAN. I DON'T WANT TO SOUND LIKE I'M EXCUSING WHAT HAPPENED, BUT IT'S TRUE.
"...AND PRETTY MUCH THE WHOLE WORLD KNOWS WHAT HAPPENED NEXT."
...AND SO WHAT WE'RE OFFERING HERE AT CRYOGENETICS IS THE FUTURE. A BETTER FUTURE. HEALTHIER. MORE YOUTHFUL. ALIVE.
BUT YOU DON'T HAVE TO TAKE MY WORD FOR IT. I HAVE A SURPRISE FOR YOU TODAY. YOU MIGHT SAY IT'S A REAL... BLAST FROM THE PAST. HA! HA!
CryoGenetics
MEET THREE YOUNG MEN WHO'VE BEEN CLIENTS OF CRYOGENETICS SINCE 1987! WELCOME DREW, CHAD, AND STEVE— THE LOST BOYS OF PASADENA!
CryoGenetics

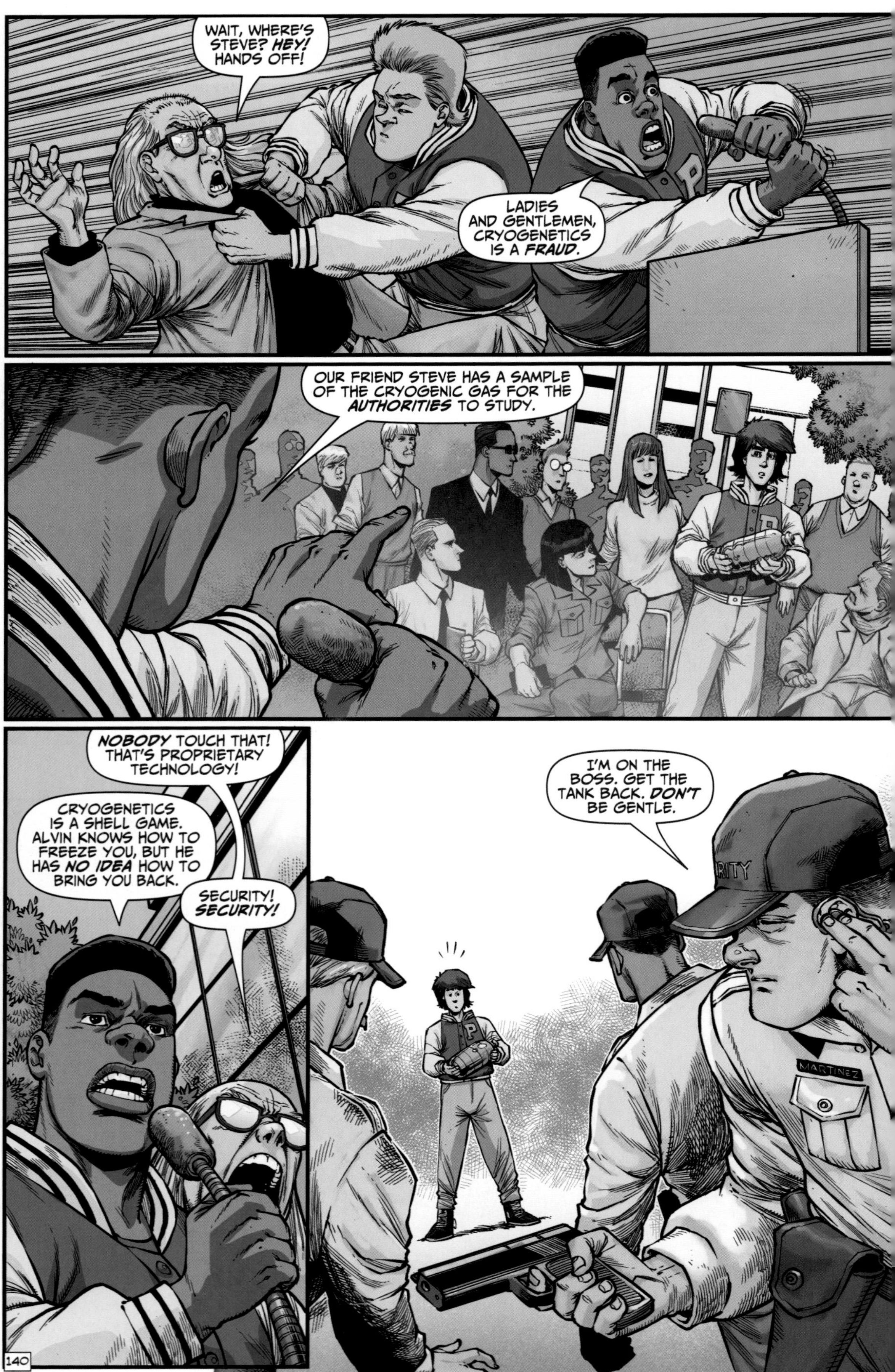
WAIT, WHERE'S STEVE? HEY! HANDS OFF!
LADIES AND GENTLEMEN, CRYOGENETICS IS A FRAUD.
OUR FRIEND STEVE HAS A SAMPLE OF THE CRYOGENIC GAS FOR THE AUTHORITIES TO STUDY.
NOBODY TOUCH THAT! THAT'S PROPRIETARY TECHNOLOGY!
CRYOGENETICS IS A SHELL GAME. ALVIN KNOWS HOW TO FREEZE YOU, BUT HE HAS NO IDEA HOW TO BRING YOU BACK.
SECURITY! SECURITY!
I'M ON THE BOSS. GET THE TANK BACK. DON'T BE GENTLE.
MARTINEZ

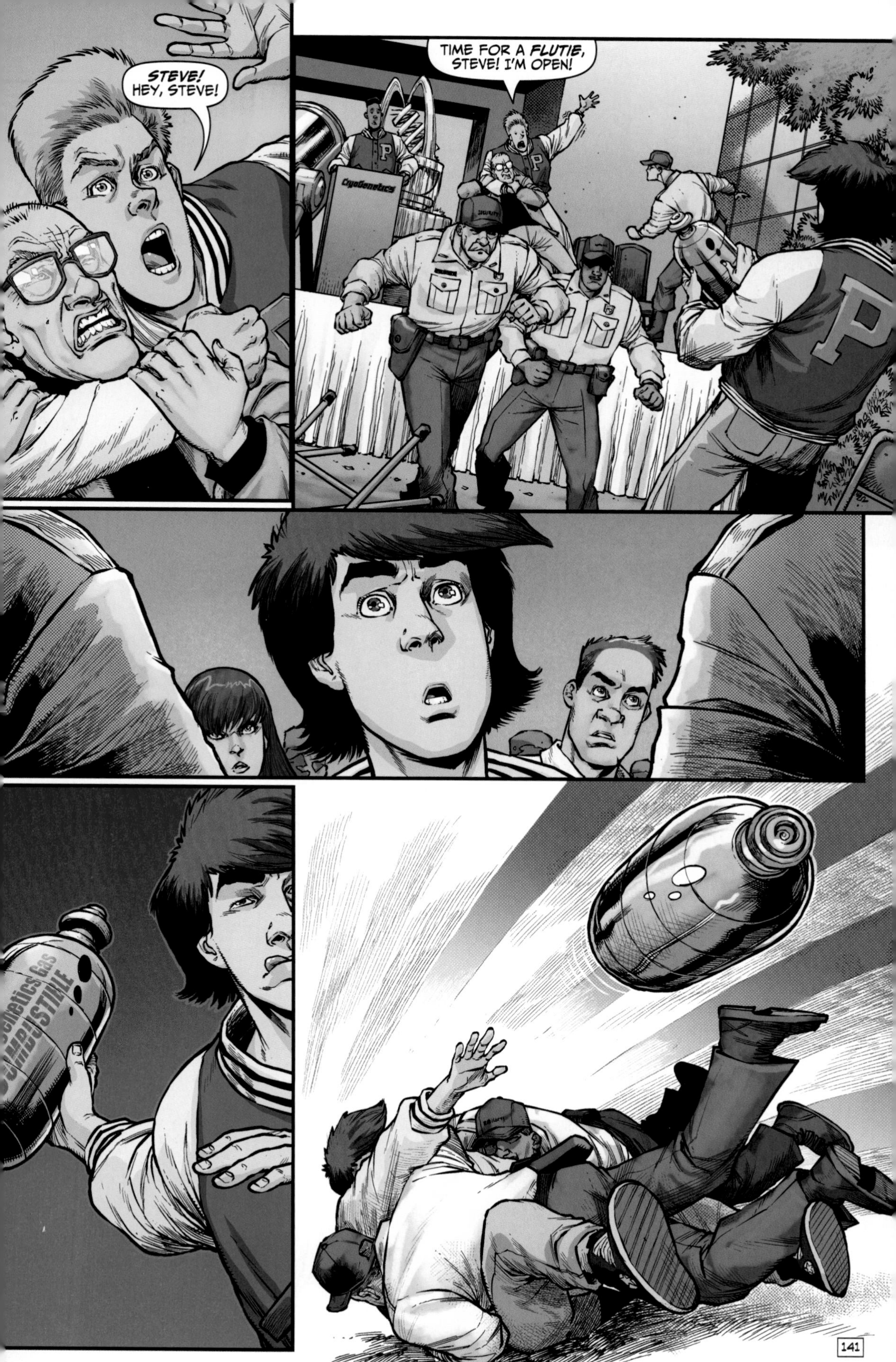
STEVE! HEY, STEVE!
TIME FOR A FLUTIE, STEVE! I'M OPEN!

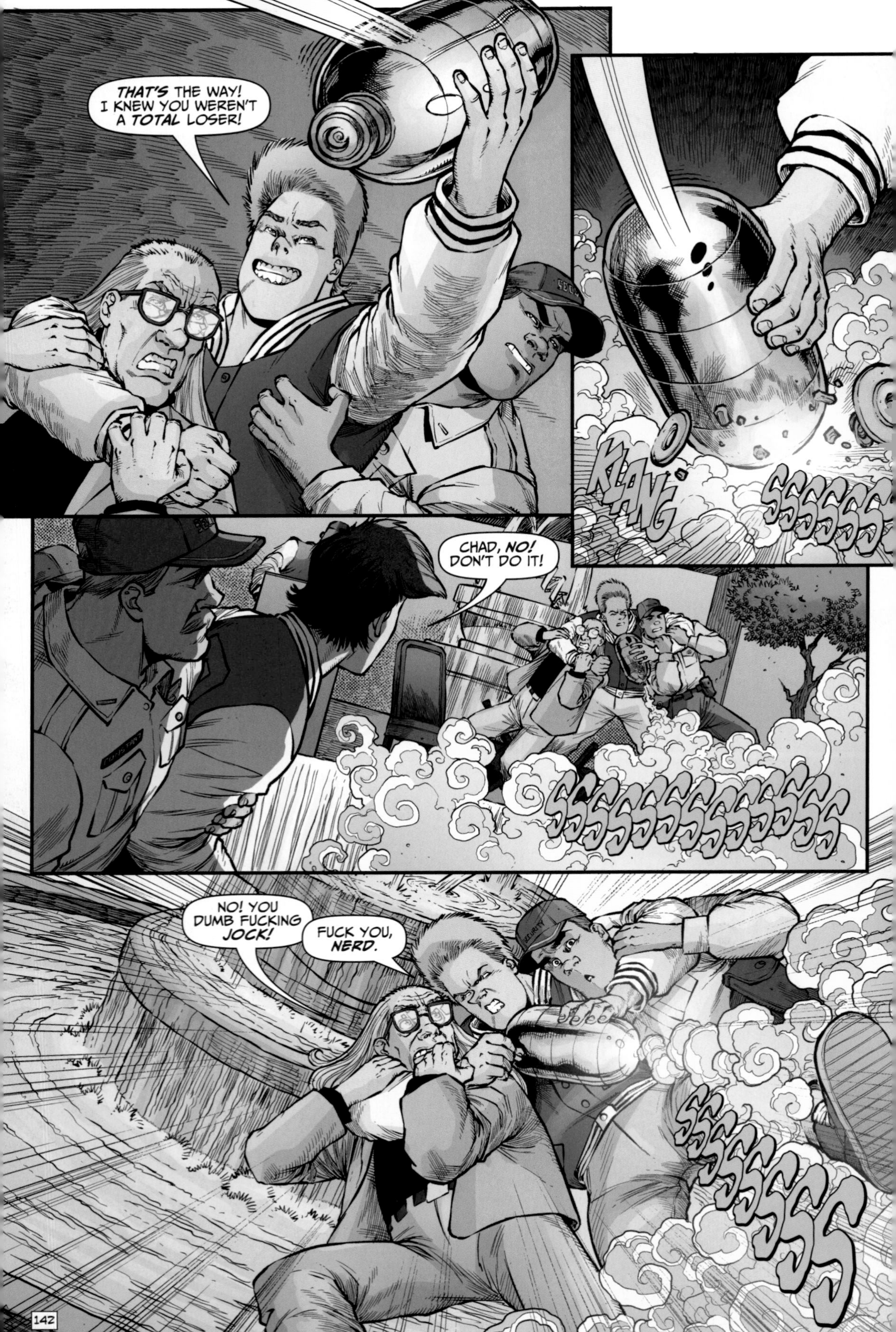
THAT'S THE WAY! I KNEW YOU WEREN'T A TOTAL LOSER!
KLANG
SSSSSS
CHAD, NO! DON'T DO IT!
SSSSSSSSSSSSSSS
NO! YOU DUMB FUCKING JOCK!
FUCK YOU, NERD.
SSSSSSSSSSS

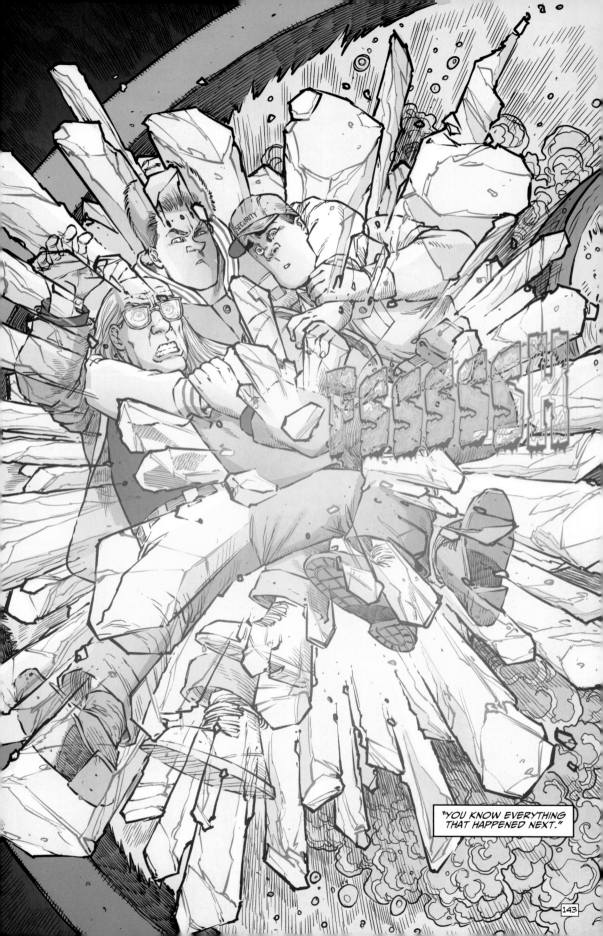

"YOU KNOW EVERYTHING THAT HAPPENED NEXT."

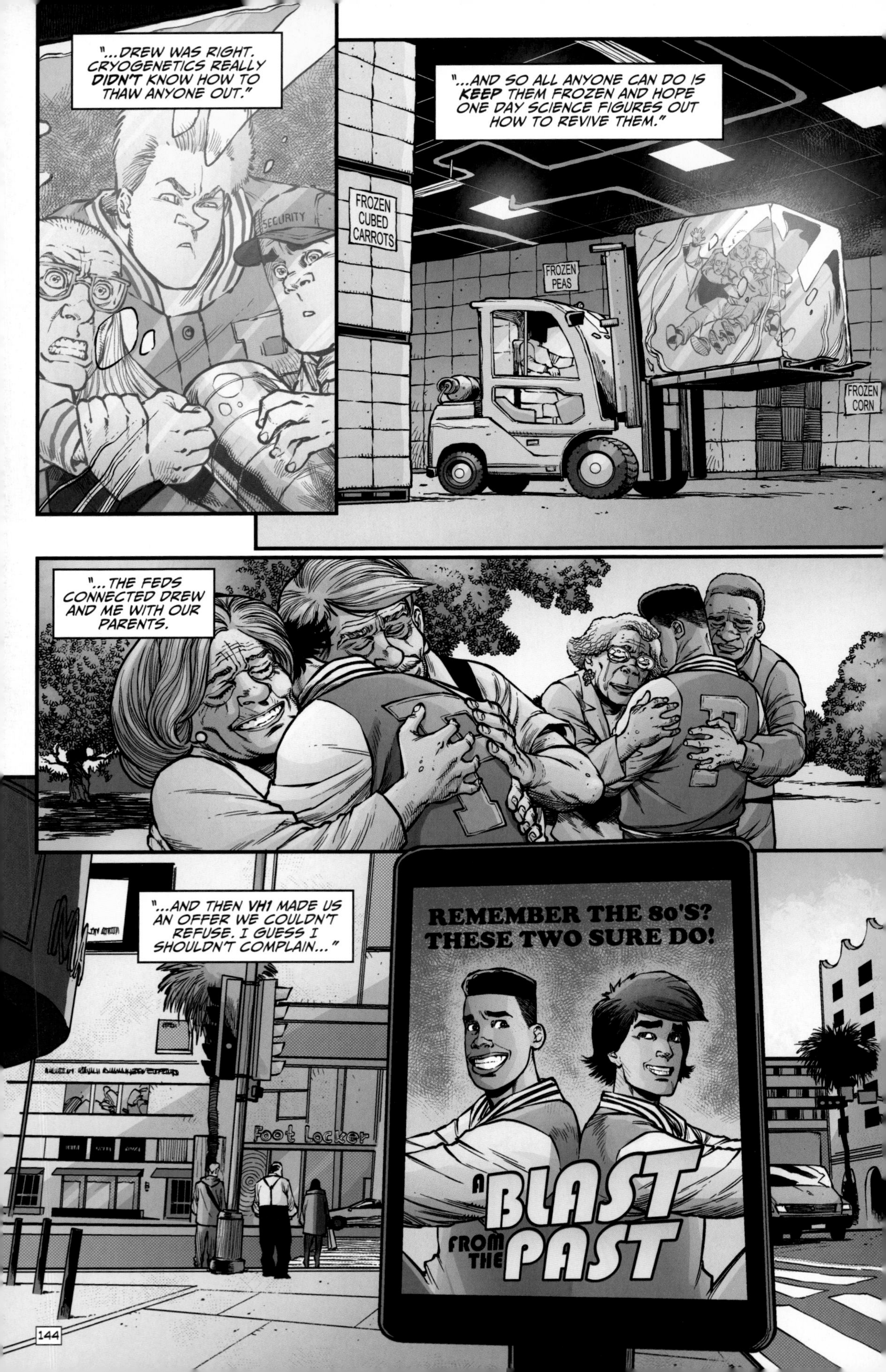
"...DREW WAS RIGHT. CRYOGENETICS REALLY DIDN'T KNOW HOW TO THAW ANYONE OUT."
SECURITY
"...AND SO ALL ANYONE CAN DO IS KEEP THEM FROZEN AND HOPE ONE DAY SCIENCE FIGURES OUT HOW TO REVIVE THEM."
FROZEN CUBED CARROTS
FROZEN PEAS
FROZEN CORN
"...THE FEDS CONNECTED DREW AND ME WITH OUR PARENTS.
"...AND THEN VH1 MADE US AN OFFER WE COULDN'T REFUSE. I GUESS I SHOULDN'T COMPLAIN..."
Foot Locker
REMEMBER THE 80'S? THESE TWO SURE DO!
A BLAST FROM THE PAST

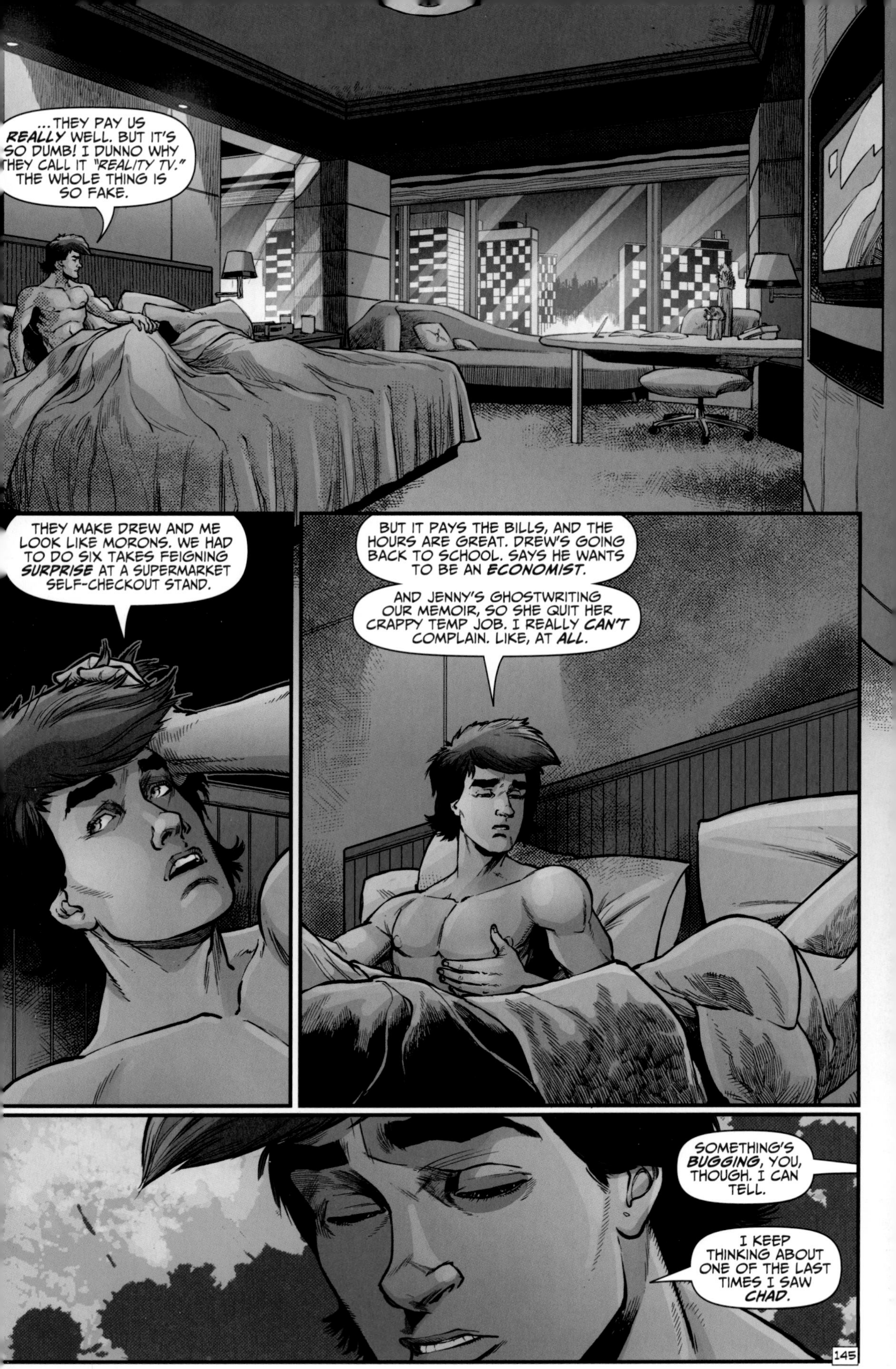
...THEY PAY US REALLY WELL. BUT IT'S SO DUMB! I DUNNO WHY THEY CALL IT "REALITY TV." THE WHOLE THING IS SO FAKE.
THEY MAKE DREW AND ME LOOK LIKE MORONS. WE HAD TO DO SIX TAKES FEIGNING SURPRISE AT A SUPERMARKET SELF-CHECKOUT STAND.
BUT IT PAYS THE BILLS, AND THE HOURS ARE GREAT. DREW'S GOING BACK TO SCHOOL. SAYS HE WANTS TO BE AN ECONOMIST.
AND JENNY'S GHOSTWRITING OUR MEMOIR, SO SHE QUIT HER CRAPPY TEMP JOB. I REALLY CAN'T COMPLAIN. LIKE, AT ALL.
SOMETHING'S BUGGING, YOU, THOUGH. I CAN TELL.
I KEEP THINKING ABOUT ONE OF THE LAST TIMES I SAW CHAD.

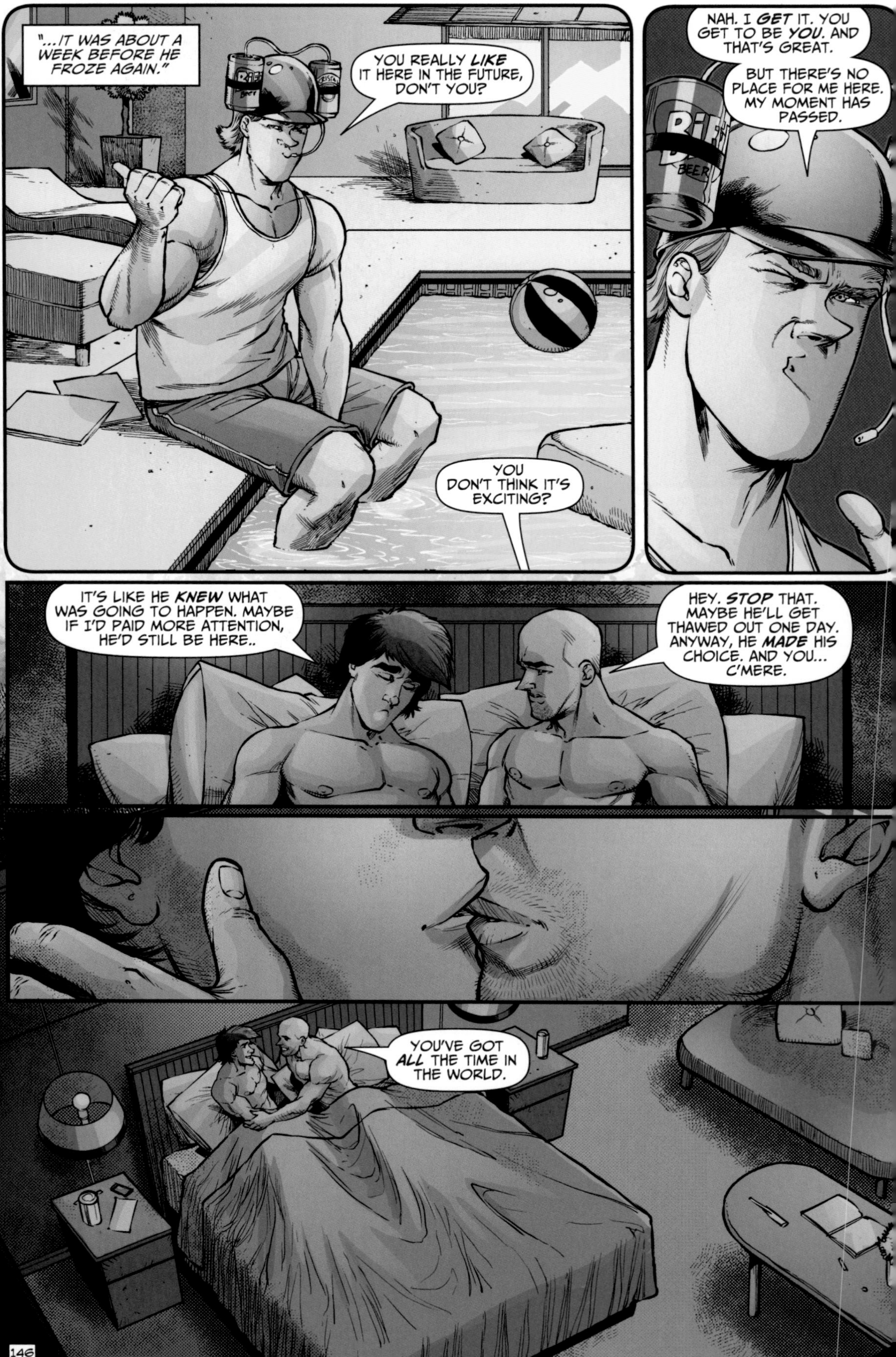
"...IT WAS ABOUT A WEEK BEFORE HE FROZE AGAIN."
YOU REALLY LIKE IT HERE IN THE FUTURE, DON'T YOU?
YOU DON'T THINK IT'S EXCITING?
NAH. I GET IT. YOU GET TO BE YOU. AND THAT'S GREAT.
BUT THERE'S NO PLACE FOR ME HERE. MY MOMENT HAS PASSED.
IT'S LIKE HE KNEW WHAT WAS GOING TO HAPPEN. MAYBE IF I'D PAID MORE ATTENTION, HE'D STILL BE HERE..
HEY. STOP THAT. MAYBE HE'LL GET THAWED OUT ONE DAY. ANYWAY, HE MADE HIS CHOICE. AND YOU... C'MERE.
YOU'VE GOT ALL THE TIME IN THE WORLD.

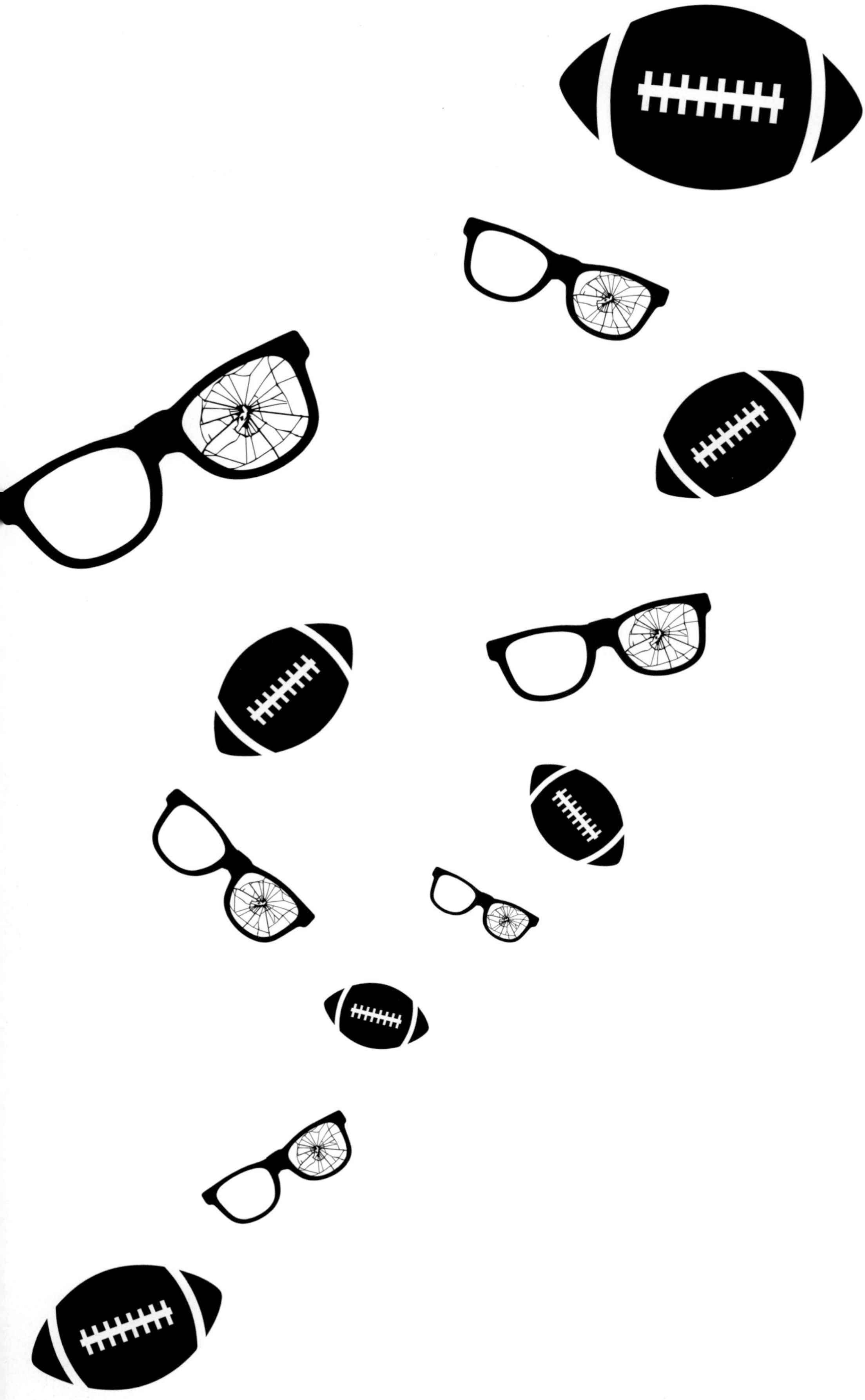

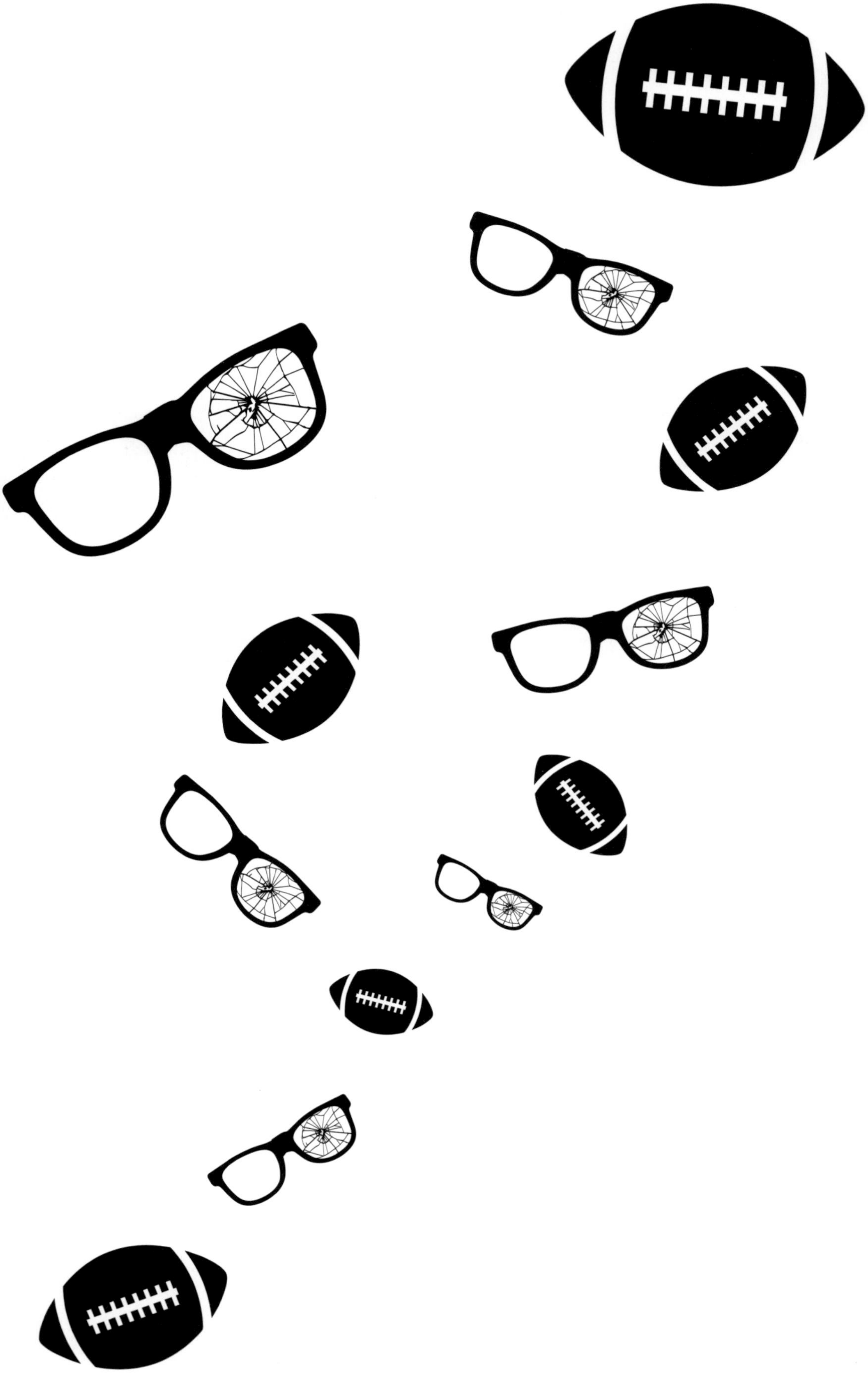

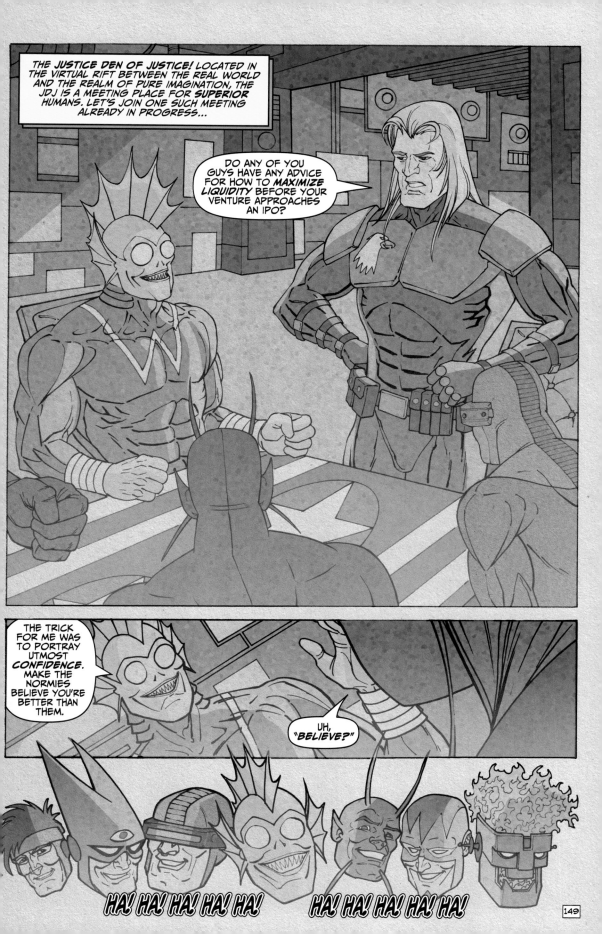

THE *JUSTICE DEN OF JUSTICE!* LOCATED IN THE VIRTUAL RIFT BETWEEN THE REAL WORLD AND THE REALM OF PURE IMAGINATION, THE JDJ IS A MEETING PLACE FOR *SUPERIOR* HUMANS. LET'S JOIN ONE SUCH MEETING ALREADY IN PROGRESS...

DO ANY OF YOU GUYS HAVE ANY ADVICE FOR HOW TO *MAXIMIZE LIQUIDITY* BEFORE YOUR VENTURE APPROACHES AN IPO?

THE TRICK FOR ME WAS TO PORTRAY UTMOST *CONFIDENCE.* MAKE THE NORMIES BELIEVE YOU'RE BETTER THAN THEM.

UH, *"BELIEVE?"*

HA! HA! HA! HA! HA!   HA! HA! HA! HA! HA!

149

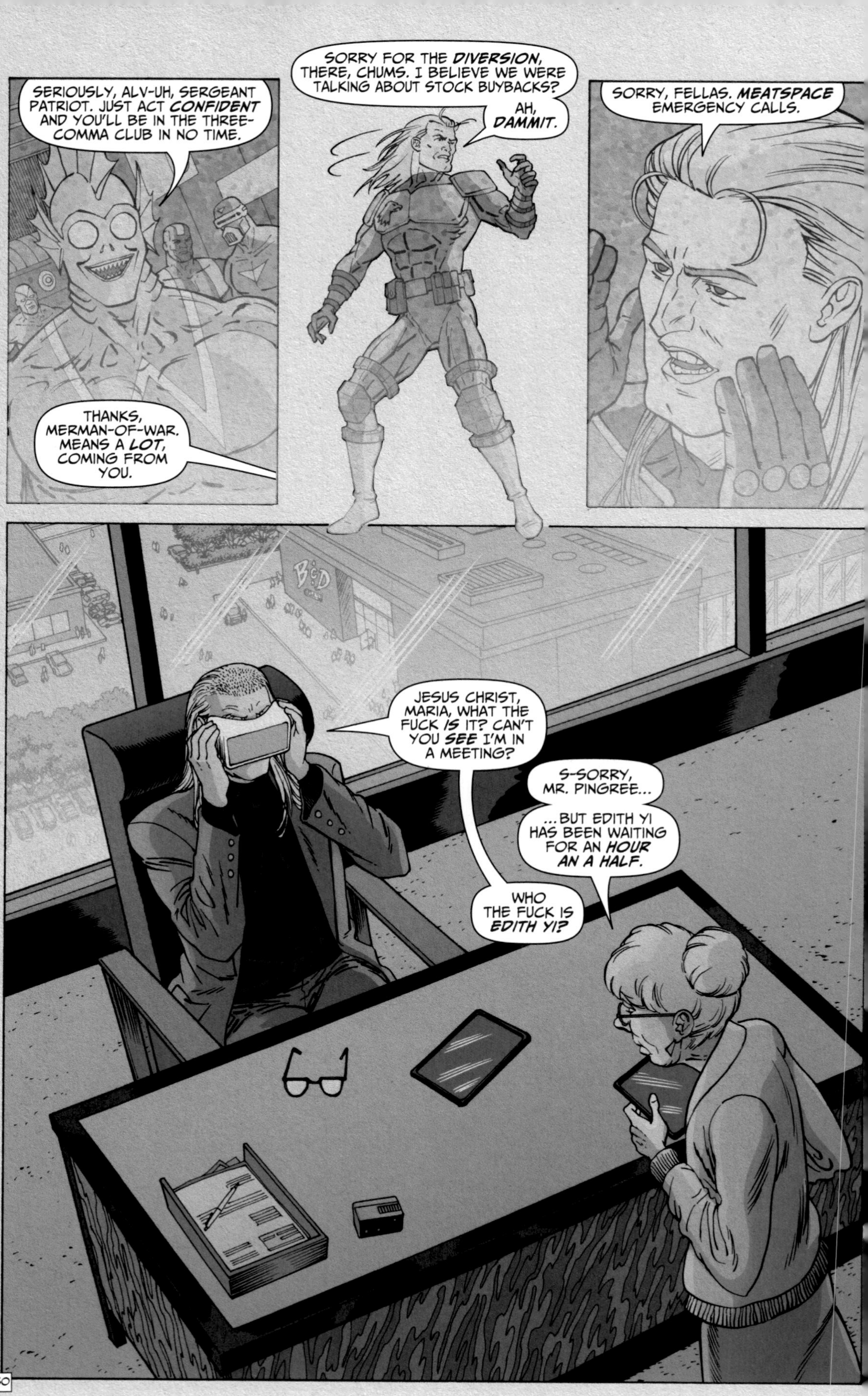
SERIOUSLY, ALV-UH, SERGEANT PATRIOT. JUST ACT CONFIDENT AND YOU'LL BE IN THE THREE-COMMA CLUB IN NO TIME.
THANKS, MERMAN-OF-WAR. MEANS A LOT, COMING FROM YOU.
SORRY FOR THE DIVERSION, THERE, CHUMS. I BELIEVE WE WERE TALKING ABOUT STOCK BUYBACKS?
AH, DAMMIT.
SORRY, FELLAS. MEATSPACE EMERGENCY CALLS.
JESUS CHRIST, MARIA, WHAT THE FUCK IS IT? CAN'T YOU SEE I'M IN A MEETING?
S-SORRY, MR. PINGREE...
...BUT EDITH YI HAS BEEN WAITING FOR AN HOUR AN A HALF.
WHO THE FUCK IS EDITH YI?

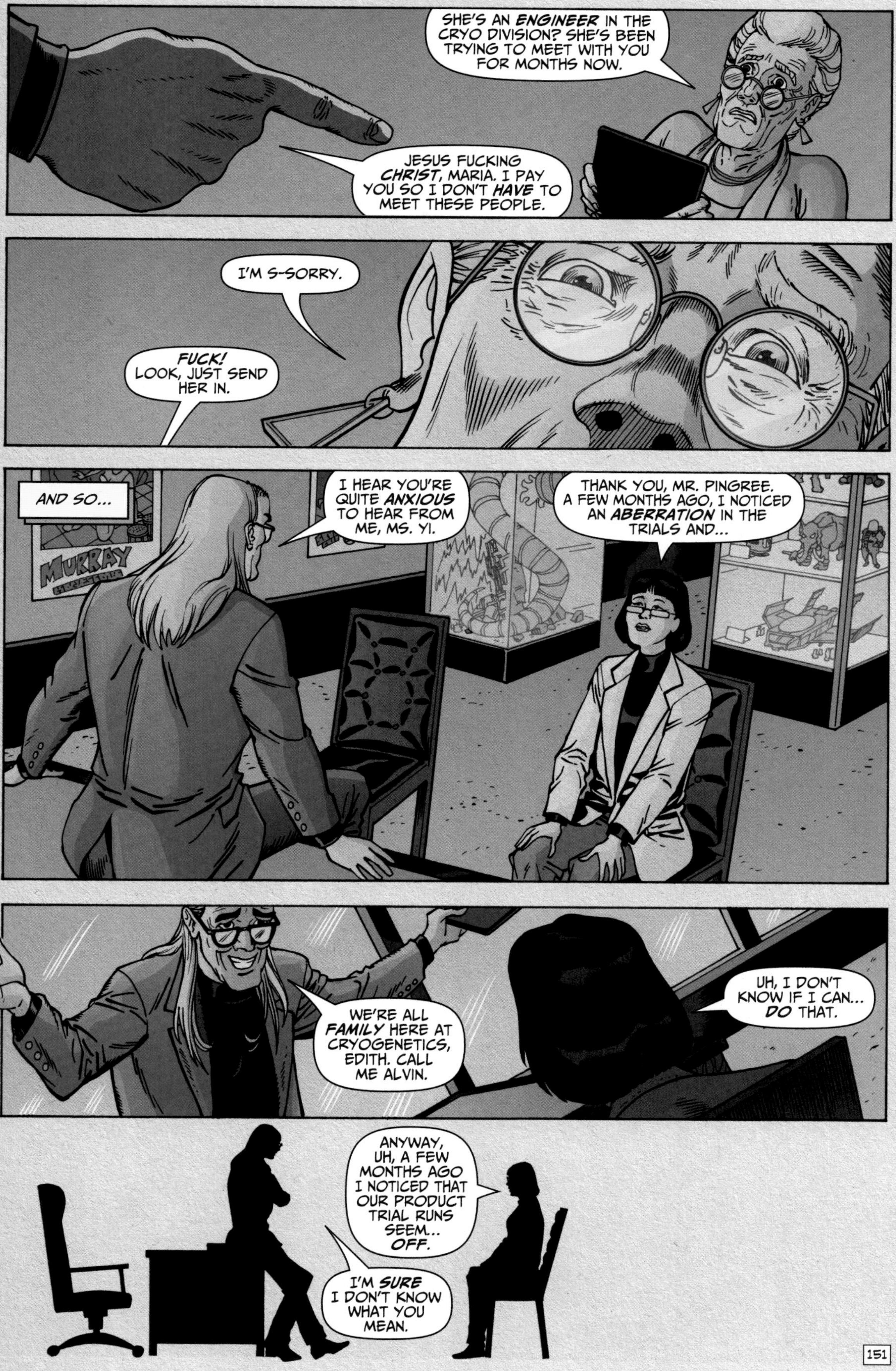
SHE'S AN ENGINEER IN THE CRYO DIVISION? SHE'S BEEN TRYING TO MEET WITH YOU FOR MONTHS NOW.
JESUS FUCKING CHRIST, MARIA. I PAY YOU SO I DON'T HAVE TO MEET THESE PEOPLE.
I'M S-SORRY.
FUCK! LOOK, JUST SEND HER IN.
AND SO...
MURRAY
I HEAR YOU'RE QUITE ANXIOUS TO HEAR FROM ME, MS. YI.
THANK YOU, MR. PINGREE. A FEW MONTHS AGO, I NOTICED AN ABERRATION IN THE TRIALS AND...
WE'RE ALL FAMILY HERE AT CRYOGENETICS, EDITH. CALL ME ALVIN.
UH, I DON'T KNOW IF I CAN... DO THAT.
ANYWAY, UH, A FEW MONTHS AGO I NOTICED THAT OUR PRODUCT TRIAL RUNS SEEM... OFF.
I'M SURE I DON'T KNOW WHAT YOU MEAN.

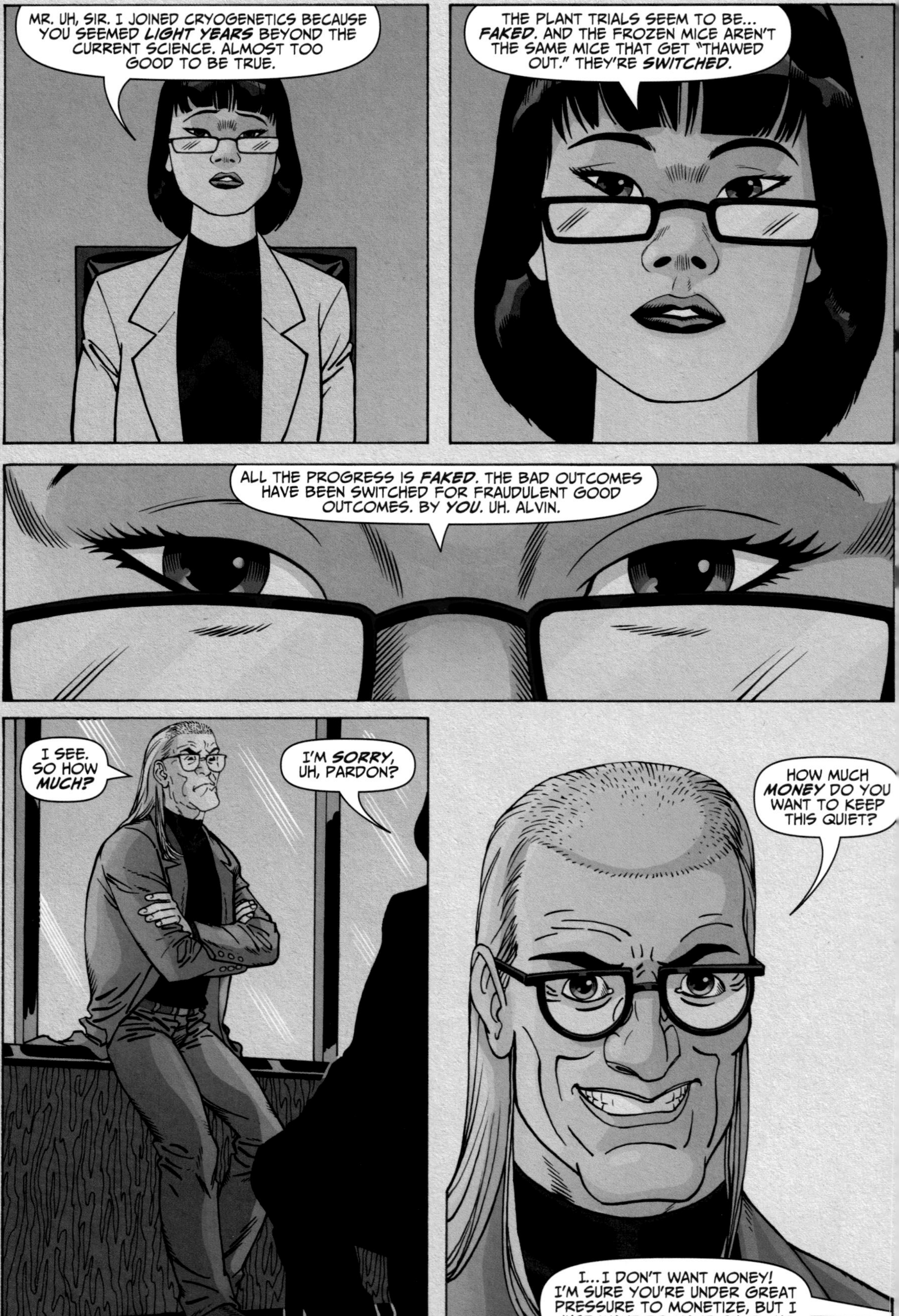
MR. UH, SIR. I JOINED CRYOGENETICS BECAUSE YOU SEEMED LIGHT YEARS BEYOND THE CURRENT SCIENCE. ALMOST TOO GOOD TO BE TRUE.
THE PLANT TRIALS SEEM TO BE... FAKED. AND THE FROZEN MICE AREN'T THE SAME MICE THAT GET "THAWED OUT." THEY'RE SWITCHED.
ALL THE PROGRESS IS FAKED. THE BAD OUTCOMES HAVE BEEN SWITCHED FOR FRAUDULENT GOOD OUTCOMES. BY YOU. UH. ALVIN.
I SEE. SO HOW MUCH?
I'M SORRY, UH, PARDON?
HOW MUCH MONEY DO YOU WANT TO KEEP THIS QUIET?
I...I DON'T WANT MONEY! I'M SURE YOU'RE UNDER GREAT PRESSURE TO MONETIZE, BUT I JUST WANT TO MAKE SURE THE SCIENCE IS RIGHT.

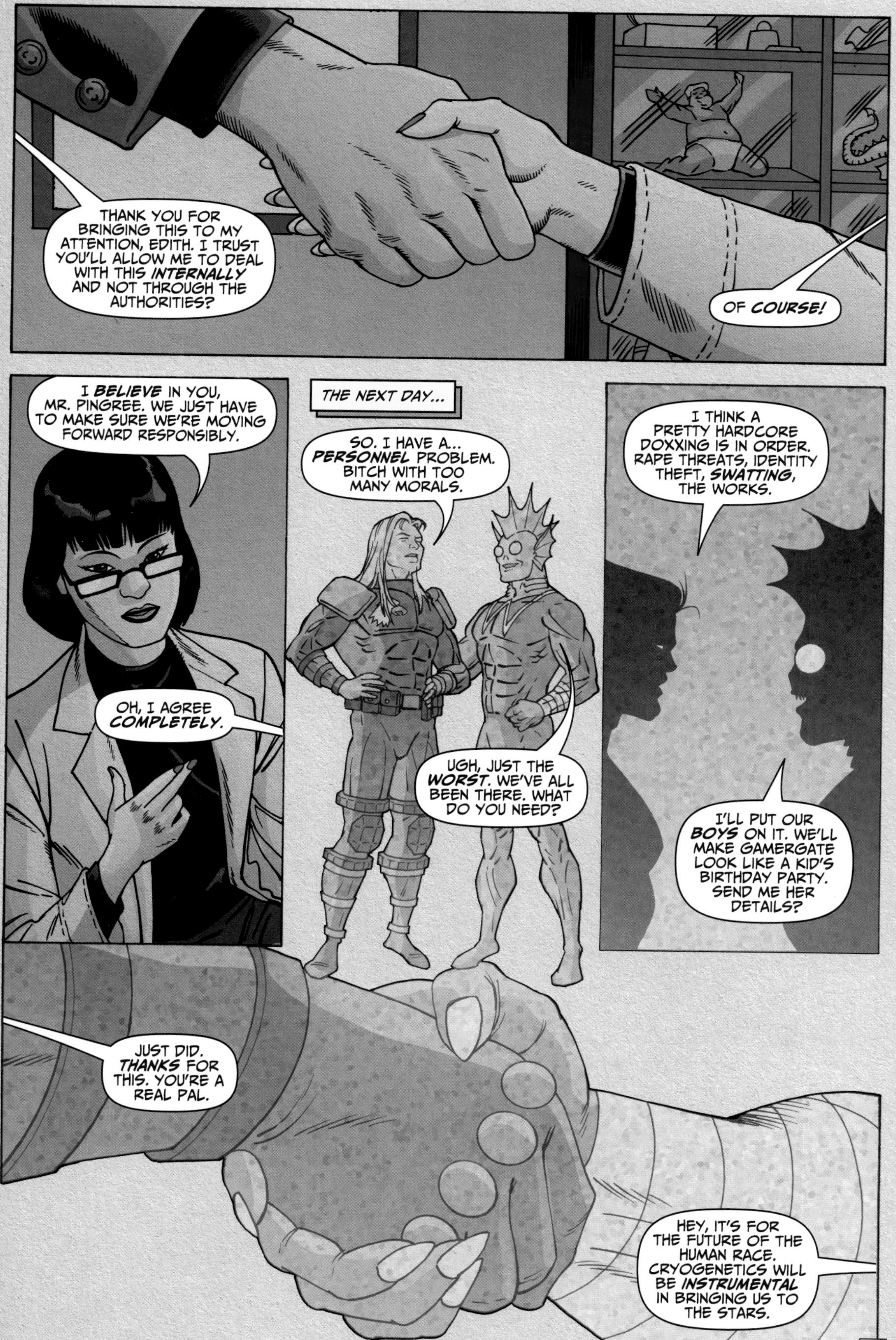

THANK YOU FOR BRINGING THIS TO MY ATTENTION, EDITH. I TRUST YOU'LL ALLOW ME TO DEAL WITH THIS *INTERNALLY* AND NOT THROUGH THE AUTHORITIES?
OF *COURSE!*
I *BELIEVE* IN YOU, MR. PINGREE. WE JUST HAVE TO MAKE SURE WE'RE MOVING FORWARD RESPONSIBLY.
OH, I AGREE *COMPLETELY*.
THE NEXT DAY...
SO. I HAVE A... *PERSONNEL* PROBLEM. BITCH WITH TOO MANY MORALS.
UGH, JUST THE *WORST*. WE'VE ALL BEEN THERE. WHAT DO YOU NEED?
I THINK A PRETTY HARDCORE DOXXING IS IN ORDER. RAPE THREATS, IDENTITY THEFT, *SWATTING*, THE WORKS.
I'LL PUT OUR *BOYS* ON IT. WE'LL MAKE GAMERGATE LOOK LIKE A KID'S BIRTHDAY PARTY. SEND ME HER DETAILS?
JUST DID. *THANKS* FOR THIS. YOU'RE A REAL PAL.
HEY, IT'S FOR THE FUTURE OF THE HUMAN RACE. CRYOGENETICS WILL BE *INSTRUMENTAL* IN BRINGING US TO THE STARS.

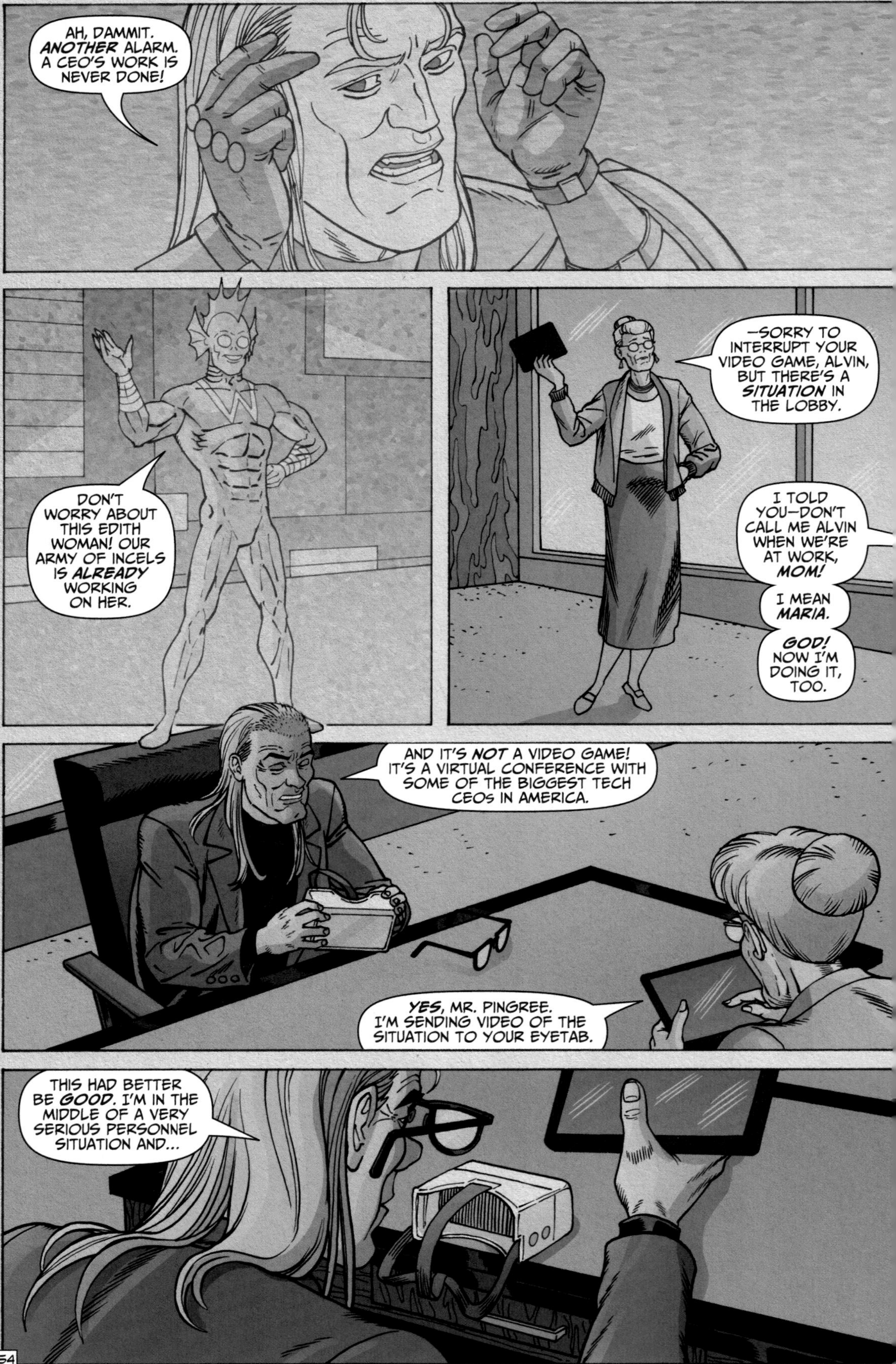

AH, DAMMIT. ANOTHER ALARM. A CEO'S WORK IS NEVER DONE!
DON'T WORRY ABOUT THIS EDITH WOMAN! OUR ARMY OF INCELS IS ALREADY WORKING ON HER.
—SORRY TO INTERRUPT YOUR VIDEO GAME, ALVIN, BUT THERE'S A SITUATION IN THE LOBBY.
I TOLD YOU—DON'T CALL ME ALVIN WHEN WE'RE AT WORK, MOM!
I MEAN MARIA.
GOD! NOW I'M DOING IT, TOO.
AND IT'S NOT A VIDEO GAME! IT'S A VIRTUAL CONFERENCE WITH SOME OF THE BIGGEST TECH CEOs IN AMERICA.
YES, MR. PINGREE. I'M SENDING VIDEO OF THE SITUATION TO YOUR EYETAB.
THIS HAD BETTER BE GOOD. I'M IN THE MIDDLE OF A VERY SERIOUS PERSONNEL SITUATION AND...

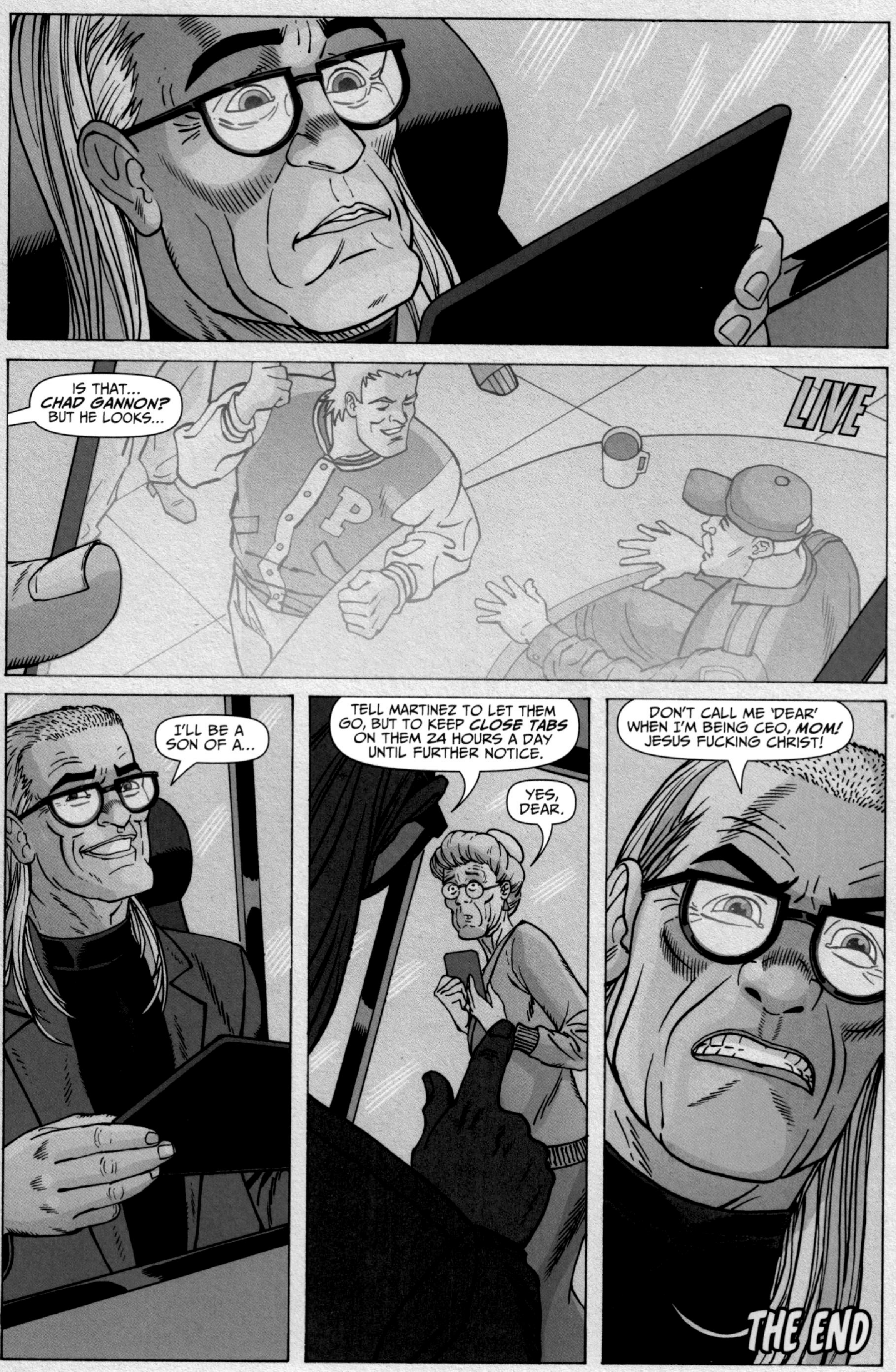
IS THAT... CHAD GANNON? BUT HE LOOKS...
LIVE
I'LL BE A SON OF A...
TELL MARTINEZ TO LET THEM GO, BUT TO KEEP CLOSE TABS ON THEM 24 HOURS A DAY UNTIL FURTHER NOTICE.
YES, DEAR.
DON'T CALL ME 'DEAR' WHEN I'M BEING CEO, MOM! JESUS FUCKING CHRIST!
THE END

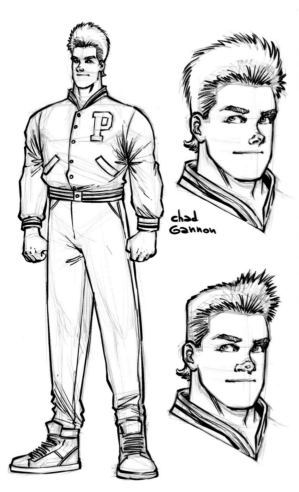

chad
Gannon

From the moment AHOY Editor-in-Chief Tom Peyer and I asked Alan Robinson to draw **PLANET OF THE NERDS**, Alan immediately became an equal creator. These two pages reproduce the very first time Alan drew our time-traveling jocks. It was eerie how quickly and effortlessly he took to the characters and themes of the book.

— PAUL CONSTANT

While Steve's bowl cut (at right) certainly represents a common 1980s look—I had this exact haircut until I turned 19 years old—that lush, feathered helmet of hair is more befitting of a protagonist: noble, dignified, huge. Alan deserves all the credit for not making the hair and clothing into an exaggerated joke in every panel; the '80s look is undeniably funny, but it's not just a visual gag.

Chad's design only required two minor tweaks. I believe Tom was the one who suggested his hair should be much higher and spikier and just generally 1980s-ier. And I thought Chad should have an upturned nose, because most of the cruelest bullies I remember from '80s TV shows and movies had Kevin Bacon-style schnozzes for some reason. Alan incorporated both notes and turned around the new design within minutes, quickly transforming Chad from a big doofy football bro into the Alpha Jock that we know and love and fear and loathe.

Drew
Johnson

Pleated pants are very difficult to draw and Alan nailed Drew's pants on the first try. Take it from someone whose first job was restocking the Maine Mall Sears men's department: these are some high-quality pleats, right here.

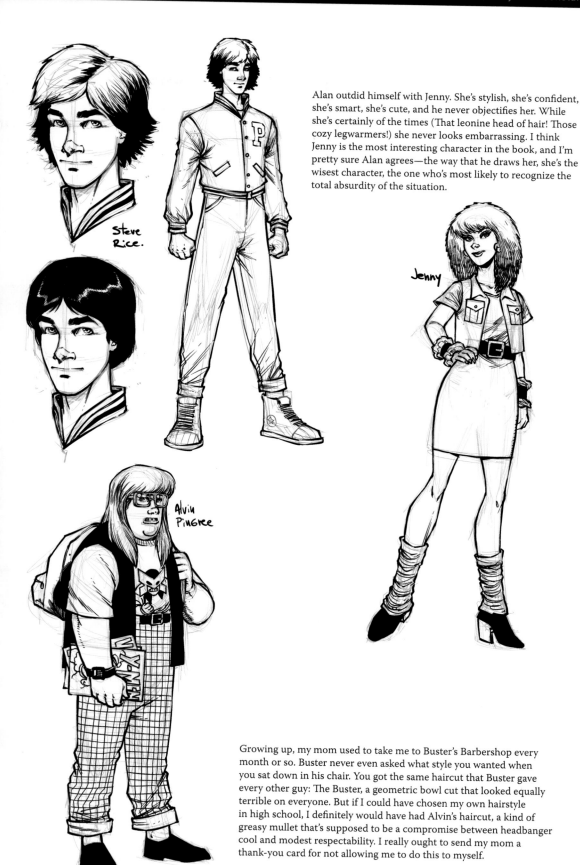

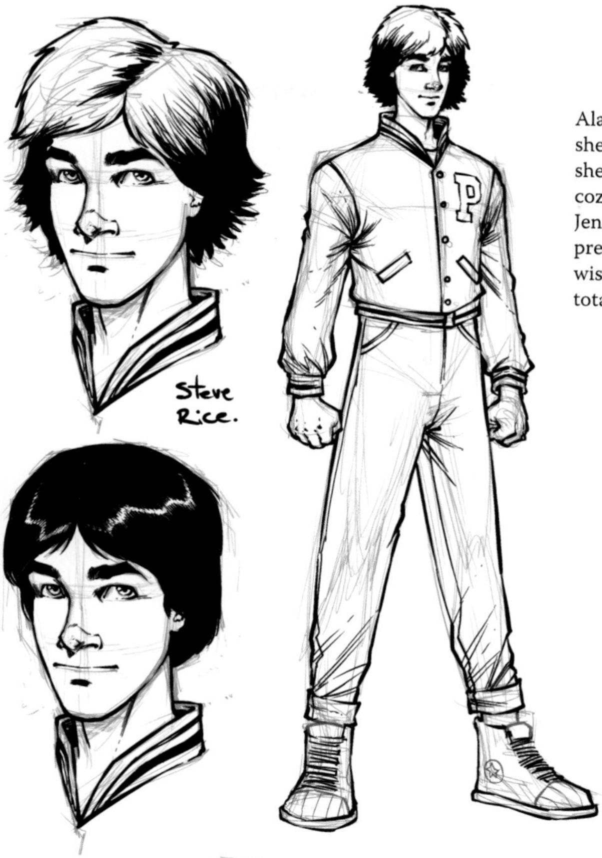
Steve
Rice.

Alan outdid himself with Jenny. She's stylish, she's confident, she's smart, she's cute, and he never objectifies her. While she's certainly of the times (That leonine head of hair! Those cozy legwarmers!) she never looks embarrassing. I think Jenny is the most interesting character in the book, and I'm pretty sure Alan agrees—the way that he draws her, she's the wisest character, the one who's most likely to recognize the total absurdity of the situation.

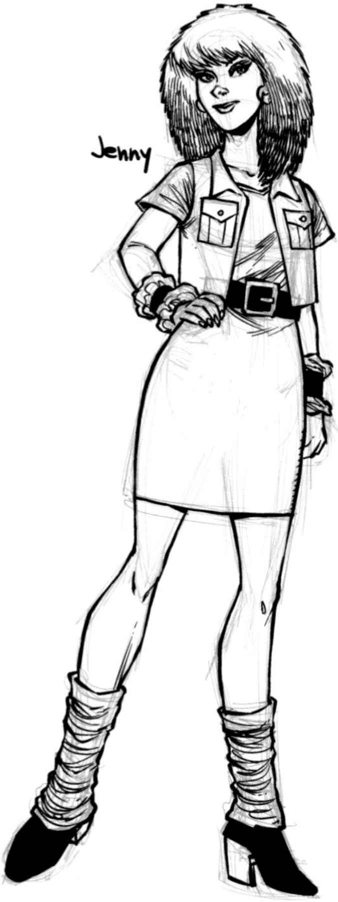
Jenny

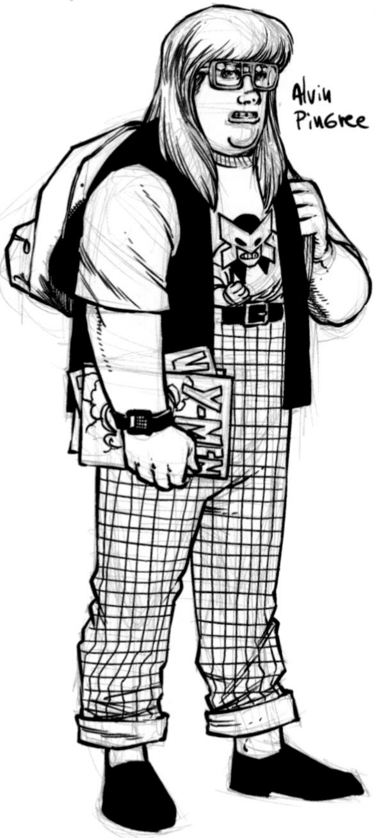
Alvin
Pingree

Growing up, my mom used to take me to Buster's Barbershop every month or so. Buster never even asked what style you wanted when you sat down in his chair. You got the same haircut that Buster gave every other guy: The Buster, a geometric bowl cut that looked equally terrible on everyone. But if I could have chosen my own hairstyle in high school, I definitely would have had Alvin's haircut, a kind of greasy mullet that's supposed to be a compromise between headbanger cool and modest respectability. I really ought to send my mom a thank-you card for not allowing me to do this to myself.

PLANET OF THE NERDS #1, PAGE 1 LAYOUT, PENCILS & INKS by Alan Robinson

When I was called by Tom and Paul to do ***PLANET OF THE NERDS***, it was a dream project for me, so I felt an obligation to be as accurate and precise as possible with the art and references. I started looking for '80s images and films right from the begining. I was a boy in 1987 and didn't remember the imagery of those years that well. I do remember though, that there was a LOT of hair, everywhere. And of course, shoulder pads.

For the first page, I wanted it to have impact, and at the same time to give us an idea of what our guys are like. In this image, we present our heroes and our villain, only it seems the villains are Chad, Steve and Drew, and Alvin's the victim.

I also had a lot of fun working on mock-up covers for the comics strewn in front of Alvin.

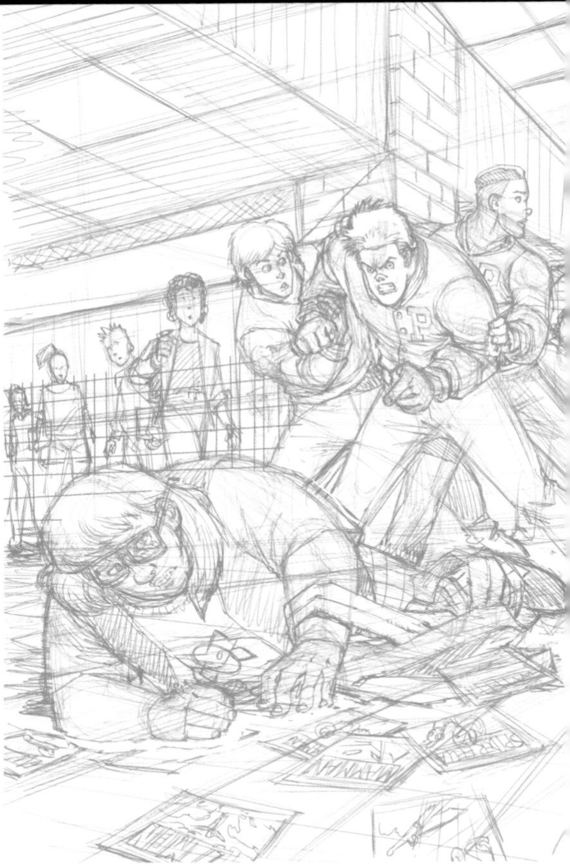

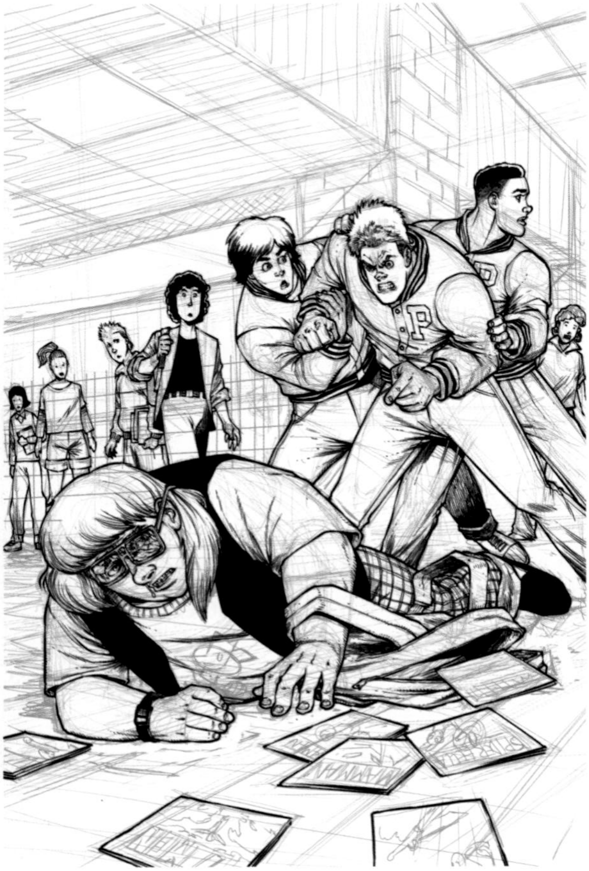

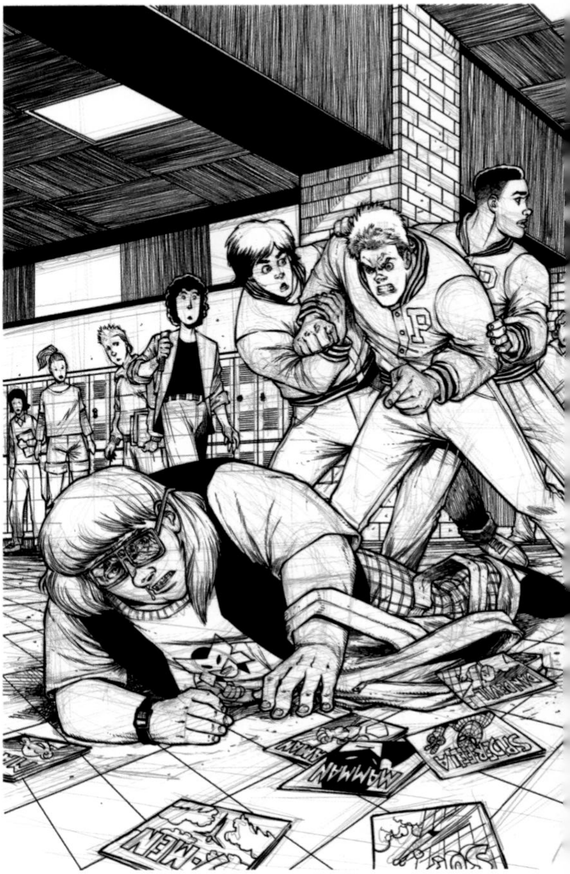

is is my first cover for AHOY, and what better honor than king it for ***PLANET OF THE NERDS***? For this image, I nted the guys to look as low as possible—helpless and sad. ey are in an era where they don't belong. There's no place they ı call home, so that turns into anger and sadness at the same ne. I think you can still see their personalities in this image, and t's why I was happy with the result, plus I had a hell of a time awing it.

— ALAN ROBINSON

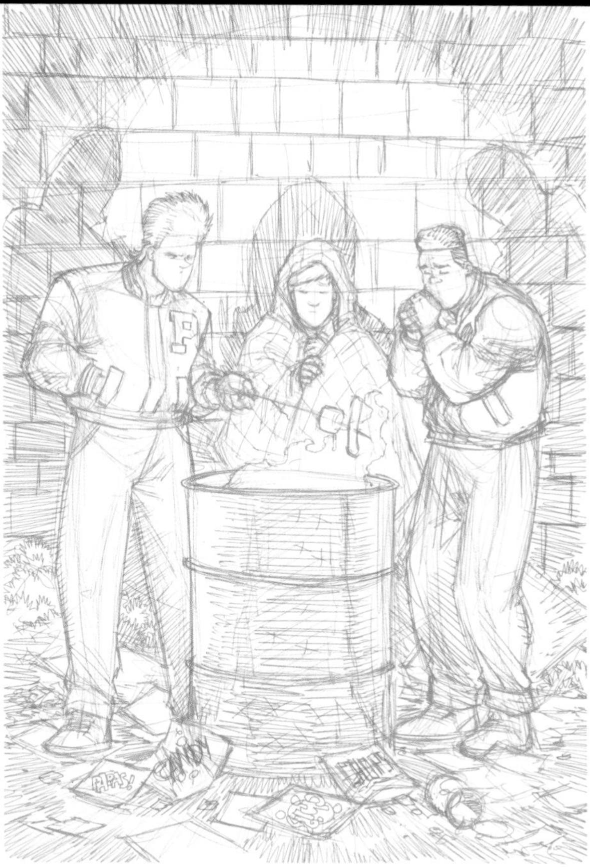

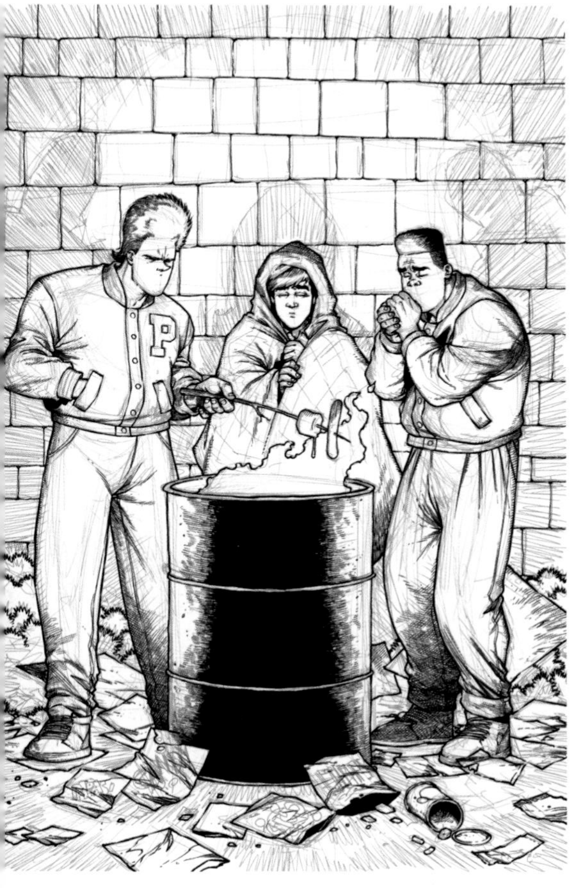

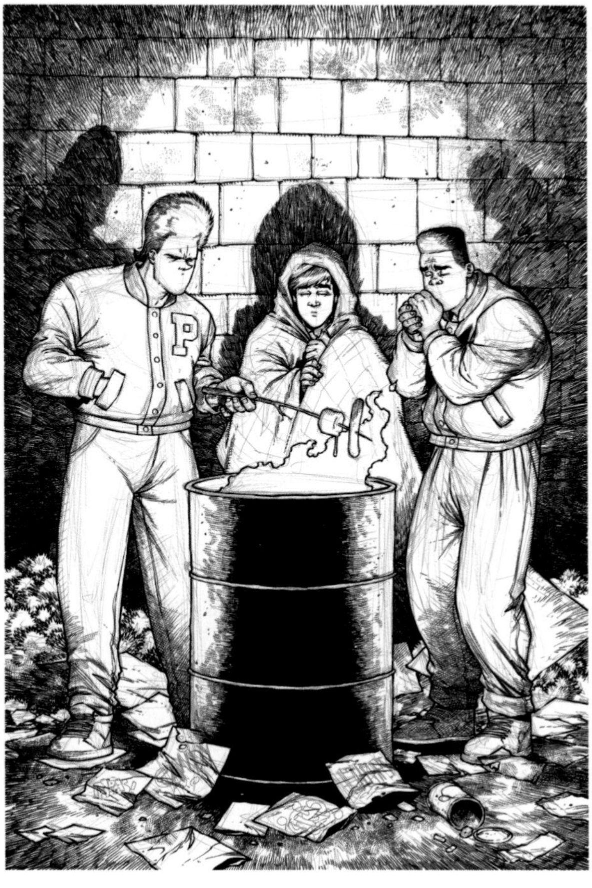

BIOGRAPHIES

PAUL CONSTANT is the co-founder of *The Seattle Review of Books*, an award-winning site for book news, reviews, and interviews. He has written journalism and cultural criticism for the *Los Angeles Times*, i09, the *Seattle Times*, the *New York Observer*, and *BuzzFeed News*, and he currently works as a fellow for Seattle-area public policy incubator Civic Ventures.

ALAN ROBINSON has been drawing comics professionally for more than ten years, working for IDW Publishing, Dark Horse and Beyond Reality Media, on titles such as *Back to the Future*, *V-Wars*, *Star Wars*, *Warden*, *Terminator* and *Secret Battles of Genghis Khan*. He lives in Concepcion, Chile, with his wife Jessica and their lovely kids Matilda and Agustin.

RANDY ELLIOTT, a Syracuse native, has been working professionally in comics since 1988. Over the last 30 years he has created work for publishers like DC, Wildstorm, Dark Horse, Marvel, Archie and Valiant, working on titles as diverse as *Dragonlance*, *Stormwatch*, *Justice League Europe*, *Excalibur*, *Turok*, *Bionicle* and *Scooby-Doo*.

LEE LOUGHRIDGE is a color artist who has created award-winning work for Marvel, DC, Dark Horse and Image Comics throughout his 25-year career.

FELIPE SOBREIRO is a Brazilian artist and colorist. He has worked for all major comic book publishers, including Marvel, DC, Image, Dark Horse, IDW, Heavy Metal and others.

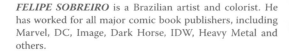

ROB STEEN is the illustrator of *Flanimals*, the best-selling series of children's books written by Ricky Gervais, and *Erf*, a children's book written by Garth Ennis.

DAVID NAKAYAMA is an illustrator, concept artist, and art director probably best known for his Marvel Comics cover art (*X-Men*, *Deadpool*, *Ant-Man and the Wasp*, *Rocket Raccoon*). He's also freelanced for Hasbro, Upper Deck, and *Official Playstation Magazine UK* among many, many others. As an Art Director at Jam City, he led the art teams for *Marvel Avengers Academy* and the new blockbuster hit on mobile *Harry Potter Hogwarts Mystery*.